Six Crises of the World Economy

José A. Tapia

Six Crises of the World Economy

Globalization and Economic Turbulence from the 1970s to the COVID-19 Pandemic

palgrave
macmillan

José A. Tapia
Drexel University
Philadelphia, PA, USA

ISBN 978-3-031-38734-0 ISBN 978-3-031-38735-7 (eBook)
https://doi.org/10.1007/978-3-031-38735-7

This Palgrave Macmillan imprint is published by the registered company Springer Nature Switzerland AG
The registered company address is: Gewerbestrasse 11, 6330 Cham, Switzerland

The function of social science is quite different from that of the natural sciences—it is to provide society with an organ of self-consciousness.

Joan Robinson, *Freedom & Necessity—An Introduction to the Study of Society* (1971).

A genuine economic crisis [...] is a situation in which a large number of debtors find themselves unable to meet their obligations when due; accompanied, preceded, or followed by a marked falling-off in the demand for goods. Separating the financial phenomena from the industrial, for analytical purposes, a financial crisis is a situation in which a large number of debtors are unable to meet their obligations [...] An industrial crisis is a marked falling-off in demand for goods.

Minnie Throop England, "Economic crises", *Journal of Political Economy* (1913).

The arrival of European capitalism in North America was accompanied first by the extermination of the indigenous Amerindian population and the theft of their lands by English emigrants, then by the establishment at the start of the 19th century of a capitalist raw-materials production for English industry, and the enslavement of four million black Africans who were sold to America by European slave-traders [...] The establishment of the capitalist world economy brings in its wake [...] a growing insecurity of existence across the whole globe, corresponding to the accumulation of capital in a few hands.

Rosa Luxemburg, *Introduction to Political Economy* (1910)

A mis profesores, Jesús Medina, *El Trivial,* Santiago Llanos, *El Pelanas,*
y Don Ernesto, *El Búho,* que tanto me enseñaron

Contents

Preface

This book is about the crises of the world economy that have occurred from the 1970s to the present. It makes the specific case that the global economy went through six crises during this period of half a century, the first crisis occurred in the mid-1970s, and the sixth crisis occurred in 2020, at the time of the COVID-19 pandemic. Crises of the global economy are periods of substantial slowdown in world economic activity—as measured by investment, money value of the economic output, industrial production, trade, unemployment, etc.—in which many national economies, though not all, are technically in recession. To pose the existence of crises in the global economy implies that the world economy is a proper construct which has conceptual substance given by its own dynamics; it implies also that the usual view that takes national economies as units of economic analysis is an approach with major limitations. The book provides data illustrating the global and regional manifestations of these crises of the world economy, elaborates on the concepts of the world economy and economic crisis, and discusses the theories that have been used to explain them. Its general thrust is to argue that the world economy, not national economies, is the major unit to be analyzed when trying to understand the economic reality of our time, particularly the reality of crises. These crises are discrete, countable phenomena, distinct states of an entity that can be properly called the world or global economy, or world capitalism.

The book is written from a political economy perspective in which major theoretical influences are the world-system school, institutional economics, and ecological economics, with Immanuel Wallerstein, Wesley C. Mitchell, and Nicholas Georgescu-Roegen being the most representative authors of these schools. Now, the world-system school takes its inspiration largely from Marx, Wesley Mitchell was a leading author of mainstream economics, while ecological economics, which was born late in the past century, is marginal in the discipline and focuses on problems that were largely ignored by Marx, Mitchell, Keynes, and neoclassical economists. So, it could be thought that the theoretical underpinnings of this book are mostly eclectic. However, in writing it I have made a major effort to be consistent, both internally and with the facts. It is true—as Albert Einstein emphasized in physics and Tjalling Koopmans in economics—that theory guides research by focusing attention on specific issues and variables.[1] However, reality is persistent and often insists on showing its true nature screaming out for those who want to understand how and why things happen that the gaze is misdirected, that the focus must be shifted. It means theory needs change. In an interview in which he was asked about the Great Recession, a recipient of the Nobel Memorial prize in economics, Eugene Fama, claimed that he had no idea about what causes recessions.[2] We can be sympathetic to him; nobody can be knowledgeable about everything. However, Fama also meant that, in general, economics as a discipline has today no clue about what causes economic crises. If that is the case, what is then the relevance of the discipline to understand the major issue—crises—of economic life?

I try to provide some answers to these questions. In this book, I argue that the main feature of economic crises is a temporary interruption of capital accumulation, which is manifested as a slowdown of economic activity, almost always associated with financial turmoil which is both an effect and a cause of the malfunction of the real economy.

[1] Heisenberg (1971), *Physics and beyond*, 63; Bernstein (1973), "The secrets of the old one", *New Yorker*, March 10, 44–101, March 17, 44–91; Koopmans (1941), "The logic of econometric business-cycle research", *Journal of Political Economy* 49(2):157–181.

[2] Cassidy (2010), "Interview with Eugene Fama: After the blowup," *New Yorker* Jan 11, 28 *et seq.*.

The embryo of this book was a paper that I wrote in 2013 and presented in January 2014 at the annual meeting of ASSA/AEA in Philadelphia. I titled the paper "From the Oil Crisis to the Great Recession: Five crises of the world economy" and dated the crises in the mid-1970s, early 1980s, early 1990s, around the turn of the century, and in 2008–2009. In 2013, it was common to refer to the Great Recession as a global recession or a crisis of the world economy—the term Global Financial Crisis had been often applied to the 2008–2009 crisis—but referring to several crises of the world economy beyond the Great Recession was a rarity, indeed I thought my use was somewhat of an innovation. However, as I began to work on this book project, an IMF publication appeared in which four recessions of the world economy were identified and dated 1975, 1982, 1991, and 2009.[3] Obviously, these four crises identified by IMF authors as recessions of the world economy are the same crises that I date more loosely in the mid-1970s, early 1980s, early 1990s, and 2008–2009. For the IMF authors there was not, however, a global recession around the turn of the century, though they identified "downturns of the world economy" in 1998 and 2001.[4] To a large extent, this book has been written "in conversation" and often in controversy with Kose and Terrones, the speakers of the IMF in these matters.[5] In the book, I discuss the criteria to justify my chronology of crises, including the theoretical reasons and empirical data which in my view provide ample support for the idea that there was a crisis of the global economy around the turn of the century.

The book is written for a public of informed readers interested in economic and social issues, undergraduate and graduate students, and

[3] Kose & Terrones (2015), *Collapse and revival—Understanding global recessions and recoveries.*

[4] Kose & Terrones (2015), *Collapse*, 65.

[5] The book by Kose and Terrones has the usual disclaimers explaining that it is not the official position of the IMF, the publishing institution. But a note in the book introduces M. Ayhan Kose as Director of the World Bank Group's Development Prospects Group and previous Assistant to the Director of the Research Department at the IMF, and Marco E. Terrones as a Deputy Division Chief in the Research Department of the IMF.

professionals in the social sciences. Statistical analyses including some *P*-values, correlations, and regression results that require some knowledge of statistics are included very sparsely, in footnotes, and in appendices at the end of the book. The rest of the book only assumes general literacy on science and economic issues and knowledge about our modern world.

Philadelphia, USA José A. Tapia

Abbreviations

The following list of abbreviations includes all the acronyms and abbreviations used in the text. Many of them like US, EU, USSR, OECD, IMF, ILO, or GDP refer to states, groups of states, countries, agencies of the United Nations system, or common concepts in economics, they are relatively well known for anyone who reads in English and will be used without explanation in the text. They are explained here considering that many readers of this book may not be as familiar with English. The list also includes abbreviations that will be used in the text but will be explained when they appear for the first time.

AEA	American Economic Association
BIS	Bank for International Settlements
ch.	chapter
CO_2	carbon dioxide
COMECON	Council for Mutual Economic Assistance
CPI	consumer price index
DSGE	dynamic stochastic general equilibrium (models)
EKC	environmental Kuznets curve
EU	European Union
fn	footnote
G20	Inter-governmental forum including a group of 20 countries—the seven G7 countries plus Argentina, Australia, Brazil, China, India, Indonesia, South Korea,

	Mexico, Russia, Saudi Arabia, South Africa, Turkey, and the EU, with Spain as a permanent observer.
G7	Group of 7, inter-governmental forum including Canada, France, Germany, Italy, Japan, the United Kingdom, and the United States
GATT	General Agreement on Tariffs and Trade
GDP	gross domestic product
GHG	greenhouse gasses
ILO	International Labor Organization
IMF	International Monetary Fund
l.h.s.	left-hand scale
mbpd	million barrels per day
MECW	Marx & Engels Collected Works
NATO	North Atlantic Treaty Organization
NBER	National Bureau of Economic Research (semi-official US research institute)
OECD	Organization for Economic Cooperation and Development
OLS	ordinary least squares
OPEC	Organization of the Petroleum Exporting Countries
PPP	purchasing power parities
r.h.s.	right-hand scale
RBC	real business cycle (theory, models)
UK	United Kingdom
UN	United Nations
US$	United States dollar
US, USA	United States of America
USSR	Union of Soviet Socialist Republics
WDI	World Development Indicators, the database of the World Bank
WGDP	world GDP
WTO	World Trade Organization

List of Figures

List of Tables

CHAPTER 1

Introduction

According to Immanuel Wallerstein,

> Today we have a capitalist world-economy. It encompasses the entire globe, but there isn't anything else [...] It starts in the end of the 19th century, but it's the first time in human history where there's only one historical system on the planet at a given time. And that does change a lot of things.[1]

It was also Wallerstein who claimed that social scientists like to set turning points to clarify the story they are trying to tell. This device

> becomes a basic building block of their analyses of the immediate phenomena they are studying. The choice of turning points constitutes a basic framework within which we all operate. But choosing different turning points can change entirely the logic of the analyses. What are considered to be the "turning points" can mislead as readily as they can clarify.[2]

[1] Wallerstein (2013), "Interview with G. Williams (2013)", *Journal of World-Systems Research* 19(2), 202–210.

[2] Wallerstein (2011), *Modern World-System III: The Second Era of Great Expansion of the Capitalist World-Economy, 1730s–1840s*, xiii.

J. A. Tapia, *Six Crises of the World Economy*,
https://doi.org/10.1007/978-3-031-38735-7_1

This book makes the case that there have been six crises of the world economy since the 1970s to the present. The assertion that an entity called "the world economy" had six crises since the 1970s to the start of the third decade of the twenty-first century provides key insights into the basic dynamics of economic and social conditions and into a variety of issues worthy of consideration in social science. As it will be shown in the next chapter, significant evidence of six major "slumps" of the global economy, i.e., world recessions or crises, is provided by a variety of economic indicators. These six world economic crises occurred

(i) in the mid-1970s, when most national economies went through recessions that were considered part of the so-called First Oil Crisis;
(ii) in the early 1980s, in what sometimes was called the Second Oil Crisis;
(iii) in the early 1990s, when most Western economies suffered major recessions at the same time that the USSR and the Soviet bloc crumbled;
(iv) around the turn of the century, when mild recessions affected high-income economies and major economic disturbances occurred in many Asian countries, Russia and Latin America;
(v) in the late 2000s when the Great Recession started and in many European countries extended to the early years of the 2010s; and
(vi) in 2020, when the world economy had a major contraction at the time of the COVID-19 pandemic.

Business cycle chronologies of national economies such as those produced by the NBER or other institutions are to a substantial extent consistent with these six crises of the world economy—which, obviously, had different manifestations in different nations and economic regions.

Modern discussions of economic crises often turn quickly to empirical data, focusing on national statistics on national income, unemployment, financial markets, or other economic indicators. In this way the assumption is made, often implicitly, that the discussion of crises must focus on a unit of analysis that cannot be other than a national economy.[3] Regretfully, the concept of crisis itself is often used without much definition, as if it were evident. To face this issue upfront, in this book a world economic crisis is defined as a period of at least a year and no longer than a few years in which there is a strong drop of the accumulation of capital or, in other terms, capital formation, or business investment. This concept will be discussed further in Chapter 4.

In the aftermath of the world economic crisis that erupted in 2008, there were multiple attempts to generate inventories of crises, usually focusing on finance and banking. In *Misunderstanding Financial Crises*, Gary Gorton explained that identifying crises or, more specifically, setting a chronology in which the start date and the end date of the crises is established, is a relatively controversial issue in mainstream economics.[4] Gorton cited studies by IMF economists Laeven and Valencia, by Reinhardt and Rogoff, and by Bordo et al.[5] While Laeven and Valencia referred to 124 systemic banking crises over the period 1970–2007, in *This Time is Different* Reinhardt and Rogoff considered a period of several centuries in which Britain, the United States, and France had, respectively, 12, 13, and 15 banking crisis episodes. But Reinhardt and Rogoff concluded that the frequency of crises declined in the period after World War II. Writing in 2001, Bordo et al. had asked themselves whether the crisis problem was growing more severe. They examined the period 1880–2000, concluding that the frequency of financial crises since 1973 had been rivaled only by the 1920s and 1930s, but in their view, there was "little evidence that crises have grown longer or output losses have

[3] The idea that in studying macroeconomic issues the proper unit of analysis must be the national economy has a long tradition coming back to Simon Kuznets, who in the 1930s led with Wesley C. Mitchell the development of national income accounts at the NBER. For Kuznets (1966), "if the study of economic growth is oriented to policy problems, the study should be centered on units that possess the major policy-making power" (*Modern economic growth: Rate, structure, and spread*, 17). I have used national data for economic analyses for instance in Tapia (2017), *Rentabilidad, inversión y crisis: Teorías económicas y datos empíricos*) and Tapia (2013), "Does investment call the tune? Empirical evidence and endogenous theories of the business cycle", *Research in Political Economy* 28, 229–259.

[4] Gorton (2012), *Misunderstanding financial crises: Why we don't see them coming.*

[5] Laeven & Valencia (2008), "Systemic banking crises: A new database," *IMF Working Paper* No. 08/224; Reinhart & Rogoff (2009), *This time is different: Eight centuries of financial folly*; Bordo et al. (2001), "Is the crisis problem growing more severe?", *Economic Policy* 16(32), 51–82.

become larger." This conclusion, as we will see in the next chapter, is untenable considering the contractions of WGDP in 2009 and 2020.

In an update of their inventory of crises, Luc Laeven and Fabián Valencia estimated in 2012 that during the period 1970–2011, there were worldwide 146 *banking* crises, 218 *currency* crises, and 66 episodes of *sovereign debt* crisis and debt restructuring.[6] The authors provided careful formal definitions of each type of crisis. A common fundamental feature of these three types of crises as defined by Laeven and Valencia is financial stress due to the inability of private financial enterprises or government institutions to face due payments. This leads to bank runs and liquidations (*banking crisis*), devaluation of the national currency (*currency crisis*), or sovereign debt defaults (*sovereign debt crisis*). Laeven and Valencia maintained that these three types of crises often overlap in a "twin" or "triplet" crisis, i.e., a period in which two or three of these types of financial crisis occurs at the same time.

Many countries experienced banking crises in 2008, but for Laeven and Valencia, problems in the financial sector were severe enough to classify them as systemic banking crises only in later years, specifically 2009 for Denmark, Germany, Greece, Ireland, Mongolia, and Ukraine; 2010 for Kazakhstan; and 2011 for Nigeria and Spain. Though obviously Laeven and Valencia focused on national economies as the units in which crises can occur, they accepted that some banking crises "do not originate domestically but are imported from abroad when foreign subsidiaries of domestic banks get in trouble."

Reinhart and Rogoff saw financial crises occurring in waves, and Laeven and Valencia agreed with that view. When Laeven and Valencia examined the distribution of banking crises since the 1970s to 2012 (Fig. 1.1), they found a large peak of "crisis activity" in 2008, but the rest of the crises are loosely spread out: in the 1980s and 1990s there were many financial crises, with only the mid-1980s and the last two years of the century showing financial calm. Clear peaks of crisis activity can be observed in the mid-1970s and the early 1980s, and in three clusters during the 1990s, corresponding to the crises of the transition economies of Eastern Europe, of Latin American countries during the so-called *tequila* crisis in the mid-1990s, and of East Asian countries during the so-called Asian financial crisis around 1998. For Laeven and Valencia

[6] Laeven & Valencia (2012), "Systemic banking crises database: An update," *IMF Working Paper* 12/163.

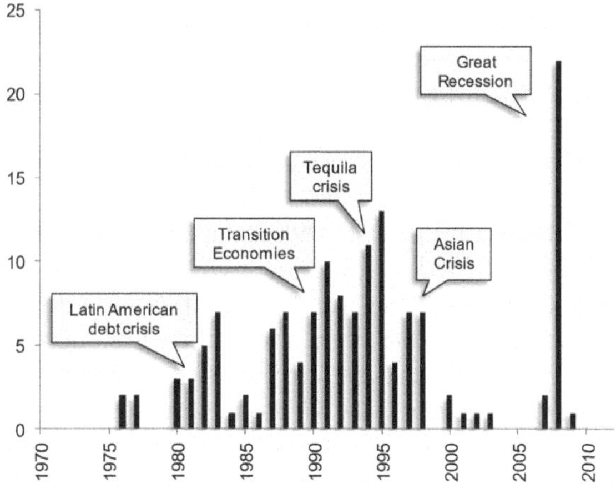

Fig. 1.1 Number of national economies undergoing a systemic banking crisis each year (Reproduced from Laeven & Valencia (2012), Systemic banking crises database: An update)

there are "crisis cycles," that "frequently coincide with credit cycles" and considering 129 banking crises episodes for which credit data are available, they found that 45 episodes were preceded by a credit boom.[7]

As obvious intellectual derivatives of the Great Recession, two outstanding studies on financial crises in advanced economies were published in the past ten years in the *American Economic Review*. In the first one, Schularick and Taylor (2012) analyzed the factors contributing to 79 major banking crises, each one dated in a unique year in a panel of 14 advanced economies in the 138 year period 1870–2008.[8] In the second one, Romer and Romer (2017) examined 24 countries of the OECD in the period 1967–2012.[9] Starting from the narrative OECD reports on the national economies of the organization and coming from the idea that financial problems fall along a continuum, Romer and Romer attributed in a remarkable exercise of eyeballing a value between 0 and 15

[7] Laeven & Valencia (2012), "Systemic banking crises".

[8] Schularick & Taylor (2012), "Credit booms gone bust: Monetary policy, leverage cycles, and financial crises, 1870–2008", *American Economic Review* 102(2), 1029–1061.

[9] Romer & Romer (2017), "New evidence on the aftermath of financial crises in advanced countries", *American Economic Review* 107(10): 3072–3118.

(with 0 for no distress, 1 for disruption of minimal importance, and 15 for extreme crisis with maximum distress) to an index of financial distress severity for each half year in the sample they analyzed. This 16-point scale was so wide that the value 15 was not attributed to any period of the sample (the highest value of severity of financial stress assessed by Romer and Romer was 14 points for the first half of 2009 in Iceland, followed by 13 points for the second half of 1998 in Japan). Other aspects of these two studies will be discussed in subsequent chapters of this book.

The aforementioned analyses were focused on the financial sector, with the real economy considered mostly as the outcome variable of the disturbances in money markets and credit activities. However, in *Misunderstanding Financial Crises* Gary Gorton affirmed that financial crises "are an integral part of business cycles". Gorton, for whom the 2008 financial crisis in the United States was to a large extent a bank panic on the market of sale-and-repurchase securities (the REPO market), bank runs and panics "are not irrational events. Panics happen when information arrives about a coming recession. It is the fact that there are potential problems with banks that causes a run".[10] This observation points to a more fundamental underlying dynamic: that as a rule financial crises are preceded by disturbances in the real economy in which goods and services are produced and sold. This fact was noted more than a century ago by Wesley C. Mitchell, and half a century before Mitchell by Karl Marx.[11]

In this book, it is argued that the dozens of financial crises counted by different observers in the past half century are just the national manifestations of six large downturns in world economic activity. These crises of the real economy of the world system had different manifestations in the financial sphere.

To assert that there have been six crises in the world economy since 1970 to the present implies that these crises are discrete, countable phenomena, representing distinct states of an entity that can be properly called world or global economy. In the same way that a human body is not just an aggregate of four limbs, a trunk, and a head, the global economy is not only the aggregation of the two-hundred-and-some national economies, but an integrated unity of a higher order. To

[10] Gorton (2012), *Misunderstanding*, 5, 74.

[11] Mitchell (1913), *Business cycles*, 576–579; Marx (1981), *Capital: A critique of political economy—Volume 3* [1894], Parts 4 & 5.

count and to measure are two basic endeavors of science. But to count something, first it is necessary to clarify what is to be counted to avoid getting entangled in fuzzy reasoning and logical contradictions. The Sokal affair demonstrated that unfortunately these are not rare in the social sciences.[12]

The remainder of this book discusses empirical and theoretical issues related to the crises of the world economy, including their characteristics, causes, and implications. It presents an alternative view to understanding these crises emphasizing empirical data but also taking a historical and global perspective. Chapter 2 provides evidence on the six crises of the global economy in the past half century. Data on capital formation, output growth, unemployment rates, monetary aggregates, industrial activity, and rates of return on capital show that in the mid-1970s, in the early years of the three following decades, in 2008–2009 and in 2020 there were significant stoppages of capital accumulation and slowdowns of world economic activity. Chapter 3 on globalization, national economies, and global crises provides an outline of economic history as well as some major historical developments linked to each one of the crises posed in the book. Chapter 4 discusses how "economic crisis", "recession", and other terms related to the recurrent fluctuations of modern economies are understood by different authors and schools of thought. The view of some authors in the world-system school according to which crises are economic circumstances that can last even decades is critiqued based on both theoretical and empirical reasons. Chapter 5 focuses on the evidence that a world economy exists, justifying an economic analysis at this level, and discusses how old is the "world economy". Chapter 6 on causal theories of the business cycle is a general review of theories explaining why economic crises occur. In mainstream economics, economic crises are mostly viewed as anomalies of the economic system, departures from the equilibrium that is essential to the system, therefore they can only occur in response to exogenous factors. The general view adopted in this book and developed in more detail in Chapter 6 is that the reduction of profitability before crises, explained both by long-run and short-run processes, reduces investment thus leading to a drop of demand that appears as a recession and is often associated with financial turmoil. Chapter 7 on nature, oil, profits, and crises discusses the

[12] Sokal (2010), *Beyond the hoax: Science, philosophy and culture*.

links between natural resources, economic activities, and the crises of the world economy. Oil price "shocks" that would have been exogenously caused by OPEC manipulations, wars or revolutions have been often mentioned as exogenous causes of economic crises. Versus this idea, the evidence presented in Chapter 7 shows that prices of mineral raw materials peaking immediately before each crisis and quickly falling in its aftermath are endogenously determined phenomena. Raw materials rise in price under conditions of strong demand and their prices drop when the demand quickly drops because of a recession. Chapter 8 discusses and rejects the notion of long waves (Kondratieff waves), often defended by authors who are favorable to the idea of the world economy as an appropriate unit for economic, social, and historical analysis. The chapter also discusses the notion of social structures of accumulation. Chapter 9 considers the crisis that started in 2020 and was obviously triggered by the COVID-19 pandemic. The procedures and actions to fight the pandemic, which implied an almost total interruption of business activity in major sectors of the economy, triggered an economic depression that otherwise could have had quite different characteristics, as for many observers a crisis was developing in the underground and was ready to erupt in 2020, when governments began to implement isolation policies to strangle the dissemination of the virus. Chapter 10 closes the book by presenting some general conclusions and discussing the prospects for the world economy after many months of Russian invasion of Ukraine and new alignments in the world economy to a large extent because of that war. The appendices present technical issues and models some of which require knowledge of statistical methods. Appendix A presents some monetary issues. Milton Friedman showed that in national economies "money leads," i.e., that changes in the volume of the monetary mass predict the evolution of the real economy. That seems to be also true in the global economy. Reasons are given to explain the phenomena using a conceptual scheme that largely differs from Friedman's monetarism. Appendix B discusses data concerning monetary aggregates and credit, as reported for the world economy and several national economies in the WDI database of the World Bank. Appendix C presents statistical models that justify the assertion that economic growth is the main cause of greenhouse emissions and therefore climate change. Appendix D is a technical note on the profit rate and its evolution in time. Appendix E includes a numerical table with the data used in the most important analyses of the book.

CHAPTER 2

Evidence of Six Crises

A variety of economic indicators provide consistent evidence that the global economy went through a crisis six times in the past five decades. As proposed in this book, these six crises occurred in the mid-1970s, in the early years of the next three decades, around 2000, at the end of the first decade of the present century, and in 2020. If more precision is required, the six crises in the world economy can be dated—somewhat arbitrarily, as it will be explained later in this chapter—in the years 1975, 1980–1982, 1991–1993, 2001–2002, 2008–2009, and 2020, so that the world economy was in crisis for a total of 12 years in a period of half a century. This chronology of six crises of the global economy is to a large extent consistent with business cycle chronologies for national economies. This chapter provides evidence to sustain this chronology of six world economic crises.

According to the NBER, since the mid-1970s there were seven US recessions dated (*i*) Fall 1973 to Winter 1975; (*ii*) Winter to Summer 1980; (*iii*) Summer 1981 to Fall 1982; (*iv*) Summer 1990 to Winter 1991; (*v*) Winter to Fall 2001; (*vi*) Fall 2007 to Summer 2009); and (*vii*) Winter 2019 to Spring 2020. Putting together the two contiguous recessions of 1980 and 1981, the six periods in which, as it will be shown, data show significant downturns of the global economy coincide with the dates in which according to the chronology of the NBER there were recessions in the United States. This is not surprising, considering that the

J. A. Tapia, *Six Crises of the World Economy*,
https://doi.org/10.1007/978-3-031-38735-7_2

US economy is still the main national component in the world economy in value terms.[1]

Many other economies, though of course, not all, conform quite well to the chronology of crises of the global economy proposed in this book. That is the case for instance of Germany where, according to Beate Schirwitz, between 1970 and 2006, recessions ocurred from (*i*) Winter 1974 to Spring 1975, (*ii*) Winter 1980 to Fall 1983, (*iii*) Winter 1992 to Winter 1993, (*iv*) Fall 1995 to Winter 1996, and (*v*) Fall 2002 to Fall 2003.[2] Excepting the recession of the mid-1990s that seems to be a specifically German recession, all others fit the pattern of crises of the world economy proposed here. For Portugal in the period 1978–2010 recessions were dated October 1983 to June 1984, March 1991 to November 1993, May 2001 to February 2006, and May 2007 to November 2009 in a chronology of the Portuguese business cycle authored by Vitor Castro, who wrote that "[t]hese contractions coincide quite remarkably with world crises."[3] In Colombia, as reported by Carlos Alberto Duque, in the period 1967–2019 there were major economic downturns with economic growth about zero or negative in 1975, 1982–1983, 1990, 1998–2000, and 2009, and "the Colombian economy followed a similar pattern to other Latin American countries like Brazil, México, and Argentina."[4] In Spain, according to the Business Cycle Dating Committee of the Spanish Economic Association, there were recessions from (*i*) Fall 1974 to Spring 1975, (*ii*) Summer 1978 to Spring 1979, (*iii*) Winter 1992 to Summer 1993, (*iv*) Spring 2008 to Fall 2009, and (*v*) Fall 2010 to Spring 2013. These recessions conform quite well to the chronology of world economic crises proposed here,

[1] Using market exchange rates for computing national GDPs in US dollars and the WGDP in real terms, the size of the US economy in 2019 was 18.3 trillion in 2010 US dollars, versus 11.5 trillion for China and 84.9 trillion for the world economy. However, with GDPs computed using PPP rather than exchange rates, China is since 2017 the biggest economy of the world, with a GDP for the year 2019 of 22.5 trillion international dollars of 2017, compared with 20.5 trillion for the United States and 130.0 trillion for the world (as reported in the WDI database in November 2020).

[2] Schirwitz (2009), "A comprehensive German business cycle chronology", *Empirical Economics* 37(2), 287–301.

[3] Castro (2015), "The Portuguese business cycle: Chronology and duration dependence", *Empirical Economics* 49(1), 325–342.

[4] Duque (2022), "Economic growth and the rate of profit in Colombia 1967–2019: A VAR time-series analysis", *Review of Radical Political Economics* 54(3), 1–19, Figure 2.

but furthermore, as I have argued elsewhere,[5] the increase of the unemployment rate from 10.6% in 2001 to 11.5% in 2002 is quite substantive evidence that at that time there was a recession in the Spanish economy, in which case the Spanish business cycle is fully consistent with the chronology of crises of the world economy proposed in this book.

Since the 1970s to the present, the Japanese economy had recessions in (*i*) Fall 1973 to Spring 1975, (*ii*) Winter 1977 to Fall 1977, (*iii*) Winter 1980 to Winter 1983, (*iv*) Spring 1985 to Fall 1986, (*v*) Winter 1991 to Fall 1993, (*vi*) Spring 1997 to Winter 1999, (*vii*) Fall 2000 to Winter 2002, (*viii*) Winter 2008 to Winter 2009, and (i*x*) Fall 2018 to Spring 2020.[6] Out of these nine Japanese recessions, six are fully consistent with the six crises of the world economy proposed here, while the three recessions of 1977, 1985–1986, and 1997–1998 are superimposed on that pattern.

The crises of the global economy in past decades can be identified using a variety of economic indicators. In the classical descriptions of the business cycle, that is, the recurrent alternation of periods of expansion and contraction in the market economy, drops in investment are a major characteristic of what have variously been called economic crises, downturns, slumps, recessions, or depressions.[7] In what follows, levels of capital formation, rates of output growth, unemployment rates, monetary aggregates, and industrial activity as measured by a chemical index will be used to support an annual chronology of crises of the world economy. During years identified as crisis years, a large proportion of the national economies of the world were in economic recession as defined by the usual criteria.

[5] Tapia (2017), *Rentabilidad, inversión y crisis—Teorías económicas y datos empíricos*, 18–22.

[6] Government of Japan, Cabinet Office (2013), "The provisional determination of business-cycle peak and trough", August 21, 2013, www.esri.cao.go.jp/en/stat/di/130821rdates.html, accessed September 2022; Anonimous (2021), "Japan recession lasted for 19 months through May 2020, government panel says", *The Japan Times*, December 1, www.japantimes.co.jp/news/2021/12/01/business/economy-business/japan-recession, accessed September 2022.

[7] Mitchell (1913), *Business cycles*; England (1913), "Economic crises", *Journal of Political Economy* 21(4), 345–354 are outstanding examples of the old literature on business cycles and economic crises. For modern reviews see Zarnowitz (1985), "Recent work on business cycles in historical perspective", *Journal of Economic Literature* 23(2), 523–580; Knoop (2004), *Recessions and depressions: Understanding business cycles*; Glasner & Cooley (1997), *Business cycles and depressions: An encyclopedia*.

Most of the indicators of the world economy used in what follows are available from the generally trusted source of the World Bank. When comparisons are possible, these data are generally consistent with those of other economic institutions such as the Organization for Economic Cooperation and Development (OECD), the International Monetary Fund (IMF), the Bank for International Settlements, or Eurostat. The Bank for International Settlements (BIS), based in Basel, Switzerland is an international financial institution owned by central banks that promotes international monetary cooperation and serves as a bank for central banks. Eurostat is the statistical branch of the European Commission.

The fact that the World Bank is a generally trusted source does not mean however that there are no problems with the statistics in its WDI database, which are obtained from a laborious and complex process of aggregation of national statistics. These in turn are produced by national economic and statistical agencies which must use the available data on production and consumption, coming usually from tax records and little else. It is obvious that the resulting statistics must be plagued by major errors. This makes economic statistics "soft" numbers which have to be taken with "many grains" of salt as it was noted, perhaps with too much emphasis, by Oskar Morgenstern.[8] During the writing of this book, I had the opportunity to notice how the World Bank changes the reported data from time to time. For instance, according to the WDI database of the World Bank, accessed in 2014, the rate of growth of Japan's GDP in the year 1970 had been −1.0%, while the same rate had been estimated by the same source as 0.4% in 2020 and 2.5% in September 2022. These values imply significant differences in economic terms. Despite these and other problems, it is my view that the World Bank's statistics for national economies and for the global economy are useful, when used with the proper care, to learn about the economic realities of our time. Indeed, it is based on these statistics that I claim in this book that the crises of the world economy occurred in specific years. But let us look at the data.

[8] Morgenstern (1950), *On the accuracy of economic observations*; Bagus (2011), "Morgenstern's forgotten contribution: A stab to the heart of modern economics", *American Journal of Economics and Sociology* 70(2), 540–562 is an exaggerated attack on economic statistics based on Morgenstern ideas.

Capital Formation and Output of the Global Economy

Since the 1930s when Wesley Mitchell and Jan Tinbergen produced the early empirical analyses of the business cycle, it is accepted that drops in investment are the key component of recessions.[9] World Bank investment data from the global economy are available for the period since 1969, as data on gross capital formation and gross fixed capital formation.[10] These data can be used as quantifiers of the rate at which capital accumulation proceeds. A rising formation of capital means acceleration of capital accumulation and economic expansion; a decline in the formation of capital means a stoppage of the accumulation of capital, that is, an economic crisis.

Figure 2.1 shows gross capital formation and gross fixed capital formation as shares of world GDP (WGDP), as reported by the World Bank in its WDI database in 2013 and in 2022. The figures reported in 2013 and 2022 differ by several percentage points, revealing how largely uncertain are these global indicators, and how large can be the differences between revisions of the statistical estimates. Nevertheless, the 2013 and 2022 series are largely consistent in terms of upward and downward oscillations. Gross capital formation shows somewhat sharper oscillations than gross fixed capital formation. According to the definitions provided in the metadata of the WDI database, *gross fixed capital formation* includes purchases of plant, machinery, and equipment; land improvements such as fences, ditches, and drains; construction of roads, railways, schools, offices, hospitals, private residential dwellings, and commercial and industrial buildings; it also includes the net acquisitions of valuables; *gross capital formation* consists of gross fixed capital formation plus net changes in the level of inventories. Both indicators are rough measures of investment in the economy, and it would be arguable which one of the two could or should be considered a more proper index of total investment as a key component of effective demand in a Keynesian or neoclassical framework, or capital accumulation in the Marxian sense. At any rate, the series of gross total

[9] Mitchell (1927), *Business cycles: The problem and its setting*; Tinbergen (1939), *Statistical testing of business-cycle theories*.

[10] The World Development Indicators (WDI) database is available at https://www.databank.worldbank.org/source/world-development-indicators. Most data used in this book are from this source.

and gross fixed capital formation in Fig. 2.1 reveal sharp drops of investment in 1974–1975, 1979–1983, 1989–1993, 2000–2002, 2008–2009, and 2019–2020. Overall, the measures of gross capital formation for total capital and fixed capital show that investment substantially declined in the mid-1970s, in the early years of the three following decades, in 2009, and in 2020. These are the six crises of the world economy proposed in this book.

Figure 2.2 shows together the most recent series of capital formation and the annual rate of growth of WGDP. The six crises of the world economy are marked by obvious drops of WGDP growth in 1975, 1982, 2009, and 2020, and substantive declines in the early 1990s and the years around the turn of the century. In all cases, the drop in the growth of the world economy coincides with a drop in capital formation. Considering the size of the contraction of the world economy as gauged by the rate of growth of WGDP, the crisis of 2020 associated with the COVID-19

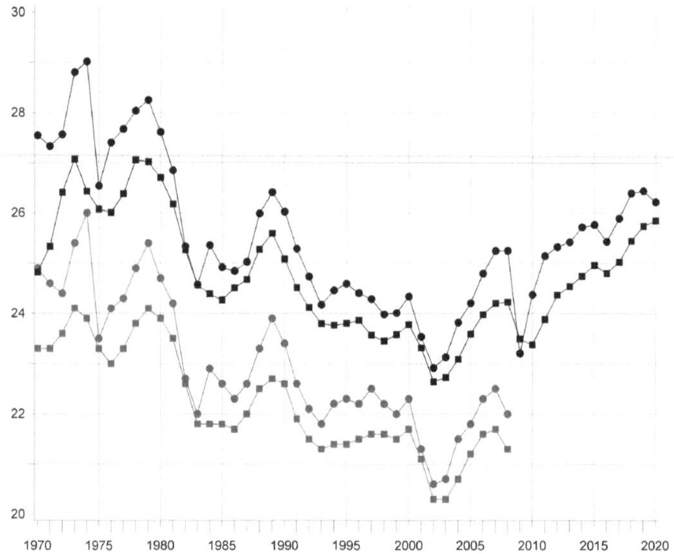

Fig. 2.1 Gross capital formation (dots) and gross fixed capital formation (squares) as percent of WGDP (as reported by the WDI database in 2022 [upper lines] and 2013 [lower lines])

pandemic has been the most severe crisis of the world economy since data are available, as in the series shown in Fig. 2.2, reported by the World Bank in 2022, the growth of the world economy in 2020 was −3.3%, compared with −1.3% in 2009, at the time of the Great Recession. There are however other ways of assessing the severity of the crises in recent decades.

Figure 2.3 shows data on gross capital formation (top panel) and gross fixed capital formation (bottom panel) in the global economy adjusted for inflation, in trillion US$ of 2010, in the period 1971–2020. In each panel of Fig. 2.3, a year is identified as a year of crisis if there was a decline in

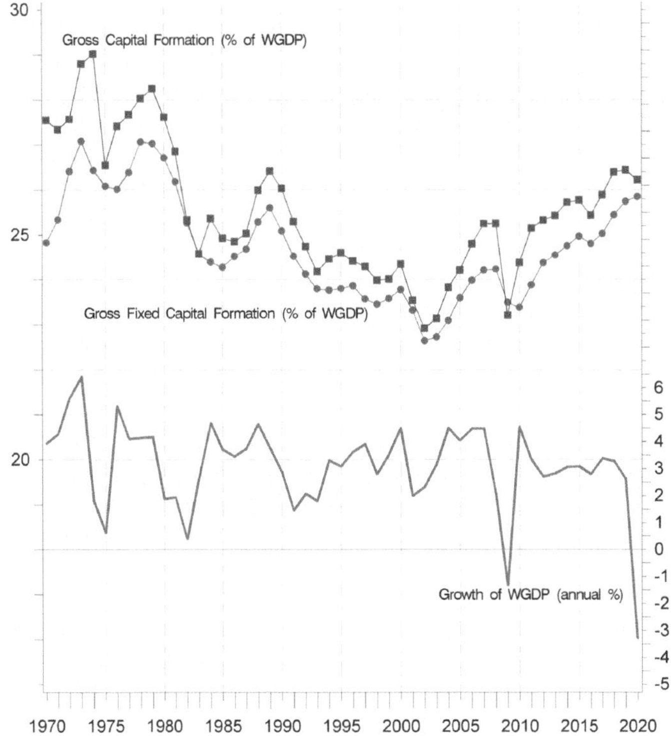

Fig. 2.2 Annual rate of growth of WGDP, gross capital formation and gross fixed capital formation as a percentage of WGDP (Author's elaboration from WDI data accessed September 2022)

capital formation in real terms. Crisis years identified that way are marked with a gray bar. The two measures of capital formation identify crisis years in a slightly different way. Declines in gross capital formation identify a total of 12 crisis years—1975, 1980, 1981, 1982, 1991, 1992, 1993, 2001, 2002, 2008, 2009, and 2020—while declines in gross fixed capital formation identify only eight crisis years—1974,1975, 1982, 1991, 1992, 1993, 2002, 2009, and 2020. Both panels of Fig. 2.3 show that in the past five decades, considering annual data the rising trend in gross capital formation was interrupted six times, and each interruption lasted between one and three years. If declining gross fixed capital formation is used as identifying criterium of the crisis years, then the crisis of the early 1990s was the longest crisis, lasting three years, from 1991 to 1993. Considering gross capital formation the crises of the early 1980s and the early 1990s both lasted three years, 1980–1982 and 1991–1993, respectively.

Let us examine for instance the crisis that as defined by a contraction in gross capital formation lasted one year, 1975, while defined by the contraction of gross fixed capital formation lasted two years, 1974 and 1975. In neither of these two years the rate of growth of the world economy was negative, but it had a major drop in both years, as it went from 6.4% in 1973 to 1.8% in 1974, and then dropped even more to 0.6% in 1975. It is obvious that 1975 was a crisis year meaning an interruption of capital accumulation or a significant contraction of the rate of growth of the world economy, but there are also reasons to extend that crisis to 1974.[11] The fact that different criteria to identify crisis years produce slightly different results with respect to the concrete years in which crises of the world economy occurred seems to be a good reason why it might be preferable to refer to "the crisis of the mid-1970s" rather than choosing quite arbitrarily one of several possible criteria to define "crisis" and thus refer either to the crisis of 1974–1975 or to the crisis of 1975.

Figure 2.3 also shows the years in which recessions of the global economy occurred according to the IMF chronology.[12] The IMF chronology and the chronology proposed here are largely consistent as

[11] Besides a sudden drop in the rate of growth of WGDP, in 1974 there was a worldwide contraction of the monetary mass and credit to the private sector, as it will be shown later in this chapter.

[12] Kose & Terrones (2015), *Collapse and revival—Understanding global recessions and recoveries*.

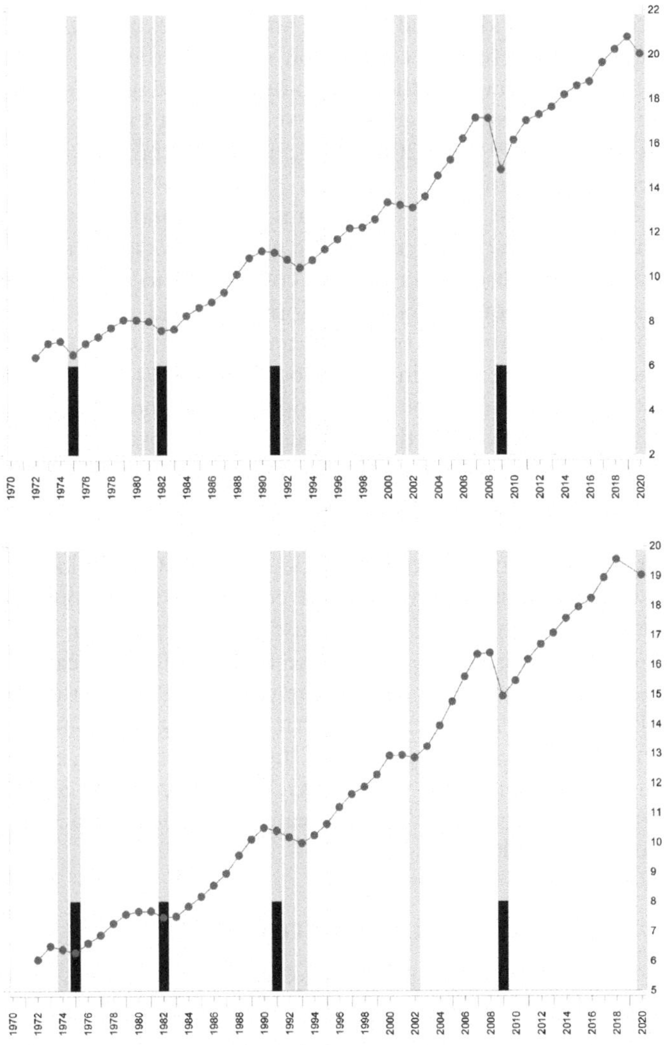

Fig. 2.3 Gross capital formation (top panel) and gross fixed capital formation (bottom panel) in the world economy (trillion 2010 US$). Gray bars mark the years in which the specific measure of capital formation declined. Black bars mark the four years in which recessions of the world economy took place according to the IMF chronology by Kose and Terrones (2013). (Author's elaboration from WDI data accessed September 2022)

all the recession years identified by Kose and Terrones are included in the crisis years defined here by a contraction of any of the two measures of capital formation. However, the chronology of Kose and Terrones does not identify any recession longer than a year and does not detect anyone occurring between 1991 and 2009. These issues will be discussed in more detail later in this chapter.

Table 2.1 shows the peaks and troughs of the annual series of capital formation to estimate the severity of the crises, that can be measured by the peak to trough absolute or relative contraction in capital formation. The contraction of both gross capital formation and gross fixed capital formation—either in absolute or relative terms—identify the Great Recession as the most severe crisis in the period 1971–2020, with a decline of 2.3 trillion dollars in gross capital formation, which amounts to a contraction of 13.5% between 2007, the peak year, when gross capital formation was 17.2 trillion, and 2009, the trough year of the Great Recession, when gross capital formation dropped to 14.8 trillion (as estimated in 2010 US$). The crisis of 1990–1993, was the mildest one, as during the three years that it lasted, implied only a decline of just 0.23 trillion dollars, or 1.7%, in gross capital formation. Of course, all these considerations must be taken with a grain of salt, because first, the precision of all these numbers must be necessarily low and second, 2020, the year in which the series of capital formation ends, is the year of the deepest contraction of WGDP to date. What is certain is that according to the most recent figures on the annual rate of growth of the global economy, the deepest downturn occurred in 2020, with a WGDP contraction of 3.3%, which is a contraction 2 percentage points greater than the contraction of the Great Recession in 2009.

Consumption

Since the early studies on the business cycle, it is known that both consumption and investment grow in the upturn and fall in the downturn of the cycle, but investment is a more volatile variable and the drop in investment in the recession is more pronounced.[13] For the period 1971–2020 the coefficients of variation of gross capital formation and consumption (both measured as a percentage of WGDP) are 4.3 and 2.1,

[13] Mitchell (1913), *Business cycles*, Ch. VIII; Tinbergen (1950), *The dynamics of business cycles*, Ch. 13.

Table 2.1 Severity of the crises of the world economy measured by the peak-trough contraction in gross capital formation (GCF, upper panel, trillion US dollars of 2010) or gross fixed capital formation (GFCF, lower panel)

	GCF		*Contraction*	
Year	*(tUS$)*		*tUS$*	*Percent*
1974	7.1	Peak		
1975	6.5	Trough	0.6	8.5
1979	8.0	Peak		
1982	7.5	Trough	0.5	6.2
1990	11.1	Peak		
1993	10.4	Trough	0.8	7.1
2000	13.3	Peak		
2002	13.1	Trough	0.2	1.7
2007	17.2	Peak		
2009	14.8	Trough	2.3	13.5
2019	21.4	Peak		
2020	20.6	Trough	0.8	3.7
1973	6.5	Peak		
1975	6.3	Trough	0.23	3.46
1981	7.7	Peak		
1982	7.5	Trough	0.22	2.81
1990	10.5	Peak		
1993	10.0	Trough	0.52	4.94
2001	12.9	Peak		
2002	12.8	Trough	0.09	0.69
2008	16.4	Peak		
2009	14.9	Trough	1.46	8.90
2019	20.0	Peak		
2020	19.0	Trough	1.00	4.98

respectively. Indeed, the share of consumption in GDP usually *grows* in recessions, as investment decreases sharply and GDP itself stagnates or shrinks.

Figure 2.4 shows an indicator of total consumption in the world economy between 1970 and 2020. This measure of consumption as a share of world output is quite stable, oscillating between 55 and 60% of WGDP during the whole period. Consumption grew dramatically as a share of GDP during the Great Recession, in 2009, and the same

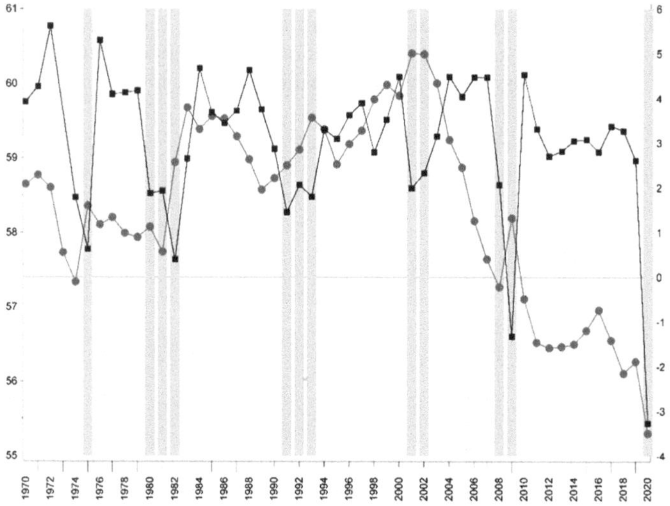

Fig. 2.4 Final consumption expenditure of households and nonprofit institutions serving households (% of WGDP, dots, l.h.s.) and annual growth of world GDP (%, squares, r.h.s.). Gray bars mark the years of crisis as indicated by a contraction in gross capital formation (Author's elaboration from WDI data accessed September 2022)

happened in the crises of the mid-1970s and the early 1980s. Investment, though being a smaller proportion of the aggregate economy, contracts intensely during the recession, so that the proportion accounted for consumption in WGDP grows. However, as shown in Fig. 2.4, that was not the case in the recession of 2020, when consumption dramatically dropped because of the restrictions on commerce imposed by the policies of isolation implemented to fight the COVID-19 pandemic. This is one of the elements that make the crisis of 2020 very different to the other five crises of the past half century.

Unemployment

Unemployment rates provide the most intuitive illustration of the crises of the world economy since the 1970s to the present. Because unemployment is a lagged indicator and starts declining or rising in each cyclical fluctuation months after economic activity starts expanding or contrasting, respectively, plotting together national unemployment rates, crises appear as clusters of rising unemployment rates which reach a peak that marks with a lag of about a year the end of the crisis and the start of the new expansion. Regretfully, for most countries, there are no appropriate series of historical unemployment rates beyond the most recent decades. Figure 2.5 presents unemployment data since 1972 for selected countries. The figure shows clusters of peaks in unemployment rate graphs centered approximately in 1975, 1982, 1993, 2001, and 2010, and the graphs show upturns of the unemployment rate in basically all countries in 2020.

The WDI database provides a series of 1991–2020 ILO estimates of the world unemployment rate. The WDI indicates that these harmonized estimates use strict data selection criteria and enhanced methods to ensure comparability across countries and over time. Using this series, the annual absolute change in unemployment correlates −0.92 ($n = 30$, $P < 0.0001$)

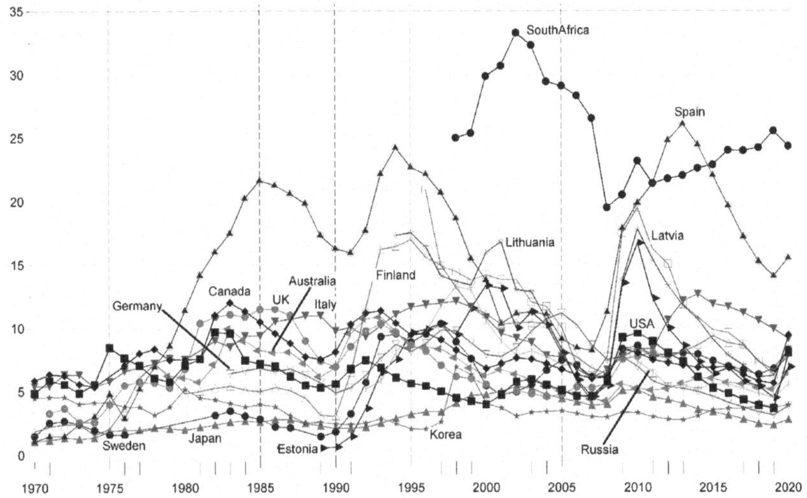

Fig. 2.5 Unemployment rate as percent of the labor force, selected countries (Author's elaboration from WDI data accessed September 2022)

with the annual rate of growth of the world economy. This is a confirmation of Okun's law—the negative correlation between the growth of output and change in unemployment—at the global level.[14]

Monetary Aggregates

A basic characteristic of capitalism is to be an economy which is fully based on money. Indeed, the term "money economy" was proposed by Wesley Mitchell to differentiate the modern industrial economy based on business enterprises from former types of economic organization in which money existed but fulfilled a much minor role in economic life.[15]

Monetary disturbances are always part of economic crises. The evolution of monetary aggregates also provides evidence that the global economy went through six crises since the crisis of the mid-1970s to the worldwide recession of the COVID-19 pandemic in 2020. Figures 2.6 and 2.7 show what the World Bank denominates "broad money", which is very similar to what economists have referred to since many decades ago as M2, corresponding basically to money bills in circulation and demand bank accounts.[16] Figure 2.7 shows how in the crises of the twentieth century a rapid expansion of money as compared with output announced during the crisis, while during the crisis itself, money ceased growing and contracted. Thus in 1972 broad money reached a peak of 64.7% in WGDP units, to drop to 60.7% in 1974; then in 1980, broad money that had reached 66.1% contracted to 63.8% in 1978; in 1992 it shrank to 88.3% after peaking at 93.3% three years earlier; in 2001, it dropped to 95.5% after peaking in 2000 at 99.2%; after a quick buildup between 2005 and 2008, in 2009 broad money peaked at 110.5% to drop to 107.6 in 2010. Thus the pattern is solid, with monetary expansions preceding the

[14] Okun's law can be considered as indirect evidence in favor of the labor theory of value, as it shows that the rate of growth of total output (in money value) is correlated negatively with the change in unemployment, or positively with the change in employment.

[15] Mitchell (1913), *Business cycles,* Ch. 2; Groseclose (1961), *Money and man.*

[16] In 2013 the only measure of money in the world economy that was reported in the WDI database of the World Bank was M2. In later years "broad money" was added, both series had almost identical values. After 2019, M2 was no longer reported.

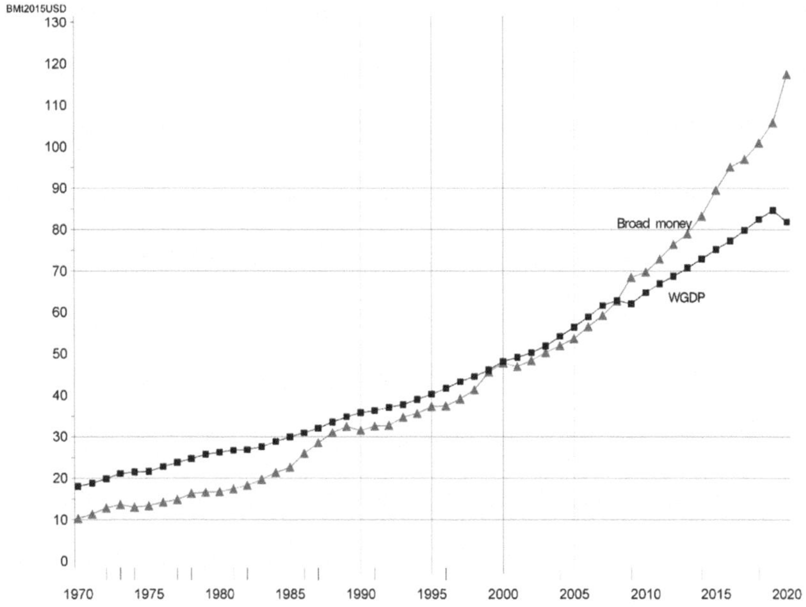

Fig. 2.6 Broad money and global output (WGDP) both in trillion of 2015 US dollars. (Author's elaboration from WDI data accessed September 2022)

downturns, in which the rule is monetary contraction.[17] Figure 2.7 also shows two indicators of credit, a wide one including all domestic credit to the private sector and a restricted one including just credit supplied to the private sector by banks. The monetary mass as indexed by broad money appears at an intermediate range between the two types of credit, and credit also reveals a pattern of escalation in the years leading to the crisis. Interestingly, the Great Recession appears as the moment when, for the first time since data are available, the monetary mass in the global economy, as measured by broad money, exceeded WGDP.

[17] See Appendix A for a brief econometric discussion of the hypothesis that "money leads" in the world economy. Appendix B describes how the World Bank dramatically changed its estimates for M2 in the years around the Great Recession. For a period that I believe coincided with the time of the COVID-19 pandemic, the World Bank ceased reporting money aggregates for the world economy.

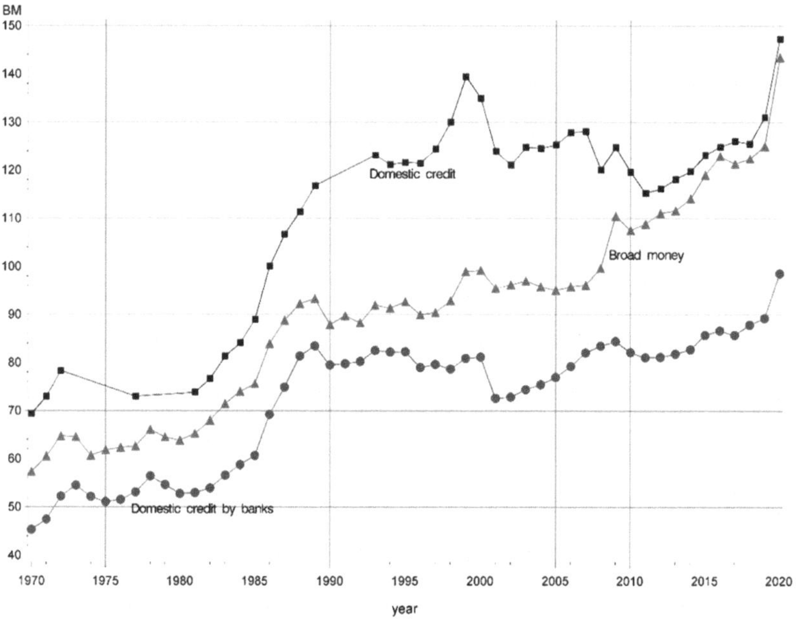

Fig. 2.7 Broad money and credit to the private sector (both as percent of WGDP) (Author's elaboration from WDI data accessed September 2022)

Economic Activity as Measured by a Chemical Index

Evidence that reinforces the chronology of six crises of the global economy in the mid-1970s, in the early years of the next three decades, in 2008 and in 2020 is also provided by the series of global emissions of CO_2, a variable that, to my knowledge, has been never used as an economic indicator.

Figure 2.8 presents three series of global emissions of CO_2. The series at the bottom comprises only emissions generated in energy-related activities; the intermediate series comprises the combustion of fossil fuels and industrial processes; the series at the top includes also emissions implied by changes in land use, added to all other processes in which CO_2 is produced. These series are estimated from data on consumption and trade of fossil fuels, production of cement, deforestation or forestry activities,

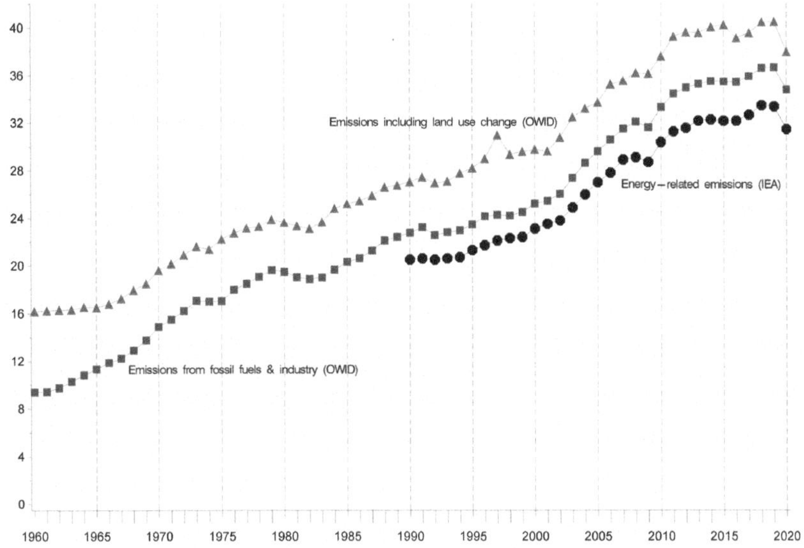

Fig. 2.8 CO_2 global emissions, gigatons, estimates from two sources, International Energy Agency (IEA) and Our World In Data (OWID), accessed September 2022

etc. Since at the global level net trade is zero, errors in estimating trade of fuels may introduce errors when estimating national CO_2 emissions, but they are irrelevant to estimate global emissions. The three series present a steady growth which is clearly interrupted in times of downturn of the world economy, like 2009 and 2020, but also the mid-1970s and the early years of the next three decades. Figure 2.9 plots annual changes in WGDP and in CO_2 emissions produced by fossil fuel combustion and industrial activity. The two series are highly correlated (the correlation coefficient is 0.72) revealing the quite obvious fact that economic activities are the source of emissions so that, for instance, when the world economy contracted by 0.83 trillion dollars in 2009, emissions of CO_2 contracted by 0.46 gigatons. Even more dramatically, in 2020 the world economy contracted by 2.8 trillion dollars while emissions dropped by 1.9 gigatons. According to the WDI database, world emissions of CO_2 from the combustion of fossil fuels decreased by 5% in the year 2020, obviously because of the economic depression associated with the COVID-19 pandemic. Then they increased by 5.3% in 2021, because of the economic rebound that was acclaimed with joy by most politicians.

The interruptions in the past half century by periods of economic turmoil (in which, as data show, both capital formation and total global output significantly slowed down) of the almost linear increase of emissions did not pass unobserved to natural scientists studying the dynamics of climate change. Indeed, the periods in which CO_2 emissions ceased growing where mentioned in climate change publications using terms from the economic and financial literature. Thus, the mid-1970s were referred to as the First Oil Crisis; the early 1980s as the Second Oil Crisis or the Savings & Loans Crisis; the crisis of the early 1990s was related to the collapse of the Soviet bloc and the USSR; the late 1990s was the time of the Asian Financial Crisis; and finally, 2008–2009 was the Great Recession or Global Financial Crisis. In these five occasions, the growth of

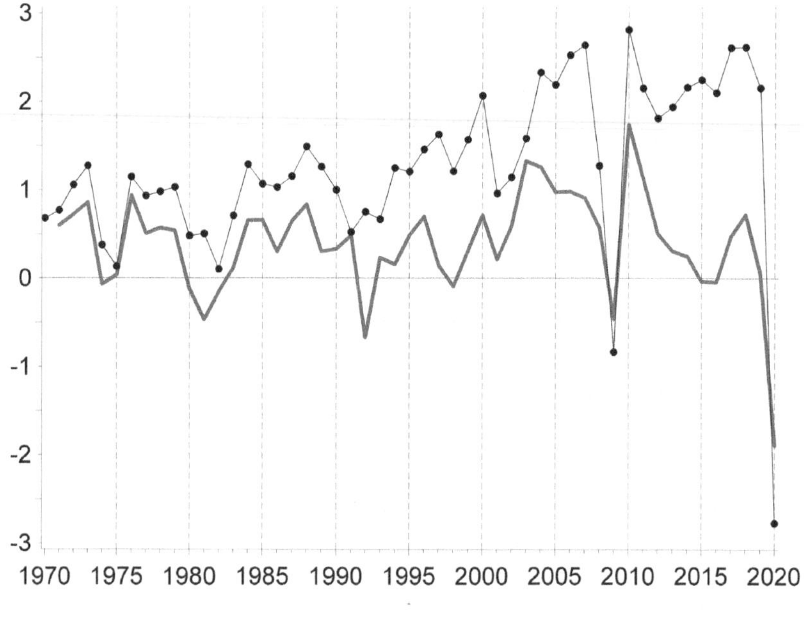

Fig. 2.9 Annual change in global CO_2 emissions (gigatons, gray line) and annual change in WGDP (trillion US 2015 dollars, dots) (Author's elaboration from OWID and WDI data)

annual emissions of CO_2 ceased and emissions declined at least for one or two years.[18] This is what has happened in the period of history for which data on national CO_2 emissions are available, they indeed slowed down or contracted during the Great Depression of the 1930s and in every occasion in which national economies passed through a recession.[19] As shown in Fig. 2.9, the annual change in emissions is strongly correlated with the annual change in global economic output. Furthermore, the rates of annual growth of WGDP are also significantly correlated with the annual increases of atmospheric concentrations of CO_2—which are not estimated from economic data, but directly measured from air samples. To discuss that correlation, however, is quite technical and goes beyond the scope of this book.[20]

For the years 1971–2020, the Pearson correlation coefficient of the annual rate of growth of WGDP with the annual rate of growth of CO_2 global emissions is 0.82 ($n = 50$, $P < 0.001$). When lagged one year, the rate of growth of broad money in 2015 US$ correlates 0.44 with WGDP growth ($n = 50$, $P < 0.001$) and 0.31 with the rate of growth of CO_2 emissions ($n = 50$, $P = 0.027$). These variables represent different indicators of the global business cycle and therefore, they are highly correlated.

Profitability

The idea that economic crises are preceded and caused by drops in profits and profit rates was proposed by Marx in some of his unpublished manuscripts and entered briefly into mainstream economics in the first half of the twentieth century when it was sustained by Wesley Mitchell. This issue will be thoroughly discussed in Chapter 6.

18 Peters et al. (2012), "Rapid growth in CO_2 emissions after the 2008–2009 global financial crisis", *Nature Climate Change* 2(1), 2–4.

19 Tapia & Carpintero (2013), "Chapter 3—Dynamics and economic aspects of climate change", in Kang & Banga, eds., *Combating climate change: An agricultural perspective*, 29–58.

20 Tapia, Ionides & Carpintero (2012), "Climate change and the world economy: Short-run determinants of atmospheric CO_2", *Environmental Science & Policy* 21, 50–62.

Profit rates have been investigated rarely by mainstream economists, and always at the level of national economies.[21] Much more commonly profit rates have been the concern of researchers working in a Marxian framework. With the profit rate defined usually as the ratio of total annual profits to total advanced capital, a usual point of controversy is how to estimate the value of capital to be used as the denominator of the rate. Participants in these debates have proposed either replacement costs or historical costs of fixed capital as denominator of an estimated profit rate.[22] Going beyond national data, Minqi Li and coworkers, Esteban Ezequiel Maito, and Michael Roberts, produced several years ago estimates for the rate of profit for the world economy.[23] Another attempt to estimate the world rate of profit has been done recently by Basu et al.[24] This attempt by Basu et al. seems to be a much better one, both because practical and theoretical considerations. On the practical side, Basu et al. have included in their computations a larger number of countries and have provided estimates using different exchange rates, either nominal or PPP-based. From the point of view of theory, Basu et al. demonstrate that the world profit rate must be a weighted mean of the national profit rates, but the proper weight for this weighted average must be the national share of capital in a world capital, not the national GDP share in WGDP, which

[21] Nordhaus (1974), "The falling share of profits", *Brookings Papers on Economic Activity* 1, 169–217; Feldstein & Summers (1977), "Is the rate of profit falling?", *Brookings Papers on Economic Activity* 1, 211–228; Blanchard, Rhee & Summers (1993), "The stock market, profit, and investment", *Quarterly Journal of Economics* 108(1), 115–136.

[22] Andrew Kliman (2012), thoroughly discussed these issues in *The failure of capitalist production*. In *Theory as critique—Essays on* Capital Paul Mattick Jr. (2019) sustains that overall, economic statistics about profits or capital are not valid to test the corresponding Marxian concepts because Marx's profit rate is a non-observable variable. According to Duque García (2022), this was also the view of Althusser and Balibar. To discuss these issues goes beyond the scope of this book.

[23] Li et al. (2007), "Long waves, institutional changes, and historical trends: A study of the long-term movement of the profit rate in the capitalist world-economy. *Journal of World-Systems Research* 13(1), 33–54; Roberts (2012), "A world rate of profit", https://www.gesd.free.fr/mrwrate.pdf; Maito (2018), "The tendency of the rate of profit to fall since the nineteenth century and a world rate of profit", in Carchedi & Roberts, eds., *World in crisis*, 129–156.

[24] Basu et al. (2022), "World profit rates, 1960–2019", University of Massachusetts Amherst, Economics Department Working Paper Series 318, https://doi.org/10.7275/43yv-c721.

had been the usual weight in previous attempts to estimate the world profit rate.

Figures 2.10 and 2.11 presents, respectively, four of the estimates of the profit rate for the United States and four of the world profit rate estimates by Basu et al.

Obviously, because of the lack of data for many countries, the problems with the data themselves, and the lack of theoretical consensus on how to compute the profit rate from the data in national statistics, the reliability of the graphs in Figs. 2.10 and 2.11 as accurate estimates of the level of profitability of capital in the United States or in the world economy is just relative. However, taken together, these series provide a glimpse or a general idea of how the fluctuations of the actual profit rate may have actually been.

The four series in Fig. 2.10 have relatively different shapes and, considering the whole period, their long-term trends look like quite inconsistent. All of them show nevertheless drops of the estimated rate

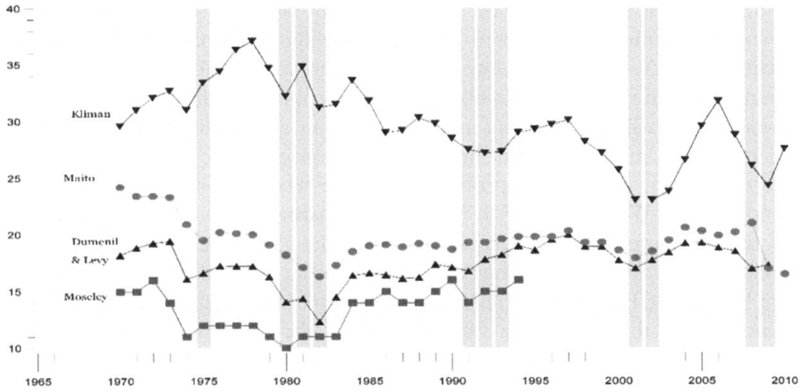

Fig. 2.10 Annual rates of profit (%) for the US economy, as estimated by Andrew Kliman, Gerard Dumenil & Dominique Levy, and Fred Moseley, and for the world economy as estimated by Esteban Maito. Gray bars mark the years of crises of the world economy as defined by a decline of year-to-year gross capital formation (Author's elaboration from data in Kliman (2012), *The failure of capitalist production*; Moseley (2000), "The rate of profit and stagnation in the US economy," in Baiman, Boushey & Saunders, eds., *Political economy and contemporary capitalism*, 59–67; and Maito, "The historical transience of capital: The downward trend in the rate of profit since the XIX century")

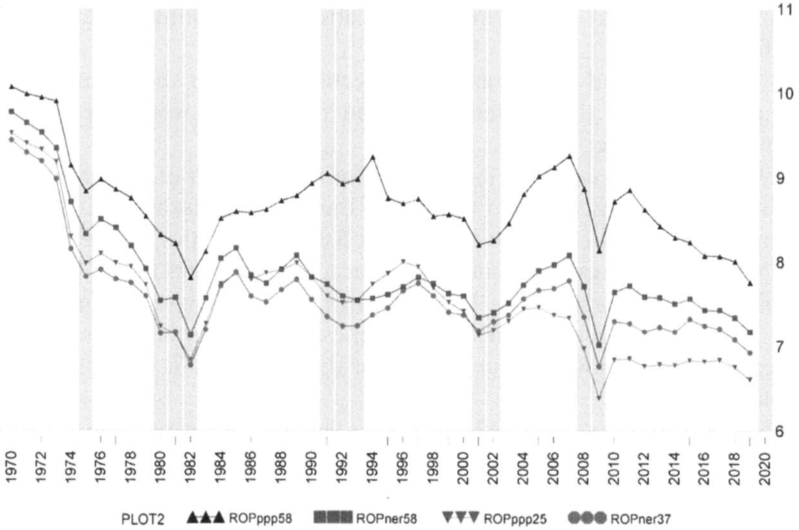

Fig. 2.11 Four estimates of the annual rate of profit (r. h. s. scale, %) for the world economy, as computed by Deepankar Basu, Julio Huato, Jesus Lara Jauregui, and Evan Wasner. Gray bars mark the years of crises of the world economy as defined by a decline of year-to-year gross capital formation (Author's elaboration from Basu et al. data in dbasu.shinyapps.io/World-Profitability/ and WDI on gross capital formation in the world economy. The data used by Basu et al. to estimate the annual profit rate for the world economy are from the Extended Penn World Table 7.0. The variable name in the figure legend indicates the exchange rates to aggregate national data that were used in these four estimates: either nominal exchange rates ("ner" in the name of the variables in the figure legend) or PPP-based exchange rates ("ppp" in the name of the variable). The number at the end of the variable name is the number of countries used in the computations, the largest number corresponds to the estimation when all available observations were included; the smallest one is when only countries for which all observations are available for all selected years were included)

of profit in the years immediately preceding the crises proposed in this book; in all of them there are also recoveries of profitability in the years following the crises. Thus, all estimated profit rates show drops in profitability in n1973–1974, in the late 1970s, in the late 1980s–early 1990s, around 2000, and in the years immediately before the 2008 crash. In his book on *Capitalism*, Anwar Shaikh's estimates of the rate of business profit for the US economy show obvious declines in 1973–1975, 1978–1983, 1988–1990, 1998–2002, and 2006–2009, which is also consistent with my chronology.[25] And the same looks applicable to the estimates of profitability computed by Li, Xiao, and Zhu in their study of long-term trends of profit rates in the capitalist world economy.[26] Of course, considering that the United States is in value terms the largest part of the world economy, it would be implausible that the evolution of the profit rate in the United States were very different to the evolution of the rate of profit at the level of the global economy.

The estimates of a world rate of profit by Basu et al. shown in Fig. 2.11 are also consistent with my chronology of crises of the world economy. Note that all series, except one in one occasion, show declines before the crisis and increases during the crisis. With all the uncertainties associated with the national or international estimates of the rate of return on capital, they provide in my view an additional layer of evidence supportive of the existence of crises of the world economy in the cited years. Production in the market economy is production for profit, and declining levels of profitability tend to reduce investment—generating large masses of hoarded money that reduce demand and often go to speculative channels increasing the risk of financial troubles. All these phenomena are known from long ago, though to a large extent have been generally ignored in mainstream economics. The statistical associations of falling profits with falling investment and the subsequent outflows of money toward speculative activities and hoarding have been repeatedly found at

[25] Shaikh (2016), *Capitalism: Competition, conflict, crises*, Figures 6.1, 246, and 6.2, 249.

[26] Li, Xiao & Zhu (2007), "Long waves, institutional changes, and historical trends: A study of the long-term movement of the profit rate in the capitalist world-economy", *Journal of World-Systems Research* 13(1), 33–54.

the level of national economies.[27] Figure 2.12, showing profits for business corporations in the United States between 1948 and 2019 shows that profitability declines coinciding with every run into recession, for instance, profits peaked in 2007 and started to decline immediately before the Great Recession; after recovering in the early years of the next decade, they reached another peak in 2017 and since that year they started a decline that was indeed announcing a crisis when the economy was closed down by the COVID-19 pandemics. Overall, statistics for the national economies and the global economy are consistent with the view that drops in profitability precede economic crises.

Fig. 2.12 Corporate business profits (billions of dollars, log scale) before (upper line) and after taxes (lower line), without inventory valuation adjustment and capital consumption adjustment. Shaded areas are recessions, according to the NBER chronology (Modified from the website of the FRED database, Federal Reserve Bank of St. Louis, accessed October 14, 2020. Data from the US Bureau of Economic Analysis)

[27] I have explored these statistical associations at the level of the US economy, for instance in the chapter "Investment, profit and crises: Theories and evidence", in Carchedi & Roberts, eds., *World in crisis* and, in Spanish, in the book *Rentabilidad, inversión y crisis: Teorías económicas y datos empíricos.*

Stylized Facts

Mohammed H. I. Dore, a theorist of the business cycle, defined the stylized facts pertaining to a phenomenon as "the enduring empirical regularities that are its defining characteristics."[28] In Dore's view there are ten stylized facts (SF) of business cycles, that can be summarized as follows: (SF1) long-term growth, so that after the recession each expansion reaches and overcomes the level of the previous expansion; (SF2) recurrent but not periodic cycles; (SF3) procyclical inflation[29]; (SF4) procyclical profits; (SF5) procyclical real wages, but procyclical wage share in GDP, so that at the peak the profit share is generally low; (SF6) procyclical labor productivity; (SF7) procyclical investment; (SF8) procyclical credit and monetary aggregates; (SF9) countercyclical unemployment, and (SF10) increasing synchronization of international cycles.[30] In the preceding sections, it has been shown how these stylized facts of business cycles are found in the crises of the world economy since the 1970. Thus, in the past half century, over a long-term growth of the world economy (SF1) crises have occurred recurrently but not periodically (SF2), with expansions of investment—measured by gross capital formation or gross fixed capital formation—coinciding procyclically (SF7) with expansions of economic activity, as indexed in inflation-adjusted money terms by WGDP. A "chemical index"—CO_2 emissions—provides a clear proxy for global industrial activity. Countercyclical increases of rates of unemployment (SF9) have coincided with the periods of crisis in which the rate of growth of the world economy has dropped. Some data were also presented at least suggestive that at the level of the global economy, profits tend to increase procyclically, declining before crises (SF4).

[28] Dore (1993), *The macrodynamics of business cycles*, 21–28; Dore (1997), "Stylized facts", in Glasner & Cooley. eds., *Business cycles and depressions—An encyclopedia*, 662–664.

[29] In economic parlance, a variable is procyclical when it grows and declines in parallel with economic activity, as it happens, for instance, with consumption of electricity, sales of luxury goods, or deaths because of car crashes; a variable is countercyclical when varies "against the cycle", that is, increasing when the economy contracts and decreasing when the economy expands; the rates of unemployment, business failures, consumption of very cheap foods and suicide deaths are typical countercyclical variables.

[30] See the cited entry by Dore (1997) in *Business cycles and depressions—An encyclopedia* and also Dore (1993), *The macrodynamics of business cycles*, 21–28.

It was also shown that credit and monetary aggregates (broad money) vary procyclically (SF8). For Victor Zarnowitz, considered an authority on the empirical facts of business cycles, "monetary aggregates usually experience only reduced growth rates, not absolute declines, in connection with ordinary recessions," so that only "in cycles with severe contractions do substantial downward movements interrupt the pronounced upward trends in these series."[31] Obviously, Zarnowitz was thinking in national economies and not in the world economy when he wrote this sentence which, on the other hand, if applied to the global economy indicates that the recessions that took place in 1974, 1990, and 2001—when there were absolute declines in broad money measured in 2015 USS (Fig. 2.5, p. 22)—were indeed "severe contractions." Now, considering broad money measured in 2010 US$, 1992 was also a crisis year in which the monetary mass contracted. Measuring broad money in WGDP units, the monetary mass contracted in all the aforementioned years, but also in others: 1974, 1979, 1980, 1990, 1992, 1994, 1996, 2001, 2004, 2005, 2010, and 2017. It also jumped at the time of the Great Recession from 99.7% in 2008 to 110.5% in 2009 and continued growing at quite unprecedented rates, reaching 143.5% in 2020 (Fig. 2.7, p. 24), very likely as a consequence of the extreme actions taken by central banks around the world to prevent a major melting of the world financial structure. Zarnowitz considered monetary disturbances as a sign of severe economic circumstances and all the former facts are very suggestive that the world economy is sailing since the Great Recession in very troubled waters.

It was also Zarnowitz's view that during the 1950s and 1960s, cyclical downturns in the Western world assumed the form of retardations of growth rather than absolute declines, but these slowdowns and the intervening speedup phases continued to show a high degree of international diffusion. Then growth slackened and the "classical" business cycles, with absolute declines in output and employment, reappeared in the 1970s, and the tendency for business cycles to be roughly synchronized across the major economies became visible again. This tendency toward international synchronization of business cycles (SF10) has been long considered

[31] "Recent work on business cycles in historical perspective: A review of theories and evidence", *Journal of Economic Literature* 1985, 23(2), 523–580.

a non-controversial stylized fact of business cycles.[32] Statistical analyses of 1970–1993 series of output, investment, and consumption in the G7 countries by Gregory, Head, and Raynauld revealed a "world business cycle" with downturns in the mid-1970s, early 1980s, and early 1990s. All the series had important national components, but they also revealed major common components, particularly in output and investment.[33] Also, in their panel study of 14 developed countries over almost 140 years, Schularik and Taylor found that country fixed effects are highly statistically significant to predict financial crises, what was interpreted by the authors as just revealing the consensus view that financial crises tend to happen in waves often afflicting multiple countries.[34] This is just an indirect confirmation of the international synchronization of financial crises as a component of economic crises and a business cycle of the global economy.

The occurrence of increasingly synchronized downturns of the major national economies around the turn of the century, in 2008–2009 and in 2020 appears to be strongly consistent with the idea that, across countries, cycles are not only synchronized, but integrated parts of the same phenomenon. The crises, cycles, and fluctuations "pertain" to the world economy. This was forcibly put by Robert Brenner two decades ago, when he wrote that "the oft-heard notion that the U.S. economy is essentially self-contained and can be analyzed as such is profoundly misleading."[35]

How Many Crisis years and How Many Crises?

As it was mentioned, in their 2015 book Kose and Terrones identified four recessions of the global economy precisely dated in the four years 1975, 1982, 1991, and 2009. They also considered that "global downturns" had occurred in 1998 and 2001, but they did not consider

[32] See the cited works by Dore (1993, 1997) and Zarnowitz (1985), as well as Oppenlaender (1997), "Characteristics and classification of business cycle indicators", in Oppenlaender, ed., *Business cycle indicators*, 25–32.

[33] Gregory, Head & Raynauld (1997), "Measuring world business cycles", *International Economic Review* 38(3), 677–701.

[34] Schularik & Taylor (2012), "Credit booms gone bust: Monetary policy, leverage cycles, and financial crises, 1870–2008", *American Economic Review* 102(2), 1029–1061.

[35] Brenner (2002), *The boom and the bubble: The US in the world economy*.

these as belonging to any global recession and indeed they considered the period 1991–2001 as a long phase of global expansion. In the chronology of the present work economic crises of the world economy are dated in the mid-1970s, the early years of the next three decades, 2008–2009 and 2020; or, more precisely, defining crisis year as a year of contraction in gross capital formation, 1975, 1980–1982, 1991–1993, 2001–2002, 2008–2009, and 2020. This chronology is consistent with the chronology of Kose and Terrones, except that in this book crises are dated somewhat loosely, or when dated more precisely using strict criteria of contraction of investment, some crises are longer than a year and an extra recession or crisis of the world economy is identified in around 2000.

Now, the question is whether it is defensible to date global recessions loosely as it is argued in this book. Is it not easier and more accurate to refer to the global recession of 1975 rather than refer loosely to a global recession of the mid-1970s? Talk about the global recession of 1975 can be a convenient way to be brief, but at the same time can be a way to losing precision. Or more exactly, to convey a misleading precision based on economic data which are quite imprecise. Dating global recessions specifically in a year ignores that the distribution of recessions of individual national economies during a crisis of the global economy usually has a bell-shape distribution, so that many national economies are in recession in different but contiguous years. Thus, as Fig. 2.13 shows, 34.5% of 142 national economies for which GDP growth data is available at the WDI database were in recession—defined by negative annual GDP growth—in 1982 (the only year of the global recession according to Kose & Terrones) but the proportion was almost as high, 31.2%, in 1983. In each of the four years 1990–1993 the proportion of national economies with negative growth was between 27.7% and 30.7%. Apparently using a less strict definition of national recession (probably based on quarterly data, so that a year contains a recession if GDP growth is negative in two consecutive quarters) Kose and Terrones found that about half of all national economies were in recession in 1992, but a slightly smaller proportion, over 45%, were in recession in 1991 and also in 1993 (Fig. 2.14). Thus, dating the global recession in "the early 1990s" in a sense is also *more precise* than dating it "in 1991." The use of confidence limits and intervals (rather than the clumsy *P*-values) has been adopted as a standard for publication in many disciplines (though not much in economics) precisely to convey the imprecision of measurements and estimates.

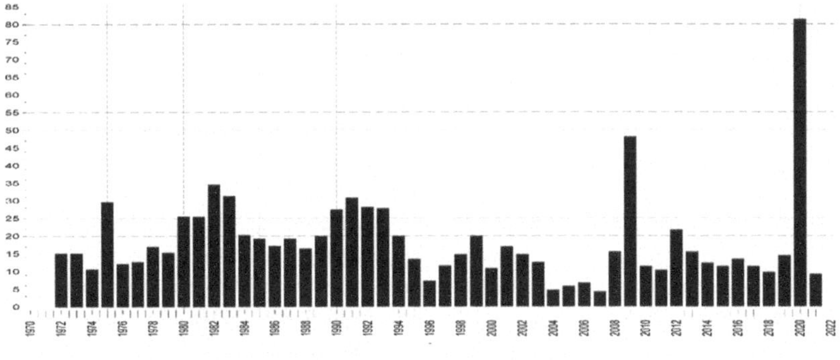

Fig. 2.13 Proportion of the national economies with annual GDP growth data available in 2022 in the WDI database that were during each year in recession as defined by negative annual GDP growth (Author's elaboration from WDI data accessed September 2022)

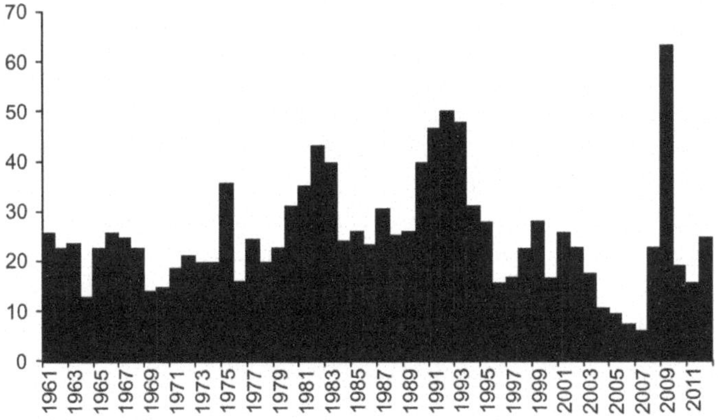

Fig. 2.14 Proportion of national economies that were in recession during each year according to Kose & Terrones (Author's elaboration from Fig. 7.1-A in Kose & Terrones, 2015)

In dating global recessions in specific years which exclude a global recession around the turn of the century, Kose and Terrones follow a kind of scholastic atheoretical *tatonnement* in which they grope for a definition of global recession. They declare that a fundamental question which has anchored debates of economists on the Great Recession and the associated global financial crises is what the nature of a global recession is, and admit that understanding of this issue is surprisingly limited, "primarily reflecting widespread confusion" about the very definitions of the underlying concept:

> A recession, by definition, implies a contraction in national gross domestic product (GDP). But the global economy rarely contracts because countries that experience recessions seldom do so in a way that is synchronized enough to translate into an outright decline in world GDP. This difficulty in describing a global recession, in turn, makes it challenging to concretely define a global recovery. Although there are simple rules of thumb to describe a national recession, such as two consecutive quarters of decline in national output, it is not easy to map such rules in a global context. For example, it is difficult to create quarterly GDP series for the world economy because most countries do not have reliable quarterly series over extended periods.[36]

Since quarterly data are unavailable for the global economy, Kose and Terrones cannot apply the usual definition of a recession as identified by two consecutive quarters of negative growth.

Considering the data at hand, which are annual rates of growth of WGDP (see Fig. 2.2 earlier in this chapter, p. 15), Kose and Terrones noticed indeed that except in the Great Recession, and only in 2009, the annual rate of global economic growth has been always positive, indeed it was, respectively, 0.7%, 0.4%, and 1.4% in 1975, 1982, and 1991, three years in which they identify global recessions. To overcome this problem, they reach the rate of growth of output per capita and claim that a recession.

> can be called global when there is a contraction in world real output per capita accompanied by a broad, synchronized decline in various other measures of global economic activity. This has happened four times over the past half century: in 1975, 1982, 1991, and 2009.

Of course, to define the condition of an economy, the world economy in this case, based on the growth of GDP per capita is to mix up the change in economic activity with a demographic rate that has nothing to

[36] Kose & Terrones (2015), *Collapse*, 13.

do with the economy, as the rate of growth of GDP per capita is just the rate of growth of GDP minus the rate of population growth.[37]

Now, World Bank estimates of the rate of growth of WGDP per capita have changed. In 2015 the WDI database reported negative rates of growth of WGDP per capita measured in 2010 US dollars for 1974 (−0.2%), 1975 (−1.1%), 1982 (−1.3%), 1991 (−0.2%), and 2009 (−3.3%). Using this criterion, the recession of the mid-1970s would have had a duration of 2 years. In 2022, in the WDI database the per capita GDP growth for the world (the metadata is unclear on how the aggregation is done) is negative for 1974 (−0.1%), 1975 (−1.2%), 1982 (−1.4%), 1991 (−0.2%), 2009 (−2.5%), and 2020 (−4.3%).

Again, this would imply a two-year recession in the mid-1970s, not the one-year global recession that Kose and Terrones dated 1975. For getting the mid-1970s recession concentrated in one year, Kose and Terrones had to apply two sets of weights to combine the national economies and compute the rate of global growth. Thus, "when measured by market weights, the duration of the 1991 global recession is two years, but the duration of other episodes is just one year. With the purchasing-power-parity weights, the duration of all four global recessions is one year."[38]

How the signs of the estimated growth of GDP per capita for the world economy change in successive rounds of the continuous process of computation of global statistics is illustrated in Fig. 2.15, that presents data obtained from the WDI database in 2019 and 2022. While the growth of per capita WGDP for the years 1975, 1982, 1991, 1992, and 1993 was positive, above the zero line in the data reported in 2019, it was negative in the data reported in 2022. This shows that dating global crises or recessions taking as main criterium the level of one number that is quite imprecisely computed leads to major inconsistencies. A further consideration is the absurdity of introducing world population growth to assess the condition of expansion or contraction of the global economy. Kose and Terrones assert that "real world GDP growth per capita is a primary measure of the wellbeing of the typical world citizen."[39] This

[37] Let GDP per capita = i, GDP = y, and population = p, then $i = y/p$, and by differentiation $di/i = dy/y - dp/p$, so that the rate of growth of GDP per capita (di/i) is equal to the rate of growth of GDP (dy/y) minus the rate of growth of population (dp/p).

[38] Kose & Terrones (2015), *Collapse*, 34.

[39] Kose & Terrones (2015), *Collapse*, 26.

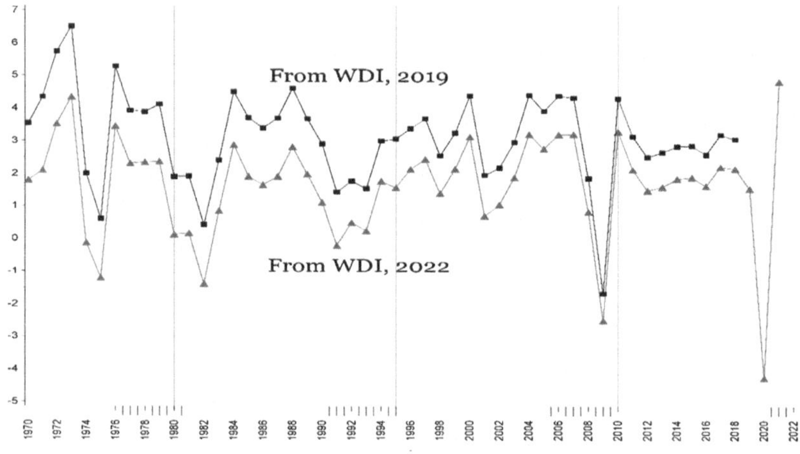

Fig. 2.15 Annual growth of WGDP per capita, as reported in the WDI database in 2019 and 2022 (Author's elaboration from WDI data)

is just a misleading statement as the number they are describing is just an average of figures with major differences, almost like in the joke that "statistics teaches us that if you put your feet in an oven and your head in a refrigerator, you are at a comfortable temperature"; furthermore, the figures that are averaged are rates of growth, while the well-being of citizens, if we assume it as connected with income, as measured by GDP per capita figures, is linked with the level of income, not with its rate of change. But discussing more in detail these issues is beyond the scope of this book.

To frame their identification of global recessions and expansions, Kose and Terrones cited the classical definition of business cycles by Burns and Mitchell, in which a national business cycle "consists of expansions occurring at about the same time in many economic activities, followed by similarly general recessions, contractions, and revivals which merge into the expansion phase of the next cycle."[40] But this is a partial quotation, the full definition by Burns and Mitchell is the following one:

[40] Kose & Terrones (2015), *Collapse*, 29.

> Business cycles are a type of fluctuation found in the aggregate economic activity of nations that organize their work mainly in business enterprises: a cycle consists of expansions occurring at about the same time in many economic activities, followed by similarly general recessions, contractions, and revivals which merge into the expansion phase of the next cycle; this sequence of changes is recurrent but not periodic; in duration business cycles vary from more than one year to ten or twelve years; they are not divisible into shorter cycles of similar character with amplitudes approximating their own.[41]

Thus, Kose and Terrones leave aside two important elements of Burns and Mitchell's definition of national business cycles: first that they are "recurrent but not periodic," second, that they vary in duration "from more than one year to ten or twelve years." This duration according to the definition of Burns and Mitchell is not consistent with Kose and Terrones's view in which a business cycle of the global economy lasted 18 years between the two recessions they date 1991 and 2009. Of course, Burns and Mitchell were referring to national economies, and we are dealing here with the global economy. At any rate, the important question posed here is, are there good reasons to sustain that a global crisis or recession occurred at the turn of the century? Previous sections of this chapter have shown a variety of data providing evidence on crisis periods of the global economy in the past half century, including one at the turn of the century. Let us summarize that evidence: first, broad money stagnated in 1999 and 2000 and contracted in 2001 (Fig. 2.6); second, global economic activity as indexed by CO_2 emissions (Figs. 2.7 and 2.8) was depressed in the years around 2000—as compared with the rate of growth in 1997, CO_2 emissions grew significantly less in 1998, 1999, 2001, and 2002 (Fig. 2.8); third, all estimates of profit rates show that returns of capital declined in the late 1990s and early years of the twenty-first century (Figs. 2.9 and 2.10); fourth, according to World Bank data, a considerable proportion of the countries for which GDP growth information is available had negative GDP growth in the years around 2000 (Fig. 2.13); and fifth and probably most important, capital formation strongly dropped in 2001–2003, so that considering gross capital formation or gross fixed capital formation (Figs. 2.1, 2.2, and 2.3) as proxies for investment, global investment reached in 2001–2003 its lowest levels

[41] Burns & Mitchell (1946), *Measuring business cycles*, 4.

since the 1960s (Fig. 2.1). To state that a world recession or economic crisis occurred around the turn of the century is just to summarize a variety of evidence revealing a major hitch in the process of accumulation of capital in those years. To conclude that in 1999 and 2002 there were only "global downturns" that "fall short of qualifying as a global recession"[42] looks like a scholastic conclusion based on a purely numerical approach that involves "cherry picking" and ignores the real dynamics of the global economy.

Kose and Terrones wrote their book about ten tears ago and concluded that the world economy had had only four recessions in 1975, 1982, 1991, and 2009. This chapter has tried to prove that this chronology is weakly supported by the evidence, as data suggest first, that there was also another recession at the turn of the century, and second, that some of these "recessions" were clearly longer than a year.

Now, in 2022, at the time of this writing, it is undeniable that another crisis of the world economy ocurred in 2020, though it was a very peculiar crisis associated with the COVID-19 pandemic. That crisis will be discussed in Chapter 9.

[42] Kose & Terrones (2015), *Collapse*, 65.

CHAPTER 3

Globalization, National Economies, and Global Crises

In the view of two American historians, Alfred A. Eckes and Thomas Zeiler, the term "globalization" probably was used for the first time in 1983, though the process of globalization had its origins centuries ago, dating back at least to the explorations of Marco Polo. However,

> we believe strongly that the modern age of globalization did not arrive until the last quarter of the twentieth century. Parallel developments in technology, business, and public policy, as well as the end of the Cold War, permitted phenomenal synergies in the marketplace and weakened the hold of states on cross-border contacts.[1]

As it will be discussed in Chapter 5, though there are widely differing opinions on how old the world economy is, there is little disagreement that the process of globalization was already an undeniable reality in the late decades of the twentieth century. This chapter focuses on this period of modern globalization. Even restricting the decades under consideration to the most recent past, a detailed narrative of the process of globalization and the national and international aspects of the crises of the world economy in that period would amount to a global economic and political history of the modern world, which would go much beyond the scope of this book. Instead, to provide some context for the assertions on the

[1] Eckes & Zeiler (2003), *Globalization and the American century*, 6–7.

J. A. Tapia, *Six Crises of the World Economy*,
https://doi.org/10.1007/978-3-031-38735-7_3

global economy and world economic crises, this chapter will present a general outline of key economic and political developments in the post-World War II period and some national and regional manifestations of the crises of the world economy since the 1970s onward.[2]

From World War II to the "First Oil Crisis" of the Mid-1970s

The defeat of Germany and Japan by the United States, the Soviet Union, Great Britain, and the other allied nations in World War II, the proclamation of the People's Republic of China in 1949, and the rapid process of decolonization in the late 1940s and the 1950s shaped a new world that was quite different from the colonial world ruled by European empires that had existed both before and after World War I. A major feature of the world of the Cold War that started in the late 1940s and lasted for four decades was to be mostly though not fully divided into two major economic and political areas, led, respectively, by the two superpowers that had emerged victorious from World War II.

Very soon after the end of World War II major changes occurred in the world system. As the Soviet Union consolidated its control on Eastern Europe, in 1947 India and Pakistan became independent from the British empire, Mao Zedong proclaimed the People's Republic of China in 1949, and in 1950–1953 in the Korean War the North, supported by China and the USSR, fought the South, supported by the United States. Perhaps because both the United States and the USSR were now armed with nuclear weapons, the Korean War did not evolve into World War II. But the Cold War was set.

In its early stages, the conflict between the United States and the USSR for world supremacy had important links with decolonization, as movements fighting for the independence of the colonies were often led by communist organizations and sustained by the USSR or China. With few exceptions, in the twenty years following the end of World War II, the French, British, Dutch, and Belgian colonies in Asia and Africa became independent states. The United States tried to fill the hole and substitute the European influence in these regions, if not as a colonial authority at

[2] Most facts that I mention in this chapter are consensual and for that reason I will support my assertions sparsely with specific references.

least as influential power. It failed on many occasions, though overall, it maintained its superpower status in the world at large.

In the mid-1950s, what the communist parties called "the socialist camp" included the centrally planned economies of the USSR, Eastern Europe and the Balcans, and the large portion of Asia represented by China, Mongolia, North Korea, and North Vietnam. These countries ruled by communist parties in unique-party regimes comprised a large proportion (almost a quarter) of the land surface of the Earth (the USSR and China had areas about 15% and 6.5% of the Earth's land, respectively) and an even bigger share (almost a third) of the 2.5 billion world population (China and the USSR had populations of 550 and 180 million, respectively). The nations of the "socialist camp", particularly those in Europe, had significant economic links between them and with the USSR. Immediately after the end of World War II the USSR had pillaged the economies of these nations, for instance by removing industrial facilities from Germany and taking them to its territory and by forcing Hungary to pay in concept of war reparations as much as high as half the GDP of prewar years. Once governments under heavy Soviet influence if not absolute control had been established in these countries, cooperation and trade between them were promoted by the Council for Mutual Economic Assistance (COMECON), that was formed under Soviet leadership in 1949, and in 1950 integrated the USSR, Bulgaria, Czechoslovakia, Hungary, Poland, Romania, Albania, and East Germany.[3]

The political influence of the USSR on the countries of the "socialist camp" ranged from basically absolute control in Eastern Europe to moderate or minor influence in China, North Korea, North Vietnam Yugoslavia, and Albania. The attainment of power by communist parties had led to the expropriation of owners of economic resources, either land or industrial capital, and thus the economic system of these nations was basically one of state ownership and control and central planning, following in general lines the model of the Soviet Union.

In the rest of the world, national economies were organized under free-enterprise and free-market principles under US hegemony, what was sometimes called *Pax Americana*. The nations of Western Europe were the key allies of the United States and benefitted from the US financial

[3] Arrizabalo (2016), *Capitalismo y economía mundial*, 305–310.

aid of the Marshall plan for reconstruction. The agreements of the 1944 Conference of Bretton Woods took about a decade to be fully implemented, but in the mid-1950s the Western world and especially Western Europe had in place a system with more or less liberalized free trade and warranted stability of exchange rates under the hegemony of the US dollar.[4] As the key currency of the international system, the dollar was the only one having a direct convertibility with gold.

In the early 1950s, decolonization was starting in Africa and Asia, but Africa was almost totally a collection of European colonies. Independent countries that at the time had an established market system, and a free-enterprise economy, occupied the Western hemisphere, that is the American continent and the Caribbean, plus Western Europe, parts of Asia, and Oceania. In these countries, the political system was generally organized under democratic principles with freely elected governments, but there were many exceptions. In many nations of the free-enterprise system, the market economy operated under military or civil dictatorships often allied with the United States, like those of Chiang Kai-Shek in Taiwan—at the time occupying a seat in the United Nations as "Republic of China"—, Sarit Dhanarajata in Thailand, the *apartheid* regime in South Africa, Batista in Cuba, the PRI in Mexico, Trujillo in the Dominican Republic, or Francois Duvalier "Papa Doc" in Haiti. In Argentina, after a decade in which the freely elected government of General Juan Domingo Perón often resorted to organized violence and dictatorial rule to uphold strongly nationalistic and populist economic policies—that never went beyond the limit of the market system—, a *coup d'état* in 1955 started a period of three decades in which civil governments and military dictatorships alternated almost once per decade. In Brazil something similar happened, though the start of the period of military government was in the mid-1960s. In Southern Europe, the military regime of Francisco Franco and the civil dictatorship of the Estado Novo in Portugal, both solid anti-communist allies of the United States, lasted from the 1930s to the 1970s.

In the free-market economies of Europe, North America, Oceania, and Japan, the 1950s and 1960s were years of steady economic growth and reinforcement of the welfare state, often under the leadership of political

[4] Hobsbawn (1994), *Age of Extremes*, 274–275; Kotz (1987), "Long waves and social structures of accumulation", *Review of Radical Political Economics* 19(4), 16–38; Arrizabalo (2016), *Capitalismo y economía mundial*, 292–304.

parties of social democratic adscription. Overall, in Western capitalism, the 1950s and 1960s were a period of income growth and modernization following Western models, either under democratic regimes and elected governments or under dictatorial rule. In Africa and Asia the newly independent states sometimes remained subjected by multiple cultural, economic, and political links to the old metropolis—both French and British governments took care of this, the UK even formalized these links in its Commonwealth of Nations—but not infrequently the new nations developed strong relations with the Soviet bloc, as it was common that they often had become independent of the European metropolis because of guerrilla activities or even open wars led by nationalist movements with a strong influence of Marxist ideas, Soviet sympathies and not rarely, open or covert support of the USSR in the fight for independence. This is best exemplified by the case of Vietnam, where the communist-led fight for independence from France in the late 1940s continued after the French defeat in Diem Bien Phu with the war against the US intervention and culminated in 1976 with the unification of the country as Socialist Republic of Vietnam—which immediately, in 1978, joined the COMECON and signed a treaty of Friendship and Cooperation with the USSR.[5]

The North Atlantic Treaty Organization (NATO), established in 1949, integrated ten countries in Western Europe—Great Britain, France, Belgium, the Netherlands, Luxemburg, Denmark, Norway, Iceland, Italy, and Portugal—with the United States and Canada in the other side of the Atlantic. It was intended to face the Soviet Union, at the time increasingly assertive in Eastern Europe. When NATO expanded in 1955 by integrating West Germany, the USSR and the countries of Eastern Europe in the Soviet sphere of influence formed the Warsaw Pact, initially including Albania, Bulgaria, Czechoslovakia, East Germany, Hungary, Poland, Romania, and the Soviet Union. These countries were often collectively called the Soviet bloc, a bloc which soon shrank by the defection of Albania, which aligned with China in the ideological conflict splitting the communist world since the late 1950s.

The opposition of "capitalism" and "communism" or "West" and "East", or more concretely, between the countries, respectively, led by the United States and the Soviet Union with NATO and the Warsaw Pact as

[5] Soon (1980), "The Soviet-Vietnamese Treaty", *Southeast Asian Affairs* 1980, 54–65.

military cores, maintained its high levels of tension in the 1950s, before and after the stalemate in the Korean War. There is agreement, however, that the highest level of tension took place in the early 1960s, after the Cuban revolution of 1959 and the consolidation of the Cuban revolutionary government as a Soviet ally. At the time Jan Tinbergen, a clever observer of the world economy, described the situation in these terms:

> The world is in the process of a great transformation. In a considerable part of it, a new economic order, "communism," is being vigorously tried out. Elsewhere an old order is passing as one country after another throws off the yoke of colonialism. The wholesale introduction of Western techniques and ways of life is shaking the foundations of numerous beliefs and attitudes, for good or for evil. A spurt of population growth accompanies this development. All of these changes, with their multiple potentialities for conflict, are taking place in an era in which mankind has just discovered the possibilities of nuclear warfare.[6]

After the Cuban government led by Fidel Castro joined the Soviet sphere of influence, and the United States stationed nuclear weapons in a NATO nation, Turkey, the Soviet attempt of installing nuclear missiles in Cuba led to the missile crisis of 1962. This was the time generally agreed as the one when the Cold War was closest to become World War III.

A usual way to simplify the history of the mid decades of the twentieth century is to view the period of the Cold War as a time when the world was mostly or even wholly divided into East and West, or into two camps or blocs, one socialist, or communist, the other capitalist. However, the insufficiencies and limitations of this scheme and these denominations are obvious, as the 1960s saw the emergence of two phenomena that largely question the validity of the two-camp view. On the one hand, a major split, reaching the level of undeclared war in 1969, arose in the late 1950s between the communist parties of the Soviet Union and the People's Republic of China[7]; the "socialist camp" had ceased to exist, or now was an angrily divided camp; on the other hand, this was the time in which the movement of the so-called non-aligned countries emerged. Many nations recently independent from the colonial rule of Great Britain, France,

[6] Tinbergen (1962), *Shaping the world economy—Suggestions for an international economic policy*, 3.

[7] Baby (1976), *Los orígenes de la controversia chino-soviética*.

Belgium, or the Netherlands, adopted more or less non-aligned positions versus American and Soviet influence.

While the self-proclaimed popular democracies or socialist republics of the COMECON intensified trade and cooperation between themselves and obtained some substantial gains in economic standards with most of the productive activities under State control, in the rest of the world Keynesian economics was quite predominant and influential in economic policy. In many countries of Latin America, Africa, and Asia, many of them of recent independence, Keynesianism was applied under the guise of development policies intended to reach full economic independence through import-substitution industrialization.

As it will be discussed more in detail in Chapter 5, the division of most of the world into two blocs or camps during the four decades between the Korean War and the disappearance of the Soviet Union in 1991 is frowned upon by authors who defend the world-system theory and claim that a world system and a world economy have been a reality for decades, or even centuries. For instance, Minqi Li maintains that, after the revolution of 1949, China remained as a component of the capitalist world system and was forced to operate "under the basic laws of motion of the system".[8] This view fits poorly with the fact that since the 1950s until the late 1970s China was largely isolated from world markets and the economic institutions operating in the country—mostly peasant cooperatives and state-owned industrial enterprises—had very little to do with the usual economic institutions in capitalist economies. The economic separation between the Soviet sphere of influence and the West is also illustrated by the fact that Eastern Europe did not participate in the Marshall Plan and the USSR and most countries in its sphere of influence were ineligible for IMF or World Bank assistance, as they did not participate in the financial order derived from Bretton Woods and based in the hegemony of the US dollar. External financing for Eastern Europe was credit from the USSR for the acquisition of raw materials and equipment from the Soviet Union itself. By 1953, 64% of Eastern European exports went to Eastern countries, while only 14% went to Western Europe, and less than 1% to the United States, Canada, and Latin America.[9]

[8] Li (2011), "The rise of the working class and the future of the Chinese revolution", *Monthly Review* 63(2), 38.

[9] Hart & Spero (2010), *The politics of international economic relations*, 380–381.

Leaving aside the issue of whether China and the countries in the Soviet bloc pertained in the 1950s and 1960s to something that could be properly called a world system or world economy, what is undeniable about the quarter century after World War II is the following: first, that European colonial empires disappeared almost completely and several dozen new nations in Asia and Africa became independent states; second, that this was a general period of economic prosperity in the Western "capitalist" world; and third, that in the centrally planned economies of Eastern Europe and Asia an steady expansion of output and incomes in the 1950s supported by internal trade was followed by relative stagnation in the 1960s. An important historical event in 1958–1961 was the so-called Great Leap Forward in China, a major fiasco in the policies of Mao Zedong to advance quickly in the process of industrialization by the transformation of the peasant cooperatives into improvised steel mills. The World Bank estimates 27.3% and 5.6% the respective contractions of China's GDP in 1961 and 1962 (Table 3.1). For the human cost of that fiasco estimates range from several million to 45 million as the mortality burden of the famine derived from the lack of attention to agricultural work.[10] The highest values in such a wide range of estimates are usually those of research authored and published after the 1980s in China, where the present government is openly hostile to Mao's legacy and severely restricts the access to official archives.

An important feature of the three decades after World War II was the end of the business "boom-and-bust" cycles of economic expansion and depression that had been so prominent in the decades before World War I and during the 1920s and 1930s. Recessions were considerably milder during these years of the so-called Golden Age of Western capitalism. Some Keynesian economists even claimed that the business cycle had been tamed[11]; others proposed the term *growth cycle* to mean that the alternation was no longer between economic expansions and contractions, but between faster and slower growth.[12] Of course, all that does not mean that there were no major recessions in particular countries. For example,

[10] Wemheuer (2011), "Sites of horror: Mao's great famine", *China Journal* 66, 155–164.

[11] Bronfenbrenner (1969), *Is the business cycle obsolete?*; Samuelson (1967), *Economics*, 7th ed., 254–255.

[12] Klein (1997), "Growth cycles", in Glasner & Cooley, eds., *Business cycles and depressions: An encyclopedia*, 289.

Table 3.1 GDP growth rates of selected national economies, 1961–2021

Year	*Arg*	*Aus*	*Bra*	*Can*	*Chn*	*Chl*	*Egy*	*Fin*	*Fra*	*Ger*	*Ind*	*Ita*	*Jap*	*Pol*	*Rus*	*Sau*	*SAf*	*Spa*	*Swe*	*Swi*	*USA*	*UK*
1961	5.4	2.5	8.6	3.2	−27.3	5.2	5.2	7.6	5.0		3.7	8.2	12.0				3.8	11.8	5.7		2.3	2.7
1962	−0.9	1.3	6.6	7.4	−5.6	4.0	3.9	3.0	6.8		2.9	6.2	8.9				6.2	10.0	4.3		6.1	1.1
1963	−5.3	6.2	0.6	5.3	10.3	5.8	10.5	3.3	6.2		6.0	5.6	8.5				7.4	9.6	5.3		4.4	4.9
1964	10.1	7.0	3.4	6.6	18.2	2.6	11.5	5.2	6.7		7.5	2.8	11.7				7.9	5.3	6.8		5.8	5.5
1965	10.6	6.0	2.4	6.3	17.0	1.0	4.9	5.3	4.9		−2.6	3.3	5.8				6.1	6.3	3.8		6.4	2.1
1966	−0.7	2.4	6.7	6.7	10.6	11.2	5.0	2.4	5.3		−0.1	6.0	10.6				4.4	7.2	2.1		6.5	1.6
1967	3.2	6.3	4.2	3.1	−5.8	3.6	0.8	2.2	4.9		7.8	7.2	11.1				7.2	4.3	3.4		2.5	2.8
1968	4.8	5.1	9.8	5.0	−4.1	3.6	−1.6	2.3	4.5		3.4	6.5	12.9				4.2	6.6	3.6		4.8	5.4
1969	9.7	7.0	9.5	5.0	16.9	3.9	5.3	9.6	7.1		6.5	6.1	12.5			6.0	4.7	8.9	5.0		3.1	1.9
1970	3.0	7.2	10.4		19.3	1.8	5.6	4.8	6.1		5.2	5.3	2.5			58.6	5.2	4.3	7.3		−0.3	6.3
1971	5.7	4.0	11.3		7.1	9.4	4.1	2.4	5.3	3.1	1.6	1.8	4.7			20.5	4.3	4.6	0.9		3.3	3.5
1972	1.6	3.9	11.9		3.8	−1.0	3.1	7.7	4.5	4.3	−0.6	3.7	8.4			22.9	1.7	8.1	2.3		5.3	4.3
1973	2.8	2.6	14.0		7.8	−5.0	3.5	7.0	6.3	4.8	3.3	7.1	8.0			24.2	4.6	7.8	4.0		5.6	6.5
1974	5.5	4.1	8.2		2.3	2.4	1.6	3.2	4.3	0.9	1.2	5.5	−1.2			16.2	6.1	5.6	3.2		−0.5	−2.5
1975	0.0	1.3	5.2		8.7	−12.9	8.9	1.8	−1.0	−0.9	9.1	−2.1	3.1			−8.9	1.7	0.5	2.6		−0.2	−1.5
1976	−2.0	2.6	10.3		−1.6	3.8	13.3	0.3	4.4	4.9	1.7	7.1	4.0			17.8	2.2	3.3	1.1		5.4	2.9
1977	6.9	3.6	4.9		7.6	10.4	9.0	0.2	3.5	3.3	7.3	2.6	4.4			7.1	−0.1	2.8	−1.6		4.6	2.5
1978	−4.5	0.9	5.0		11.3	7.7	8.6	2.9	4.0	3.0	5.7	3.2	5.3			−5.2	3.0	1.5	1.8		5.5	4.2
1979	10.2	4.1	6.8		7.6	8.4	4.5	7.1	3.5	4.2	−5.2	6.0	5.5			11.9	3.8	0.0	3.8		3.2	3.7
1980	1.5	3.0	9.2		7.8	8.0	10.0	5.4	1.6	1.4	6.7	3.4	2.8			5.7	6.6	2.2	1.7		−0.3	−2.0
1981	−5.2	3.3	−4.2		5.1	6.5	7.3	1.3	1.1	0.5	6.0	0.8	4.3			1.9	5.4	−0.1	0.5	1.6	2.5	−0.8
1982	−0.7	3.3	0.8		9.0	−11.0	9.9	3.1	2.5	−0.4	3.5	0.4	3.3			−20.7	−0.4	1.2	1.2	−1.3	−1.8	2.0
1983	4.3	−2.2	−2.9		10.8	−5.0	5.1	3.1	1.2	1.6	7.3	1.2	3.6			−16.1	−1.8	1.8	1.9	0.6	4.6	4.2
1984	1.6	4.6	5.4		15.2	4.1	9.7	3.2	1.5	2.8	3.8	3.2	4.4			−4.7	5.1	1.8	4.2	3.0	7.2	2.3
1985	−5.2	5.3	7.9		13.4	4.0	5.8	3.5	1.6	2.3	5.3	2.8	5.2			−9.8	−1.2	2.3	2.2	3.7	4.2	4.1
1986	6.2	4.0	7.5		8.9	5.4	4.7	2.8	2.3	2.3	4.8	2.9	3.3			17.0	0.0	3.3	2.7	1.9	3.5	3.2

(continued)

Table 3.1 (continued)

Year	Arg	Aus	Bra	Can	Chn	Chl	Egy	Fin	Fra	Ger	Ind	Ita	Jap	Pol	Rus	Sau	SAf	Spa	Swe	Swi	USA	UK
1987	2.7	2.5	3.5		11.7	6.5	3.8	3.6	2.6	1.4	4.0	3.2	4.6			−6.6	2.1	5.5	3.4	1.6	3.5	5.4
1988	−1.1	5.7	−0.1		11.2	7.3	5.5	5.2	4.7	3.7	9.6	4.2	6.7			13.1	4.2	5.1	2.6	3.3	4.2	5.7
1989	−7.2	3.9	3.2		4.2	9.9	4.9	5.1	4.3	3.9	5.9	3.4	4.9			−0.5	2.4	4.8	2.7	4.3	3.7	2.6
1990	−2.5	3.6	−4.4		3.9	3.3	5.7	0.7	2.9	5.3	5.5	2.0	4.8		−3.0	15.2	−0.3	3.8	0.8	3.7	1.9	0.7
1991	9.1	−0.4	1.0		9.3	7.8	1.1	−5.9	1.0	5.1	1.1	1.5	3.5	−7.0	−5.0	15.0	−1.0	2.5	−1.1	−0.9	−0.1	−1.1
1992	7.9	0.4	−0.5		14.2	11.2	4.5	−3.3	1.6	1.9	5.5	0.8	0.9	2.5	−14.5	4.0	−2.1	0.9	−1.2	0.0	3.5	0.4
1993	8.2	4.0	4.9		13.9	6.6	2.9	−0.7	−0.6	−1.0	4.8	−0.9	−0.5	3.7	−8.7	−1.4	1.2	−1.0	−2.1	−0.1	2.8	2.5
1994	5.8	4.0	5.9		13.0	5.0	4.0	4.0	2.4	2.4	6.7	2.2	1.1	5.3	−12.6	0.6	3.2	2.4	3.9	1.3	4.0	3.8
1995	−2.8	3.8	4.2		11.0	8.9	4.6	4.2	2.1	1.5	7.6	2.9	2.6	7.1	−4.1	0.2	3.1	2.8	3.9	0.5	2.7	2.5
1996	5.5	3.9	2.2		9.9	6.8	5.0	3.7	1.4	0.8	7.5	1.3	3.1	6.1	−3.8	2.6	4.3	2.7	1.6	0.5	3.8	2.4
1997	8.1	3.9	3.4		9.2	7.4	5.5	6.3	2.3	1.8	4.0	1.8	1.0	6.4	1.4	1.1	2.6	3.7	3.1	2.3	4.4	4.9
1998	3.9	4.6	0.3	2.8	7.8	4.2	5.6	5.5	3.6	2.0	6.2	1.8	−1.3	4.6	−5.3	2.9	0.5	4.4	4.3	3.1	4.5	3.2
1999	−3.4	4.9	0.5	4.0	7.7	−0.3	6.1	4.4	3.4	1.9	8.8	1.6	−0.3	4.7	6.4	−3.8	2.4	4.5	4.2	1.7	4.8	3.0
2000	−0.8	3.9	4.4	4.9	8.5	5.0	6.4	5.8	3.9	2.9	3.8	3.8	2.8	4.6	10.0	5.6	4.2	5.2	4.8	4.0	4.1	3.7
2001	−4.4	2.0	1.4	1.4	8.3	3.2	3.5	2.6	2.0	1.7	4.8	2.0	0.4	1.3	5.1	−1.2	2.7	3.9	1.4	1.6	1.0	2.1
2002	−10.9	4.0	3.1	3.4	9.1	3.2	2.4	1.7	1.1	−0.2	3.8	0.3	0.0	2.0	4.7	−2.8	3.7	2.7	2.2	0.0	1.7	2.1
2003	8.8	3.1	1.1	3.8	10.0	4.7	3.2	2.0	0.8	−0.7	7.9	0.1	1.5	3.5	7.3	11.2	2.9	3.0	2.3	0.0	2.8	3.0
2004	9.0	4.2	5.8	3.9	10.1	6.7	4.1	4.0	2.8	1.2	7.9	1.4	2.2	5.0	7.2	8.0	4.6	3.1	4.3	2.8	3.9	2.4
2005	8.9	3.2	3.2	5.0	11.4	5.8	4.5	2.8	1.7	0.7	7.9	0.8	1.8	3.5	6.4	5.6	5.3	3.7	2.9	2.9	3.5	2.6
2006	8.0	2.7	4.0	4.2	12.7	6.0	6.8	4.0	2.4	3.8	8.1	1.8	1.4	6.1	8.2	2.8	5.6	4.1	4.7	4.0	2.8	2.6
2007	9.0	3.8	6.1	6.9	14.2	5.2	7.1	5.3	2.4	3.0	7.7	1.5	1.5	7.1	8.5	1.8	5.4	3.6	3.4	4.0	2.0	2.3
2008	4.1	3.6	5.1	1.0	9.7	3.8	7.2	0.8	0.3	1.0	3.1	−1.0	−1.2	4.2	5.2	6.2	3.2	0.9	−0.5	2.8	0.1	−0.2
2009	−5.9	1.9	−0.1	−2.9	9.4	−1.1	4.7	−8.1	−2.9	−5.7	7.9	−5.3	−5.7	2.8	−7.8	−2.1	−1.5	−3.8	−4.3	−2.1	−2.6	−4.2
2010	10.1	2.2	7.5	3.1	10.6	5.9	5.1	3.2	1.9	4.2	8.5	1.7	4.1	3.7	4.5	5.0	3.0	0.2	6.0	3.3	2.7	2.1
2011	6.0	2.5	4.0	3.1	9.6	6.2	1.8	2.5	2.2	3.9	5.2	0.7	0.0	4.8	4.3	10.0	3.2	−0.8	3.2	1.9	1.5	1.5
2012	−1.0	3.9	1.9	1.8	7.9	6.2	2.2	−1.4	0.3	0.4	5.5	−3.0	1.4	1.3	4.0	5.4	2.4	−3.0	−0.6	1.2	2.3	1.5

Year	*Arg*	*Aus*	*Bra*	*Can*	*Chn*	*Chl*	*Egy*	*Fin*	*Fra*	*Ger*	*Ind*	*Ita*	*Jap*	*Pol*	*Rus*	*Sau*	*SAf*	*Spa*	*Swe*	*Swi*	*USA*	*UK*
2013	2.4	2.6	3.0	2.3	7.8	3.3	2.2	−0.9	0.6	0.4	6.4	−1.8	2.0	1.1	1.8	2.7	2.5	−1.4	1.2	1.8	1.8	1.9
2014	−2.5	2.6	0.5	2.9	7.4	1.8	2.9	−0.4	1.0	2.2	7.4	0.0	0.3	3.4	0.7	3.7	1.4	1.4	2.7	2.4	2.3	3.0
2015	2.7	2.2	−3.5	0.7	7.0	2.2	4.4	0.5	1.1	1.5	8.0	0.8	1.6	4.2	−2.0	4.1	1.3	3.8	4.5	1.7	2.7	2.6
2016	−2.1	2.7	−3.3	1.0	6.8	1.8	4.3	2.8	1.1	2.2	8.3	1.3	0.8	3.1	0.2	1.7	0.7	3.0	2.1	2.0	1.7	2.3
2017	2.8	2.3	1.3	3.0	6.9	1.4	4.2	3.2	2.3	2.7	6.8	1.7	1.7	4.8	1.8	−0.7	1.2	3.0	2.6	1.6	2.3	2.1
2018	−2.6	2.9	1.8	2.8	6.7	4.0	5.3	1.1	1.9	1.1	6.5	0.9	0.6	5.4	2.8	2.5	1.5	2.3	2.0	2.9	2.9	1.7
2019	−2.0	2.1	1.2	1.9	6.0	0.8	5.6	1.2	1.8	1.1	3.7	0.5	−0.2	4.7	2.2	0.3	0.1	2.1	2.0	1.2	2.3	1.7
2020	−9.9	0.0	−3.9	−5.2	2.2	−6.0	3.6	−2.3	−7.9	−4.6	−6.6	−9.0	−4.5	−2.5	−2.7	−4.1	−6.4	−10.8	−2.9	−2.4	−3.4	−9.3
2021	10.3	1.5	4.6	4.6	8.1	11.7	3.3	3.5	7.0	2.9	8.9	6.6	1.6	5.7	4.8	3.2	4.9	5.1	4.8	3.7	5.7	7.4

The countries in the table are Argentina (Arg), Australia (Aus), Brazil (Bra), Canada (Can), China (Chn), Chile (Chl), Egypt (Egy), Finland (Fin), France (Fra), Germany (Ger), India (Ind), Italy (Ita) Japan (Jap), Poland (Pol), Russia (Rus), Saudi Arabia (Sau), South Africa (SAf), Spain (Spa), Sweden (Swe), Switzerland (Swi), the United States (USA), and the United Kingdom (UK). All data, including the empty cells, from WDI as reported in October 2022. The listed countries include all the G20 countries except Mexico, Korea, and Turkey. Chile, Egypt, and Switzerland which are included in the table, are not members of the G20

Argentina had in 1963 a severe recession in which GDP decreased 5.3%, and India's GDP shrank 2.6% in 1965 (Table 3.1). In the United States the NBER defines a recession as a period in which "a significant decline in economic activity spreads across the economy and can last from a few months to more than a year." In the NBER chronology, in the post-World War II period until 1975 the US economy had recessions in 1953, 1957, 1960, and 1969. These four recessions were however shorter than a year, and in none of them the *annual* growth of GDP was negative (Table 3.1).

The world was quite in turmoil in the late 1960s and the year 1968 was remarkable for many reasons. France was paralyzed by strikes of students and workers; Czechoslovakia, that had gone into reform policies ill-received by the USSR was invaded by troops of the Warsaw Pact; in Mexico, students were savagely repressed at the Tlatelolco massacre; the Cultural Revolution started in China; in the United States, opposition to the Vietnam War multiplied and political leaders were murdered; social unrest was widespread in the world. Immanuel Wallerstein referred to a world revolution that would have occurred in 1968 or rather 1966–1970.[13] If all that unrest can be properly called a revolution, it is obvious that was a failed one.

According to World Bank estimates, the rate of growth of the global economy declined from 5.8% in 1969 to 3.9% in 1970; the monetary mass as indexed by broad money contracted in 1969 to 53.1% of WGDP from 55.8% in 1969 (see Table E-1 on p. 297). The United States had negative GDP growth in 1970 (Table 3.1). These data and others suggest significant turbulence and slowdown of the world economy around 1970.[14] The period of fast and steady growth of Western capitalism following World War II was reaching its end.

In the 1960s the role of the dollar as a key stone of the international financial system eroded as the political and economic hegemony of the United States declined versus the rising economic power of Japan and the Western European nations. A negative balance of payments of the United States, public debt steadily growing because of the expenses of the Vietnam War and Great Society programs, and the consequent increasing

[13] Wallerstein (2009), "Crisis of the capitalist system: Where do we go from here? The Harold Wolpe Lecture, University of KwaZulu-Natal, 5 November 2009", *MR Online*.

[14] As it was mentioned in Chapter 2, the rate of growth of Japan's GDP in 1970 that was reported in the WDI database during the past ten years had major modifications.

flows of dollars (the so-called Eurodollars) moving around the world made increasingly untenable the gold convertibility of the US dollar. The so-called London Gold Pool—a 1961 agreement of eight central banks (of seven European countries and the United States) to cooperate in the maintenance of the Bretton Woods system of fixed-rate convertible currencies and a fixed gold price of the US dollar—collapsed in 1968 as dollars printed in the United States and sent overseas to pay for whatever were increasingly returned to the United States to be exchanged for gold. With -0.3% GDP growth in the United States in 1970 (Table 3.1), in 1971 President Nixon imposed wage and price controls, a surcharge on imports and major restrictions to the dollar convertibility into gold. In two years it was evident that neither the gold parity of the dollar nor the fixed exchange rates could be maintained, and Japan and the nations of the European Economic Community decided to let their currencies to float, ending the Bretton Woods system.[15]

The next recession of the US economy according to the NBER chronology started in November 1973 and lasted 16 months. In this downturn the US GDP shrank for two consecutive years, with growth rates of –0.5% in 1974 and –0.2% in 1975. This recession of the US economy was part of the world economic crisis that started soon after the Yon-Kippur War of October 1973, when the members of the Organization of Arab Petroleum Exporting Countries proclaimed an oil embargo against Canada, Japan, the Netherlands, the United Kingdom, and the United States. At that time economic troubles were expected as effects of these actions. Indeed, between the start of the embargo in October 1973 and its end few months later, the price of oil almost tripled from less than 4 US$ per barrel to quite over $10 and significant declines in economic activity were observed in most countries of the Western world.[16] Starting a tradition that would last until today, the economic troubles were blamed on the oil exporting countries, and the economic downturn was baptized as "The Oil Crisis". When other downturns occurred in later years and were also blamed on oil and the Arab oil exporters, the deep recession

[15] Hagiwara (2013), "The demise of the Keynesian regime, financial crisis, and Marx's theory", in Yagi et al. eds., *Crises of global economies and the future of capitalism*, 91–108; Butkiewicz & Ohlmacher (2021), "Ending Bretton Woods", *The Economic Historian*, November 28.

[16] Klein (1997), "Growth cycles".

of the mid-1970s was renamed "The First Oil Crisis". More on this in Chapter 7.

Technically, considering the only data available, which are annual series, the world economy did not contract in the mid-1970s, since according to the World Bank the global output still grew at rates of 1.8% in 1974 and 0.6% in 1975 (Fig. 2.2 on page 15, Table E1, page 297). This represented a major deceleration in the world economy, since the rate of growth of WGDP had been estimated to be 6.4% in 1973 and over 3.9% in all the years since 1960. As shown in Chapter 2, worldwide gross capital formation shrank in 1975 and gross fixed capital formation also did in 1974, and again in 1975.

The crisis was followed by a quick recovery, the world economy surged in 1976 at a rate of 5.0% and continued increasing at rates of 4.0% in 1977 and 4.2% in 1978. Sharp declines in GDP growth in 1974, in 1975, or in both years, followed by quick recoveries, were observable in many national economies. The contraction of the US economy by 0.2% in 1975 was followed by an expansion of 5.4% in 1976 (Table 3.1). The British GDP that had increased by a remarkable 6.5% in 1973 had respective contractions of 2.5% in 1974 and 1.5% in 1975, to return to growth at rates around 3% in the late 1970s. In 1975 and 1976 Switzerland's GDP spectacularly shrank, respectively, by 7.3 and 1.4%, to grow again by 2.4% in 1976.[17] Western Germany grew just 0.9% in 1974, contracted 0.9% in 1975, and grew again 4.9% in 1976. In Japan GDP grew at high rates even over 8% in 1971–1973, then economic growth became negative, −1.2%, in 1974 to recover quickly with growth of 3.1% in 1975.

In Latin America, Brazil's economy that had been growing at rates over 8% between 1970 and 1974 grew just 5.2% in 1975 and returned to fast growth in 1976 with 10.3% (Table 3.1). Argentina, that grew at rates between 1.6% and 5.7% in 1970–1974, stagnated at 0% in 1975 and contracted 2.0% in 1976.

An interesting aspect of the mid-1970s crisis of the world economy is that it coincided with important political changes in several countries. For decades Portugal had resisted the wave of decolonization following World War II that during the 1950s and 1960s eliminated the colonial empires of Britain, France, the Netherlands, and Belgium. In Portugal

[17] These were rates reported in the WDI database in 2020, but accessed in October 2022, the database does not report GDP growth figures for Switzerland for the years before 1981, see Table 3.1.

however, the government of the anticommunist Estado Novo installed by Oliveira Salazar in the 1920s and led from 1968 by Marcelo Caetano, and member of NATO since the establishment of the Atlantic Treaty, had preserved a colonial empire in Africa with a total area twenty times larger than metropolitan Portugal. The Portuguese dictatorship was however undermined by the protracted colonial wars that convinced many in the Portuguese military of the futility of the colonial effort. In April 1974, a bloodless left-wing military coup in Lisbon, the Carnation Revolution, led the way for the independence of the overseas territories, as well as for the restoration of civil liberties. The Portuguese economy that had expanded at quite high rates between 6.6% and 12.6% in 1970–1974, grew just 1.1% in 1974—the year of the coup—and in 1975 went through an important contraction with GDP growth of –4.3%. In 1976 there was an important recovery with the economy expanding at 6.9%.[18] Thus, in the recession of the Portuguese economy in the mid-1970s the effects of national political developments are inextricably linked with the general economic aspects of the crisis in its global character.

Portugal's neighbor in the Iberian Peninsula, Spain, had been also under authoritarian rule after a civil war in 1936–1939 was followed by decades of military dictatorship. Initially isolated by its connections with the powers defeated in World War II, Nazi Germany and fascist Italy, the regime led by Generalísimo Franco soon found an accommodation with the anticommunism of the Cold War and in 1953 the Spanish government agreed with the installation of four US military bases in Spanish territory. Investment from the United States and other Western countries arrived in significant quantities that together with abundant foreign currency from tourism and from Spanish immigrants in Germany and other European countries fed a large economic boom, so that between 1960 and 1974 the Spanish economy grew at annual rates always over 4% and several years at rates over 10%. Since the 1960s underground political activity undermined general Franco's regime and 1975 was a key year in which the dictator died, economic growth dropped to just 0.5%—after 5.6% growth in 1974—, and a political process of transition evolved to a progressive

[18] As reported in the WDI database, accessed October 2022.

instauration of civil liberties in 1976 and 1977, years in which economic growth somewhat recovered to rates around 3%.[19]

In Chile, the Unidad Popular government of Salvador Allende had reached power in 1970, starting a program intended to peacefully transform Chile into a socialist country. Chile's GDP grew a remarkable 9.4% in 1971, but with the opposition of national and international capital to Allende's government, GDP growth went down in 1972 to –1.0%, followed by an even worst contraction, –5.0%, in 1973 (Table 3.1). This was the year of the *coup d'état* in which after months of economic and political turmoil caused by the Chilean wealthy, the Chilean right-wing forces, and the US CIA, the Unidad Popular government was suppressed by the Chilean armed forces led by general Pinochet. President Allende was killed during his resistance to the September 11 coup in the presidential palace. Following Allende's removal, under Pinochet military dictatorship the Chilean economy grew 2.5% in 1974. Despite sympathies and support of Western governments and corporations, and the advice of *Chicago Boys* like Milton Friedman, the Chilean economy under Pinochet contracted by an abysmal 12.9% in 1975. To a large extent, Chile's economy was largely dependent on exports of copper ore, which significantly dropped in 1974 and 1975 when the world economy halted.

The mid-1970s were also the time of important changes in China, until that time quite isolated from the world economy. In 1976 Mao died and the so-called *gang of four*—promoters of Cultural Revolution policies that were largely autarkic—were removed from the leadership of the Communist Party. Two years later Deng Xiaoping, formerly accused by the Maoists to be a follower of the capitalist way and demoted, was reinstated as de facto leader of the party. Since that time, the opening of the country to foreign investment, the privatization of many enterprises, and the elimination of government policies of warranted employment and peasant cooperatives marked a quick evolution of the Chinese economy toward forms of market capitalism under authoritarian rule, with an important presence of the State in the industrial sector. In the 30 years following the death of Mao Zedong the Chinese GDP grew at breakneck rates often above 10% (Table 3.1). China became the world powerhouse of industrial goods and in 2005 had the dubious honor of displacing the United States as the main producer of emissions of CO_2.

[19] Harrison (1978), *An economic history of modern Spain*; Tortella Casares (1998), *El desarrollo de la España contemporánea: Historia económica de los siglos XIX y XX*.

In the decades after World War II started what Schularick and Taylor call the second era of finance capitalism. For these authors, in the first era that ran from 1870 to 1939,

> money and credit were volatile but over the long run they maintained a roughly stable relationship to each other, and to the size of the economy measured by GDP. The only exception was the Great Depression [...]. The second financial era, starting in 1945, looks very different, however. First, money and credit began a long postwar recovery, trending up rapidly and then surpassing their pre-1940 levels compared to GDP by about 1970. That trend continued to the present and, in addition, credit itself then started to decouple from broad money and grew rapidly, via a combination of increased leverage and augmented funding via the nonmonetary liabilities of banks. With the banking sector progressively more leveraged in the second financial era, particularly in the last decade or so [...] we have entered an age of unprecedented financial risk and leverage, a new global stylized fact that is not fully appreciated.[20]

The accumulation of private debt which was a frequent component of the national processes leading to crisis since World War II to the present is shown for 26 countries in Figs. 3.1, 3.2, 3.3, 3.4, and 3.5. The surge of debt in the US and the UK in the early 1970s is shown in Fig. 3.1, which plots the level of credit to the private sector as reported by two sources, BIS and WDI. The estimates reveal quite substantial differences, which is not surprising given that credit markets are often obscure, and in substantial ways they can operate in the shadows.[21] At any rate, the BIS and the WDI estimates evolve in relatively similar ways. In both the US and the UK, compared with GDP the amount of debt of the private sector climbed until reaching a peak before the crisis of the mid-1970s. In the UK the peak was in 1974 if private debt is measured by WDI figures or in 1972 if the debt estimate is that of BIS. In the US private debt also peaked before the 1975 crisis, either in 1972 or 1974, depending

[20] Schularick & Taylor (2012), "Credit booms gone bust: Monetary policy, leverage cycles, and financial crises, 1870–2008", *American Economic Review* 102(2), 1029–1061.

[21] For instance, they can have substantial links with money laundering which, according to Ghenne et al. ("Fighting money laundering with intelligent automation", International Institute for Analytics/SAS, 2021), could be between 2% and 5% of WGDP. Reinhart & Rogoff (*This time is different*, 2009, xxxiii) acknowledge that the amount of standing debt of sovereign states is often hidden by governments. See Appendix B for a discussion of the credit indicators included in the WDI database.

on the source. Private debt also rose and peaked before the 1975 crisis—as shown in Figs. 3.2, 3.3, 3.4, and 3.5—in several major economies. According to WDI estimates, the peak in private debt as percent of GDP occurred in 1972 in Japan, India, Korea, Peru, Mexico, and Brazil; in 1973 in Australia and South Africa, and in 1974 in Malaysia. According to WDI and BIS estimates (not shown) the debt of the private sector peaked in Greece, Finland, Italy, France, Sweden, Portugal, and other many countries in any of the four years of the period 1972–1975.

Peaks of private credit as announcers of crisis are also shown in multiple countries in Figs. 3.1, 3.2, 3.3, 3.4, and 3.5 in the late 1980s, the late 1990s, and immediately before the Great Recession. All that belongs, though, to the following sections of this chapter.

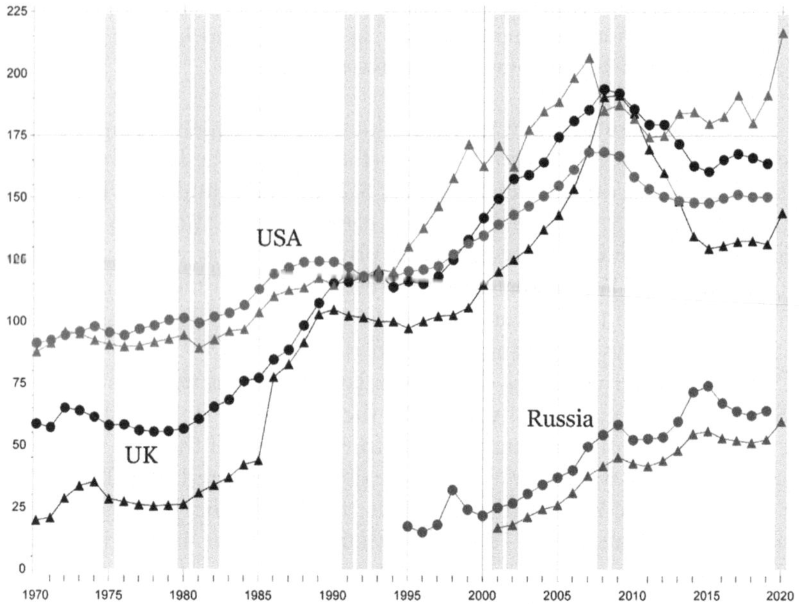

Fig. 3.1 Credit to the private sector in the US, the UK, and Russia as reported in 2020 by BIS ("ratio private non-financial credit to GDP", dots), and in 2022 by WDI ("domestic credit to the private sector, percentage of GDP", triangles). Vertical gray rectangles mark the years of world economic crisis as defined by a decline of gross capital formation

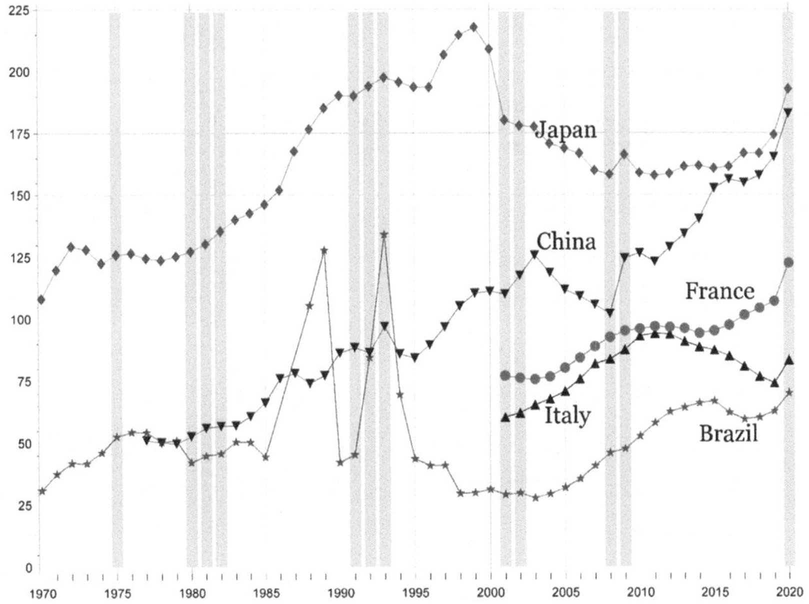

Fig. 3.2 Domestic credit to the private sector, percentage of GDP, in five countries. Vertical gray rectangles mark the years of world economic crisis as defined by a decline of gross capital formation. (Author's elaboration from WDI data, accessed October 2022)

The "Second Oil Crisis" of the Early 1980s

As in the mid-1970s, the annual rates of growth of the global economy in the early 1980s do not reveal any global recession, since WGDP grew at rates between 0.4 and 4.1% in the five years of the period 1979–1983 (Fig. 2.2, page 15, Table E-1, page 297). Though in many countries the recession hit in 1981 or 1982, and even in some in 1983, at the global level the crisis was revealed mostly in the reduced rate of growth of the global output in 1982, 0.4%. Early manifestations of the global downturn could be observed in 1979 in India, where GDP growth was –5.2% in 1979, and in the US and the UK, where the rates of growth were, respectively, −0.3% and –2.0% in 1980 (Table 3.1). In Latin America, the recession was particularly severe in 1981–1983. In Argentina there were two consecutive years of negative growth, in 1981 and in 1982.

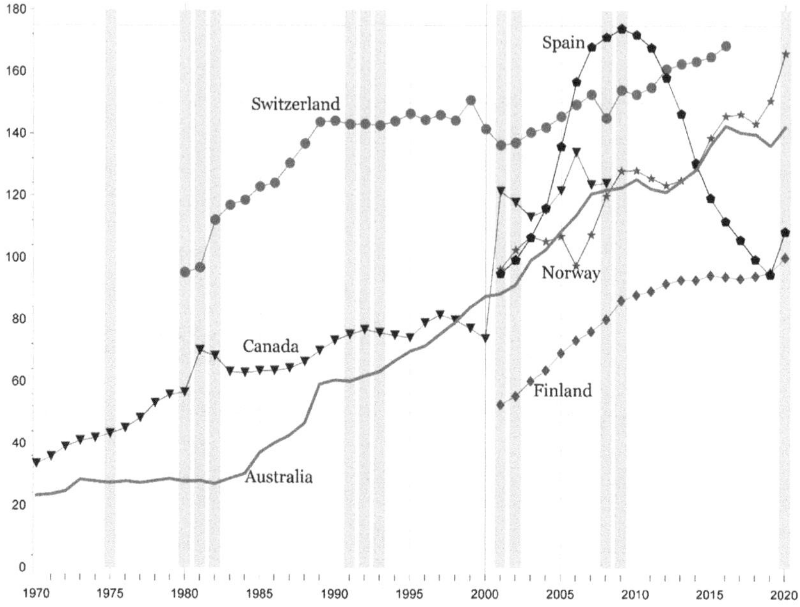

Fig. 3.3 Domestic credit to the private sector, percentage of GDP, in five countries. Vertical gray rectangles mark the years of world economic crisis as defined by a decline of gross capital formation (Author's elaboration from WDI data, accessed October 2022)

In Brazil two years of substantial negative growth, 1981 and 1983, were separated by a year of very low growth, 0.8% in 1982. Chile, still under Pinochet's military dictatorship, had relatively high levels of economic growth during the late 1970s, but the Chilean economy fell abysmally again when the global economy faltered, with remarkable rates of growth of –11.0% in 1982 and –5.0% in 1983. Chile's exports, of which copper has been always a substantial part, in the 1970s amounted to about a quarter of the nation's GDP. In constant dollars Chilean exports had been growing at rates over 11% in the five-year period 1976–1981, but in 1982 they contracted 8.9% and in the next three years they mostly stagnated growing, respectively, at rates of 4.5%, 0.0%, and 2.3%.[22] This is

[22] Computed with WDI data of Chile's exports in 2015 US$.

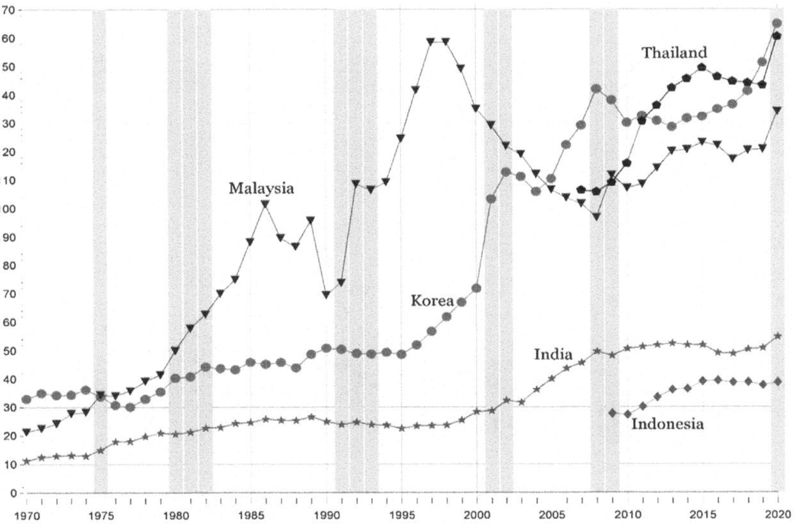

Fig. 3.4 Domestic credit to the private sector as a percentage of GDP, in five Asian countries. Vertical gray rectangles mark the years of world economic crisis as defined by a decline of gross capital formation (Author's elaboration from WDI data, accessed October 2022)

an illustration of the fact that in countries significantly integrated into the global economy global events are key determinants of economic growth. This is obvious in the case of Saudi Arabia, an economy depending almost absolutely on oil exports whose GDP plummeted in the four years 1982–1985, with a negative GDP growth as dismal as –20.7% in 1982 (Table 3.1). Australia, that had had not even one year of economic contraction between 1960 and 1982, had GDP growth of -2.2% in 1983 (Table 3.1). Illustrating how world economic crises affect countries unequally, Japan was almost unaffected by the crisis of the early 1980s. Between 1979 and 1983 the year in which Japan's GDP growth was the lowest was 1980, when the Japanese economy expanded by 2.8%.

Because unemployment levels were still high in many countries as a consequence of the crisis of the mid-1970s, the crisis of the early 1980s pushed unemployment up to two-digit rates in many major economies (Fig. 2.5, page 22) such as the US, the UK, Canada, Italy, Belgium, Turkey, Spain, and others. In Spain joblessness reached in the 1980s over

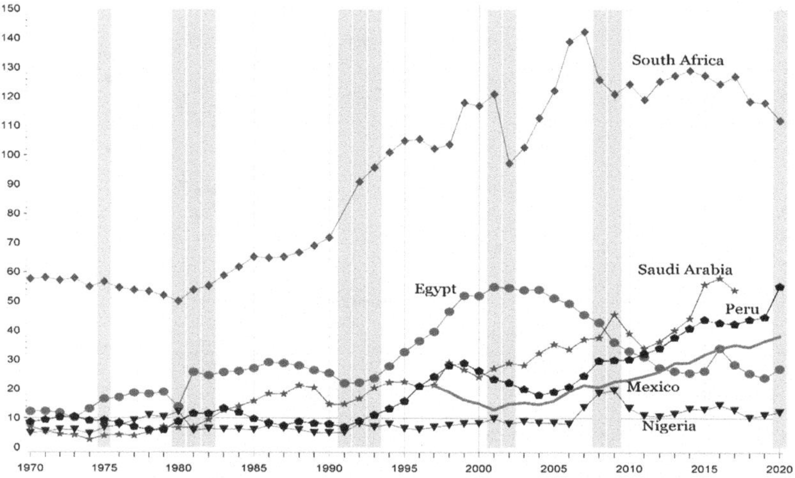

Fig. 3.5 Domestic credit to the private sector, percentage of GDP, in five countries of Latin America, Africa, and Asia. Vertical gray rectangles mark the years of world economic crisis as defined by a decline of gross capital formation. Data from WDI, accessed October 2022 (*Source* Author's elaboration from WDI data, accessed October 2022)

20% of the total labor force. Such high rates of unemployment had not been seen in Europe and North America since the Great Depression of the 1930s.

Unemployment rates at high levels because of the previous crisis of the mid-1970s were not the only reason for unemployment rates reaching very high levels in the 1980s in many countries. In Spain, where the economy had recovered in 1976 and 1977 growing at rates around 3%, the fall of GDP growth in 1978 and in 1979—when it was 0%—made unemployment to quickly soar because it was also stoked by two demographic effects: first, a baby boom in the 1950s and 1960s (that flooded the labor market with young adults looking for jobs in the 1980s—I was one of them); second, the return to the country of more than a million Spanish workers that had been during previous years employed in Germany, Switzerland, France, and other European countries and were forced by the crisis to return to Spain since the mid-1970s.

As in the previous crisis, in the years leading to the crisis of the early 1980s the accumulation of private debt was a major factor in many national economies. Thus, private debt peaked between 1977 and 1982 in the United States (Fig. 3.1), Brazil (Fig. 3.2), Australia, Canada (Fig. 3.3), India, Korea (Fig. 3.4), Egypt, Peru, and Nigeria (Fig. 3.4). According to BIS or WDI data (not shown), private debt also peaked in the years 1977–1982 in Ireland, Belgium, Switzerland, Spain, Greece, Norway, Sweden, and the eurozone at large, as well as Thailand and Russia, with these peaks usually preceding a recession of the national economy.

With the fall of the shah of Iran in 1979 and the outbreak of the Iran–Iraq war in 1980, the OPEC doubled oil prices in less than a year. The cost of oil for refineries in the United States rose from US \$13 in 1979 to \$30 in 1980 and \$37 in early 1981.[23] Thus a number of economists attributed the crisis of the early 1980s to the oil shock, naming it the Second Oil Crisis.[24] The appropriateness of this denomination and more in general the idea that oil price shocks have a major role as causes of economic crises will be discussed in Chapter 7.

The Crisis of the Early 1990s and the Demise of the Soviet Bloc and the USSR

The worker riots in East Germany in 1953, the Hungarian revolution in 1956, the turmoil in Poland in the late 1950s, and the reforms by the Dubček government of Czechoslovakia in the spring of 1968 were illustrative events of the precarious nature of the Soviet hegemony in Eastern Europe, where governments led by communist parties despite being under the strong influence of the USSR sometimes went their own way following policies unwelcome by Moscow. In several cases these processes were suppressed *manu militari* by the intervention of the USSR-led Warsaw Pact. Significant economic distress mostly connected with scarcity and inferior quality of consumer goods added to the political discontent in the USSR and the Soviet allies in Eastern Europe. It

[23] Tatom (1997), "Recessions (supply-side) in the 1970s", in Glasner & Cooley, eds., *Business cycles and depressions: An encyclopedia*, 569–572.

[24] See the entry on "Oil crises" in both Wikipedia and Encyclopedia.com.

was in that context that Mikhail Gorbachev was elected General Secretary of the Communist Party of the Soviet Union (CPSU) in 1985. The policies of *glasnost* ("openness") and *perestroika* ("restructuring") were immediately started, but in 1986 the disaster of Chernobyl triggered huge operations of cleanup and evacuation that cost the USSR a significant part of its budget, already seriously overloaded by military expenditures in weaponry and in the disastrous war in Afghanistan. In the second half of the 1980s the countries of Eastern Europe evolved out of the Soviet sphere of influence, with communist parties being removed from power around 1989. At the time either the USSR was very weak as to intervene in Eastern Europe or the Soviet leadership was not prone to do it, or both things. In 1991 Gorbachev resigned, the CPSU was removed from power, and Boris Yeltsin became the top leader of the Russian Federation that inherited the largest part of the Soviet territory and military power, including all nuclear weapons, when the Soviet Union itself broke up into 15 independent republics.

During the early 1990s market economies were quickly set by means of generalized privatization of government-owned companies in the countries of the old Soviet bloc, as well as in the former Yugoslavia and Albania, which had been centrally planned economies ruled by communist parties but not part of the Soviet sphere of influence. Germany was reunified in 1991, the same year in which the Soviet Union disintegrated. Wars started in the territory of the old Yugoslavia, that soon broke down, and in 1993 Czechoslovakia peacefully split into two independent Czech and Slovak republics. All these events undoubtedly had a role as contributors to the downturn of the world economy, as the closure of hundreds of enterprises and pure disorganization dramatically reduced economic activity in the countries of Eastern Europe and the old USSR during the sudden transition from centrally planned economies into a market economy in the early 1990s. The free fall of the economic output in the countries of the disintegrated Soviet bloc strongly reduced its capacity to import and export goods, thus impacting on the economy of many Western countries. In Finland, for instance, which was a major exporter to the USSR, the early 1990s downturn was so severe that the Finnish economy contracted, respectively, 5.9%, 3.3%, and 0.7% in the three consecutive years 1991–1993 (Table 3.1) and the unemployment rate that had been below 5% in 1988–1990, rose over 16% in 1993 and 1994 (Fig. 2.5, p. 21). At a much smaller scale something similar occurred in Sweden, where GDP grew 0.8% in 1990 and then shrank at growth rates around –1.5% in the three following years. The disruption of exports of raw materials was also an important factor to internationalize the Soviet crisis into the global economy. Thus, Russian exports of crude oil were reduced in the 1990s to a level less than half they had been in the 1980s, which for sure had an impact in raising the price of crude oil in international markets.[25]

However, the role of the Soviet bloc collapse does not seem to have been important even as a trigger of the recessions that occurred in the early 1990s in many national economies that had little or no economic links with Eastern Europe. The 1980s were a period of steady growth of the indebtedness of the private sector in many Western economies—a phenomenon that had nothing to do with the events that were developing in Eastern Europe—and data show a total debt of the private sector growing steadily during most of the 1980s in the US, the UK (Fig. 3.1), Japan, China, Canada, Indonesia, New Zealand, Australia (Fig. 3.2), Norway, Sweden, Switzerland (Fig. 3.3), the Netherlands, Finland (Fig. 3.4), Thailand, Korea (Fig. 3.5), and many other countries (not shown, as reported in both WDI and BIS data). In general, the years that led to the world economic crisis of the early 1990s were a period of accumulation of private debt which often peaked at the end of the 1980s or early in the 1990s; for instance, in 1988 in the United States and Norway, in 1989 in Switzerland, in 1990 in Japan, Australia, Sweden, and Chile, in 1992 in Finland, and in 1993 in Canada (Figs. 3.1, 3.2, 3.3, 3.4, and 3.5). In many countries, the volume of domestic credit to the private sector peaked the same year or the year before a national recession started. For instance, in both Japan and Switzerland the ratio of private debt to GDP peaked in 1990 (Figs. 3.2 and 3.3); then GDP had negative or zero growth for three consecutive years in Switzerland in 1991–1993, while in Japan GDP growth dropped in 1992 to 0.8% and went negative in 1993 (Table 3.1). In Australia debt peaked in 1990 (Fig. 3.3) and GDP growth reversed to negative in 1991. In the US

[25] Russian crude oil exports oscillated over 4.4 million barrels per day (mbpd) in the 1980s, reaching an all-time high of 5.35 mbpd in 1988. Then they dropped steadily in the next three years to a record low of 2.49 mbpd in 1994. They stayed at levels well below 3 mbpd until 1999, then quickly increased in the next two years until reaching a plateau in which they oscillated between 4.5 and 5.5 mbpd in the first two decades of the present century. From 1980 to 2021 the average was 4.65 mbpd, with the most recent data 4.51 mbpd in December 2021 and 4.62 mbpd in December 2020 (CEIC, www.ceicdata.com/en/indicator/russia/crude-oil-exports, accessed November 1, 2022).

private debt reached a plateau in the late 1980s and dropped in 1991 (Fig. 3.1), when GDP growth was −0.1% (Table 3.1). In Spain, France, and Portugal debt grew until 1993, when GDP contracted in the three countries (Table 3.1). In Latin America national recessions had started earlier, with the Argentinian economy sliding to a deep slump in 1988, 1989, and 1990 (Table 3.1), and the Brazilian's GDP growth falling to –4.4% in 1990. In both countries, private sector debt reached a peak in 1989 that was followed by a dramatic drop: 39.7% of GDP in Argentina that dropped to 15.6% in 1990; 127% in Brazil, that dropped to 42.1% in 1990.[26] In Chile, however, the world economic crisis of the early 1990s had little effect, GDP growth was steady in the late 1980s and the 1990s until 1989.

Discussions of the concept of national income often emphasize that GDP figures have little sense when prices are not determined in the market but fixed by a central authority.[27] Despite that consideration, it is increasingly common to see GDP estimates for economies under central planning and prices under centralized control. Thus, the WDI database of the World Bank reports values of GDP and GDP growth for instance for Albania for the years since 1981 onward, despite the fact that a centrally planned economy was in place in Albania until the early 1990s. Similarly, for China the WDI database reports GDP growth rates since 1961, even though market reforms and liberalized prices were not introduced in China until the late 1970s or even later. Whatever the reasons for all this, in Albania, which had a political regime strongly centralized under the government of the Communist Party since 1945 until the late 1980s, according to the WDI database GDP growth was 9.8% in 1989, the first year in which the economy was liberalized, followed by an abysmal contraction during the three following years, with GDP growth –9.6% in 1990, –28.0% in 1991, and –7.2% in 1992. In Russia where the generalized transition to a market economy started in the early 1990s, negative rates of GDP growth are reported by the WDI for all the years of that decade, except 1997 and 1999, with the deepest contraction, 14.5%, in 1992 (Table 3.1).

[26] WDI database, accessed November 2022. Figure 3.2 shows the WDI data for Brazil in which wild oscillations appear in the late 1980s and early 1990s.

[27] Maier & Easton (1999), *The data game: Controversies in social science statistics*.

Periods of economic crisis in market economies have never had major demographic or health consequences, and indeed they have regularly coincided with minor *decreases* of both fertility and mortality rates.[28] Contrarily, the transition to a market economy in Eastern Europe and the old USSR in the early 1990s had major demographic and health correlates. During the economic debacle of the early 1990s in Eastern Europe mortality skyrocketed and birth rates dropped dramatically.[29] In some of the countries formerly part of Yugoslavia and the USSR, in the new republics of the Caucasus and in Central Asia, social and economic conditions were complicated even further by local wars. The sociodemographic crisis lasted a few years in most countries of Eastern Europe, but in most republics of the former Yugoslavia and USSR it lingered for the whole decade and even further. Because of high mortality rates and very low birth rates after the transition, the Russian population shrank from a peak of 148 million in 1992 to 142 million in 2012. The burden of death from the mortality crisis of the transition in eastern Europe and the USSR has been estimated in ten million extra deaths from 1990 to 2000.[30]

In China the global economic crisis of the early 1990s revealed itself by rates of GDP growth of about 4% in 1989–1990 after eight consecutive years of two-digit rates.

[28] Ruhm (2000), Tapia & Diez Roux (2009), Tapia & Ionides (2017), and Salinari & Benassi (2022) can be illustrative of a wide literature that shows mortality rates in market economies deviate from trend upward in years of economic prosperity and downward in slumps. This fact has been often "rejected" by investigations methodologically flawed. For instance a paper claiming that the Great Recession had generated in Spain more deaths than the civil war of 1936–1939 (Cabrera de León et al., "Austerity policies and mortality in Spain after the financial crisis of 2008", *American Journal of Public Health* 108, 1091–1098) was retracted in 2018, one year after published, because of obvious statistical flaws. Since the 1970s, Harvey Brenner, Ralph Catalano, David Stuckler, and others have repeatedly "demonstrated" in papers and books (and even in a congressional report of Brenner) that recessions cause increases in mortality due to major causes, including heart disease. Except for suicides, these results could not be reproduced by other researchers, including myself—who indeed found exactly the opposite.

[29] Cornia & Paniccià, eds. (2000), *The mortality crisis in transitional economies*; Stillman (2006), "Health and nutrition in Eastern Europe and the former Soviet Union during the decade of transition: A review of the literature", *Economics & Human Biology* 4(1), 104–146; Tapia (2022), *Chernobyl and the mortality crisis in Eastern Europe and the former USSR*.

[30] Cornia (2016), "The mortality crisis in transition economies".

The Crisis of the Turn of the Century

Out of the six crises of the world economy posed in this book, the global crisis around the turn of the century was the least well-defined, since its manifestations were distributed over several years, with the national crises starting in the late 1990s and extending to the early years of the next decade. For the Japanese economy that had been growing at rates between 3.3 and 6.7% in the period 1981–1991, most of the 1990s were a period of stagnation or contraction that led to the notion that the 1990s were the lost decade of the Japanese economy. In the period 1992–1999 the highest rate of economic growth was just 2.6%, in 1995, and GDP growth was indeed negative in 1993, 1998, and 1999 (Table 3.1).

The 1990s or at least most of the decade were years of steady accumulation of private debt in the US, the UK (Fig. 3.1), Japan, China (Fig. 3.2), Switzerland, Canada, Australia (Fig. 3.3), Korea, India, Indonesia (Fig. 3.4), South Africa, Saudi Arabia (Fig. 3.5), and many other countries. Following this accumulation of private debt, recessions with a strong financial component of banking crises occurred at the end of the 1990s in South Korea (1997–1998), Indonesia (1997–2001), Malaysia (1997–1999), Thailand (1997–2000), the Philippines (1997–2001), and Russia (1998).[31] These banking crises were the financial manifestation of turbulence in national and international financial flows and major disturbances in the real economy of these national economies that had major slumps in 1998, when GDP growth was –5.1% in South Korea, –13.1% in Indonesia, –7.4% in Malaysia, –7.6% in Thailand, –0.5% in the Philippines, and –5.3% in Russia. In Singapore GDP growth was negative in 1998, –2.2%, and in 2001, –1.1%. These Asian economies had been growing at rates over 5% and even not infrequently over 10% in previous years and were considered by international financial institutions and mainstream economists as having sound macroeconomic policies and proper institutions in place.[32] Despite all that, they all tanked around the end of the century.

In Argentina, negative growth of GDP in 1999 continued for the next three years. The financial crisis erupted in 2001 and kept the country in

[31] Laeven & Valencia (2012), "Systemic banking crises database: An update", IMF Working Paper 12/163.

[32] Spence (2011), *The next convergence—The future of economic growth in a multispeed world*, Ch. 7.

financial disarray for months; the situation at the time when cash could be retrieved only in very limited amounts from bank accounts in dollars—very common at the time—, was known in Argentina as *el corralito*. In Uruguay negative GDP growth and financial distress also extended four years between 1999 and 2002; in Saudi Arabia GDP growth was negative in 1999, 2001, and 2002; in the Czech Republic in 1997 and 1998; in Jamaica, there were three years of negative GDP growth in 1996–1998, in 1999 and 2000 GDP growth was 1% or less. For Laeven and Valencia these were clearly financial crises associated with output loss, that is, they were generalized economic downturns.[33] It could be argued that the entire 1990s was a decade of economic crises around the world. However, during most of the decade the major economies in Western Europe and North America, as well as China, Australia, Brazil, and many other countries were growing at quite high rates, and the global drops in investment and output concentrated strongly around the beginning and the end of the decade when, furthermore, they coincided with banking crises in many countries. All that argues in favor of dating world crises at the beginning of the decade and at the turn of the century, when there were major reductions in capital formation, industrial activity, etc., as it was shown in Chapter 2.

The Great Recession and the 2010s

In the years before the COVID-19 pandemic of 2020 there was quite general agreement that the Great Recession had been the most important economic crisis since the 1930s. That recession started in late 2007, became manifest with the global financial crisis of 2008, and affected in a greater or lesser extent almost all national economies. Between 2008 and 2009, GDP growth dropped by several percentage points in many countries (for instance 10.0 percentage points in Argentina, 5.2 in Brazil, 3.9 in Canada, 4.9 in Chile, 13.0 in Russia, 4.7 in Spain, Table 3.1) and dropped to –2% at the global level. As we will see later, this –2% growth of WGDP looked—because it was—a phenomenal contraction of the global economy. However, as compared with the 3.3% contraction of 2020, the Great Recession of 2009 was "not that bad" (Fig. 2.2).

[33] Laeven & Valencia (2012), "Systemic banking crises database".

The global economic crisis that started late in 2007 revealed itself by strong drops in GDP growth in 2008, though it was in 2009 when annual economic growth became negative in a large proportion of nations (94 out of 196 in the WDI database, vs 30 out of 194 in 2008). The global recession involved major economic downturns in North America and Japan, but it was in Europe where its manifestations were the most severe. In the so-called emerging economies of Latin America and Asia, as well as Australia and in most nations of Eastern Europe, GDP growth slowed down significantly, but in most cases remained positive (Table 3.1).

As in the former crises of the world economy, the years leading to the crisis saw a steady growth of private debt, with the ratio of private debt to GDP reaching peaks between 2007 and 2010 in the US, the UK, Russia (Fig. 3.1), Japan, China, France, Italy (Fig. 3.2), the Eurozone (not shown) Norway, Switzerland, Spain (Fig. 3.4), Nigeria, South Africa, Saudi Arabia (Fig. 3.5), and many other countries.

In the United States the recession officially ended in the summer of 2009, and GDP expanded at annual rates of around 2% in the early 2010s, but in Europe the recession lingered with negative GDP growth in Spain, Greece, Portugal, Slovenia, Slovakia, and Hungary during one, two, or three years between 2009 and 2012. In Finland GDP growth that in 2009 was –8.1% recovered immediately to positive rates in 2010 and 2011, but was again negative in 2012, 2013, and 2014 (Table 3.1).

During the Great Recession unemployment peaked in the United States and Germany in 2009 at respective rates of 9.6% and 7.7% of the labor force and since that year unemployment rates slowly declined. However, after 2009 in several European countries in which economic growth lingered in negative territory unemployment rates remained at two-digit levels and even above 20% in some cases. Joblessness was particularly severe in Estonia, Greece, Ireland, Latvia, Lithuania, Slovenia, and Spain. In all these countries the unemployment rate soared since 2007 and peaked in 2010 at 14.4% in Slovakia, 8.4% in Finland and France, 18.7% in Latvia, and 17.8% in Lithuania. In Southern Europe unemployment continued rising, reaching in 2012 25.0% in Spain, 24.2% in Greece, 10.7% in Italy, and 9.9% in France.

Post-Keynesian and Marxist economists and commentators interpreted the Great Recession in various ways as a failure of economic policy or capitalism itself but in general put emphasis on the financial aspects of it.[34] The deregulation of banking activities since the times of Clinton and the views of Hyman Minsky on financial instability were often mentioned by radical authors as directly leading to the US financial debacle which would have spilled over to the rest of the world pushing the real economy to a contraction. As some economists said, looking at debt growth in the years leading to the crisis, it looked as a Minsky moment rather than a Marx moment.[35] This usually did not consider that for instance in the US economy profits before and after taxes, and for nonfinancial and financial industries, had a peak in the third quarter of 2006, that is, quite before the financial crisis erupted.[36]

Not much after the major heat of the global financial crisis that accompanied the Great Depression had subsided, voices were heard in the economic profession suggesting that there were reasons not to expect a quick and sustained recovery. A reputed macroeconomist, Robert Gordon, claimed that powerful forces would slow down the rate of growth of the American economy for years.[37] Gordon maintained that very likely stagnant living standards would be the reality for most Americans, because economic growth would be sapped by slowing technological progress and several "headwinds", including rising inequality, a plateau in education levels, and an aging population. His views were disputed, but many economists heed them.[38] Gordon referred mostly to the American economy, but in most countries of Europe the recovery from the Great Recession was weak and protracted and there were, as it was already mentioned, years of negative growth in the early 2010s in many European countries where, it was told, there were double-dip recessions. Interestingly, the Great Recession also put an end to double-digit rates of growth in China. The year 2010 was the last one in which China's GDP grew at a rate of over 10%.

[34] Yagi et al., eds. (2013), *Crises of global economies and the future of capitalism.*

[35] Friedman, Moseley, & Sturr, eds. (2009), *The economic crisis reader: Readings in economics, politics, and social policy.*

[36] Tapia (2012), "Statistical evidence of falling profits as cause of recession: A short note", *Review of Radical Political Economics* 44(4), 484–493.

[37] Gordon (2012), "Is U.S. economic growth over? Faltering innovation confronts the six headwinds," *NBER Working Paper* 18315; Goldfarb (2014), "Why Robert Gordon thinks economic growth is over", *The Washington Post*, 2 March.

[38] Krugman (2016), "Review: 'The Rise and Fall of American Growth' by Robert J. Gordon", *The New York Times*, January 31.

In 2019 the opinion of acknowledged authorities in the economic profession such as Larry Summers and Paul Krugman was that a recession looked likely. As the decade neared its end, excepting Donald Trump enthusiasts, expectations were that a recession was close.[39] As we now know, it started in the spring of 2020 in a completely surprising way, with an unexpected viral pandemic. That was the sixth crisis of the world economy which will be discussed more in detail in Chapter 9.

The International Synchronization of Business Cycles

Since economic analyses of all kinds have overwhelmingly focused on the working of national economies, not much knowledge has been obtained on how and why the business cycle has evolved increasingly synchronized across the countries of the world. An illustration of that process is provided by the two panels of Fig. 3.6 showing the annual rate of growth of four national economies in two periods, 1960–1990 and 1990–2020. Recessions are apparent as troughs in the curves of GDP growth. Comparing the top and the bottom panels of the figure, it is obvious that the business cycles of these four economies are more synchronized in 1990–2020 than in 1960–1985. Indeed, the Japanese recession of 1998–1999 is the only discordant note in a quartet playing quite in tune after 1990. Of course, the crises did not occur exactly in the same year and with the same intensity in the four countries, but they had a significantly similar timing, which has grown more synchronized over time.

What Fig. 3.6 illustrates for the United States, Japan, Spain, and the Netherlands could be also shown for many other countries. As argued in this book the national economies are increasingly marching in line and there are many reasons to see the slumps in 2008–2009 and at the turn

[39] Writing in *The Washington Post*, on January 7, 2019 ("The right policy as recession looms"), Larry Summers placed the odds of a recession before 2021 at about 50%. On April 26, 2019, James Freeman in *The Wall Street Journal* ("Has the recessions been cancelled? The strength of the U.S. economy continues to confound the liberal establishment") attacked Paul Krugman, Larry Summer and the Brooking Institution because of their views of an impending recession. As an example of the optimism prevailing among corporate executives, Freeman cited JPMorgan Chase CEO Jamie Dimon: "People are going back to the workforce. Companies have plenty of capital... business confidence and consumer confidence are both rather high... it could go on for years. There's no law that says it has to stop."

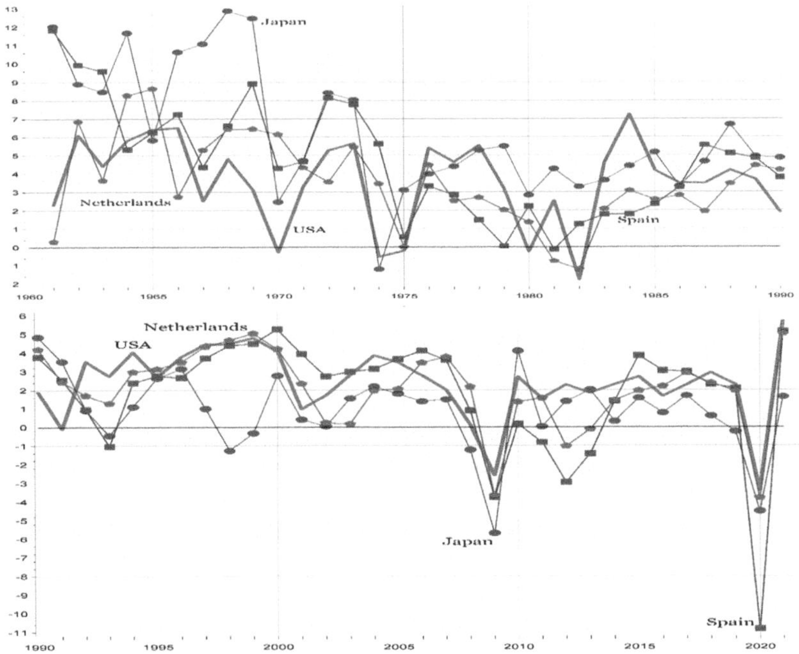

Fig. 3.6 Annual rate of growth of four national economies in 1965–1985 (top panel) and 1985–2015 (bottom panel) (Author's elaboration from WDI data, accessed October 2022)

of the century as crises of the world economy, and the same can be said about the recessions in the early 1990s, the early 1980s, and the mid-1970s. Obviously the COVID-19 pandemic was the exogenous factor that led basically all the economies of the world to recession in 2020, but there was no pandemic in 2009. Commercial ties in the form of imports and exports of both raw materials and manufactured products and financial links in the form of credit flows and foreign direct investment becoming stronger with the pass of time are an obvious explanation of the increasing synchronization of business cycles across nations.

A factor sometimes mentioned, perhaps more in the past than recently, is a supposedly leading or increasingly important role of the US economy in the context of the economy of the world which would pose the US economy as the locomotive pulling the train of the rest of the world.

US recessions and expansions being propagated to the rest of the world would be the mechanism to explain the international synchronization of business cycles. This explanation, however, does not appear defensible for several reasons. First, there is general agreement that the weight of the United States in the world economy has been declining in recent decades. Computing WGDP and its components using market exchange rates, which undoubtedly reflect the real weight of each country in the world economy better than PPP, the share of the United States in WGDP was about 27% in the early 1960s, went down to about 24% in the 1980s, recovered slightly in the 1990s but then steadily declined down to 22% in the 2010s; it was 21.5% in 2019. With very large rates of growth in the past two decades, China's GDP share in WGDP grew from less than 2% before 1985 to 13% in the 2010s and 13.6% in 2019.[40] This decreasing weight of the United States in the world economy would tend to produce less rather than more synchronization of national economies if the synchronization were caused by the hegemony of the United States in the world economy. Second, the links between the United States and economies which have been highly synchronized with the US economy in recent decades are not particularly strong. Figure 3.6 shows for instance that the expansions and recessions of Spain and the United States are highly synchronized from the 1970s on; however, Spain has much stronger commercial links with the countries of the European Union than with the United States. Third, the timing of the crises does not support the view that the United States is leading and the other economies following. The crisis of the early 1980s in the United States was indeed preceded by 0% economic growth in 1979 in Spain. Then in the 1990s negative growth hit the United States in 1991 and Spain in 1993. More generally, the crisis around the turn of the century affected Asia, Russia, and Latin America intensely, but was quite mild in North America and Europe. The American economy as an engine of the global economy is a metaphor increasingly unplausible.

[40] These shares in WGDP are computed from WDI data on national and world GDPs in 2010 US dollars. With national GDP computed using PPP the weight of the United States in the economy is smaller than the weight of China, which in 2019 accounted 17.3% of WGDP, with the United States contributing just 15.8%. In 2019 the euro area contributed 16.7% of WGDP if the share is computed by using market exchange rates and 12.4% if using PPP.

It is obvious, however, that the interconnections of the national economies have grown stronger in recent decades. The increasing worldwide synchronization of expansions and recessions was noted more than two decades ago.[41] Versus the arguable assertion by authors in the world-system school that the world economy was a reality already several centuries ago, what is unarguable is that the world economy has become a tangible reality in recent decades, when the links binding together national economic spaces—trade, capital flows, flows of people, financial shocks—became much stronger. Of course, that assertion does imply neither that there were no links between national economies in past centuries, nor that presently national economies have no autonomy at all. In fact, as Fig. 3.6 illustrates, the economies of the United States, Japan, the Netherlands, and Spain evolved quite differently after 2008. While the United States had a weak but real recovery, the Spanish, Japanese, and Dutch economies were mired in negative growth in the early 2010s. Many have claimed that the different evolution of the economies of the United States, Western Europe, and Japan after the 2009 slump illustrates how different economic policies—austerity or expansionary monetary policy (i.e., quantitative easing)—generate different economic performances. However, the synchronization of national economies makes it increasingly unbelievable that economic performance had much to do with the actions of national governments and the economic policies applied at the national level. National governments have applied different economic policies in recent decades, and economic policies having a major influence on economic growth would imply a broad desynchronization of national economies. However, what is observed is precisely the opposite.

The Demographic Globalization

This rough outline of the main economic developments and national manifestations of the crises of the world economy has not elaborated on many major aspects of the world economy in recent decades. It would miss a very important one if it were not mentioned here a major phenomenon that occurred since the 1980s, to know, the transformation of the ethnic composition of the population in many high-income countries. Attracted by possibilities of work during the periods of expansion

[41] Gregory, Head & Raynauld (1997), "Measuring world business cycles", *International Economic Review* 38(3), 677–701.

and stimulated to migrate by a variety of conditions in their countries of origin—poverty, war, lack of jobs, and political repression—millions of immigrants from Africa, Asia, Latin America, and Eastern Europe arrived in recent decades at the high-income economies of Western Europe, North America, and Oceania. Countries that until the 1970s had had an almost fully homogeneous population in ethnic and religious terms—e.g., Sweden, Finland, Spain, or Italy—were transformed by the influx of foreign-born workers that now form important minorities of the resident population. As estimated by the World Bank, the international migrant stock, that is the proportion of people born in a country other than that in which they live, as a proportion of all residents of the country, grew between 1990 and 2015 from 1.3% to 5.7% in Finland, from 2.1% to 12.7% in Spain, from 4.6% to 10.1% in Denmark, and from 6.4% to 13.2% in Britain. In countries where international migrants were already a sizable portion of the population in 1990, the international migrant stock continued growing, thus it rose from 9.2% to 16.8% in Sweden, from 9.2% to 14.5% in the United States, from 23.1% to 28.2% in Australia and from 20.9% to 29.4% in Switzerland. These migrants generate very significant monetary flows between countries, in the first place because of direct remittances to relatives in the countries of origin. Thus, in 2019 personal remittances received by residents from nonresidents amounted to 10.3% of GDP in Ukraine, 9.6% in Albania, 5.3% in Nigeria, 3.1% in Mexico and Romania, 3.0% in Ecuador and Kenya, 2.9% in India, 2.0% in Mozambique, 1.5% in Peru, 1.1% in Poland, 1.0% in Indonesia, and 0.6% in Russia. What these figures illustrate is however only part of the issue, as foreign-born residents generate huge volumes of international travel and international purchases, all of which add to the many elements that make the present world a truly global economy. Behind the known increase in the number of foreign-born people in countries as different as the United States, South Africa, Australia, Sweden, or Chile, is the less known fact that at least several thousand fatalities per year have been documented in recent years on migratory routes around the world. This estimate of casualties among those trying to escape poverty, political repression, the effects of climate change, natural disasters, or wars is for sure a significant underestimate because a large majority of migrant deaths worldwide, in deserts, jungles, oceans or cities, go unrecorded.[42] Citizenship rights,

[42] Migration data portal, "Migrant deaths and disappearances", https://migrationdataportal.org/themes/migrant-deaths-and-disappearances, accessed 10/2023.

which can be purchased by paying substantial sums,[43] are probably the major source of misery and discrimination in our world.

[43] Henley & Partners, "Leading Citizenship by Investment Programs," https://www.henleyglobal.com/citizenship-investment?page=ppc_Global_gsn_gen_cit1_tier1&gad=1&gclid=CjwKCAjwg4SpBhAKEiwAdyLwvDJvQw4qCcNnVXAQbBpCIewuFlRNcnuUbkFK_AOSxQmVa9fFM7vechoC4M4QAvD_BwE, accessed 10/2023.

CHAPTER 4

Conceptual Issues—Depressions, Recessions, Crisis Cycles, Business Cycles

The entry on *crises* in the *New Palgrave Dictionary of Economics* asserts that the term "as used in economics is principally associated with Marx," as while other writers used the term, "Marx attempted rigorously to theorize crises as they occur in capitalism."[1] Maybe this is the reason why contrary to *The New Palgrave*, most dictionaries of economics have entries neither for *crisis* nor for *economic crisis* nor for *financial crisis*.[2] You cannot find these terms either in the index or in the glossaries of most modern textbooks of economics or macroeconomics for which undergraduates often pay splendid bills.[3] In these bibles of the economic science taught to the apprentices of economists, the term *crisis* appears sometimes in the explanations of the business cycle, as a possible synonym of "recession," but in most economic textbooks to look for *crisis* will

[1] Kenway 1998 [1987], "Crises", in Eatwell, Milgate & Newman, eds., *The New Palgrave: A Dictionary of Economics*, 724–726.

[2] Ammer & Ammer (1977), *Dictionary of business & economics*; Bannock, Baxter & Davis (1998), *The Penguin dictionary of economics*; Pass et al. (1991), *The Harper-Collins dictionary of economics*; remarkably, with three volumes and an advisory board including Nobelists James Buchanan and Janos Kornai, *The New Palgrave dictionary of economics and the law* (Newman, ed., 1998) includes entries neither for "crisis" nor "economic crisis" nor "financial crisis" nor "recession" nor "business cycle".

[3] For instance, Krugman & Wells (2006), *Economics*; Gordon (2009), *Macroeconomics*; Blanchard (2006), *Macroeconomics*.

J. A. Tapia, *Six Crises of the World Economy*,
https://doi.org/10.1007/978-3-031-38735-7_4

fail to produce any hit. Before 2008, crisis was for a large majority of economists a concept to be ignored, the same as "the *D* word", depression, was a term not to be mentioned. A case particularly illustrative is that of *The Princeton Encyclopedia of the World Economy*, a 1246-page long book that was published in 2009.[4] In this encyclopedia that obviously was prepared when the Great Recession was in incubation, the reader will look in vain for entries on the business cycle, recession, depression, or crisis. For the editors of this encyclopedia the world economy obviously was not to be related to these concepts. The book includes entries on financial crisis, currency crisis and banking crisis, concepts that are discussed as unrelated to world production and affecting mostly developing countries. Considering the "state of the art" revealed by the absence of substantial discussions of the concept of economic crisis in canonic works of economics, it is not surprising at all that the Great Recession, as Nicholas Mankiw put it, "caught most economists flat-footed."[5] In recent decades the sporadic attempts of the economic profession to deal with the possibility of appearance of this not-to-be-mentioned event have been always plagued by outstanding conceptual confusion.[6]

It was not always that mainstream economics was deaf to the reality of crises. In the early decades of the twentieth century, the concept of economic crisis was often discussed in the mainstream economic literature. *Les Crises Périodiques de Surproduction* by Albert Aftalion, and *Les Crises Industrieles en Angleterre* by Michel Tugan-Baranovski were both published in 1913 in Paris, where it were also published *Les Crises Economiques* by Mentor Bouniatian in 1922, and the third edition of *Des Crises Générales at Périodiques de Surproduction* by Jean Lescure, in 1923. Minnie Throop England, an economist at the University of Nebraska, published several papers on economic crises in which she discussed the links between troubles of industrial firms to obtain the adequate revenue

[4] *The Princeton encyclopedia of the world economy*, ed. by K. A Reinert and R.S. Rajan, Princeton University Press, Princeton, NJ, 2009.

[5] Mankiw (2010), "A call for humility: Trying to tame the unknowable", *New York Times*, March 26, B6.

[6] An example of it is *The risk of economic crises*, edited by Martin Feldstein (1991), a collection of short papers and commentaries from a roundtable in which quite disparate views were exposed. In one commentary Hyman Minsky complained that the three background papers of the roundtable [by Benjamin Friedman, Paul Krugman, and Larry Summers] were "on financial, not economic, crisis; furthermore, the papers are not clear on how financial and economic crisis are related" (p. 161).

and the tensions in the financial sphere as a key component of crises.[7] She also discussed the crucial role of investment—which she called "promotion"—in crises and criticized the views that in her opinion exaggerated the role of interest rates.[8] Today she is basically forgotten, perhaps even more than Wesley C. Mitchell, who as leader of empirical economic research in the United States in the first half of the twentieth century referred repeatedly to the issue of economic crises.

In his early works, which stand out for the effort to introduce rigor and accuracy into the empirical analysis of business cycles, Mitchell meticulously discussed how different authors had understood the "business cycle," a term that had had many former incarnations including crisis cycle, trade cycle, industrial cycle, cycle of prosperity and depression, and cycle of prosperity and crisis, among others.[9] He clarified that some authors had used the term "crisis" to mean simply the transition from the phase of prosperity to that of depression, while others had used it to mean severe disruption of economic life, with significant numbers of firms under major stress or failing. For Mitchell, in the transition from prosperity to depression in business cycles such disturbances occur frequently, but not always, and for that reason he concluded that the term *crisis* is not appropriate in referring to one of the phases of the cycle. "Crisis", said Mitchell

> is a poor term to use in describing one of the four phases of business cycles. If it is to be retained, it must be defined in the colorless fashion of Lescure and Aftalion—as the mere point of intersection between prosperity and depression. But sad experience shows how much misunderstanding comes from the effort to use familiar words in new technical senses. Scientific writers can, hardly expect that readers will purge their minds of old associations and form new ones at a terminologist's bidding.[10]

[7] England (1913a), "Economic crises", *Journal of Political Economy* 21(4), 345–354; England (1913b), "An analysis of the crisis cycle", *Journal of Political Economy* 21(8), 712–734.

[8] England (1912), "Fisher's theory of crises: A criticism". *Quarterly Journal of Economics* 27(1), 95–106; England (1915), "Promotion as the cause of crises", *Quarterly Journal of Economics* 29(5), 748–767.

[9] Mitchell (1913), *Business cycles*, Chapter 1.

[10] Mitchell (1927), *Business cycles: The problem and its setting*, 378–382.

In the late nineteenth century very few economists were interested in what in the twentieth century came to be called "the business cycle" as a recurrent but not periodical alternation of prosperity and depression.[11] In earlier times when the present-day discipline of economics was called political economy, Adam Smith, David Ricardo, John Stuart Mill, and others had used a variety of terms including *trade revulsion*, *commercial panic*, *glut of markets*, or *commercial crisis* as meaning financial panics during periods of commercial stress or periods of deep industrial depression when banks failed, factories closed and products remained unsold in the market. But they, as most economists of the nineteenth century, considered these to be mostly isolated events limited to particular markets and subscribed to the idea of Jean-Baptiste Say, who denied that a "glut," that is, overproduction, could be general, affecting all markets. According to Say, in what later was called Say's law, an economic crisis understood as a situation with generalized oversupply in the market, was not possible. As it will be discussed in the rest of this chapter, the concept of economic crisis was born and developed in opposition to Say's law, to the idea of equilibrium of the market system. Marx is the main author who created a body of theory—born as a critique in opposition to the notions of classical political economy—in which the concept of economic crisis is a key element. After writing with Engels the *Communist Manifesto* (1848) in which the modern industrial economy based on the exploitation of wage labor by capital was considered as condemned to be soon eliminated, Marx continued during the rest of his life elaborating the concepts of his critique of political economy. Though he developed his economic views mostly independently, he sometimes requested the collaboration and advice of Engels, who was fully immersed in the commercial and industrial life that was known to Marx only second-hand and from his relationships with industrial workers. Both Marx and Engels were active participants of socialist movements that at the time had multiple links with activist workers and social democratic parties in Germany, France, Britain, and other countries, since 1864 integrated in the International Workingmen's Association. When Marx died, most of his views on the industrial cycle and crises where unpublished in manuscripts that later were edited by Engels or others. As it will be discussed in this chapter, Engels, who can be considered the first Marxist, modified and amended Marx's notions on

[11] Morgan (1990), *The history of econometric ideas*, 15.

economic crises and the industrial cycle, which were further transformed by twentieth century Marxists. The chapter will conclude with a schematic examination of how the idea of economic crises evolved in the economic discipline since the early decades of the twentieth century to the present.

Marx and Engels

Karl Marx strongly disagreed with Jean-Baptiste Say, to whom he addressed his most caustic comments. References to overproduction and crisis are common in Marx's work, though they are widely scattered and mostly in works such as the second and third volumes of *Capital* and the *Theories of surplus value* that Marx left as unpublished manuscripts and were edited by others. The opinion that Marx never produced a complete theory of crisis is commonly accepted.[12] In Marx's view, the evolution of capitalism—a term that Marx rarely used, he generally talked about "the modern factory system" or "the bourgeois economy"—is basically a succession of periods of accumulation of capital separated by crises, in an alternating process that he called "industrial cycle," or "crisis cycle."[13] As Marx explained in *Capital*, the enormous capacity of capitalism

> for expanding with sudden immense leaps, and its dependence on the world market, necessarily give rise to the following cycle: feverish production, a consequent glut of the market, then a contraction of the market, which causes production to be crippled. The life of industry becomes a series of periods of moderate activity, prosperity, overproduction, crisis and stagnation. The uncertainty and instability to which machinery subjects the employment, and consequently the conditions of existence, of the operatives becomes a normal state of affairs, owing to these periodic turns of the industrial cycle.[14]

[12] Schumpeter (1954), *History of economic analysis*; Medio (1987), "Trade cycle," in Eatwell, Milgate & Newman, eds., *The New Palgrave—A dictionary of economics*, 666–671; Mandel, "Introduction", in Marx (1981) [1894], *Capital*, Volume 3, ed. by F. Engels, 38.

[13] Clarke (1994), *Marx's theory of crisis*; Mattick (1981), *Economic crisis and crisis theory*.

[14] Marx (1977) [1867], *Capital—A critique of political economy*, Volume I, ch. 15, 581–582.

This quotation makes it obvious that the industrial cycle Marx was thinking of was something that occurred every few years, not every few decades. Otherwise, the corresponding "uncertainty and instability" would be of little concern for "the operatives" who take care of the machinery as the only means to gain a living.

Marx viewed the mode of production based on the hegemony of capital as a world system and his analysis of long-term trends was based on the abstraction of a capitalist market extended to the entire world, so that the unit to be analyzed is a unique world economy. He was not shy, however, about examining and commenting concrete economic data belonging to the national economies of his time. In the period since his early publications on economic issues in the 1840s until the publication of the first volume of *Capital* in 1867, Marx often paid attention to the concrete timing of commercial crises in England and other countries. In the first volume of *Capital*, Marx proposed that crises had a decennial periodicity, but he and Engels before him seem to have ruminated a long time on the issue. Thus, in "The principles of communism," written in 1847 and used as preparatory material for the *Manifesto of the communist party*, Engels wrote that since the beginning of the century, the condition of industry had

> constantly fluctuated between periods of prosperity and periods of crisis; nearly every five to seven years, a fresh crisis has intervened, always with the greatest hardship for workers, and always accompanied by general revolutionary stirrings and the direct peril to the whole existing order of things.[15]

In his speech "On the Question of Free Trade" to the Democratic Association of Brussels at its public meeting of 1848, Marx referred to "the average period of from six to seven years [...] during which modern industry passes through the various phases of prosperity, overproduction, stagnation, crisis, and completes its inevitable cycle."[16] But then in the *Manifesto*—published as an anonymous text the same year—the two friends referred to "periodical convulsions" and "commercial crises

[15] Engels (1969) [1847], "The principles of communism", in *Marx & Engels Selected Works*, Volume 1, 81–97.

[16] *Marx & Engels Collected Works* (2010), 6, 450–465, the quoted passage is on p. 458. Hereafter, *Marx & Engels Collected Works* will be abbreviated *MECW*.

that by their periodical return put the existence of the entire bourgeois society on its trial," but they did not give any specific periodicity for "the cycle."[17]

In 1852, Marx wrote in a piece for *The New-York Daily Tribune* that modern industry and commerce

> pass through periodical cycles of from 5 to 7 years, in which they, in regular succession, go through the different states of quiescence—next improvement—growing confidence—activity—prosperity—excitement—over-trading—convulsion—pressure—stagnation—distress—ending again in quiescence.

At that time when British commerce was booming, Marx explained that "the most superficial knowledge of commercial history from the beginning of the nineteenth century, suffices to convince anybody that the moment is approaching when the commercial cycle will enter the phase of excitement, in order thence to pass over to those of over-speculation and convulsion," Marx made fun of "bourgeois optimists" who at the time were claiming this time would be different and the prosperity would not end in crisis. The phase of excitement of commerce, Marx wrote, "is only the precursor of the state of convulsion. Excitement is the highest apex of prosperity; it does not produce the crisis, but it provokes its outbreak."[18]

The crisis that Marx had seen approaching in 1852 indeed began in 1854. Writing in January 1855 for the *Neue Oder-Zeitung*, he referred to the years 1825, 1836, 1847, and 1854 as turning points in which "the commercial cycle has again reached the point where overproduction and overspeculation turn into a crisis"[19] (note that in the chronology proposed by Marx here, four crises occur with starting years separated by respective periods of 11, 11 and 7 years). The same month, this time in the *New-York Daily Tribune*, Marx referred with mockery to the views on the crisis of "free-traders" (economists and businessmen, presumably), which were endeavoring to show that the crisis,

[17] Marx & Engels 2010 [1848], *Manifesto of the communist party*, in *MECW* 6, 477–520.

[18] Marx (2010) [1852], "Pauperism and free trade—The approaching commercial crisis", *MECW* 11, 357–363.

[19] Marx (2010) [1855], "The crisis in trade and industry", *MECW* 13, 571–578.

instead of flowing from the natural working of the modern English system, and being altogether akin to the crises experienced at periodical intervals almost since the end of the 18th century, must, on the contrary, proceed from accidental and exceptional circumstances. According to the tenets of their school, commercial crises were out of the question.[20]

Four years later, while developing the materials that eventually were published in *Capital*, Marx was still thinking over the periodicity of "the cycle." On March 2, 1858, he wrote from London to his entrepreneur-consultant in the textile firm Ermen and Engels:

> Can you tell me how often machinery has to be replaced in, say, your factory? Babbage maintains that in Manchester the bulk of machinery is renovated on average every 5 years. This seems to me somewhat startling and not quite trustworthy. The average period for the replacement of machinery is one important factor in explaining the multi-year cycle which has been a feature of industrial development ever since the consolidation of big industry.

On March 4, Engels replied from Manchester:

> As to the question of machinery, it's difficult to say anything positive; at all events Babbage is quite wrong. The most reliable criterion is the percentage by which a manufacturer writes down his machinery each year for wear and tear and repairs, thus recovering the entire cost of his machines within a given period. This percentage is normally 7 1/2, in which case the machinery will be paid for over 13 1/3 years by an annual deduction from profits [...] 13 1/3 years is admittedly a long time in the course of which numerous bankruptcies and changes occur; you may enter other branches, sell your old machinery, introduce new improvements, but if this calculation wasn't more or less right, practice would have changed it long ago. Nor does the old machinery that has been sold promptly become old iron; it finds takers among the small spinners, etc., etc., who continue to use it. We ourselves have machines in operation that are certainly 20 years old [...] Babbage's assertion is so absurd that were it true, England's industrial capital must continually diminish and money simply be thrown away. A manufacturer who turns over his capital 5 times in 4 years, hence 6 1/4 times in 5 years, would, in addition to his average profit of 10%, have to earn annually a further 20% on approximately 3/4

[20] Marx, "The commercial crisis in Britain" [1855], *MECW* 13, 585–589.

of his capital (the machinery) if he was to recoup without loss his outlay on the old machinery—i.e. would have to make 25%. This would, of course, vastly increase the cost price of all articles—more, almost, than it would be increased by wages in which case where is the advantage of machinery? [...] Ten to twelve years are enough to bring about changes in the character of the bulk of machinery, thereby necessitating its replacement to a greater or lesser extent. The period of 13 1/3 years will vary, of course, depending on bankruptcies, breakage of essential parts where a repair would prove too expensive, and similar contingencies, so one could make it a bit shorter. But certainly not less than 10 years.

On March 5 Marx replied enthusiastically:

My best thanks for your explanations about machinery. The figure of 13 years corresponds closely enough to the theory, since it establishes a unit for *one epoch of industrial reproduction* which *plus ou moins* coincides with the period in which major crises recur; needless to say, their course is also determined by factors of a quite different kind, depending on their period of reproduction. For me the important thing is to discover, in the immediate material postulates of big industry, one factor that determines cycles.[21]

The first volume of *Capital* was published in Germany nine years later, in 1867. Apparently, what Engels had suggested in his letter of March 1858 on the period for full replacement of industrial capital was accepted by Marx as a base for fixing a periodicity of the industrial cycle. However, perhaps because crises with a periodicity of 13 years did not fit with what had happened in England since the late eighteenth century, Marx reduced the period to just ten years. Thus, he wrote in *Capital* that to the extent that the durability of fixed capital develops with the development of the capitalist mode of production,

so also does the life of industry and industrial capital in each particular investment develops, extending to several years, say *an average* of ten years. If the development of fixed capital extends this life, on the one hand, it is cut short on the other by the constant revolutionizing of the means of production, which also increase steadily with the development of the capitalist mode of production. This also leads to changes in the means of

[21] The three quoted letters of 1858 in *MECW* 40, 278–284.

> production; they constantly have to be replaced, because of their moral depreciation, long before they are physically exhausted. We can assume that, for the most important branches of large-scale industry, this life cycle is now *on average* a ten-year one. *The precise figure is not important here.* The result is that the cycle of related turnovers, extending over a number of years, within which the capital is confined by its fixed component part, is one of the material foundations for the periodic cycle in which business passes through successive periods of stagnation, medium activity, overexcitement and crisis. The periods for which capital is invested certainly differ greatly, and do not coincide in time. But a crisis is always the starting point of a large volume of new investments. It is also, therefore, if we consider the society as a whole, more or less a new material basis for the next turnover cycle.[22]

Marx never developed this vague idea of a decennial crisis cycle based on the period of renovation of fixed capital.[23] But he repeatedly said that he was referring to the *average* duration of the cycle, therefore he was implicitly acknowledging that the cycle is an irregular one. A century and a half later, we should consider the 10-year irregular cycle of Marx as a quite decent approximation to the economic reality of capitalism, since one of the major characteristics of the "cycle" that appears clearly in the empirical data of two centuries is its irregular character that makes both expansions and recessions as well as the whole "cycle" quite variable in length, but not much different from ten years.[24]

Interestingly, the decennial periodicity of crisis seems to have been a view shared by other authors at the time Marx proposed it. Thus, in a communication to the Manchester Statistical Society, John Mills—a friend of Stanley Jevons—referred in 1868 to commercial and credit disturbances showing "with a striking uniformity in the period of their occurrence" a decennial wave:

> It is an unquestionable fact that about every ten years there occurs a vast and sudden increase of demand in the loan market, followed by a great revulsion and a temporary destruction of credit. In the present century

[22] Marx (1981), *Capital—A critique of political economy*, Volume 2, ed. by F. Engels [1885], 264. Emphasis added (JAT) except in the remark on the "precise figure".

[23] Mattick (1981), *Economic crisis and crisis theory*, Chapter 2.

[24] According to Burns & Mitchell (1946), *Measuring business cycles,* vary from more than one year to ten or twelve years".

> six of these events have been distinctly marked. In 1815-6, 240 country banks failed; in 1825, 70 banks shared the same fate; in 1836-9 a similar revulsion took place [...] and of what occurred in 1847, 1857 and 1866 I scarcely need remind you...

Mills concluded that the ten-year periodicity of commercial crises was an undeniable fact.[25]

When Marx referred to the industrial cycle, he loosely used the terms *crisis, depression, glut, collapse*, or *stagnation of trade* with similar meaning, all of them referring to periods in which there is an interruption of the process of accumulation of capital. These moments of crisis must be brief, since they "are never more than momentary, violent solutions for the existing contradictions, violent eruptions that reestablish the disturbed balance for the time being."[26] David Ricardo viewed capitalism leading toward a final stage of chronic stagnation, which would be the logical consequence of a long-run decline in profitability because of the need for using increasingly poor lands for cultivation. Contrary to this view, Marx saw overproduction and a falling rate of profit triggering crises in which capital destruction and the increase in the rate of exploitation led to a recovery of the profit rate, and with it, a restart of the accumulation of capital. For Marx, permanent crises "do not exist."[27]

Versus Marx's view that capitalism is either in a status of expansion through quick capital accumulation or in a *temporary* status of crisis or depression that occurs about once every ten years, it was Engels who developed the idea of long-drawn crises.

He seems to have arrived at the idea of long depressions after hesitation. In a letter to Bebel in May 1883, Engels apparently suggests that a five-year cycle was observable:

> Generally speaking, it is only since 1847 (because of Californian and Australian gold production which resulted in the world market becoming fully established) that the ten-year cycle has clearly emerged. Now, when America, France and Germany are beginning to break England's monopoly

[25] Mills (1868), "On credit cycles and the origin of commercial panics", *Transactions of the Manchester Statistical Society*, 5–40.

[26] Marx (1981), *Capital—A critique of political economy*, Volume 3, ed. by F. Engels [1894], ch. 15, 357.

[27] Marx (1968), *Theories of surplus value*, Part II, 497.

> of the world market and when, therefore, overproduction is beginning, as it did before 1847, to assert itself more rapidly, the quinquennial intermediate crises are also recurring (...) The period of prosperity no longer reaches its full term; overproduction recurs after only 5 years...[28]

Thus, in May 1883, two months after Marx died, Engels was claiming that crises were occurring at quinquennial intervals rather than decennially. Then three years later, in 1886, in the preface to the first English edition of *Capital*, Engels remarked that the decennial cycle "of stagnation, prosperity, overproduction and crisis, ever recurrent from 1825 to 1867, seems indeed to have run its course; but only to land us in the slough of despond *of a permanent and chronic depression*."[29] Six years later, in the third volume of *Capital*, which Engels finished editing in 1894, he insisted, this time in a footnote, that

> the acute form of the periodic process, with its former ten-year cycle, appears to have given way to a more chronic, long drawn-out alternation between a relatively short and slight business improvement and a relatively long indecisive depression.[30]

As in so many other things, Engels' interpretation became "the Marxist truth." The idea of extended depressions or crises lasting for years permeated Marxism and critical thought to the present day. It became common that Marxist authors referred to crisis or stagnation without much precision, but mostly meaning long periods, lasting decades, even centuries for some authors in the world-system school.

The Marxists and the NBER

Engels's suggestion that acute crises recurring approximately at decennial intervals had been displaced by protracted cycles and longer periods of depression does not fit with the empirical data of the last decades of the nineteenth century. Thus, with a careful study of the evolution of a variety

[28] *MECW* 47, 23. I saw this letter cited in T. Kuczyinsky. "Marx and Engels on long waves", in Vasko, ed. (1987), *The long-wave debate*, 35–47.

[29] Marx (1977) [1867], *Capital—A critique of political economy*, Volume 1, 113. Italics added.

[30] Engels in Marx (1981), *Capital*, Volume 3, ed. by F. Engels, ch. 30, 620, fn. 8.

of economic indicators in England, France, Germany, and the United States, Wesley Mitchell concluded in 1913 that between 1890 and 1910 recurrent crises had interrupted European prosperity every few years, so that it could be said without grave inaccuracy that for England, France and Germany there had been

> crisis in 1889-90, depression until 1894, revival in 1894-1895 running up to a flood tide of prosperity in 1899, crisis in 1900, depression until 1903-04, revival followed by great prosperity culminating in 1906, crisis in 1907, depression in 1908, and revival once more in 1909.[31]

For Mitchell, these dates did not fit the United States economy where, for instance, there occurred a panic in 1893 that was not accompanied by a crisis in Europe. Furthermore, the European crisis of 1900 was scarcely felt in America, where business activity continued to expand in the face of European depression until 1903–1904. At any rate, what Mitchell was showing is that one century ago major differences in the chronology of business cycles could be observed among advanced countries.

Mitchell's work contributed to the establishment of the NBER, which has produced a chronology of business cycles in the United States since 1854. According to this chronology, 33 cycles with a mean duration of 4–5 years (56 months) have occurred to the present. The NBER has identified 11 recessions of the US economy since 1945, lasting on average about one year (11 months) each, with intercalated expansions lasting on average 5 years (59 months) each. Note that these averages say nothing about a regular cycle, as the observed "cycles" vary widely in length. The NBER chronology includes seven recessions of the US economy since 1970, with starting dates in 1973, 1980, 1981, 1990, 2001, 2007, and 2020.

If crises, as Marx viewed them, are "violent eruptions" or momentary solutions of inner contradictions, in empirical terms it seems logical to make them equivalent to the recessions of the NBER, which being on average as short as a year, would qualify as temporary. Marx saw crises as moments in which the circuit of capital is interrupted, and because levels of profitability are insufficient, capital is frozen—and thus ceases to be capital—in the form of unsold commodities, unpaid debts, unused machinery, or hoarded money—all of which are observed in the recessions

[31] Mitchell (1913), *Business cycles*, 86.

defined by the NBER. This interruption of the process of accumulation of capital implies that a fraction of what was the total social capital before the crisis is either temporarily excluded from claiming a share in the produced surplus value or permanently eliminated as capital, at the same time that wageworkers lose their jobs, wages drop and conditions of work deteriorate.[32] The elimination of capital during crises is illustrated, for instance, by the financial assets reaching trillions that were wiped out in 2008. A key component of the panic of 2008 was the demise of Lehman Brothers which had been valued at $635 billion. This was about ten times the value of Enron, and six times the size of WorldCom, both of which had melted down in the "mild" recession that had occurred earlier in the decade.[33]

Since the average rate of profit that regulates accumulation is the ratio of surplus value produced to total capital in society, by raising the numerator through the greater exploitation of the labor force implied by falling wages and longer working days imposed *de facto* if not *de iure*, and by reducing the denominator by eliminating substantial fractions of the total capital available in society, each crisis poses the conditions for an increase of profitability and the start of a renewed accumulation of capital. Similarly, the subsequent period of capital accumulation, by increasing the organic composition of capital and creating conditions for business costs to increase, reducing profit margins, brings forth the conditions for another crisis. Both a permanent expansion in which the accumulation of capital occurs smoothly, and a permanent crisis in which capital does not accumulate, would represent an equilibrium state that is badly conceivable from Marx's dynamic perspective of capital accumulation. Contrary to the views of Malthus, Keynes, Kalecky, and the *Monthly Review* school, all of whom viewed capitalism as inherently prone to stagnation, Marx saw it as a system in which a ceaseless accumulation of capital is interrupted by temporary crises.

Many authors in the Marxist tradition have nevertheless understood crises as protracted phenomena, lasting many years, and separated by periods of even several decades. It seems obvious that a major influence

[32] Mattick (1969), *Marx and Keynes—The limits of the mixed economy*; Clarke (1994), *Marx's theory of crisis*.

[33] The financial assets destroyed worldwide by the 2008 crisis are estimated by Rickards (2012, *Currency wars—The making of the next global crisis*, 211) in $6 trillion, while McNally (2010, *Global slump—The economics and politics of crisis and resistance*, 13–17) estimate is much higher, $35 trillion.

on this notion were Engels's views. However, after the 1930s, the influence of the Keynesian school was very important, as Keynes theorized that there is a tendency for capitalism to stagnate, and this tendency will be intensified by the development of capitalism. But the view of long and protracted crises can be also found among authors writing in the Marxian tradition with a strong anti-Keynesian stance, like Paul Mattick senior, who in *Marx and Keynes* highlighted the stark differences between Marxian economic theory and Keynesian economics.[34] He was however the same author who in 1934 theorized about the permanent crisis of capitalism and later exposed the view that "the crisis of 1929 was actually a continuation of the unresolved economic crisis preceding World War I".[35]

The idea of protracted capitalist crises is frequent in both the French *régulation* school, and the *Monthly Review* school which are two of the most important left-wing economic trends of the last decades of the twentieth century. Writing in the early 1980s and probably referring to a crisis that for him had started several years earlier, Michel Aglietta, a typical representative of the French *régulation* school, referred to the Great Depression of the 1930s as a violent and relatively brief crisis, while "for us the crisis is blurred and longer."[36] Similarly, writing on the economic conditions in March 1991, the editors of *Monthly Review*—at that time Paul M. Sweezy and Harry Magdoff—commented that the recession then underway was "widely expected to be the most serious since the Second World War."[37] The editors of *Monthly Review* theorized that

> what will happen in the future is largely determined by what has happened in the past. Largely but not entirely. The past establishes the possibilities of the future—a framework, a set of parameters within which choices must be made. If there is a science of history, it has to do not with predictions but with identifying and studying these determinations of the past with

[34] Mattick (1969), *Marx and Keynes*.

[35] Mattick (1934), "The permanent crisis: Henryk Grossman's interpretation of Marx's theory of capitalist accumulation", *International Council Correspondence* 1(2), 1–20; Mattick (1978), *Economics, politics, and the age of inflation*, 116–117.

[36] Aglietta (1982), *Mientras Tanto* (Barcelona), 3, 103 (my translation into English, JAT).

[37] Anonymous (1991), "Review of the month—Where are we going?" *Monthly Review* 42(10), 1–15.

> a view to making meaningful choices for the future. Capitalism is essentially a process of capital accumulation driven by the desire of capitalists and other affluent citizens to increase their wealth and future incomes. If this process takes place smoothly and with only minor interruptions, the system prospers. On the other hand, if there are major blockages, the system falls on hard times. One form of the malfunctioning of the accumulation process is the business cycle with its recurring periods of recession/ depression which have characterized capitalist development since the early nineteenth century. Another form is longer periods of stagnation in which the upswing phase of the cycle is weak and the downswing phase deep and prolonged. On the whole the formative phase of capitalism as we know it today—roughly the nineteenth century—was one in which, despite the ups and downs, the system prospered and expanded mightily. The buildup of basic industries and infrastructure virtually from scratch demanded relatively enormous amounts of capital, while on the other side of the equation supplies were still meager. The result was that the periodic breakdowns of the accumulation process tended to be brief and soon forgotten in the rush to take advantage of the seemingly endless opportunities (....) Gradually, however, the underlying situation changed (...) The old relationship in which the demand for capital tended to run ahead of the supply was now reversed.

Sweezy and Magdoff saw the chronic stagnation of capitalism growing strong in the first decade of the twentieth century but "what might have developed into a prolonged period of stagnation was cut short by the First World War, and it was only in the 1930s that the full depth of the problem was revealed." Then the depression of the 1930s did not end either, but "merely disappeared in the great mobilization of the forties". The three decades following World War II saw a vigorous expansion because the conditions for capital accumulation were "exceptionally favorable," though they were also "essentially temporary." Indeed "the war, as the stagnation that precede it, it never ended," and "the direct and indirect effects of military spending put a floor under the American economy which precluded any return to the stagnation of the 1930s." What the authors of this editorial, who were very likely Paul M. Sweezy and Harry Magdoff, concluded was that finally conditions had evolved to the point that, what was happening at the beginning of the 1990s was "not a routine recession but a relapse into chronic stagnation with no remedy in sight."

Despite the forecast of stagnation of *Monthly Review*, the world economy strongly expanded in the 1990s at annual growth rates between 3% and 4%, while the US GDP grew at rates between 2.4% and 4.9% during eight consecutive years.

Three elements of the predominant thought on economic issues in left-wing circles are present in the 1991 views of *Monthly Review* just cited. The first is the idea that the business cycle is just a minor component of longer waves "in which the upswing phase of the cycle is weak and the downswing phase deep and prolonged." The second is the idea that elements external to the economy itself—the military spending of World War II first and Cold War later—were keeping capitalism alive. And third, the crisis was becoming permanent, in the form of chronic stagnation. Since the years of the Great Recession, these views have been common in authors writing on economic issues from a left-wing perspective who generally claim that from the late nineteenth century there have been four crises, occurring respectively in the 1890s, the 1930s, the 1970s–1980s, and then the one that started in 2007. This view of four crisis, with two great depressions or contractions in the 1890s and the 1930s, a great stagflation in the 1970s, and the Great Recession starting in 2007 has been sometimes espoused by conservative quarters like those of the Foreign Policy Research Institute,[38] but usually is a scheme applied by left-wing authors and radical economists to the US economy and often extended in a fuzzy manner to the entire capitalist system. The scheme involves crises lasting many years, even more than a decade.[39] Thus, Leo Panich wrote in 2013 that the economy was going through "a great capitalist crisis, really only the fourth crisis of such scale after the so-called Great Depression of 1873–1896, the more familiar Great Depression of the 1930s, and the global stagflation and profitability crisis of the 1970s."[40] Anwar Shaikh, who differentiated among "general crises" involving a widespread collapse of the system and "partial crises and business cycles which are a regular feature of capitalist history," stated a length of 15 years for one of these crises that he refers to as "the

[38] Kurth (2011), "A tale of four crises: The politics of great depressions and recessions", *Orbis* 55(3), 500–523.

[39] Foley (2010), "The political economy of post-crisis global capitalism"; Shaikh (1983), "Economic crises" in Bottomore et al., eds., *A dictionary of Marxist thought*, 138–143.

[40] Panitch (2013), "Crisis of what?", *Journal of World-Systems Research* 19(2), 129–135.

Great Stagflation of 1967–1982."[41] Robert Brenner referred to a persistent stagnation of the US economy lasting from 1973 to 1993.[42] Andrew Kliman claimed that the US economy never fully recovered between what he calls "the slump/recession of the 1970s" and the start of the Great Recession in late 2007.[43] For Michael Roberts crisis conditions existed for 17 years in the US economy in 1965–1982, and then for a similarly extended period since 1998 to 2009.[44]

Perhaps Hillel Ticktin and Paul Mattick Junior are the authors who take the idea of the permanent crisis more to the extreme. Thus, Tiktin claimed in 2017 that capitalism had been for more than a decade in a worldwide crisis, "a genuine crisis of the capitalist system, not just part of a minor or major cycle, which had been functional to the system for centuries." But in the same paper, Ticktin claimed that capitalism had been in a permanent crisis "since the long depression of 1873, which lasted 20 years in the UK. Its fundamental solution was war, Cold War, or expectation of war plus imperialist wars combined with exploitation of conquered territories."[45] Along similar lines, Paul Mattick Jr. claimed in 2011 that the "present crisis" was just the continuation of the crisis of the 1970s.[46] As David McNally wrote in 2010,

> there is a markedly unhelpful tendency in many radical analyses to treat the entire forty year period since 1970 as a "crisis," a "long downturn" or even a "depression." Yet [...] such assessments miss the mark by a country mile. They either ignore, or thoroughly downplay the dramatic social, technical, and spatial restructuring of capitalist production that occurred across the neoliberal period, all of which [...] led to a volatile but nonetheless

[41] Shaikh (2011), "The first great depression of the twenty-first century", *Socialist Register*, 47.

[42] Brenner (2002), *The boom and the bubble—The US in the world economy.*

[43] Kliman (2012), *The failure of capitalist production—Underlying causes of the Great Recession*, 11, 24, and 48.

[44] Roberts (2009), *The Great Recession: Profit cycles, economic crises—A Marxist view*, 33.

[45] Ticktin (2017), "The permanent crisis, decline and transition of capitalism," *Critique* 43(3), 359–386.

[46] Clegg & Benanav (2011), "The economic crises in fact and fiction: Paul Mattick," *Brooklyn Rail*, June.

real process of sustained capitalist expansion, much of it centered in East Asia.[47]

For many reasons, David McNally's analysis of the Great Recession as a global slump can be considered a major contribution and a comprehensive investigation of the best quality. But even McNally, who brings clarity to many issues that are quite obscure in the analyses of other authors, gets entangled in the simple issue of establishing a plain chronology of the development that he describes. Thus, he says the world economy went through sustained expansion in 1948–1973, world slump in 1973–1982, and sustained expansion again in 1982–2007, and just a few pages later, he asserts that in the twelve years following 1969, "world capitalism would undergo two deep, demoralizing slumps."[48] But just a detailed consideration of the cited chronology is needed to know that with expansion in 1948–1973, slump in 1973–1982, and expansion in 1982–2007, only one and not two slumps can be placed in 1970–1982. Furthermore, to consider as McNally does that the period 1982–2007 was a period of expansion ignores the quite clear crises of the world economy that occurred in the early 1990s and at the turn of the century.

Rolando Astarita is an Argentinian Marxist who has strongly criticized the idea that the world economy has been in a state of stagnation in recent decades. Astarita cites IMF data showing that as a share of GDP, investment in 1986–1993 and 1994–2001 was respectively 18.8% and 19.6% in the US and 31.4% and 32.4% in the Asian emerging economies. In per capita terms, the growth of the global output in 2003–2007 was greater than in the five years of highest growth of the 1960s.[49] These data prove substantial expansion—not secular stagnation—during most of the 1990s and the early years of the century before the start of the Great Recession.

[47] McNally (2010), *Global slump—The economics and politics of crisis and resistance*, 36.

[48] McNally (2010), *Global slump*, 26, 31.

[49] Astarita (2009), *El capitalismo roto*, 224–225.

Mainstream Economics—Keynesians and Monetarists

In 1936 John Maynard Keynes published *The General Theory of Employment, Interest and Money*, the book that during three decades was an almost undisputed canonic text. In *The General Theory*, Keynes used the term "crisis" only a few times, and often with quotation marks, as if he thought it was not a very proper term. He also used very sparely the terms "recession", and "depression" while the term "slump" was used repeatedly, indeed more than twenty times. The term "trade cycle" is all around the book, often in capitals, for instance, in reference to

> another characteristic of what we call the Trade Cycle which our explanation must cover if it is to be adequate; namely, the phenomenon of the crisis—the fact that the substitution of a downward for an upward tendency often takes place suddenly and violently, whereas there is, as a rule, no such sharp turning-point when an upward is substituted for a downward tendency.[50]

In this passage Keynes appears to be emphasizing the violent character of the fluctuations of the market system by using "crisis" as a frequent form of appearance of a phase of the trade cycle. However, the only time in which the term "business cycle" appears in *The General Theory* is in a passage where Keynes emphasized exactly the opposite, as if making an effort to present a mild view of the ups and downs of capitalism that many in the 1930s saw as frankly catastrophic:

> it is an outstanding characteristic of the economic system in which we live that, whilst it is subject to severe fluctuations in respect of output and employment, it is not violently unstable. Indeed it seems capable of remaining in a chronic condition of sub-normal activity for a considerable period without any marked tendency either towards recovery or towards complete collapse. Moreover, the evidence indicates that full, or even approximately full, employment is of rare and short-lived occurrence. Fluctuations may start briskly but seem to wear themselves out before they have proceeded to great extremes, and an intermediate situation which is neither desperate nor satisfactory is our normal lot. It is upon the fact that fluctuations tend to wear themselves out before proceeding to extremes

[50] Keynes (1936), *The General Theory of Employment, Interest and Money*, ch. 22.

> and eventually to reverse themselves, that the theory of business *cycles* having a regular phase has been founded.[51]

In the three decades after World World II economic fluctuations were mild everywhere and economists were increasingly confident in their ability, based on Keynesian theory, to advice policies that would prevent any kind of violent oscillation of the economy that could be properly referred to with the world *crisis*. Melting together Keynesian and pre-Keynesian ideas, Paul Samuelson became a canonic author in the field for his *Economics*, the textbook that has been translated into 41 languages and has gone through 19 editions since first published in 1948. Writing in 1985, two radical economists, Samuel Bowles and Richard Edwards, explained how the Keynesians had modified his views on the business cycle:

> Not so long ago Keynesian economists thought that the alternating pattern of expansion and recession known as the business cycle was on its way to extinction. Through its control over interest rates and the money supply (monetary policy) and taxation and expenditure (fiscal policy), they thought the government could encourage investment (capital formation) and keep the economy on a smooth course of stable economic growth.
>
> MIT Professor Paul Samuelson, the first Nobel prize winner in economics, is among the most distinguished of the early Keynesians and was an early exponent of this theory. In 1955 he told the Joint Economic Committee of the U.S. Congress, "With the proper fiscal and monetary policies, our economy can have full employment and whatever rate of capital formation it wants."
>
> The hopes of the Keynesians were to be fulfilled briefly during the 1960s when the economy experienced the longest period in U.S. history without a recession. Celebrating the end of the business cycle, Samuelson declared "Business cycle theorists have done themselves out of a job."
>
> He even rewrote the section on business cycles in his famous textbook. In the third edition (1955) he had described the business cycle in the present tense: "Such, in brief, is the so-called business cycle that has characterized the industrial nations of the world." The 1967 edition, however, read: "Such, in brief is the so-called 'business cycle' that *used to characterize* the industrial nations of the world."

[51] Ch. 18, italics in the original.

> But during the 1970s and 1980s the business cycle returned with a vengeance. The recession of 1974–1975 drove the unemployment rate to 8.5 percent, at the time a post-Great Depression record; the recession of 1980–1982, called by some the 'great recession', pushed the unemployment rate to 10.7 percent in the fall of 1982.
>
> Professor Samuelson rewrote his business cycle chapter again. The 1980 edition reads: "Such, in brief, is the so-called 'business cycle' that has characterized the industrial nations of the world...". [52]

If Samuelson was the uncontested leader of academic Keynesianism, in the 1960s and 1970s, Milton Friedman became the leader of the anti-Keynesian field that was to become marginally dominant in economics in the last decades of the century. The 900-page long *A Monetary History of the United States 1867–1960*, authored in 1963 by Friedman and Schwartz, was one of the major contributions of which the theory of monetarism cemented its intellectual prestige. In the book, the term "economic crisis" did not appear even once. Samuelsonian Keynesians and Friedmanite monetarists were at odds in many things, but they agreed that governments, by applying the proper economic policy (Keynesians) or by not doing anything, as the market equilibrates itself (monetarists), could avoid any major economic disturbance. For most of the second half of the twentieth century economics excluded economic crises from its visual field. Articles with titles referring to "economic crises" or even to "the crisis cycle" like those Minnie Throop England had authored in the 1910s would be unthinkable in the major economic journals. But facts are stubborn and after the great convulsions of the world economy in the mid-1970s and the early 1980s, the notion of economic crises rose its head again, mostly among heterodox economists and non-economists—historians, sociologists, political scientists, and Marxists of all kinds. Many of them were unclear and ambiguous on the issue of economic crises, but the situation was as bad or even worst in the field of mainstream economics that, as it was explained early in this chapter, basically ignored the notion of economic crisis, even with the concept of "the Great Moderation" according to which the smart application of macroeconomic knowledge and monetary policies had been able to prevent any major

[52] Bowless & Edwards (1985), *Understanding capitalism*, 355.

economic disruption in the advanced economies for two decades.[53] This was in the late 1990s and early 2000s, before the Great Recession, when the idea of a "New Economy" of ever-growing prosperity was also prominent in discussions about the US economy.[54] In this intellectual context of the economic discipline, it was not surprising at all that, as it has been often mentioned in the aftermath of the Great Recession, the economic profession did not expect at all that such a crisis could even occur.[55]

Some major economists, for instance, Paul Volker, have even blamed the crisis of the Great Recession on the profession itself, because "an unjustified faith in rational expectations, market efficiencies, and the techniques of modern finance."[56] Of course, to make the economic profession responsible for economic crises is also to accept that the economic profession is able to prevent them from applying the appropriate policies. That is a point of view that, considering the achievements of "economic science" in recent years, and the dozens of economic crises that have occurred in the past two centuries of full-blown capitalism, looks quite a bit arrogant and naive.

A best-seller "phenomenon" in economics was the book *Capital in the Twenty-First Century*, by Thomas Picketty, which since its publication in French in 2013 was the object of innumerable translations, acclamations, reviews, and commentaries. A major characteristic of Picketty's book, which indeed is an important work with many virtues, is to say almost nothing about economic crises. As Robert Solow put it in a review of Picketty's book, we can imagine an economy growing at 2% a year "perhaps with occasional hiccups, to be ignored."[57]

[53] Bernanke (2004), Remarks on The Great Moderation by Governor Ben S. Bernanke at the meetings of the Eastern Economic Association, Washington, DC, February 20.

[54] Knoop, *Recessions and depressions*, 173.

[55] Cassidy (2010), "After the blowup," *The New Yorker*, January 11.

[56] Cited by Gorton (2012), *Misunderstanding financial crises*, vii–ix.

[57] Solow (2014), "Thomas Piketty is right: Everything you need to know about *Capital in the twenty-first century*", *The New Republic*, April 22.

CHAPTER 5

A World Economy

Among authors who favor the world-system theory, in which the world economy is the key component, there are major differences in the dating of the birth of a global economic system, or world-system, or world economy. Some, such as Barry Gill and André Gunder Frank, date it many centuries ago, with "the fundamental cyclical rhythms and secular trends of the world system having existed for some 5000 years."[1] However, Thomas Kuczynski dated the birth of a world capitalist economy in the nineteenth century, concretely in the depression that followed the 1825 crisis, and Andrew Tylecote dated the first truly international boom in the 1850s.[2] Immanuel Wallerstein sets the start of the world economy (henceforth, I will suppress the hyphen when not needed for grammar conventions) around the sixteenth and seventeenth centuries and is perhaps representative of majority views in the world-system school

[1] Frank & Gill (1992), "The five thousand year world system: An interdisciplinary introduction", *Humboldt Journal of Social Relations* 18(1), 1–79.

[2] Kuczyinsky (1978), "Kondratieff cycles: Appearance or reality?", in Flinn, ed., *Proceedings of the 7th international economic history congress, Volume II*; Tylecote (1993), *The long wave in the world economy: The present crisis in historical perspective*, 207.

J. A. Tapia, *Six Crises of the World Economy*,
https://doi.org/10.1007/978-3-031-38735-7_5

in which probably all authors would agree that a world economic system has had a real existence since at least a few centuries ago.[3]

Against the view that world capitalism was already a reality in the late nineteenth century, it could be argued that if such an entity actually existed, it was just in an embryonic form compared with the present world. Furthermore, if an entity called world capitalism existed in the late nineteenth century, that entity went through serious existential during half a century of world wars and revolutions.

Comparing Britain, France, Germany, and the United States in the periods 1879–1914 and 1919–1932, Oskar Morgenstern concluded that in the period before World War I, the international synchronization of business cycles was significantly greater than in the postwar period.[4] This can be plausibly interpreted as revealing a temporary reversal in the process toward the formation of an integrated global economy in which crises of national economies become increasingly synchronized. Overall, it seems quite proper to consider the period between 1914 and 1945 as a three-decade interruption or slowdown of the process of globalization, which is just another name for the development and establishment of a world capitalist economy.

After World War II, the process of globalization restarted in a peculiar way. The development and strengthening of economic links between countries and the international exchange of products advanced at the same time that many nations in Africa and Asia became politically independent of their European metropolis, and a large portion of the world's land, population, and economic activity aggregated in "the socialist camp" became quite neatly isolated from increasingly integrated Western capitalist markets. In the two decades of Pax Americana that followed 1945 and can be characterized as a period of prosperity and growth of world capitalism, the Marshall Plan was applied to the reconstruction of Western European economies and production and commerce considerably grew around the world. It is indeed in this period when Michael Spence, the co-recipient of the 2001 Nobel Memorial Prize in Economic

[3] Wallerstein (2011), *Modern world-system III: The Second era of great expansion of the capitalist world-economy, 1730s–1840s*; Shannon (1989), *An introduction to the world-system perspective*, 21, 43, 136, etc.

[4] Morgenstern (1959), *International financial transactions and business cycles*, Ch. II.

Sciences, situates the origin of the global economy.[5] Against the assertion dating the start of the world economy in the 1950s it could be argued that, at that time, there were actually two different poles of economic integration. With the formation of the Council for Mutual Economic Assistance (COMECON) that lasted from 1949 to 1991 under the command of the USSR, a huge portion of Eurasia, from Central Europe to the Pacific Ocean, was economically separated from the rest of the world. After the Sino-Soviet split in the late 1950s, the Chinese economy went into a period of quite a strict autarky, while the USSR and Eastern Europe became considerably integrated through the bilateral and multilateral COMECON agreements that assured the member countries' stability of prices for commerce as well as a steady supply of specific raw materials, often through a process of bartering.

In the 1950s and 1960s, globalization, as a process of increasing integration of Western market economies, steadily advanced. This became evident in the mid-1970s when serious downturns across Western economies occurred with substantial synchronization. At the same time, different processes were bringing back toward world capitalism the third of the world's population that for several decades had been mostly separated from it in the countries of Eastern Europe and the USSR. Back in the 1920s and 1930s, the Soviet Union had made successful efforts to be involved in trade with capitalist countries, and between the 1950s and the 1980s, the economies of Eastern Europe developed increasingly important links through borrowing and trade with Western economies and with international financial institutions under Western control, like the IMF. But it was only when economic reforms started in China in the late 1970s, and then the centrally planned economies of Eastern Europe and the USSR imploded around 1990, that this large fraction of the economy of the world became rapidly an integral part of the world economy in the sense of integration in world markets and world capitalism. Before 1990, the Soviet bloc countries had traded with the Western capitalist world, but to a large extent, their economies were isolated from it. In the case of the People's Republic of China, the isolation from the world market during the Maoist period was even greater, but this changed very fast in the 1980s. As estimated by the World Bank, between 1960 and 1978 exports had represented less than 5% of China's GDP, but they

[5] Spence (2011), *The next convergence—The future of economic growth in a multispeed world*, ch. 4.

grew quickly thereafter to 5.9% in 1980, 17.9% in 1995, and a peak of 36.0% in 2006. With the Great Recession, they dropped from 32.6% in 2008 to 24.7% of GDP in 2009 and have been around 20% in recent years. Also estimated by the World Bank, exports of the Russian Federation in 1989 when Russia was still part of the USSR accounted for 21.9% of GDP, but went down to 18.2% in 1990 and just 13.3% in 1991, to jump to 62.3% of GDP in 1992. Thereafter, the share of exports in the Russian Federation GDP oscillated between 25% and 45%.[6] Given the extreme disorganization of the Russian economy in the early 1990s and the difficulty of computing money estimates of the value of production in a system that was going through a chaotic transition from central planning to market economy, it is obvious that these numbers must be taken as very rough approximations. At any rate, these estimates of the contribution of exports to the GDP of China and Russia illustrate how in just a decade China became fully integrated into the world market, to become in the 1990s a world leader in exports, while the link of Russia with the world economy was significantly strengthened following the disappearance of the USSR in 1991. The integration of the Eastern European countries of the old Soviet bloc into the global economy was even stronger, as by the turn of the century most of them, including the Baltic nations that had belonged to the USSR, had become members of both the European Union and NATO.

In 2008, when it became obvious that the economic troubles that had started in the United States were being generalized across the world, a famous economist commented that the synchronization of the world business cycle was "something of a mystery."[7] But, was it?

The World Economy as a Historical Notion

A key component of the Marxian view of modern society that has been often labelled as historical materialism is the emphasis on the tendency of the capitalist system to evolve toward a world system. The idea was stated 174 years ago in the *Manifesto of the communist party*:

[6] Exports share in GDP for China and Russia from WDI, accessed November 2022.

[7] Krugman (2008), "Synchronized sinking", *New York Times,* August 23.

> The discovery of America, the rounding of the Cape, opened up fresh ground for the rising bourgeoisie. The East-Indian and Chinese markets, the colonisation of America, trade with the colonies, the increase in the means of exchange and in commodities generally, gave to commerce, to navigation, to industry, an impulse never before known, and thereby, to the revolutionary element in the tottering feudal society, a rapid development [...] steam and machinery revolutionised industrial production. The place of manufacture was taken by the giant, modern industry; the place of the industrial middle class by industrial millionaires [...]
>
> Modern industry has established the world market, for which the discovery of America paved the way. This market has given an immense development to commerce, to navigation, to communication by land.[8]

Half a century later, in her doctoral dissertation presented at the University of Zurich in 1897 Rosa Luxemburg elaborated on the same idea:

> It is an inherent law of the capitalist method of production that it strives to materially bind together the most distant places, little by little, to make them economically dependent on each other, and eventually transform the entire world into one firmly joined productive mechanism.[9]

It seems the idea of Rosa Luxemburg describes quite properly the general development of the past two centuries. Now, the construct that we call world economy or global economy or, perhaps better, world capitalism, is obviously a historical concept, similar to notions such as "European colonialism" or "Middle-East empires." It is unarguable that this kind of historical concept has validity in a historical period but not in others. As a construct of social science, the notion of world economy has gained validity and credibility with the passing of time and in the twenty-first century has an almost obvious validity that it had not before. Medieval theologians argued over when in the gestation period the human fetus is infused with a soul, thereby becoming human, and similar endless arguments would be possible about identifying a concrete

[8] Marx & Engels [1848] (1969), *Manifesto of the communist party*.

[9] Luxemburg (2013), *The industrial development of Poland* (1897), in Hudis, ed., *The complete works of Rosa Luxemburg, Volume I—Economic writings I*.

birthdate for world capitalism when the capitalist economies of major nations became sufficiently entangled to constitute a global system.

In 1984, despite the existence of the USSR and the many countries in the Soviet economic and political sphere, and a Chinese economy still largely autarkic in which the market had been rising but still had little role, Immanuel Wallerstein claimed that "there are today no socialist systems in the world economy any more than there are feudal systems because there is only one world system. It is a world-economy and it is by definition capitalist in form."[10] Many found it difficult to agree with statements of that kind. However, the demise of the USSR and the centrally planned economies of Eastern Europe, and the accelerated integration of China and the rest of the "socialist camp" in the world market, have updated the concept of the world economy which, as a unique entity seems today rather undeniable. The global economy, or the world-economy, with or without hyphen, is a reality that according to IMF authors has its own business cycles and global recessions.[11]

To make the case that the Great Recession of 2007–2009 was a world economic crisis is an easy task when, for instance, major drops in GDP growth were registered in 2008 and 2009 in almost all countries of the world. The annual rate of economic growth dropped in China from 14.2% in 2007 to 9.6% in 2008 and 9.2% in 2009; in Brazil, the pre-crisis GDP growth, 6.1% in 2007, declined to 5.2% in 2008 and dropped to −0.3% in 2009; Germany's GDP growth was 1.1% in 2008 and −5.1% in 2009. As estimated by the World Bank, the output of the world economy increased by 4.0% in 2007 and by 1.4% in 2008, decreased by 2.1% in 2009, and grew again by 4.0% in 2010. But, have these figures of world output or WGDP any real meaning?

WGDP figures are subject to the same criticisms that are leveled against GDP as a national economic indicator. In the view proposed by Paul A. Samuelson in the 1950s, GDP per capita represents some kind of psychic income and is therefore a good proxy for human well-being, a

[10] Wallerstein (1984), *The politics of the world-economy: The states, the movements and the civilizations*, 35.

[11] Kose & Terrones (2015), *Collapse and revival: Understanding global recessions and recoveries*.

point of view that has been seriously criticized from different perspectives.[12] On the other hand, in recent decades the introduction in GDP computation of hedonic adjustments, of imputed rents supposedly yielded by owned residences to their owners, and even of activities very poorly measured, raises considerable issues when the purpose is to use GDP as a proper measurement of the level of economic activity.[13] Despite all this, national GDP figures ***do provide a rough index of the intensity of economic activity, which has unarguable economic meaning***. This is supported by the fact that GDP growth correlates strongly with other more "tangible" economic figures, such as employment or unemployment rates, indices of industrial production, investment or consumption, or emissions of CO_2 or greenhouse gases in general. Though statistics for many of these variables are not available for the world economy, the growth of WGDP is strongly correlated with the growth of CO_2 emissions (Fig. 2.9, page 27), a fact that has major implications for climate change.

Leaving aside considerations on the proper understanding of WGDP, it does not seem arguable that in any explanation of the processes converging into the Great Recession major roles are played by factors such as the dissemination of mortgage-based US securities to international markets, the cross-national ownership of national debts, the international role of old and new currencies (the dollar and the euro), the massive displacement of manufacturing from the "industrialized countries" toward China and other "emerging" economies in the past three decades, the astounding increase of international trade and foreign investment in past decades and the emergence of a global elite. With Chinese factories assembling "German" Volkswagens, "American" Chevrolets, and "Japanese" Hondas, and with Ford pulling together its Escort models in Germany from parts produced in 15 countries, it is hard to argue that the relevant object of social and economic relevance to be analyzed is not a world system of which national economies are components.

[12] See, for instance, the views of Richard Easterlin in *Happiness in economics* (2003), and *The reluctant economist* (2004) and the essays by Esteva on "Development", by Robert on "Production", and by Latouche on "Standard of living" in Sachs, ed. (1992), *The development dictionary*.

[13] Maier & Imazeki (2013), *The data game,* ch. 7. In June 2014, *The New York Times, The Wall Street Journal* and other newspapers reported on the decision of the statistical authorities of the UK to consider black market activities including prostitution and sales of illegal drugs in the computation of British GDP.

Writing in 2010, the German financial journalist Wolfgang Münchau, associate editor of the *Financial Times*, claimed that the Great Recession could not be considered in any way "a case of bad people wrecking an otherwise good system." It was a story of systems failure and, furthermore, the crisis was "not a story that can be fully or even adequately understood in the context of America alone," but an issue requiring a global perspective. In looking for answers to the questions of what ultimately led to the Great Recession "one invariably encounters the global economy, the global monetary system, and the global financial system." For Münchau—who as many economic commentators basically focuses on financial markets and ignores the real economy in explaining the Great Recession— the main cause of the Great Recession was "an inherently unstable global economic system." Since finance is global, concluded Munchau, serious attention needs to be paid "to global forms of governance."[14]

The idea that this is "the same world system" that always existed is indefensible. In 1929, at the peak of world trade before the large contraction of international commerce during the 1930s, both US exports and imports amounted to about 6% of US GDP, while in the early 2000s, exports amounted to 10% of GDP and imports about 15%, the gap revealing the outstanding debility of the US economy as an exporter. But the weight of international trade in the national economy measured by the ratio of trade (the sum of exports and imports) to GDP which was 11.1% in 1929, had dropped to 7.7% in 1938, and from there had risen to 8.1% in 1950, 10.8% in 1970, 20.5% in 1980, and 26.0% in 2000.[15] Thus, as measured by the trade to GDP ratio, the insertion of the US economy in the world system had multiplied by more than three in the period from 1929 to 2000. Despite the anti-free trade traditions from the times of Alexander Hamilton, and the strong isolationist trends in American political thought, since its early years, the United States had been a major player in the growing international trade, for instance, with major exports of cotton. Since the nineteenth century, the United States had been a major promoter of globalization, for example, through capital exports, with US foreign direct investment growing from 2.6 billion US$

14 Münchau (2010), *The meltdown years: The unfolding of the global economic crisis*, 1–2, 6, 209.

15 Eckes & Zeiler (2003), *Globalization and the American century*, Table A9, 268.

in 1914 to 11.8 billion in 1950, 78.2 billion in 1970, and 1.29 trillion in 2000.[16] But the United States was not only exporting capital but receiving foreign capital. Foreign direct investment in the United States that had been $7.1 billion US$ in 1914, and only 1.9 billion in 1937, grew to 3.4 billion in 1950, 13.2 billion in 1970, 397 billion in 1990, and 1.21 trillion in 2000.[17]

Statistics from other countries also provide startling illustrations of the present interpenetration of national economies. For example, figures for imports and exports in the early 2000s in terms of GDP were close to 40% for Canada, Azerbaijan, and New Zealand, 70% for the Czech Republic, and around 90% for Angola, Tajikistan, and Estonia. The cheapening of transport and communication costs since the 1930s to recent years has been staggering. Ocean-freight and port charges have been cut by more than half, air transportation by four-fifths, and international telephone calls by more than 99%.[18]

As I write this chapter, a can of Planters Deluxe Mixed Nuts that I bought last week in a nearby supermarket is on my table. It contains cashews, almonds, hazelnuts, pistachios, and pecans. On the side of the can, with small but quite readable characters is printed the following: CONTAINS PRODUCT FROM: INDIA, INDONESIA, MEXICO, MOZAMBIQUE, NIGERIA, TURKEY, U.S.A., VIETNAM. In a sense, this small can is a full illustration of our world economy.

The Management of the World Economy in the Twenty-First Century

In September 2013, when the world economy slowly recovered from the Great Recession it was reported that to maintain the perspectives of recovery, the European Central Bank promised to keep its benchmark interest rate at a record low indefinitely. "The world has become more interdependent," was the reaction of Norbert Reithofer, chief executive of the German automaker BMW. "When Ben Bernanke [then chairman of the US Federal Reserve] makes a statement, it has an effect on the

[16] Eckes & Zeiler (2003), *Globalization,* Table A6, 265.

[17] Eckles & Zeiler (2003), *Globalization,* Table A.8, 267.

[18] Yarbrough & Yarbrough (2006), *The world economy: International trade,* 6–10.

Indian rupee, it has an effect on the Turkish lira, it has an effect on the South African rand."[19]

Before Donald Trump became the 49th President of the United States in 2016 and opened a period of commercial wars and protectionist policies, the fact that the world had largely become a unique global economic space was increasingly recognized in economic and financial news and by world elites. World financiers, industrialists, and governments worked to assure financial stability in the interconnected world in which financial assets are increasingly at risk of being devalued by worldwide turmoil. To a large extent that was achieved by the bailouts that mostly in every country except Iceland saved banks and insurance companies from bankruptcy during the global financial crisis of 2007–2008 and its aftermath. The rationale for those bailouts was "to avoid the world another Great Depression." According to Ben Bernanke, the Fed Chair at the time of the Great Recession, now a recipient of the Nobel Prize in economics, the disruptions of financial markets in 1930–1933 affecting especially households, farmers, and small firms led to a credit squeeze, cut aggregate demand and helped convert the downturn of 1929–1930 into a protracted depression.[20] Thus, to supposedly save the world economy, in 2009 and the early 2010s banks and the financial industry in general were bailed out in every country where they were at risk.[21] This was a major step toward giving world financial elites assurance of their interest being protected by national governments everywhere.

In 1999 the Group of Twenty or G20 had been formed as a global forum for discussion of policies to promote global financial stability among the governments and central banks from 19 countries (USA,

[19] Appelbaum (2013), "In surprise, Fed decides to maintain pace of stimulus", *New York Times*, September 18, A1, B5.

[20] Bernanke (1983), "Nonmonetary effects of the financial crisis in the propagation of the Great Depression", *American Economic Review* 73(3), 257–276.

[21] Against the common view that the Great Depression in the US lasted the entire 1930s, the economic recovery after the extreme contraction of the early 1930s started in 1934, when GDP grew by 11%, and continued with 9% growth in 1935. The unemployment rate dropped 11 percentage points in four years since its depression peak in 1933. But all this happened immediately after the massive bank failures of 1933. If Bernanke's idea that bank failures were key to maintain the depression is correct, it seems quite logical to think that the massive bank failures of 1933 should have been followed by a protracted depression of the real economy. They were followed, however, by immediate recovery.

China, Russia, France, UK, Germany, Japan, Italy, Canada, Australia, Argentina, Brazil, Mexico, Saudi Arabia, South Africa, Turkey, India, South Korea, and Indonesia) and the EU. Members of the G20 account for some 90% of WGDP, 80% of world commerce, and two-thirds of the world population. Intended as a council, its agenda was expanded after 2008 during the years of the Great Recession and heads of government or heads of state, as well as finance ministers and ministers of foreign affairs, have periodically conferred at summits ever since. The G20 had a few years of healthy life in the wake of the global financial crisis and its sequence of meetings after 2008 was considered the closest thing the world had ever seen to a board of directors for worldwide issues.[22] Another institution which could claim a role in global governance, the IMF, had languished in the early 2000s but the G20 "breathed new life into the IMF by positioning it as a kind of Bank of the G20 or proto-world central bank."[23] Characteristically, Michael Spence has claimed that the G20 should be such a world-level institution of governance, required by the existence of the global economy.[24] Perhaps it is proper to say here, just in passing, that the increasingly frequent use of the word "governance" as opposed to "government" for such institutions as the G20 or the executive offices of the European Union seems to express the ambivalence of national elites. These are increasingly conscious of their timid movements toward supranational government institutions, but at the same time are strongly attached to the nationalism that has been one of their most cherished ideologies and the most effective tool to maintain their power. Of course, these world elites are also highly suspicious of ideas of world government, which are usually linked in their minds to communism or revolution.

For a while Russia held the chair of the G20, and hosted the eighth G20 summit in September 2013, which was billed by the media as a contest between Obama and Putin, with the US trying to garner support for military action against the Syrian government of Bashar al-Assad,

[22] Rickards (2012), *Currency wars—The making of the next global crisis*, 127–133; Rothkopf (2008), *Superclass—The global power elite and the world they are making*.

[23] Rickards (2012), *Currency wars*, 133.

[24] Spence (2011), *The next convergence*, Ch. 40.

and Russia opposing any such action. The summit of the G20 in Brisbane, Australia, in November 2014, had raised poor expectation after the events in Ukraine and the Russian annexation of Crimea. Its results were commented by journalists as "Much promised, less delivered."[25] Given the sanctions applied by the US and the European Union to Russia because of the annexation of Crimea in 2014 and the events in Ukraine, the 30-year agreement for the sale of Russian natural gas to China, and the increasing tensions between China and several countries in East Asia because of sovereignty on disputed islands, there was a lot suggesting that the G20 was basically dead even before Donald Trump became US President and inaugurated a period of commercial wars and military bravados. This new chapter of foreign relations in the twenty-first century was somewhat interrupted in 2020 by the COVID-19 pandemics. Then in February 2022, Russia launched its invasion of Ukraine that was plainly rejected by the US, the US allies worldwide, and the countries of NATO, but was seen with indifference or even acquiescence by China, India, Iran, and other countries. Western sanctions against Russia were a new hit against world commerce. At the time of this writing, the world economy is basically a ship adrift with nobody at the helm. It could be said that even the captain's cabin is empty, but rather is occupied by thugs fist-fighting to gain the helm. For the moment, they did not reach for their guns. At any rate, there is nothing resembling any "governance" of the world economy, and it is not to be expected that there will be one soon.

It can be argued that the acknowledgment of the existence of a global economy may contribute to some change in general views of opinion leaders and public opinion. As part of his discussion of the global economy and global issues in *The next convergence,* Michael Spence discussed the ideas of nationalism, social cohesion, and identity that, he said, unify countries or continents. Then he asserted that some modification of the notion of "us" that goes beyond national borders, a sense of a fully collective commonality of interest, is going to be needed, as nationalism, which sometimes facilitates farsighted collective choice within the

[25] Yueh (2020), "G20 summit: Much promised, less delivered", *BBC News*, November 16.

country, can get in the way when it comes to global cooperation.[26] That was written just eleven years ago, but unfortunately, it sounds now terribly outdated. Whoever says it, it is good to hear that nationalism can be an obstacle to cooperation. In the twentieth century, nationalism was a basic component of policies and political strategies that lead to the oppression of peoples and the two world wars. Unfortunately, nationalism, promoted under various garbs by Vladimir Putin, Xi Jingpin, Nancy Pelosi, Donald Trump, Georgia Meloni, and so many others has been rising its ugly head in recent years. But it is more important than ever for humanity to put nationalism in the garbage bin if we want to end the twenty-first century without a third world war or a major environmental disaster.

[26] Spence (2011), *The next convergence*, 35.

CHAPTER 6

Why Do Crises Occur? Causal Theories

Business cycles, trade cycles, boom-and-bust cycles, and macroeconomic fluctuations refer in economic parlance to the recurrent alternation of business activity between two phases, one of expansion, boom, or recovery; the other of recession, depression, slump, bust, or downturn. These are however modern ways of expression coined in twentieth-century economics. In the earlier times of political economy, the usual way to refer to periods of decay or distress in economic activity were terms such as "gluts," "panics," "crises," "revulsions", or "stagnations," loosely qualified with adjectives such as "commercial," "financial," or "industrial." Such a variety of terms to mention the phenomenon may be a symptom of the large confusion about its nature and causes; indeed, in modern economics is common to find the view that no subject in the history of economics has been "more puzzling" than the business cycle. "Although numerous theories have been suggested since the cycle was first recognized late in the 18th century, none of them has succeeded in providing a full explanation of this phenomenon. The causes of the cycle suggested by these theories seem to cover every kind of economic and noneconomic factor one could imagine".[1]

Theories of the business cycle attempt to provide a general explanation of why the phenomenon occurs, and they must therefore involve

[1] Kim (1988), *Equilibrium business cycle theory in historical perspective*, 1.

J. A. Tapia, *Six Crises of the World Economy*,
https://doi.org/10.1007/978-3-031-38735-7_6

some intuition of causality. In such sense, the earliest conjectures on the business cycle were probably the underconsumption theories proposed at the turn of the eighteenth century by Lord Lauderdale, Thomas R. Malthus, and Simonde de Sismondi, authors who attributed downturns in business activity, "general gluts," to economic circumstances, that is, to endogenous factors.[2] General gluts of markets would occur because purchasing power available in society would not be sufficient to buy the output produced. These underconsumption theories were rejected by Jean-Baptiste Say and David Ricardo in what has been called the general glut controversy.

Say's Law and the General Glut Controversy

Though the lives of Adam Smith and David Ricardo overlap with the second half of the eighteenth century, neither of them said much on the crises that recurred more or less every ten years in Britain during that period.[3] In the rare occasions in which disturbances of the economy are mentioned in *The Wealth of Nations*, Smith did not relate them to output or employment, but presented them as episodes in which there were general complaints of scarcity of money. As Smith put it,

> when the profits of trade happen to be greater than ordinary [...] over-trading becomes a general error both among great and small dealers [...] they buy upon credit, both at home and abroad, an unusual quantity of goods, which they send to some distant market in hopes that the returns will come in before the demand for payment. The demand comes before the returns, and they have nothing at hand with which they can either purchase money, or give solid security for borrowing. It is not any scarcity of gold and silver, but the difficulty which such people find in borrowing, and which their creditors find in getting payment, that occasions the general complaint of the scarcity of money.[4]

[2] Mitchell (1927), *Business cycles—The problem and its setting*, ch. 1.

[3] Glassner (1997), "Adam Smith", and "David Ricardo", in Glasner & Cooley, eds., *Business cycles and depressions—An encyclopedia*, 627–629, 580–582; Schumpeter (1954), *History of economic analysis*, 181–193, 469–479.

[4] Smith (1937) [1776], *An inquiry into the nature and causes of the wealth of nations*, 406.

Despite isolated remarks like this, the general view in *The Wealth of Nations* was one of a general propensity of markets to equilibrate by themselves.

The general glut controversy was probably the first time when economists argued about why economic crises occur, though the term "crisis" was not used at the time. What is remarkable is that to a large extent the controversy is still alive, and authors dealing with it continue disagreeing about the major issues that were discussed more than two centuries ago, few years after Smith's death.[5]

In the general glut controversy, the disagreement was on what later would be called the law of markets, or Say's law, on the possibility of a general glut of the markets, i.e., on demand being too small for buying the produced supply.

In his *Treatise on Political Economy*, whose first edition appeared in 1803, Jean-Baptiste Say had examined the evolution of trade between Brazil and England, showing that the only way for Brazil to obtain the products of England was for Brazil to supply England other products. Say extended this analysis to claim that a demand for a good or set of goods can only be expressed by an equivalent supply of other goods:

> It is worth while to remark, that a product is no sooner created, than it, from that instant, affords a market for other products to the full extent of its own value. When the producer has put the finishing hand to his product, he is most anxious to sell it immediately, lest its value should vanish in his hands. Nor is he less anxious to dispose of the money he may get for it; for the value of money is also perishable. But the only way of getting rid of money is in the purchase of some product or other. Thus, the mere circumstance of the creation of one product immediately opens a vent for other products.[6]

Thus if too much of a given commodity appears in the market it can be only either because too much of it has been produced for the needs of the market or because too little has been produced of other goods so that there is insufficient purchasing power. Both things are possible and both

[5] Sowell (1963), "The general glut controversy reconsidered", *Oxford Economic Papers* 15(3), 193–203.

[6] Say (1880) [1826], *A treatise on political economy, or the production, distribution, and consumption of wealth*, 134–135.

may lead to a glut in specific markets, but in Say's view, since sellers are anxious "to dispose of the money" they get from their sales, a situation in which excess supply of *all* commodities appears at the same time is impossible.

Say could not deny the existence of periods in which business activity slowed down and goods were unsold. He referred to them as periods in which "circulation [of commodities] is interrupted", usually

> by the obstacles thrown in its way, [rather] than by the want of proper encouragement. Its greatest obstructions are wars, embargoes, oppressive duties, the dangers and difficulties of transportation.

These are, of course, obstacles coming from outside of the economy. For the occurrence of such a period of "political diseases," in which there is scarcity of some commodities and oversupply of others, there must be present

> some violent means, or some extraordinary cause, a political or natural convulsion, or the avarice or ignorance of authority, to perpetuate this scarcity on the one hand, and consequent glut on the other. No sooner is the cause of this political disease removed, that the means of production feel a natural impulse towards the vacant channels, the replenishment of which restores activity to all the others.[7]

The cause of crisis was therefore exogenous, it was outside of the economic system.

David Ricardo accepted Say's view on these issues. For Ricardo the value of a commodity is determined by the labor involved in the production process. Thus, the aggregate value of all commodities to be sold had to be equivalent to the purchasing power created in the process of production. For Ricardo, money is immediately used for purchasing goods to be consumed or invested to produce new commodities, so that a general glut could not occur.

[7] Say (1880) [1826], *A treatise*, 138, 145.

Say's views were rejected by Thomas Malthus and Simonde de Sismondi, both saw gluts as possible, though for Sismondi, such situations were not only possible but common in modern commercial nations.[8]

The way Malthus put it in his *Principles of Political Economy* was as follows:

> It has been thought by some very able writers, that although there may easily be a glut of particular commodities, there cannot possibly be a glut of commodities in general; because, according to their view of the subject, commodities being always exchanged for commodities, one half will furnish a market for the other half, and production being thus the sole source of demand, an excess in the supply of one article merely proves a deficiency in the supply of some other, and a general excess is impossible. M. Say, in his distinguished work on political economy, has indeed gone so far as to state that the consumption of a commodity by taking it out of the market diminishes demand, and the production of a commodity proportionably increases it. It is by no means true, as a matter of fact, that commodities are always exchanged for commodities. An immense mass of commodities is exchanged directly, either for productive labour, or personal services: and it is quite obvious, that this mass of commodities, compared with the labour with which it is to be exchanged, may fall in value from a glut just as any one commodity falls in value from an excess of supply, compared either with labour or money. In the case supposed there would evidently be an unusual quantity of commodities of all kinds in the market, owing to those who had been before engaged in personal services having been converted, by the accumulation of capital, into productive labourers; while the number of labourers altogether being the same, and the power and will to purchase for consumption among landlords and capitalists being by supposition diminished, commodities would necessarily fall in value compared with labour, *so as very greatly to lower profits*, and to check for a time further production. But this is precisely what is meant by the term glut, *which, in this case, is evidently general not partial.* M. Say, Mr. Mill, and Mr. Ricardo, the principal authors of these new doctrines, appear to me to have fallen into some fundamental errors in the view which they have taken of this subject.[9]

[8] Routh (1975), *The origin of economic ideas*, 134–148; Schumpeter (1954), *History*, 615–625.

[9] Malthus (1836), *Principles of political economy*, italics added.

The reference to an immense mass of commodities "exchanged directly, either for productive labour, or personal services" is extremely confusing, as if Malthus were denying that the personal services offered for sale by a hairdresser or a dentist are not a commodity. At any rate, what is interesting in this quotation is how the issue of profitability came up relatively disguised in the controversies on Say's law. In his rebuttals to Malthus, Ricardo interpreted that Malthus's denial of his conclusion is a denial of logic, as it is a contradiction in terms to say that there is unemployed capital because its owner cannot find laborers, at the same time that there are unemployed workers because there is no capital to employ them. But the view of Malthus was not that capital is unemployed because its owner cannot find laborers but rather because the producer is worried about obtaining a sufficient profit, "because the capitalist is uncertain that he will be able to sell his output at prices that would yield a sufficient rate of return."[10]

Simonde de Sismondi also rejected Say's law, though his views were different from Malthus's. As noted by Amartya Sen, Malthus's views on many issues, particularly on population and on the uselessness of social action to face human misery, were largely passed into mainstream economics.[11] Contrarily, Sismondi remained an outsider and a critic of political economy who was largely forgotten by later economists. Indeed, Sismondi often emphasized his disagreements with "the establishment" of political economy, i.e., with Say, Ricardo, and Malthus. He was referring to them when he wrote that if we

> were not fascinated by the mystical words which certain economists have pronounced over us, the first thing we should acknowledge would be the glut of all the markets, and the sufferings which all producers experience from the difficulty of selling.[12]

[10] Cited in Maclachlan (1999), "The Ricardo-Malthus debate on underconsumption: A case study in economic conversation", *History of Political Economy* 31(3), 563–574.

[11] Sen (1994), "The political economy of hunger", in Serageldin & Landell-Mills, eds., *Overcoming global hunger*, 85–90.

[12] Introduction to *Inquiries into Political Economy*, by M. Mignet, in Sismondi (1847), *Political economy & the philosophy of government—A series of essays from the works of M. de Sismondi with an historical notice of his life & writings*, 214–215.

For Sismondi, the most fundamental question in political economy was the problem of balancing consumption with production. Economic crises present themselves as congestions in markets, when no buyers are found for products offered at prices ensuring a profit. Sismondi argued that the classical theory is powerless to explain the basic working of the economic system in which crises of overproduction periodically recur and cause major convulsions of the system, which falters leading to bankruptcies, unemployment, and mass pauperization of workers. Smith and Ricardo had asserted that the quantity of production spontaneously adjusts to the size of the population and its needs, so that prices and profits will move capital and labor to the branches where they are most demanded, and the price mechanism and free competition will restore the equilibrium if any unbalance arises. Thus, the commercial crises were seen by Ricardo as no more than fleeting disturbances, but Sismondi disagreed.[13] Indeed, Sismondi saw the gluts of general overproduction as the consequence of the inner logic of the system, because

> the market for any manufacture extends to every purchaser to whom the articles [...] can be offered at a lower price than can be done by rival manufactures. All those which can be undersold are driven from the market, and then the one which has been able to do this prospers, and makes no account of the loss of those over which it has triumphed; circulating capital is dissipated, fixed capital remains unemployed and soon falls to ruin; workmen are dismissed; they suffer in indigence or perish from want. The manufacture which has been undersold makes every effort to recover the market [...] The master is content with less profit; often he goes on, even at a loss, to maintain his credit; he gives up making a rent on his buildings and machines; he engages his famishing workmen to be satisfied with the lowest wages, rather than be dismissed and lose everything [...] the two rival manufactures will strive against one another in order to gain purchasers, who are only sufficient for the consumption of what is produced by one of them; the market is glutted to the ruin of industry.[14]

For the participants in the general glut controversy probably there was not any clear winner of the intellectual dispute, at least no one accepted to have been convinced by the reasoning of the other side. But in terms of influence on the field of political economy that evolved few decades

[13] Grossman (1924), *Simonde de Sismondi and his economic theories.*

[14] Sismondi (1847), *Political economy*, 2009–2010.

later into economics, the general glut controversy ended with the defeat of Malthus and Sismondi, whose theories were rejected as wrong.[15] John Stuart Mill summed up the controversy in favor of Say and Ricardo.[16] Subsequently, most members of the nascent academic field of economics were skeptical about the possibility of a general glut of markets. Crises of overproduction—it was the general view of the discipline—were not possible.

In the twentieth century the underconsumption theories of the participants in the general glut controversy regained some influence in heterodox economics, where underconsumption ideas were espoused, more or less openly, by John Hobson, Rosa Luxemburg, John Maynard Keynes and the school of economic thought associated with *Monthly Review* and the American left-wing economists Paul Baran and Paul M. Sweezy. But underconsumptionism continued having quite a bad reputation in mainstream economics, as for instance Gottfried Haberler's opinion was that underconsumption theories have a scientific standard quite lower than other theories of the business cycle.[17] Joseph Schumpeter suggested something similar, asserting that underconsumption theory, "as Marx well knew, is beneath discussion since it involves neglect of the elementary fact that inadequacy [...] of the wage income to buy the whole product at cost-covering prices would not prevent hitchless production in response to the demand of non-wage earners either for 'luxury' goods or for investment."[18]

Karl Marx on Crises of Overproduction

About half a century after the general glut controversy took place, Marx thoroughly studied and criticized the views of the participants in the controversy. A superficial reading of his "economics", particularly the so-called schemes of reproduction of the second volume of *Capital*, can suggest that Marx agreed with Say's law, but a careful examination of

[15] Sowell (1972), *Say's Law: An historical analysis*, 9.

[16] Schumpeter (1954), *History*, 620–621.

[17] Haberler (1937), *Prosperity and depression—A theoretical analysis of cyclical movements*.

[18] Schumpeter (1954), *History*, 740.

Marx's works shows this is not the case.[19] Indeed, Marx explicitly criticized Say's view on the impossibility of lack of demand for the produced supply and Ricardo's agreement with that view. In his manuscripts on *Theories of Surplus Value* Marx cited Ricardo saying that no man produces

> but with a view to consume or sell, and he never sells, but with an intention to purchase some other commodity, which may be immediately useful to him, or which may contribute to future production. By producing, then, he necessarily becomes either the consumer of his own goods, or the purchaser and consumer of the goods of some person. It is not to be supposed that he should, for any length of time, be ill-informed of the commodities which he can most advantageously produce, to attain the object which he has in view, namely, the possession of other goods; and, therefore, it is not probable that he will continually produce a commodity for which there is no demand.[20]

For Marx, this was Ricardo repeating "the childish babble" of J. B. Say, because, obviously, capitalists do not produce in order to consume their products. Furthermore, once commodities have been produced the capitalist

> does not have the choice of selling or not selling. He must sell. In the crisis there arises the very situation in which he cannot sell or can only sell below the cost price or must even sell at a positive loss [...] Ricardo even forgets that a person may sell in order to pay, and that these forced sales play a very significant role in the crises. The capitalist's immediate object in selling, is to turn his commodity, or rather his commodity capital, back into money capital, and thereby to realise his profit.[21]

In *Capital* and in many journalistic contributions, Marx presented economic crises in which overproduction is a key element as an intrinsic component of what he called capitalist mode of production or modern industrial system. Marx viewed crises as recurrent occasions for the

[19] Fonseca (1998) in "The general glut cntroversy" asserts incorrectly that Marx agreed with Say's law.

[20] Ricardo, as cited in MECW 32, 133. Also in Marx (1968), *Theories of surplus value*, 2, ch. XVII, 8, 502.

[21] *MECW* 32, 133–134. Also in Marx (1968), *Theories of surplus value*, 2, ch. XVII, 8, 502–503.

temporary and abrupt resolution of the antagonisms that developed inside the system based on wage labor. He agreed with Sismondi and Malthus in asserting not only the possibility but the persistent tendency of the system to get into periods in which markets are full of unsold products. But he rather aligned with Ricardo and against Malthus and Sismondi in rejecting the idea that crises are due to insufficient consumption.

Marx argued that during the process of circulation of capital—which extends since the money is spent in raw materials and in the payment of labor power until the commodities produced with the former are sold in the market and may last weeks, months or even years—changes in the productivity of labor and in the real value of commodities can occur, so that elements of crisis gather and develop that "cannot in any way be dismissed by the pitiful proposition that products exchange for products". For Marx the comparison of value in one period "with the value of the same commodities in a later period is no scholastic illusion [...] but rather forms the fundamental principle of the circulation process of capital".[22] Because of changes in value during the period of circulation, commodities that had identical values at a time could have different values at a later time thus making just hypothetical the equality assumed by Say's law. Versus the notion that Say had advocated, that commodities are produced for consumption or exchange, Marx emphasized that the actual motive of production is obtaining money profits, as "in capitalist production what matters is not the immediate use value but the exchange value and, in particular, the expansion of surplus value. This is the driving motive of capitalist production."[23] Commodities are produced with the only intention of transforming them by sale into a money revenue which is greater than the money that has been spent to pay costs in the production process. The difference between sales revenue and production costs is profit. As a rule, workers will immediately spend their wages to pay for necessities, but the profit obtained from the sale of produced commodities can be used by capital owners to purchase immediately commodities for consumption or production, or can also be hoarded for a shorter or longer time. The possibility of a lack of demand for the produced commodities is held precisely by the time lag between the sale of the produced

[22] *MECW*, 32, 126. Also in Marx (1968), *Theories of surplus value*, 2, ch. XVII, 6, 492–499.

[23] *MECW*, 32, 126.

commodities—in which money is acquired by capitalist firms—and the purchase of other commodities—in which the expenditure of that money takes place. If money is held for a while, there is a breakdown in the circle of exchange, and a general glut occurs.

Marx understands total demand as the sum of three components, wages that workers receive and must almost immediately spend to purchase life necessities; profits that capital owners spend in consumption goods; and profits that are invested, either in purchasing capital goods or in paying wages. The stimulus for investment spending is profitability, so the degree in which profits are reinvested depends on profitability and high profitability will lead to large investment and low hoarding, while low profitability will lead to high hoarding and low investment. As Marx put it, investment, that is, accumulation of capital, is determined "by the ratio of surplus value to the total amount of the capital advanced, that is, by the rate of profit, and not so much by the rate of profit as by the total amount of profit."[24] Perhaps the best illustration of the link that Marx saw between profitability and investment is a quotation of the English trade unionist Thomas Dunning that Marx included at the end of the first volume of *Capital*:

> Capital eschews no profit, or very small profit, just as Nature was formerly said to abhor a *vacuum*. With adequate profit, capital is very bold. A certain 10 per cent. will ensure its employment anywhere; 20 per cent. certain will produce eagerness; 50 per cent., positive audacity; 100 per cent. will make it ready to trample on all human laws; 300 per cent., and there is not a crime at which it will scruple, nor a risk it will not run, even to the chance of its owner being hanged. If turbulence and strife will bring a profit, it will freely encourage both. Smuggling and the slave-trade have amply proved all that is here stated.[25]

In the manuscripts that Engels edited and published as Volume 3 of *Capital*, Marx presented profitability, the rate of profit, as being subjected to forces that push it to decrease along time; though other influences raise it, in the long run, says Marx, the profit rate will fall. By asserting

[24] *MECW*, 32, 171. A slightly different translation in Marx (1968), *Theories of surplus value*, 2, 542.

[25] Thomas Dunning as cited in Marx (1977) [1867], *Capital, Volume I*, ch. 31, fn. 15, 926.

this tendency Marx was not breaking with economic ideas at the time but, contrarily, following the views of Adam Smith, David Ricardo, and John Stuart Mill, though certainly he had his own understanding of this tendency of the profit rate to fall. Overall, as presented in Volume 3 of *Capital*, the tendency of profitability to decline can be understood as leading to periods in which the stimulus for investment is low and thus investment is insufficient for demand to equalize or overcome supply, so that a glut of markets, a commercial or industrial crisis occurs in which businesses fail, significant portions of total capital are eliminated, unemployment soars, and wages suffer major cuts because of the pressure of mass joblessness. Thus, the crisis operates as a mechanism to eliminate the glut, raise profitability, and restart a new period of high investment, that is, capital accumulation, which will evolve eventually toward another crisis. These mechanisms would lead to crises occurring repeatedly. Contrary to this view, presented by Marx in unpublished manuscripts, Marx presented overproduction as basic mechanism of crisis in the first volume of *Capital*[26]; and is that view which is presented by Engels in his book [27]*Anti-Duhring*, apparently approved by Marx himself.

Marx rejected the view that a decline in wages implying a lack of purchasing power in society can be a causal factor of crisis. Indeed, Marx scorned as "sheer tautology to say that crises are caused by the scarcity of effective consumption" because crises "are always prepared by precisely a period in which wages rise generally and the working-class actually gets a larger share of that part of the annual product which is intended for consumption". If crises were caused by insufficient consumption, this should put the crisis away.[28] However, he also wrote that the ultimate reason "for all real crises always remains the poverty and restricted consumption of the masses", which seems to maintain the opposite view.[29] Both assertions are in manuscripts that were published

[26] Marx (1977) [1867], *Capital, Vol. I*, ch. 15, 581–582.

[27] See in Engels (2010), *Anti-Duhring* [1878], MECW Volume 25, 9, the statement about Marx; 263, 271–274 and other pages for overproduction crises.

[28] Marx (1981) [1885], *Capital, Volume 2, ed. by F. Engels*, ch. 20/4, 486–487. Statistics from recent decades also support this notion, see for instance Tapia (2013), Boddy & Crotty (1975), and Weisskopf (1978).

[29] Marx (2017), *Marx's economic manuscript of 1864*–1865, ed. by F. Moseley, 577. Also in Marx (1981), *Capital, Volume 3, ed. by F. Engels*, ch. 30, 615.

only by Engels after Marx's death, and evidence suggests that the assertion mocking the view that crises are caused by scarcity of consumption was written in 1878, while the passage on the poverty and restricted consumption of the masses had been written in the mid-1860s. It might be Marx had changed his mind. At any rate, these two passages which are indeed quite inconsistent have been the basis for opposite interpretations of Marx's theory of crisis by Marxists. In favor of those who think the explanation of crisis by lack of consumption is not genuine Marx is the fact that in the only volume of *Capital* that was published by Marx himself it is emphasized that the movement of wages depends on the accumulation of capital and not the other way around: "To put it mathematically: the rate of accumulation is the independent, not the dependent variable; the rate of wages, is the dependent, not the independent variable."[30] This is fully consistent with the fact that wages tend to increase when accumulation is proceeding fast, but decline when accumulation drops in the crisis.

The "cotton famine" that the American Civil War generated in the English textile industry was for Marx "the greatest example of an interruption in the production process through scarcity and dearness of raw material".[31] Thus Marx also considered the possibility of crises triggered not by overproduction or a fall of the rate of profit endogenously caused by the economic system but by changes in the conditions of production depending on external factors—for instance, a poor harvest because of bad weather.[32]

Though Marx presented crises as a key element of the capitalist mode of production in the first volume of *Capital*, the only one published during his life, to a large extent his views on crises are contained in the manuscripts that were published by Engels as third volume of *Capital* after Marx's death. Other, even more important passages of Marx on crises are in the manuscripts that were published decades after Marx's death by Karl Kautsky, and even later under Soviet editorship as *Theories of surplus value*. Thus, Marx's followers in the late nineteenth century an early twentieth century could have only a skimpy view of Marx's ideas on

[30] Marx (1977) [1867], *Capital*, Volume 1, 776–779.

[31] Marx [1894] (1981), *Capital*, Volume 3, 575. See also ch. 15, section 6, of *Capital*, Volume 1.

[32] MECW 32, 162. Also in Marx (1968), *Theories of surplus value*, 2, 533.

crises that were not particularly clear and to a large extent were presented to the public under the interpretation of Engels or others who had edited Marx's manuscripts.[33]

From *Crises Commerciales* to Astronomical and Biological Cycles

The French physician Clément Juglar got interested in economic issues and without paying much attention to preexisting theories went directly to examining the empirical data on periods of economic turbulence. In *Des Crises Commerciales et de leur Retour Périodique en France, en Angleterre et aux États-Unis*, published in 1862, five years before Marx published the first volume of *Capital*, Juglar described commercial crises as returning in variable periods of 5–10 years. They were not strictly periodical because they could be *triggered* by specific events like wars, bad harvests, or the like, but for Juglar the particular event triggering the crisis was not important as the crisis would have occurred anyway. That is so because there is a basic predisposing cause which for Juglar is the change in the conditions of credit. Prosperity conditions fed credit of merchants to consumers to sell goods as well as credit of bankers to industrialist to expand production and start new businesses. All that feeds an increase in prices which in turn stimulates credit and leads to imprudence, abuses, and excesses in both markets of goods and in the stock market, feeding accumulated tensions. Eventually, any event triggers the crisis and liquidation occurs eliminating unhealthy speculation and weak enterprises. "A crisis is just a general liquidation to allow for businesses to restart on a more solid ground."[34]

Juglar had presented commercial crises as intrinsic components of the modern economy, but as necessary evils that opened periods of business prosperity. He was not alone at the time in emphasizing that "curative" role of crisis. Thus, for example, the entry on "commercial crises"

[33] My understanding of Marx's crisis theory follows from my reading of *Capital*, *Theories of surplus value* and a few other works and newspaper articles by Marx on crises. It has also been influenced by the interpretations of Henryk Grossmann, William J. Blake, Paul Mattick, Simon Clarke, Paul Mattick Jr, and Michael Heinrich (references in the bibliography list), as well as many exchanges and conversations with Rolando Astarita.

[34] My translation from the French, as cited by Besomi (2005), "Clément Juglar and the transition from crises theory to business cycle theories".

in a *Dictionnaire universel théorique et pratique du commerce et de la navigation* published in 1859 presented them as

> inevitable, but the disadvantages do not overcome the immense benefits that people derive of businesses. The crises of this kind are growing pains; and better is activity and wealth with commercial crises [...] than inaction and poverty. The rich and prosperous countries are sometimes in crisis; poor countries are permanently so. Moreover, commercial crises are transitory in nature. Sudden drops in the value of things attract buyers, facilitate consumption, eliminate glut and cause the liquidation of faulty businesses. When they occur, the producers or holders of goods incur loses, but buyers and holders of circulating capital have unexpected gains; certain private fortunes are destroyed, others are increased; there is individual suffering, but from the social point of view, there is not the same impoverishment, and the disadvantage of the crisis was bought by the disappearance of the weak enterprises. Thus, after a quite limited time we often see after the crisis that businesses get back with more vigor and vitality than ever.[35]

Juglar, who sometimes referred to the process of prosperity followed by crisis and liquidation as a "circle" or "cycle," viewed the whole process as an endogenous development in which prosperity led to crisis and crisis led to prosperity. From the point of view of the economic theory of Smith and Ricardo this was not a good explanation, it implied self-generated market failures with supply exceeding demand and demand exceeding supply. If causes of crisis were going to be consistent with economic theory, they had to be looked somewhere else, outside of the economic realm.

This was probably the main reason why during the second half of the nineteenth century the nascent discipline of economics basically denied the reality of crises.[36] Though the new discipline adopted many ideas from Malthus, it rejected the Malthusian view on the possibility of gluts, while the more radical ideas of Sismondi and Marx were basically ignored.[37] But downturns of the economy, sometimes mild, other times intense or protracted, were recurrently observed. They generated major distress and they begged for explanation. In the first Annual Report of

[35] My translation from the text of Garnier's entry in the cited *Dictionnaire*, quoted in Besomi (2012) "Clément Juglar and his contemporaries on the causes of commercial crises", *Revue européenne des sciences sociales* 47(143).

[36] Kim (1988), *Equilibrium business cycle theory in historical perspective*, 22.

[37] Morgan (1990), *The history of econometric ideas*; Routh (1975), *The origin*, 262–271.

the Commissioner of Labor of the United States of America, published in 1886, the list of causes of economic crisis reported to various committees in Congress occupied four pages and included for instance improper use of machinery, destruction of capital during war, influence of sanitary conditions, capitalists escaping taxation, speculation in railroads, too many hours of labor, intemperance, distrust of paper money, corruption of municipal governments, and undue influence of agitators.[38] The confusion and lack of clarity on the causes of economic crises illustrated by this list had to stimulate further attempts to explain crises, identifying their causal factors. Indeed, in the decades before the start of World War I, the "cycle" of prosperity and depression displaced "crises" from economists' minds, and crises theories were displaced by business cycle theories.[39] This was the time when three exogenous theories that attribute business cycles to astronomical or biological causes were proposed.

William Stanley Jevons in England and Henry Ludwell Moore across the Atlantic explained the fluctuations of the economy by changes in weather, these determined in turn by astronomical phenomena—sun spots in Jevons's view, the position of the Earth with respect to planet Venus in Moore's.[40]

The attribution in the 1880s by William S. Jevons of business cycles to astronomical influences on weather may have much to do with the fact that astronomical and meteorological knowledge had identified sunspots in the 1870s as being related to recurrent changes in climate. Jevons thought that solar spots causing in turn climate changes and subsequent agricultural disturbances disseminating to the whole economy could be the cause of economic downturns. As evidence supporting his theory, he presented statistical associations that he considered "entrancing." However, when other people examined them, they found these associations disappointing and unconvincing. It was even impossible to find a cycle of agricultural prices that conformed to sunspot cycles.[41] Juglar, who had meticulously studied the fluctuations of finance and commerce,

[38] Hull (1926), *Industrial depressions—Their causes analysed and classified with a practical remedy for such as result from industrial derangements.*

[39] Schumpeter (1954), *History*, 1123; Kim (1988), *Equilibrium business cycle theory*, 22.

[40] Morgan (1990), *The history*, 18–33.

[41] Morgan (1990), *The history*, 23–26.

rejected as speculative Jevons's sunspot theory. For Juglar changes in business conditions were recurrent, but *not periodical*. Exogenous factors, like the weather or sunspots, would be just disturbing influences, not true causes.

In 1920 the geographer Ellsworth Huntington proposed autonomous changes in the rate of death as the factor stimulating or depressing business.[42] The view of Huntington was that when mortality rises, it causes sadness and a drop in spending, which leads to a slowdown of business activity; conversely, a decrease in mortality would be followed by increasing spending and prosperity. Thus, business cycles are caused by oscillations in the death rate, these in turn caused by epidemics and other random events.[43] Quite similar were the views of Maurice Hexter, who claimed in 1925 that the business cycle was linked to emotions of optimism and pessimism these in turn caused by changes in the death rate.[44]

These views of Jevons, Moore, Huntington, and Hexter are today scarcely considered or even known. The astronomical theories—in which the exogenous influence on agriculture is a major intermediate element of the causal chain—were badly damaged by the authoritative demonstration by Wesley Mitchell that agricultural output correlated very little with the general condition of business in the economies of the time.[45] These authors are however good illustrations of exogenous theories of the business cycle in which the alternation of economic conditions between prosperity and crisis is attributed to noneconomic phenomena.

Wesley Mitchell

Wesley Clair Mitchell is a rare phenomenon in economics. He had a long professional life in which major positions in the profession and in government service were frequent. His treaty on *Business Cycles* published

[42] Huntington (1920), *World-power and evolution.*

[43] Huntington was however noticing a correlation that has been interpreted in recent years as indicative of causality in the other direction. See Tapia (2005), "Increasing mortality during the expansions of the US economy, 1900–1996", *International Journal of Epidemiology* 34(6), 1194–1202; also fn. 28 in ch. 3, p. 69.

[44] Hexter (1925), *Social consequences* of *business cycles*.

[45] Mitchell (1913), *Business cycles*, 239; Mitchell (1951), *What happens during business cycles*, 57–58.

in 1913 became a major reference for economists, he was one of the founders of the New School for Social Research and of the NBER, the semiofficial institution where he was director of research until 1945. But Mitchell consistently maintained economic ideas that today would probably be considered extremely radical, as they deny basic tenets of our institutions. For example, to Mitchell the usual notion that the actual function of the economy is to produce goods and services for the needs and wants of the people was a myth. In his view, the basic element explaining the modern industrial economy was the business activity of a miriad of private firms each one seeking monetary gain.

Wesley Mitchell's *Business Cycles* is an impressive book not only for its volume—600 pages in big quarto format—but for its content which includes a general review of extant theories about the cycle, a compilation of statistical data on cycles in the US, England, Germany, and France, and a meticulously crafted theory of the business cycle inferred from the observed data. In Mitchel's scheme, the business cycle is a basic characteristic of "the money economy", an ancient institution

> which after a checkered history has attained its fullest development in our own day [...] The essential feature of this institution is not the use of money as a medium of exchange; but the fact that economic activity takes the form of making and spending money incomes. Instead of producing the goods their families require, men "make money," and with their money incomes buy for their own use goods made by unknown hands [...] Natural resources, mechanical equipment, and industrial skill are factors of fundamental importance under any form of economic organization. But where money economy dominates, natural resources are not developed, mechanical equipment is not provided, industrial skill is not exercised, unless conditions are such as to promise a money profit to those who direct production. The elaborate cooperative process by which a nation's myriad workers provide for the meeting of each other's needs is thus brought into precarious dependence upon factors which have but a remote connection with the material conditions of well-being—factors which determine the prospects of making money.[46]

In the concluding section of *Business Cycles*, Mitchell wrote:

[46] Mitchell (1913), *Business cycles*, 21–22.

> The present theory of business cycles deals almost wholly with the pecuniary phases of economic activity. The processes described are concerned with changes in prices, investment of funds, margins of profit, market capitalization of business enterprises, credits, the maintenance of solvency, and the like—all relating to the making of money, rather than the making of goods or to the satisfaction of wants [...] Modern economic activity is immediately animated and guided, not by the quest of satisfactions, but by the quest of profits. Therefore business cycles are distinctly phenomena of a pecuniary as opposed to an industrial character. To dip beneath the business considerations relating to profit and loss, to deal with "psychic income" and "psychic cost," even to deal with physical production and consumption in other than their pecuniary bearings, is to distort the problem. For the processes actually involved in bringing about prosperity, crises, and depression are the processes performed by business men in endeavoring to make money.[47]

For Mitchell, the underlying cause of the business cycle in which economic activity alternates between expansion and contraction is the fact that the economy is organized on the basis of money:

> So far as I have been able to trace them, these recurrent alternations of expansion and contraction in economic activity occur only in communities where the production and distribution of goods are carried on mainly by business enterprises managed for profit, and where most people get their livings by making and spending money incomes. Communities otherwise organized undergo fluctuations in fortune, and may not enjoy so high a standard of living as the most fortunate money economies; but they seem to be exempt from cyclical contractions in employment.[48]

Mitchell used his overwhelming erudition on economic issues to make very insightful comments on how the causes of business cycles could have changed through history. He wrote that.

> business cycles are much later in appearing than economic, or even strictly financial crises. In England itself they seem not to have begun before the close of the eighteenth century. But when they did appear, it was in the form of an extension over all branches of industry of difficulties not unlike

[47] Mitchell (1913), *Business cycles*, 596–597.

[48] Mitchell (1944), "The role of money in economic history", *Journal of Economic History* 4(supp.), 61–67.

> those which had been suffered for more than a hundred years by large capitalists, bankers, and speculators in stocks. With this extension in scope came a shifting in the relative importance of the causes. In the past, the undermining of credit had usually been caused by war, by the making of peace, or by some violation of financial obligations on the part of government. In the future, the undermining of credit was to be caused more frequently by stresses engendered within the world of business itself.[49]

As early as 1913, Mitchell was highlighting the endogenous character of business cycles that has been repeatedly denied by mainstream economics during the twentieth century.

The basic characteristic of modern market societies, "money economies" in Mitchell's terminology, is to be structured as an array of productive units that organize themselves and manage to generate money profits. During periods of economic depression many business enterprises fail, opportunities for profit are scarce with prices going down, credit markets are frozen, buying is very cautious, and unemployment rates grow. However, all of this eventually reduces the cost of business, raises profits for the surviving firms, expands the physical volume of trade, and triggers a new period of expansion. In Mitchell's view the expansion increases employment and enhances competition between firms in using up raw materials and labor in the quest for profits, and credit becomes overabundant to finance investment. Greater and greater capacity is so created, and step by step, processes develop that encroach profits, until eventually some enterprises strongly indebted cannot face their cash needs for due payments. Bankruptcies start to occur, and they may or not trigger a panic with bank runs, but what these isolated bankruptcies always cause is a more or less generalized chain of broken payments and retraction of demand that leads soon to a new downturn. The cycle is so closed, and a new one starts.[50]

Given the size and scope of Mitchell's *Business Cycles* it seems quite likely that only few interested economists, and perhaps a handful of businessmen and politicians, read it. An interesting coincidence refers, however, to the year in which the book was published.

Mitchell had reviewed in *Business Cycles* recent downturns, and he had concluded that crises in the United States became panics much more

[49] Mitchell (1913), *Business cycles*, 584.

[50] Mitchell (1913), *Business cycles*, Ch. XI—How prosperity breeds a crisis, 475–511.

frequently than in England, France, or Germany. In these countries, however, the shock of confidence created by a heavy failure of a major corporation or bank

> would have been allayed by the prompt' intervention of the other banks. A syndicate of the strongest financial institutions in the country would have taken charge of the embarrassed concern and guaranteed payment to its depositors. More important still, the central bank would have taken the lead in a policy of lending freely to all necessitous businessmen who could provide adequate security for repayment. Most important of all, a restriction of payments on the part of the leading banks would not have been made—it would not even have been feared [...] The process of liquidation would have proceeded with its concomitant decline in prices and trade; but the transition from prosperity to depression would have been far less violent.[51]

The same year that *Business Cycles* was published, the Federal Reserve System of the United States was created. Such an institution had been envisioned by major financiers and bankers at least from the panic of 1907,[52] but circumstantial evidence suggests that Mitchell's *Business Cycles* could have been a contributing factor for the creation of the Fed.

Mitchell was a famed and respected economist and for decades a leading figure in the NBER. According to Arthur F. Burns, his *Business Cycles* was the book with the biggest influence on economic thought between Marshall's *Principles* and Keynes's *General Theory*.[53] A contrasting opinion of Joseph Dorfman is however that the theoretical contributions of Mitchell's *Business Cycles* were not appreciated by his contemporaries, because the language was unsophisticated and the method descriptive.[54] What is undeniable is that Mitchell had been under the influence of Thorstein Veblen's radical ideas, and his theoretical views were rather atypical among economists of the early twentieth century, with the statistics of his treaty on business cycles showing the

[51] Mitchell (1913), *Business cycles*, 550.

[52] Greider (1987), *Secrets of the temple—How the Federal Reserve runs the country*, ch. 9.

[53] Burns (1952), "Introductory sketch", in Burns, ed., *Wesley Clair Mitchell—The economic scientist.*

[54] Cited in Morgan (1990), *The history*, 47.

market failures and disequilibria that according to the prevalent economic theory—based on the principles of Adam Smith, Jean-Baptiste Say, and David Ricardo—should not occur. Mitchell's emphasis in institutions as stable patterns of social functioning and in the particular institution of money as a key to understand the modern economy puts him quite at odds with the majority of the profession, still viewing money as just "a veil" that can be successfully "abstracted away" to understand how the economy works. In a speech at a rare joint session of the American Economic Association and the American Society of Mechanical Engineers, in 1922, Mitchell emphasized that the practical subordination "of our common interest in making goods to our individual interest in making money produces grave consequences" among which he cited that "our dollar is not a stable unit" and the problem of business cycles, intrinsically linked to the modern rise of a money-based economy in which industry is like "an army without a general staff and without a general plan of campaign".[55] Though Mitchell had preceded these observations with the emphatic assertion that "the money economy is doubtless the best form of economic organization for promoting the common welfare that men have yet devised," his views were presenting a chiaroscuro painting of the market economy that was purely white and bright for most in the discipline. While Joseph Schumpeter, to cite a major example, had presented in his *Theory of Economic Development* the successful entrepreneur as an heroic introducer of innovations, who benefits of superprofits because of his ability to bring forth socially useful technological progress,[56] Wesley Mitchell referred to businessmen who read financial journals "as chiefly concerned to make profits or to avoid loses arising from the ups and downs of the markets," and presented an opposed view of the community as "interested in reducing the disturbances which these market ups and downs cause in the process of making and distributing useful goods."[57]

A particularly insightful comment of Mitchell on the role of credit in the generation of crises can be found in the Lecture Notes that were taken by some of Mitchell's students in the 1930s:

[55] Mitchell (1937), "Making goods and making money", in *The backward art of spending money, and other essays*, 144–147.

[56] Schumpeter (1934), *The theory of economic development: An inquiry into profits, capital, credit, interest, and the business cycle*. Schumpeter had published the German original of this book in 1912.

[57] Mitchell (1913), *Business cycles*, 596.

> almost all business undertakings are carried on upon a bookkeeping basis, in the anticipation of realizing a sum of money from sales greater than the cost [...] business enterprises commonly [...] borrowing from others in the anticipation of repayment. It is obvious enough that this whole complicated way in which we organize most of our activities exposes business to very grave difficulties whenever for any reason there is [...] some difficulty about repaying the loans [...] difficulties of that sort occur, usually at the climax of every succeeding period of cyclical prosperity which the commercial nations have undergone. During a period of great business activity loans expand very rapidly, they ordinarily expand so rapidly as to lead to some diminution in the ability of the banks to meet further demands upon them. If, then, when the credit resources of the country are already strained somewhat there is for any reason an alarm created regarding the ability of people to repay their loans, you find there will begin to develop at a rapid rate throughout the commercial system a process of liquidation, that is, a demand that people repay the money that is owed by them. This liquidation may give rise to failures; if so, it enhances the crisis, and the upshot may be a commercial panic.[58]

After a lifetime of studying business cycles, it seems Mitchell saw no way of avoiding them. Late in his life he republished with the title *Business Cycles and Their Causes* the third part of his *Business Cycles* of 1913.[59] His views on the causes of the cycle, that is to say, causes of crises, had not changed in three decades. The business cycle was an endogenous phenomenon of capitalism and changes in profitability were the key driver of the cycle. In 1944 Mitchell asked himself on *The New York Times* on "How can we operate a system of free enterprise without falling every few years into a spasm of unemployment?" His answer was that for that problem "no nation has yet found a solution that does not involve the suppression of free enterprise itself."[60] This view was and is antithetical to the main thrust of economics. At the time, Keynesian theory was already presenting a theoretical apparatus that suggested economic crises could be avoided through government action. Wesley Mitchell was saying in his characteristic subtle way that he was skeptical about it.

[58] Mitchell (1949), *Lecture Notes on types of economic theory as delivered by professor Wesley C. Mitchell*, Vol. 1, 250).

[59] Mitchell (1941), *Business cycles and their causes.*

[60] Mitchell (1944), "Test of free enterprise—Depression-proof economy is sought", *New York Times*, 18 September.

When he died, just three years after the end of World War II, his views had been largely covered by the rise of Keynesians, who attacked his contributions as lacking theory. Thus, in the second half of the twentieth century Wesley Mitchel was increasingly ignored and now is basically forgotten.

Economic Orthodoxy Before and During the Great Depression

In spite that Mitchell's *Business Cycles* had provided many elements to strengthen the view of business cycles as endogenous processes of the market economy, Mitchell was somewhat an heterodox and the views of the profession remained to a large extent in the path of David Ricardo, Jean-Baptiste Say, and John Stuart Mill, who considered that oversupply and disturbances of the economy were not possible from inner causes, so that exogenous ones had to be hypothesized and looked for. The butchery of many million in World War I crushed much orthodoxy and led to the fall of three empires and the emergence of the USSR, a new state formed by a bunch of united republics economically organized on tenets that were opposed to those of the free-market system. Curiously, it was from that source that in the late 1920s exogenous theories of the business cycle found an unexpected spring of inspiration, in the work of the Russian statistician Evgeny Slutzky.

Slutzky showed that applying some simple mathematical operations to a series of random numbers could generate apparent cycles and following this idea, the Norwegian Ragnar Frisch was the first in proposing that the fluctuations of the level of activity in modern industrial economies may be due to the effects of erratic, uncorrelated shocks upon a system of interrelated elements.[61] For Frisch in considering the causation and nature of the business cycle two things had to be investigated and defined separately, the first one was the *impulse* problem, i.e., the discontinuous shocks providing oscillating energy to the system; the second one was the *propagation* mechanism, i.e., the inner workings of the system which would extend the energy from the shock to the entire economy.

Frisch ideas generated debates inside the discipline, but they were kind of theoretical ones, and the turbulences of the 1930s were demanding

[61] Frisch (1933), *Propagation problems and impulse problems in dynamic economics.*

views on what to do, that is, on economic policy. From Mitchell's vision on business cycles it was difficult to infer any clear-cut policy position. It is not surprising, then, that when the Great Depression started, the voices of the economic profession that were heard were others, for instance those of Joseph Schumpeter or Andrew Mellow, the Treasury Secretary, in his famous "liquidate labor, liquidate capital.". In the classical tradition they considered that the best way to deal with the economic disturbance was to allow for the markets to move toward equilibrium by themselves. If a too high level of prices existed and caused oversupply of factors of production or produced goods, these conditions had to be liquidated. All that was in line with an old tradition coming back to the empirics of Clement Juglar and the theory of John Stuart Mill, David Ricardo, and Jean-Baptiste Say. The system had to shed dead wood to breathe again into life.

That view was outspokenly dismissed by John Maynard Keynes, who lecturing at the University of Chicago in 1931 commented on the extraordinary level of business activity in the previous decade—that had received the moniker of *the roaring twenties*— as follows:

> It seems an extraordinary imbecility that this wonderful outburst of productive energy should be the prelude to impoverishment and depression. Some austere and puritanical souls regard it both as an inevitable and a desirable nemesis on so much overexpansion, as they call it; a nemesis on man's speculative spirit. It would, they feel, be a victory for the mammon of unrighteousness if so much prosperity was not subsequently balanced by universal bankruptcy. We need, they say, what they politely call a 'prolonged liquidation' to put us right ... And when sufficient time has elapsed for the completion of the liquidation, all will be well with us again.

Keynes fully rejected that view. For him the explanation of the business losses, the reduction in output, and the high unemployment at the time was not the high level of investment that had occurred up to the spring of 1929, but the subsequent cessation of that investment. "I see no hope of a recovery except in a revival of the high level of investment. And I do not understand how universal bankruptcy can do any good or bring us nearer to prosperity."[62]

[62] Keynes (1987), *The General Theory and After: Part I, Preparation: Collected Writings of John Maynard Keynes, Volume 13, pt. 1* ed. by D. Moggridge, 349.

The thrill and the contained rage revealed by these quotations suggest that practitioners of economics like Keynes were somewhat feeling the missiles coming from the outside of their discipline. Commenting on the pitiful state of the economy in 1930, Albert Einstein wrote that he only dared to present his opinion on economic issues given "the hopeless confusion of opinions among the experts."[63] It was in this context of the early years of the depression in which disappointment about the ability of economics to explain the major aspects of the economic reality was widespread when Lionel Robbins published his *Essay on the Nature and Significance of Economic Science*, a work that is unanimously agreed was key for the development of economics in later decades. One of the major issues in Robbins's *Essay* was to launch an attack against Mitchell and others involved in "empirical studies."[64] To a large extent the economic profession was reluctant to empirical investigations in which economic theory was not "the guiding compass" for research. Lionel Robbins formulated that objection against Mitchell in harsh terms. For Robbins in the natural sciences there is an easy transition from the qualitative to the quantitative, but in the social sciences the same is always associated with peril and difficulty, so that if attempts to quantify such elementary concepts as demand and supply are difficult, the same attempts with respect to more complex phenomena such as price fluctuations, business cycles, and the like must be "terribly difficult and dangerous." However, as Robbins wrote in 1932, in the past decade there had been

> a great multiplication of this sort of thing under the name of Institutionalism, "Quantitative Economics", "Dynamic Economics", and what not; yet most of the investigations involved have been doomed to futility from the outset and might just as well never have been undertaken. The theory of probability on which modern mathematical statistics is based affords no justification for averaging where conditions are obviously not such as to warrant the belief that homogeneous causes of different kinds are operating. Yet this is the normal procedure of much of the work of this kind. The correlation of trends subject to influences of the most diverse character is scrutinised for "quantitative laws". Averages are taken of phenomena occurring under the most heterogeneous circumstances of

[63] Rowe & Schulmann (2007), *Einstein on politics—His private thoughts and public stands on nationalism, Zionism, war, peace, and the bomb*.

[64] Robbins (1945), *An essay on the nature & significance of economic science* (first edition, 1932).

> time and space, and the result is expected to have significance. In Professor Wesley Mitchell's *Business Cycles*, for instance, a work for whose magnificent collection of data economists are rightly grateful, after a prolonged and valuable account of the course of business fluctuations in different countries since the end of the eighteenth century, an average is struck of the duration of all cycles and a logarithmic normal curve is fitted by Davies' Method to the frequency distribution of the 166 observations involved. What possible meaning can inhere in such an operation? Here are observations of conditions widely differing in time, space, and the institutional framework of business activity. If there is any significance at all in bringing them together, it must be by way of contrast. Yet Professor Mitchell, who never tires of belittling the methods and results of orthodox analysis, apparently thinks that, by taking them all together and fitting a highly complicated curve to their frequency distribution, he is constructing something significant—something which is more than a series of straight lines and curves on half a page of his celebrated treatise. Certainly he has provided the most mordant comment on the methodology of "Quantitative Economics" that any of its critics could possibly wish.
>
> There is no need to linger on the futility of these grandiose projects. After all, in spite of their recent popularity, they are not new, and a movement which has continually invoked a pragmatic logic may well be judged by a pragmatic test [...] We have had the Historical School. And now we have the Institutionalists [...] Yet not one single "law" deserving of the name, not one quantitative generalisation of permanent validity has emerged from their efforts. A certain amount of interesting statistical material. Many useful monographs on particular historical situations. But of "concrete laws", substantial uniformities of "economic behaviour", not one—all the really interesting applications of modern statistical technique to economic enquiry have been carried through, not by the Institutionalists, but by men who have been themselves adept in the intricacies of the "orthodox" theoretical analysis.

For Lionel Robbins, the "fruitful conduct of realistic investigations" could be only undertaken "by those who have a firm grasp of analytical principle and some notion of what can and what cannot legitimately be expected from activities of this sort."[65] Obviously, Robbins's suggestion

[65] Robbins (1945), *An essay*, 113–116.

was that institutionalists like Mitchell, members of the German historical school, and other empiricists were not included among this group of anointed savants.

However, Robbins acknowledged that the elementary equilibrium theory derived from the work of Smith, Wicksell, Walras, and Marshal

> as is well known, does not provide any explanation of the phenomena of booms and slumps. It explains the relationships in an economic system on a state of rest. As we have seen, with a certain extension of its assumptions it can describe differences between the relationships resulting from different configurations of the data. But it does not explain without further elaboration the existence within the economic system of tendencies conducive to disproportionate development. It does not explain discrepancies between total supply and total demand in the sense in which these terms are used in the celebrated Law of Markets. Yet unquestionably such discrepancies exist, and any attempt to interpret reality solely in terms of such a theory must necessarily leave a residue of phenomena not capable of being subsumed under its generalizations.[66]

With this allusion to a residue of phenomena that equilibrium theory was not capable of explaining Lionel Robbins was pointing to the niche that would be soon occupied by Keynesian theory.

From the Great Depression to Keynesian Economics and Monetarism

The 1930s saw the publication of major works trying to provide explanations of economic crises. Keynes's *General Theory of Employment, Interest Rates, and Money* and Wilhelm Röpke's *Crises and Cycles* were both published in 1936; Schumpeter's *Business Cycles* appeared three years later. It is obvious that the Great Depression was a key influence for the publication of these works.

Schumpeter's *Business Cycles* saw periods of economic prosperity as basically driven by innovations, that increase profitability until its influence in production is exhausted and profits fall in a recession that will

[66] Robbins (1945), *An essay*, 119.

be overcome when new innovations set in.[67] Besides describing historical business cycles in excruciating factual detail, Schumpeter directed his criticism particularly against the so-called "self-generating theories," according to which depression arises out of prosperity and prosperity out of depression. That was the view that had been ostensibly adopted by Karl Marx, Clément Juglar, and Wesley Mitchell. Schumpeter denounced this kind of theory as a theoretically inadmissible *perpetuum mobile*.[68] In brief, Schumpeter's causal scheme was one of exogenously-produced cycles, with "innovations" being the generic name for the exogenous causes.

Wilhelm Röpke, who like Schumpeter was trying to maintain the validity of Say's law and the general principles of economics as outlined by Lionel Robbins, proposed in *Crises and Cycles* a theory of the business cycle that could be very well included among the "self-generating theories" criticized by Schumpeter, because Röpke saw crises arising out of prosperity and prosperity arising out of crisis. Trying to explain why the causal connections generating crises had been frequently ignored, Röpke pointed out how

> the scientific analysis of economic fluctuations began with the phenomenon of crises and only at a comparatively late date was it realized that the theory of crises must be incorporated into the more general theory of cycles [...] The obvious reason for this narrowness of viewpoint lies in the fact that the boom phase of the cycle, characterized as it is by full employment of the factors of production and by an altogether healthy aspect of economic life, gives the outward appearance of perfect economic equilibrium.

However, the problem was that this equilibrium frequently did not last and even was followed by the worst economic disequilibrium, so that

> when the crisis breaks out the causes are sought in all directions save for the one direction in which they should be sought, i.e., in the unhealthy and abnormal conditions created by the boom. The regular temporal sequence

[67] Schumpeter (1939), *Business cycles—A theoretical, historical, and statistical analysis of the capitalist process*.

[68] Grossman (1941), "Schumpeter's *Business cycles*," *Studies in Philosophie and Social Science* 9(1), 181–189 is a remarkable review of Schumpeter's book.

of boom and crisis (or depression) experienced during one century of capitalistic development has, of course, done much to shake this attitude and to suggest that the temporal sequence implies a causal one.[69]

Röpke saw overinvestment connected causally with a large expansion of credit as the key mechanism of the business cycle:

the central idea of the monetary theory of the trade cycle is that the periodic expansion of credit regularly brings about that dislocation of the economic process which expresses itself in over-investment and its consequences. It would be too much to contend that this is the only circumstance that can lead to an excessive increase of investment, but experience and reflection seem to show that this is undeniably the usual way in which the disruption of the economic equilibrium takes place. In this sense the monetary theory of the trade cycle is perhaps far superior to any other.[70]

Röpke rejected the view that in the crisis there is generalized overproduction, claiming that the actual problem was one of disproportionality of production, particularly between capital goods and consumption goods:

the swing from boom to depression is primarily a change in the volume of investment and of the production of capital goods while the production of consumers' goods tends to be subject to smaller fluctuations. The rising curve of investment during the boom has its counterpart in the falling curve of the depression [...] the real centre and root of the cycle is to be found in this rhythmical expansion and contraction of investment and the separate theories of the trade-cycle diverge from each other only so far as they give a different explanation of this rhythm. An increase of investment means the growth of the economic fabric, an increase and improvement in the productive equipment, and a step forward in economic development. So the swing from boom to depression reflects the fact that economic development does not proceed evenly but in rhythmical jumps whose force shakes for a time the equilibrium of the system so that contraction follows on the expansion [...] In this light the crisis and depression appear as growing pains of the economic system from which we cannot escape.[71]

[69] Röpke (1936), *Crises and cycles*, 68–69.

[70] Röpke (1936), *Crises and cycles*, 117.

[71] Röpke (1936), *Crises and cycles*, 97.

By presenting crises as "growing pains" unavoidably linked to all the benefits brought to society by economic growth, Röpke—who later had a major role in politics as economic advisor to West Germany Chancellor Konrad Adenauer—was trying to keep clear the path that economics had followed for many decades; a path that Keynes and his followers were somewhat trying to depart.

When World War II passed the influence of Schumpeter's *Business Cycles* and Röpke's *Crises and Cycles* looked like having been rather negligible in the profession, but contrarily, Keynes's *General Theory*, in the colorful words of Paul Samuelson, "caught most economists under the age of 35 with the unexpected virulence of a disease first attacking and decimating an isolated tribe of South Sea islanders".[72]

Keynes, who died in 1946, had recognized in *The General Theory* his intellectual debt with Malthus, presented as the unsuccessful pioneer in questioning the idea, later converted in one of the principles of economics, that effective demand could never be insufficient.[73] In Keynes's *General Theory* effective demand has two major components, investment and wages. For Keynes investment decisions are largely determined by the "marginal efficiency of capital", which is the term Keynes coined to refer to the expected profitability of new investment. Probably being conscious that his term would be the source of misunderstanding, Keynes explained that

> The most important confusion concerning the meaning and significance of the marginal efficiency of capital has ensued on the failure to see that it depends on the prospective yield of capital, and not merely on its current yield.[74]

By making his marginal efficiency of capital to be dependent on the expected yield of capital, Keynes inserted an important psychological component in his theory, the famous "animal spirits":

> Most, probably, of our decisions to do something positive, the full consequences of which will be drawn out over many days to come, can only be taken as a result of animal spirits — of a spontaneous urge to action rather

[72] Samuelson cited in Knoop (2004), *Recessions and depressions*, 51.

[73] Keynes (1936), *The general theory of employment, interest, and money*, ch. 3/III.

[74] Keynes (1936), *The general theory*, ch. 11, III.

> than inaction, and not as the outcome of a weighted average of quantitative benefits multiplied by quantitative probabilities. Enterprise only pretends to itself to be mainly actuated by the statements in its own prospectus, however candid and sincere. Only a little more than an expedition to the South Pole, is it based on an exact calculation of benefits to come. Thus if the animal spirits are dimmed and the spontaneous optimism falters, leaving us to depend on nothing but a mathematical expectation, enterprise will fade and die; — though fears of loss may have a basis no more reasonable than hopes of profit had before.
>
> It is safe to say that enterprise which depends on hopes stretching into the future benefits the community as a whole. But individual initiative will only be adequate when reasonable calculation is supplemented and supported by animal spirits, so that the thought of ultimate loss which often overtakes pioneers, as experience undoubtedly tells us and them, is put aside as a healthy man puts aside the expectation of death. This means, unfortunately, not only that slumps and depressions are exaggerated in degree, but that economic prosperity is excessively dependent on a political and social atmosphere which is congenial to the average business man.[75]

Wages, the other component of demand, are for Keynes quite stable, since workers spent mostly all the money they get. Though investment comes from savings and, in the long run, savings and investment must be equal, in the short run they can differ, and there can be idle cash balances—i.e., hoarding. Since the higher the level of individual income, the lower the propensity to consume and the higher the propensity to save, redistributing income flows—for instance, through fiscal policy—from high- to low-income classes will tend to stimulate the economy while, contrarily, a relocation of income toward high-income strata will tend to produce a lower level of demand and declining economic activity. As the secular process of economic development raises the income level of the whole society, the propensity to consume will decrease in the long run, so that the more developed is an economy, the more intense will be the tendency to stagnation. Government interventions are needed to correct this persistent tendency. The required deficit spending during years of stagnation will be compensated by fiscal surplus in periods of prosperity.[76]

[75] Keynes (1936), *The General Theory*, ch. 12.

[76] *The General Theory*, chapters 8/III, 11/II, 12/II, 12/III, 12/VII, 24/I and other places.

Today it is generally accepted that many of the elements of Keynesian economics had been independently developed by a Polish, Michał Kalecki. Kalecki had left-wing views that were at odds with the moderate political views of Keynes, but they had quite common ideas on why and how business cycles occur. Both considered a key issue the lack of demand, which in the case of Kalecki had been learnt from views presented by Rosa Luxemburg even before World War I.[77] Since Keynes' *General Theory* only presented a theory of comparative statics, it was left for economists following Keynes's tradition to develop such a theory, that is, a Keynesian theory of the business cycle. *The Trade Cycle* by Robin C. O. Matthews, published in England in 1959 and republished in the United States as *The Business Cycle*, can arguably be considered one of the first systematic examinations of business cycle theory from a Keynesian point of view. Matthews repeatedly cited Michal Kalecki's *Theory of Economic Dynamics*, at that time the most recent presentation of Kalecki's macrodynamic ideas.[78] In terms of causation of the business cycle, the basic idea in these books is that investment is the key variable explaining the condition of the economy, an idea that, for instance, was accepted by an early monetarist like Wilhelm Röpke, but later was rejected by Milton Friedman.[79] With investment at an appropriate level, profits are adequate, and the economy expands toward full employment, say the Keynesians. But investment is determined by *animal spirits*, by the psychological state of the entrepreneurs and the owners of money more generally, who will be at times reluctant to invest what is needed. That is the reason of both a proneness of the market economy to stagnate and the need of government action to compensate for this trend. Both are key elements of Keynesian economics.

In the English-speaking world on both sides of the Atlantic, the influence of *The General Theory* in the years following War World II largely

[77] Luxemburg (1910), *Introduction to political economy*, in *The complete works of Rosa Luxemburg—Volume I: Economic Writings 1*, ch. 6. This *Introduction*, only recently translated into English, is an interesting collection of lectures published in Germany after Luxemburg was murdered in 1919. *Selected essays on the dynamics of the capitalist economy* (Kalecky,1971) contains several articles from the 1930s where key "Keynesian" ideas are presented.

[78] Matthews (1959), *The business cycle*; Kalecki (1954), *Theory of economic dynamics—An essay on cyclical and long-run changes in capitalist economy*.

[79] Röpke (1936), *Crises and cycles*; Friedman (1969), "Money and business cycles", in *The optimum quantity of money, and other essays*.

eclipsed the views of other authors like Schumpeter or Mitchell who in the prewar years had presented observations and explanations on the business cycle which were to a large extent incompatible with those of Keynes. But the influence of Keynes also hid from view other important books that had been published in the late 1930s under the auspice of the League of Nations. Such were Haberler's *Prosperity and Depression* and the pioneer statistical studies of business cycles by Jan Tinbergen.[80] These books were closely related, since Tinbergen, who was coming from outside of economics, tried to apply statistical methods to test the theories on the business cycle that Haberler had reviewed in *Prosperity and Depression*. Haberler's contribution became a "classic" in the so-called "literary" literature on business cycles, while Tinbergen's works of the 1930s were much later considered major founding stones in the development of econometrics. However, Tinbergen's idea that using observational methods and statistical procedures was an appropriate way to test the validity of economic theories had not a major influence in economics. Indeed, this approach, which was at odds with the views on economic research and the nature of economic science of Lionel Robbins, was openly rejected with a variety of objections. Immediately after their publication, Tinbergen's studies received strong criticisms from inside the discipline, from no others than Keynes himself and the leader of the nascent anti-Keynesian field, Milton Friedman. Keynes criticized Tinbergen for not having explained "fully and carefully" the conditions that economic data must satisfy for them to allow the application of multiple regression analysis. More substantively, he rejected Tinbergen's method asserting that statistical models can reveal nothing that is not already known from "a complete theoretical analysis."[81] From a different perspective Milton Friedman considered that the annual data which Tinbergen had used in his study were "excessively crude materials for studying business cycles," and concluded that Tinbergen's methods "do not and cannot provide an empirically tested explanation of business cycle movements."[82]

[80] Tinbergen (1939), *Statistical testing of business-cycle theories, Volume I—A Method and its application to investment activity, Volume II—Business cycles in the United States of America 1919–1939.*

[81] Morgan (1990), *The history*, 121–130; Keynes (1939), "Professor Tinbergen's method", *Economic Journal* 49(195), 558–568

[82] Friedman (1940), "Review of Tinbergen's *Business Cycles in the United States*", *American Economic Review* 30(4), 657–660.

A basic component of Tinbergen's view on the business cycle that he had inferred from his statistical studies was that investment, which is the major component of economic activity oscillating respectively upward and downward in expansions and recessions, is largely determined by business profitability. Tinbergen argued that the way most enterprises decide how to deal with changing economic conditions,

> is not purely a technical one, one in which quantities only play a role. Prices and particularly profit expectations are of great importance. Most new investments are made for the purpose of making greater profits. Profit expectations will, therefore, be among the most important determinants of new investment. It should be noted that these are "expectations" containing a considerable amount of uncertainty. Modern Anglo-Saxon and Swedish economists have paid particular attention to this aspect of profits.[83]

To the possible objection that profits are only possible if the sale of products occurs, Tinbergen answered that the sale of what is produced

> is not the only element in profits. The price of the products and the cost of production are also of importance. All these elements enter here in precisely the same way in which they enter into the calculation of profits. It is, therefore, much simpler to say that profits are the determinant of investment. But how are profit expectations determined? They may be affected by extra-economic exogenous factors, such as new technical possibilities or measures of economic policy. For these reasons, some economists consider profit expectations as an entirely exogenous factor which determines investment and thereby indirectly the entire business-cycle position. But this separation of profit expectations from the entrepreneurs' experience appears to us to be exaggerated. To a very large extent, profit expectations will be based on current facts, in particular on the actual magnitude of profits. This may be observed in many sectors of the economy. Share prices are determined to a large extent by the latest dividend. There is always a strong and well-understandable tendency to extrapolate the recent past and current events into the future. There is, therefore, very much to be said for the proposition that the volume of investment depends to a considerable extent on the level of profits at the time when investment plans are made.

[83] Tinbergen (1950), *The dynamics of business cycles*, 166.

> There is a second reason why investment depends on profits. The larger the profits, the larger the possibility toward self-financing. Since each entrepreneur prefers to invest in his own enterprise and many enterprises do not have easy access to the capital market or even to bank credit, the level of profits is an important limitation of investment. Large profits may even be the cause of investments that in themselves would be hardly justified, or not at all.[84]

Tinbergen explained this in *The dynamics of business cycles*, a general exposition of his macroeconomic views that was published in English in 1950. In other occasions he insisted in the idea that investment is not exogenous, determined by *animal spirits*, but endogenous, determined by the return of capital.[85] In spite that Tinbergen's views were generally heard and in 1969 he shared with Ragnar Frisch the first Bank of Sweden Prize in Economic Sciences in Memory of Alfred Nobel, his ideas on the business cycle were basically buried in the noise of the controversies between Keynesians and anti-Keynesians.

Keynes died in 1946, and Samuelson's *Foundations of Economic Analysis* published next year became a milestone in economic theory. It was also a key starter of the increasing use of mathematical formalism in economics. Though Samuelson was sympathetic to Keynes's views and went through a detailed analysis of the Keynesian system, he asserted that to derive useful theorems it was necessary to consider "a more general dynamic system which includes the stationary Keynesian analysis as a special case".[86] On the other hand, while *The General Theory* saw a tendency to stagnation in the working of the market economy, in discussing economic dynamics Samuelson's *Foundations* mentioned the *vix medicatrix naturae*, which apparently was a suggestion that there is a general tendency of the market economy to heal and equilibrate itself.[87]

The initial rejection of Tinbergen's statistical work from all quarters, the increasing mathematical sophistication exemplified by Samuelson's *Foundations*, and the activities of the Cowles Commission in developing

[84] Tinbergen (1950), *The dynamics of business cycles*, 166–167.

[85] Tinbergen (1952), "Comments [on Orcutt's 'Toward partial redirection of econometrics']", *Review of Economics & Statistics* 34(3), 205–206.

[86] Samuelson (1966) [1947], *Foundations of economic analysis*, 276, 278 et seq.

[87] It seems Samuelson's spelling is wrong as the natural healing power of nature, a guiding principle of Hippocratic medicine, is the *vis medicatrix naturae*.

macroeconometric models integrating Keynesian principles conformed the context in which the controversy on "measurement without theory" took place.

This controversy developed after the publication in 1946 of *Measuring Business Cycles*, a book in which Arthur F. Burns helped the already very old Wesley Mitchell to expand the statistical framework that Mitchell had outlined a quarter of a century earlier.[88] By providing detailed descriptive information about the workings of market-based economies, the book developed a comprehensive picture of the empirically observed simultaneous movements of economic variables.

In a critical attack that was quite in line with the views of Lionel Robbins in his *Essay* of 1932, Tjalling Koopmans, a member of the Cowles Commission, attacked the book by Burns and Mitchell branding it as "measurement without theory" because of its explicit inductive methodology and empiricism. Koopmans reprimanded the authors for simply "observing and summarizing the cyclical characteristics of a large number of economic series" without employing a formal theoretical framework and without revealing at all "what explanations of cyclical fluctuations, if any, they believe to constitute plausible models or hypotheses."[89] Koopmans trashed the book as often dealing with "essentially irrelevant questions," showing pedestrian statistics and not providing any guidance for economic policy.

Mitchell died few months after Koopman's criticism was published. Rutledge Vining, an economist of the NBER, was the one who defended Mitchell against Koopman's criticisms. Koopman's attack against the NBER approach came from an institution, the Cowles Commission, involved in creating econometric models to understand the economy and gain control on it. For Koopman not only economic theory but also statistical theory were missing in the book by Burns and Mitchell and in the NBER approach. Mitchell and the NBER had never developed statistical models or used statistical procedures beyond computing means, standard deviations, and correlations. They had not even used the single equation regression models that Tinbergen had used in the 1930s. Thus, the accusation of lack of statistical theory might be fair, but

88 Burns & Mitchell (1946), *Measuring business cycles*.

89 Koopmans (1947), "Measurement without theory", *Review of Economic Statistics* 29(3), 161–172.

the criticism of lacking economic theory does not resist even a superficial reading of Mitchell's work, in which relations between variables are frequently analyzed and causal mechanisms are often discussed. Despite this, accusations of Mitchell being an atheoretical author floated in the atmosphere of economics until our days. Only recently some authors have tried to recover Mitchell's theoretical views, arguing that the complexity of Mitchell's business cycle theory is very hard to be formalized because of its loops and feedbacks.[90]

In any case the controversy soon subsided and in following decades Mitchell's empiricist approach to business cycle analysis was displaced and largely forgotten. The static equilibrium theory of Keynesian economics and the construction of large-scale macroeconometric models occupied its place.

The dual attack against Tinbergen by Friedman and Keynes followed a few years later by Koopman's attack on Mitchell reveals an antiempirical tendency in economics. From his regression analysis, Tinbergen had concluded that investment is an endogenous variable determined by previous profitability. Based not on regression results but on a descriptive analysis of the data, Wesley Mitchell had arrived at a similar conclusion three decades earlier. But the conclusion of profitability being a key variable to explain the evolution of investment and the economy at large was largely at odds with the theoretical views of Keynes, Friedman, and Koopmans. Thus, it was discarded and even today is uncommon to read anything about profits in the explanations of mainstream economists about business cycles and crises.

It seems plausible—though this type of statement is always difficult to prove—that the ideological environment of the 1950s and 1960s in which the Cold War ideology poisoned most intellectual waters was a key determinant of economics taking this direction. Mitchell, who had been a prudent defender of reforms and throughout his life worked to produce an economic theory that he thought could be a tool to damp the persistent boom-and-bust cycle of business activity, did not respond to attacks that his views were "atheoretical". But ten years after his death he was still under attack, this time from Austrian economics, the school of thought that had more rabidly opposed any attempt to interfere with the autonomous workings of capitalism. Commenting on a reprint of a

[90] Sherman (2001), "The business cycle theory of Wesley Mitchell", *Journal of Economic Issues* 35(1), 85–98.

book by Mitchel, Murray Rothbard stated that Ludwig von Mises had located the cause of business cycles in interferences with the free market, "while all other writers, following Mitchell, cherish the idea that business cycles come from deep within the capitalist system, that they are, in short, a sickness of the free market. The founder of this idea, by the way, was not Wesley Mitchell, but Karl Marx."[91]

Economic Data and Macroeconomic Theories

A key aspect of the development of macroeconomics in the postwar years when Koopmans and others were attacking Mitchell for lack of theory is that at the same time the large macroeconomic models of the Cowles Commission were being built using numerous a priori restrictions on variables and equations to be included. These restrictions had no other support than "theory," i.e., the preconceptions on how the economy worked—at the time mostly based on Keynes's views. As Christopher Simms has explained, since Keynesian theory viewed the business cycle as originated from many sources, in order to be useful in guiding policy decisions—often in a time frame of quarters or months—models had to have many variables and very large scale. Thus, the Cowles Foundation models included hundreds of equations and variables and since the number of observations was limited, the data could not say anything about the values of all potential coefficients linking different variables. A priori decisions were needed about particular coefficients being zero or having a predetermined sign. In doing so, the modelers "assumed away many sources of uncertainty" and they "simplified the models as if they were certain that the restrictions they were imposing were correct, even though they were only approximate."[92] Thus the Cowles Commission models, that supposedly were modeling the economy according to how the economy had worked before, were monumental mathematical structures that provided the illusion of a fine theoretical comprehension of the economic reality, when in reality they were largely built on equations that were consistent

[91] Rothbard (1959), "Why the business cycle happens".

[92] Sims (2012), "Statistical modelling of monetary policy and its effects: Nobel Prize lecture", *American Economic Review* 102(4), 1187–1205.

with the general ideas of the modelers about the economy, though not with actual observations.[93]

It is a generally accepted idea that the conversion of Keynesian thought in academic orthodoxy during the 1950s and 1960s was associated with a steady erosion of Keynesian critiques to the classical views of Smith, Ricardo, Marshall, and Pigou on Say's law and market equilibrium.[94] The consolidation of Samuelson's neoclassical synthesis and the fact that the separation of Keynesian and pre-Keynesian views was increasingly blurred led some close followers of Lord Keynes to complain about "bastard Keynesism" or "bastard Keynesianism".[95] But Keynes's theory was for many the helm to guide the economy between the Scylla of inflation and the Charybdis of stagnation—using it properly should avoid these obstacles. The IS-LM model developed by J. R. Hicks and expanded in the neoclassical synthesis of Samuelson took some ideas from Keynes ignoring others that other Keynesians considered essential.[96] Under certain restrictive assumptions these models generated oscillations resembling the business cycle. Starting with these models and using the Keynesian tools, the oscillations could be largely damped or avoided, so the Keynesians thought, so that with proper fiscal and monetary policies, the economy could be managed to reach full employment and whatever rate of GDP growth that were desired. During the 1960s the United States experienced the longest period without a recession, and the Keynesians rejoiced considering that macroeconomic policies have been proved as largely effective. The boom-and-bust dynamics of the business cycle were seen increasingly as obsolete.[97] The concept of "growth cycles" was adopted for a while as if the recently observed mild fluctuations in

[93] Nowadays macroeconometric models in the traditions of the Coles Commission are uncommon, but Ray Fair's model is one of them. In this model investment is dependent on interest rates and GDP growth, but for instance Tinbergen's result viewing investment as largely determined by profitability is ignored; see Fair (2004), *Estimating how the macroeconomy works*, 19.

[94] Leijonhufvud (1967), "Keynes and the Keynesians: A suggested interpretation", *American Economic Review* 57(2), 401–410.

[95] Robinson (1979), *The generalisation of the general theory, and other essays*, xiv; Turgeon (1996), *Bastard Keynesianism: The evolution of economic thinking and policymaking since World War II*.

[96] Keen (2011), *Debunking economics*, 2nd ed., ch. 10 and 11.

[97] Bronfenbrenner (1969), *Is the business cycle obsolete? Based on a conference of the Social Science Research Council Committee on Economic Stability*.

which economic growth oscillated in a small range of positive values had displaced the old business cycles in which there was growth in expansions and contraction in recessions.[98]

While the Keynesians were largely involved in building large econometric models which created the illusion of a hard and complex economic technology able to control the economy, Milton Friedman and Anna Schwartz focused on just a few variables, mainly measures of money stocks, prices, and general activity, and examined the behavior of these variables in detail. They showed the high correlation between money growth and both prices and real activity, evident in the data over long spans of time, and pointed out that growth of the money stock tends to precede changes in nominal income. On the basis of these relations, they argued in favor of a much simpler view of the economy than that of the Keynesians.[99] They had supposedly shown that the quantity of money was the main driving force behind business cycles so they concluded that a more stable growth of the money supply could produce greatly dampened cyclical fluctuations. Thus, Keynesians and monetarists claimed that the fluctuations of the economy could be largely eliminated, put under control. They just differed, and not much, in the means to reach this goal.[100]

In 1960 Irma Adelman and Frank L. Adelman had demonstrated that applying perturbations to the endogenous variables or random shocks to "energize" the system enabled the econometric Keynesian model of the US economy to show oscillations resembling the observed business cycles. In the words of Ira Adelman, she and her husband had not "proved that business cycles are stochastic in origin" though they had presented evidence creating "a strong presumption in favour of this hypothesis." This would be "especially significant in view of the absence (to date) of a

[98] Klein (1997), "Growth cycles", in Glasner & Cooley, eds., *Business cycles and depressions*, 289.

[99] Sims (2012), "Statistical modelling".

[100] Friedman & Heller (1968), *Monetary vs. fiscal policy—A dialogue*, is an interesting exchange between the monetarist leader and a Keynesian economist who is today mostly forgotten. In the 1960s Heller occupied important positions as economic advisor and, interestingly, was behind major tax cuts. In the book. Milton Friedman accused the "new economics" of Heller and the Keynesians to have produced very nice models that failed to provide proper forecasts on the effects of government interventions in the economy.

completely satisfactory endogenous theory of business cycles."[101] This contribution of the Adelmans that continued the old ideas of Ragnar Frisch was quite influential in pushing macroeconomics in the direction of undefined exogenous "random shocks," supposedly responsible for the recurrent periods of economic malaise.

The notion that business cycles are exogenously determined by random shocks grew in economics in the 1960s, the time during which the Cold War reached its zenit. By the end of the 1960s the period of steady growth experienced by Western countries after World War II had ended and the 1970s were characterized by increasingly severe recessions. Blaming recessions on exogenous factors, be they random shocks or political influences, may fulfill an ideological role, since the view that recessions are determined by the inner workings of the market economy is not consistent with a defense of the free-enterprise system as the best and most efficient way to organize the production of useful material things and services. But that was the notion that had to be defended against communism during the Cold War.[102] From a scientific point of view to attribute a phenomenon that recurs repeatedly but at irregular intervals to shocks that are undefined and random represents a kind of scientific nihilism. There are many phenomena like that in science: storms, and rains in meteorology; tides, floods, and earthquakes in geology; epileptic seizures and asthma attacks in medicine; the yield point of a material in engineering just to mention some examples. Each field of science looks for causes of unexplained phenomena by trying to understand what is going on, and when a particular causal theory is proposed, experiments and systematic examination of observational data when experiments are not possible are used to evaluate its scientific merit. Since the first debates on the causes of the business cycle in the early decades of the nineteenth century quite a number of theories were proposed to explain its nature and causes. Sismondi, Malthus, Marx, Juglar, Mitchel, and Tinbergen had proposed schemes in which the business cycle had endogenous causes, while exogenous causes as those proposed by Jevons, Moore, and Huntington had

[101] Adelman (1960), "Business cycles—Endogenous or stochastic?", *Economic Journal* 70, 783–796.

[102] In the early 1960s Marxist economists from the Soviet bloc had speculated with circumspection about the reasons why in the 1950s capitalist economies had just mild and unsynchronized crises. See Rumyantsev, ed. (1963), *Crisis & the capitalist cycle—A symposium*.

been utterly unconvincing. It seems a scientific attitude should have been to examine how good the fit of the theories with the economic reality was, but when Tinbergen tried this, both Keynes and Friedman crucified him. At the time when new and powerful statistical techniques were intensively applied to economic research so that both a priori reasoning and empirical data appeared as possible sources of economic knowledge, most business cycle theorists emphasized the fundamental deficiencies of economic data and the inadequacy of statistical methods for dealing with intrinsically complicated economic phenomena. They opted for a priori reasoning as a principal and more reliable source of economic knowledge.[103] Economics as a discipline revealed a strong antiempirical stance.

Business Cycles Persist

Despite the notion of "growth cycles" and the supposed "obsolescence" of the business cycle, the 1970s and the 1980s saw major recessions occurring in the countries of the Western world, often combining unemployment with inflation. Without any particular reason to think so, most economists agreed that these recessions were caused by exogenous factors, but they strongly disagreed on what these factors were exactly. Keynesians claimed that the proper policies to stabilize the cycle based on Keynesian theory had not been applied, but Milton Friedman, Friedrich von Hayek, and others who had never agreed with the Keynesian perspective claimed that these recessions were consequences of Keynesian theories and the interventionist policies derived from them. In the 1970s and 1980s the ideas of Milton Friedman and Robert Lucas gained much influence in economics and from being considered the distilled economic knowledge of the century, Keynes's *General Theory* became "a boring book" that many economists cited disdainfully.

This was the time when the criticisms against Keynesian structural modeling shifted the focus of macroeconomic research back to the business cycle and the development of macroeconomic models that could produce cyclical behavior. However, while the Keynesian models were criticized on empirical and theoretical grounds, there was not an accepted macroeconomic model. A variety of economic models appeared and could

[103] Kim (1988), *Equilibrium business cycle theory in historical perspective*, 15.

explain particular features of observed macroeconomic data, but there was not a model accepted at least by a majority of the profession that could fully explain how economies at large evolve during business cycles.

In the 1970s many macroeconomists departed from Keynesianism and the field branched in a variety of schools and trends. Many of these schools have been considered as consecutive steps for restoring the classical principles of economic dynamics that Keynes had rejected.[104] It has been said indeed that economists following Milton Friedman's monetarism, Robert Lucas's rational expectations, and the real-business cycle theory can be regarded as "all close cousins."[105]

At the vanguard in the attack against Keynes, Milton Friedman provided a vision in which the major troubles of the market economy—inflation and unemployment—were basically consequences of exogenous disturbances in the flows of money. Since the usual view was that in the modern world money flows are mostly controlled by central banks, more or less in turn influenced by governments, in the monetarist perspective the business cycle is basically a recurrent disturbance produced by the attempts of politicians or central bankers to influence the economy. With the pass of time this led to astonishing episodes, as that of Milton Friedman's coauthor, Anna Schwartz, presenting fellow monetarist Chairman Alan Greenspan as a main culprit of the Great Recession.[106]

Robert Lucas agreed with Friedman that monetary changes are responsible of fluctuations in business activity, via relative price fluctuations, and proposed rational expectations as a theory "which accounts for the observed movements in *quantities* (employment, consumption, investment) as an optimizing response to observed movements in *prices*".[107] In Lucas's view, responses of economic agents to changes in the flow of money are changes in the supply of labor and capital, but since agents are rational, they notice after a while they don't maximize utility by doing so. Consequently, disturbances are just transitory and business cycles are not only exogenous, but unimportant from the social point of view, since

[104] Knoop (2004), *Recessions and depressions*, 93.

[105] Sachs (2009), "The future of capitalism: Rethinking macroeconomics", *Capitalism and Society* 4(3), Article 3.

[106] Schwartz (2010), "Origins of the financial market crisis of 2008", in Booth, ed., *Verdict on the crash—Causes and policy implications*.

[107] Lucas (1977), "Understanding business cycles", *Carnegie-Rochester Conference Series on Public Policy* 57, 29.

changes in the supply of labor are voluntary. According to the economic science of Robert Lucas, there is no involuntary unemployment!

Income Distribution as Cause of Recession

Income distribution is a causal factor that determines the dynamic condition of the economy for authors pertaining to quite different schools of thought, who have proposed diverse, indeed opposite mechanisms to explain why changes in the distribution of income would cause economic downturns or upturns. Both too high and too low wages—which have its correspondence in too low or too high profits—have been proposed as causes of recession.

In the old view of Arthur Pigou reedited in more recent years for example by Lee Ohanian, a qualified representative of the real-business cycle school, it is too high wages that cause too high costs for business, with the consequent decay in economic activity leading to a downturn.[108] Consequently, in this view a decrease in wages would increase supply and would also have a stimulating effect on economic activity. A slightly different perspective is offered by those who also from a variety of theoretical positions support the so-called profit-squeeze hypothesis, in which high wages lead to recession through the demand side.[109] The pathway is here from high wages to low profits, and from low profits to falling investment and the lack of effective demand with unsold goods that characterizes recessions. Some authors who support the profit-squeeze hypothesis also seem to hold underconsumptionist views, since they deemphasize the role of investment in business cycles by claiming that, with a "relatively weak response of investment to profitability [...], consumption necessarily assumes the dominant role in effective demand."[110] In a purely underconsumptionist view low wages generating

[108] Pigou (1927), "Wage policy and unemployment", *Economic Journal* 37(147), 355; Ohanian (2008), "Back to the future with Keynes", *Federal Reserve Bank of Minneapolis Quarterly Review* 32(1), 10–16.

[109] Boddy & Crotty (1975), "Class conflict and macro policy: The political business cycle", *Review of Radical Political Economics* 7(1), 1–19; Boldrin & Horvath (1995), "Labor contracts and business cycles", *Journal of Political Economy* 103(5), 972–1004; Bhaduri & Marglin (1990), "Unemployment and the real wages: the economic basis for contesting political ideologies", *Cambridge Journal of Economics* 14, 375–393.

[110] Bhaduri & Marglin (1990), "Unemployment and the real wages".

low purchasing power for consumer goods reduce aggregate demand and cause recession, so that an increase in wages during a slump would tend to stimulate recovery. This is the view of many post-Keynesian economists who in this follow the ideas of Kalecki.[111] For Kalecki a rise in wages generates an expansion of profits in the sector of consumption goods and does not reduce profits in the whole economy, therefore by stimulating aggregate demand, contributes to uplift the economy. Conversely, for Kalecki and the post-Keynesians, declines in wages tend to depress economic activity. Of course, this leaves unanswered why recessions are constantly associated with wage declines, in spite of which the recovery eventually arrives.

Empirical data show consistently that the rise in profits in the late recession is followed by increased investment, which is the key for expansion of effective demand, bringing up output and, subsequently, prices and costs.[112] A high degree of coherence between most measures of profits and investment activity has been repeatedly observed, with profits leading investment. As Boldrin and Horvath put it, profits "typically spring up at the early stage of a recovery led by strong gains in labor productivity that are not matched by raises in real wages."[113] Obviously, the reverse must occur immediately before downturns, with declining profits leading to falling investment and this, in turn, leading to the vicious cycle of falling effective demand reducing profits, which in turn reduces investment and demand.

The persistence of underconsumptionist views in economics and among many commentators on social issues is so much remarkable considering that the notion was rejected from many quarters, starting with Marx and Engels, and in the past century was repeatedly proved wrong by empirical data. In the 1910s both Wesley Mitchell and Minnie Throop England wrote openly against underconsumptionist views. In his reputed monography on business cycles, Mitchell criticized what he called the

[111] Kalecki (1994), "The mechanism of the business upswing", in Foster & Szlajter, eds., *The faltering economy—The problem of accumulation under monopoly capitalism*, 127–133.

[112] Tapia (2013), "Does investment call the tune? Empirical evidence and endogenous theories of the business cycle", *Research in Political Economy* 28, 229–259. Similar analyses with updated data in "Investment, profit and crises—Theories and evidence" in Carchedi & Roberts, eds., *World in crisis*, 78–128.

[113] Boldrin & Horvath (1995), "Labor contracts".

various forms of the underconsumption theory and added that it had "never been proven that consumers' demand falls behind supply before a crisis has begun. And whatever may be the facts of this case, there is evidence that the strains which have actually precipitated the crises of recent years have appeared earlier in other branches of trade than those which cater to the wants of consumers". The same year Minnie Throop England wrote in a leading journal of economics that "broadly speaking industrial prosperity is caused by the increasing demand for capital goods to start new enterprises; conversely, industrial depression is caused by the decreased demand for capital goods."[114] Both Mitchell and England were supporting their analysis in a meticulous examination of empirical data. Two decades later, Tinbergen analyzed further data to reach the same conclusion, that the drop in investment was the major component of the decline of demand during recessions. That underconsumptionist views and statements blaming recessions on too low wages are still around attests to how difficult is to advance knowledge on social issues against notions and prejudices that are deeply ingrained in human minds by social life.

Macroeconomics in the Dark Age

In the 1980s and 1990s dynamic stochastic general equilibrium models and real-business-cycle theory were the major innovations in macroeconomics. They were conveniently abbreviated for the professional jargon as DSGE models and RBC theory.

Robert Solow, who had received the Nobel Memorial Prize in Economic Sciences in 1987, depicted DSGE models in a quite unflattering way in a statement in front of the House Committee on Science and Technology of the US Congress. For Solow, DSGE models

> take it for granted that the whole economy can be thought about as if it were a single, consistent person or dynasty carrying out a rationally designed, long-term plan, occasionally disturbed by unexpected shocks, but adapting to them in a rational, consistent way [...] Most economists are willing to believe that most individual "agents"—consumers, investors, borrowers, lenders, workers, employers—make their decisions so as to do

114 Mitchell (1913), *Business cycles*, 580; England (1913), "Economic crises", *Journal of Political Economy* 4, 345–354.

> the best that they can for themselves, given their possibilities and their information. Clearly they do not always behave in this rational way, and systematic deviations are well worth studying. But this is not a bad first approximation in many cases. The DSGE school populates its simplified economy [...] with exactly one single combination worker-owner-consumer-everything-else who plans ahead carefully and lives forever. One important consequence of this "representative agent" assumption is that there are no conflicts of interest, no incompatible expectations, no deceptions. This all-purpose decision-maker essentially runs the economy according to its own preferences. Not directly, of course: the economy has to operate through generally well-behaved markets and prices.

For Robert Solow, authors proposing DSGE models had under pressure from skeptics and from the need to explain with actual data allowed in their models some market frictions and imperfections, but overall they viewed the whole economy "as if it were like a person, trying consciously and rationally to do the best it can on behalf of the representative agent, given its circumstances. This cannot be an adequate description of a national economy."

Also, according to Solow, DSGE models make unemployment somehow voluntary, "a choice of current leisure or a desire to retain some kind of flexibility for the future or something like that." These explanations are at odds with common sense. Furthermore, since the models assume the observed economy is

> actually doing the best it can, given the circumstances [...] conscious public policy can only make things worse [...] The point I am making is that the DSGE model has nothing useful to say about anti-recession policy because it has built into its essentially implausible assumptions the "conclusion" that there is nothing for macroeconomic policy to do.[115]

Very closely related to DSGE models is the RBC theory.[116] Though RBC became immediately a major contender for mainstream status in the

[115] Solow (2010), "Prepared statement, House Committee on Science and Technology Subcommittee on Investigations and Oversight, Building a Science of Economics for the Real World", July 20.

[116] Prescott (1986), "Theory ahead of business cycle measurement", *Federal Reserve Bank of Minneapolis Quarterly Review* 10, 9–22; Plosser (1989), "Understanding real business cycles", *Journal of Economic Perspectives* 3(3), 51.

1980s, it was also immediately subjected to plain rejections.[117] In RBC theory expansions and recessions are efficient responses of the economy as a whole to productivity shocks or supply shocks—that is, again, exogenous factors. Business cycles are the manifestation and consequence of a self-equilibrating economy responding to random shocks that disturb aggregate supply. Though the shocks usually suggested are technological innovations, James Hamilton has suggested a related model in which business cycles depend on shocks in the price of oil.[118] In this conception, oil shocks are viewed as dependent on actions of producer countries or phenomena such as wars or revolutions disturbing the production of crude oil. Since these phenomena are exogenous to the economy, the whole perspective is that the business cycle is exogenously determined.

Though some DSGE models are said to incorporate Keynesian elements, both DSGE models and RBC theory are basically a continuation of the tradition of Schumpeter and Hayek, in which technological innovations or other exogenous undefined "shocks" cause economic fluctuations. Demographic changes, political influences, or variations in relative prices due to external influences have been proposed as noneconomic factors responsible for leading to recession. Crude oil, however, is always the first in the list of suspects.

The 1980s saw an important change in the general perspective of economics on business cycles. While the usual view in previous decades was that recessions were appalling consequences of either major exogenous natural, political, or institutional interferences (in the classical and monetarist views), or manifestations of the persistent tendency of the capitalist economy to stagnate requiring stimulus from government (in the Keynesian view), the RBC theory presented periods of expansion and contraction as optimal responses of the market economy to exogenous shocks. As one of the supporters of RBC theory, Edward Prescott, has put it, it is not puzzling that recessions occur but contrarily, "it would be puzzling if the economy did not display these large fluctuations in

[117] Summers (1986), "Some skeptical observations on real business cycle theory", *Federal Reserve Bank of Minneapolis Quarterly Review* 10, 23–27.

[118] Hamilton (1988), "A neoclassical model of unemployment and the business cycle", *Journal of Political Economy* 96(3), 593; Hamilton (2009), "Causes and consequences of the Oil Shock of 2007–08", *Brookings Papers on Economic Activity* Spring, 215–267; Hamilton (2011), "Historical oil shocks", NBER Working Paper 16790.

output and employment."[119] Since for RBC proponents, as for Lucas, unemployment is a choice not to work, it is costly and inefficient to try to avoid recessions. Nothing is to be done about them, *laissez-faire* is the best type of government "intervention." Lee Ohanian, one of the leading authors in the RBC field, attributed business cycles to either productivity shocks or too high wages, often consequence of government policies.[120] Was the rise of these ideas in economics in the 1980s connected with the fact that this was also the decade of Ronald Reagan in the United States and Margaret Thatcher in Britain?

Since the 1980s, James Hamilton has been the leading proponent of the view that oil prices are a major cause if not "the" cause of recessions. Hamilton has claimed that oil shocks have been responsible for 11 of the 12 recessions in the United States after World War II.[121] Though his views are not inconsistent with those of RBC theorists, Hamilton has also wondered how RBC models became dominant in economics in the 1990s, despite the fact that these models assume productivity shocks of unknown and undefined nature.[122] A different opinion is however that of Todd Knoop, who claims that in the 1990s RBC theory and monetarism got devalued among economists, since most of them disagreed with the policy conclusions of these theories, it was impossible to explain the stagflation of the 1980s by monetary factors, and empirical data showed many cases incompatible with the perfect price and wage flexibility assumed by Milton Friedman, Robert Lucas, and the RBC theorists.[123]

Whatever be the case, when the eruption of the Great Recession and the global financial crisis in 2008 surprised most economists, a variety of perspectives—mostly monetarism, RBC theory, and new Keynesian views with some minority heterodox perspectives—were present in macroeconomics. The consequence was the emergence of angry disputes on what should be done. Major conflicts among economists were brought to the fore when policies to deal with the recession were proposed. On January

[119] Prescott (1986), "Theory ahead...".

[120] Ohanian (2008), "Back to the future...".

[121] Hamilton (2011), "Historical oil shocks".

[122] Interview of James Hamilton in Parker, ed. (2007), *The economics of the Great Depression: A 21st century look back at the economics of the interwar era*, 81.

[123] Knoop (2004), *Recessions and depressions*.

28, the Cato Institute placed a full-page advertisement in *The New York Times* in which "With all Due Respect, Mr President," Barack Obama was told that

> Notwithstanding reports that all economists are now Keynesians and that we all support a big increase in the burden of government, we the undersigned do not believe that more government spending is a way to improve economic performance [...] To improve the economy, policymakers should focus on reforms that remove impediments to work, saving, investment and production. Lower tax rates and a reduction in the burden of government are the best ways of using fiscal policy to boost growth.

About 300 economists were willing to be listed in the ad as opponents of the stimulus, including Nobel laureates Edward Prescott, Vernon Smith, and James Buchanan. No much later, Paul Krugman who had been a fierce critic of that statement, started using the derogatory term "Dark Age of Macroeconomics," that he applied to the period in which "so much knowledge had been lost."[124] He did not say however what was the knowledge that had been lost. Indeed, in Krugman's disquisitions on business cycles and recessions it is hard to find any clear explanation of why recessions occur. He had asserted in 2006 that the differences between macroeconomists were very modest and that "the clean little secret of modern macroeconomics is how much consensus economists have reached in the past 70 years."[125] What a surprise that just three years later it was discovered that macroeconomics had been in a Dark Age!

Marxists and Radicals

The idea of crisis being caused by lack or insufficient consumption has been basically a constant in economic thought. Some promoters of this idea, for example Malthus, were extremely conservative, but others were critical thinkers like Sismondi, or later in the nineteenth century, Johann Rodbertus and Eugen During in Germany, and the Chartists and John

[124] Krugman (2009), "A Dark Age of macroeconomics (wonkish)", *New York Times*, Jan. 27.

[125] Krugman & Wells (2006), *Economics*, 832.

Hobson in England. Marx had openly opposed the underconsumptionist notion, that Engels strongly criticized—with Marx approval—in his *Anti-Duhring*.[126]

After Engels died in 1895 the SPD, the German Social Democratic Party, became the main carrier of socialist thinking and theoretical inheritor of the views of Marx. Karl Kautsky, Eduard Bernstein, Rosa Luxemburg, Anton Pannekoek, and Rudolf Hilferding were some of the theoretical leaders of the party, often involved in controversies on the interpretation of Marx's economic views and the political stance to be taken by the party. Between 1910 and 1916 three books were published which were to be influential contributions to what could be perhaps improperly called Marxian or Marxist economics. They were Hilferding's *Finance capital*, Luxemburg's *Accumulation of capital*, and Lenin's *Imperialism*. Hilferding's *Finance capital*, published in 1910, argued following and developing Marx's ideas that capitalism had largely evolved toward a system more dependent on banks—which became a kind of regulator of the system.[127] In 1913, in *The Accumulation of Capital: A Contribution to an Economic Explanation of Imperialism*, Rosa Luxemburg claimed against all Marxian orthodoxy that the reproduction schemes of the second volume of *Capital* were basically wrong and inconsistent with the rest of Marx's economic theory.[128] Luxemburg cited the use by the English textile industry of the cotton produced by the slaves in the plantations of the Southern United States, the imports to England of wheat produced by serfs in Tsarist Russia, the construction of railroads by British capitals in South America, and the large exports of German chemicals such as dyes to noncapitalist countries in Asia and Africa. From these and similar contemporaneous cases, she concluded that

> even in its full maturity, capitalism depends in all of its relations on the simultaneous existence of noncapitalist strata and societies [...] The accumulation process of capital is tied to noncapitalist forms of production in all of its value relations and material relations [...] The accumulation of

[126] Engels (2010) [1894], *Anti-Dűhring*, in MECW 25, 5–312. Marx contributed a chapter to this book and according to Engels read and approved the whole manuscript.

[127] Hilferding (1981) [1910], *Finance capital—A study of the latest phase of capitalist development*.

[128] Luxemburg (2015) [1913], *The accumulation of capital*, in Hudis & Le Blanc, eds. *The Complete Works of Rosa Luxemburg—Volume II, Economic Writings 2*.

> capital cannot adequately be presented under the presupposition of the exclusive and absolute dominance of the capitalist mode of production—in fact it is inconceivable in every respect without the noncapitalist spheres that form its milieu [...] capital cannot do without the means of production and labor-power of the entire planet—it requires the natural resources and labor-power of all territories for its movement of accumulation to proceed unimpeded. Since these are in actual fact overwhelmingly bound by the precapitalist forms of production that constitute the historical milieu of capital accumulation, capital is characterized by a powerful drive to conquer these territories and societies.[129]

For Luxemburg a permanent deficiency of purchasing power to buy what is produced leads capitalists as a class, with the encouragement and help of the national state, to anxiously quest for foreign markets, to sell their products, mostly in noncapitalist economies, in the underdeveloped countries. This was the basis for the will of capitalist nations to conquer colonies. Thus, a tendency of capitalism to breakdown because of lack of demand was linked which a tendency to involve in imperialist policies and war.

The ideas of Rosa Luxemburg raised a big controversy. They were rejected in the social democratic press by, among others, Otto Bauer and Anton Pannekoek, who were answered in turn by Luxemburg. But her opposition to the World War had landed her in jail and immediately after the German defeat in 1918, she was freed and then murdered by nationalist zealots in January 1919. In *Imperialism, the Highest Stage of Capitalism*, published in 1917 when the butchery was still ongoing, Lenin kind of combined the views of Hilferding and Luxemburg with those of an English economist, John Hobson. Hobson had attacked Say's law and in his *Imperialism—A Study* (1902) had scathingly criticized the colonial empires as being an embodiment of the impulse for getting markets. Lenin, leader of the left wing of the Russian social democrats, the so-called *Bolsheviks*, echoed Hobson's views and asserted as a basic component of imperialism the tendency to export capital. Marx's focus on exploitation as a key component of the social relation between workers and capitalists in a capitalist economy was displaced by Lenin to the relation between countries, with an upper stratum of workers in developed capitalist countries—the "labor aristocracy"—enjoying the crumbs of the

[129] Luxemburg (2015) [1913], *The accumulation of capital*, ch. 26

imperialist exploitation of the peoples of backward nations. Because of the lack of territories to be conquered in America, Africa, or Asia, continents that were already in full control of the capitalist nations, Lenin saw an unavoidable tendency of capitalist nations to fight each other for conquering the territories of others. This would lead, unavoidably, to war.[130]

With the triumph of the Councils (*soviets* in Russian) of Workers, Peasants, and Soldiers of the Tsarist Empire, Russia made peace with Germany, got out of World War I, and after a few years of civil war, foreign intervention and extreme social turmoil and famine, the Bolsheviks were solidly in power. They adopted the name of Communist Party and renamed as Union of Soviet Socialist Republics the remains of the Russian empire, which had lost Finland, Poland, and the Baltic nations. Soviet communism became the new ideological reference for most followers of Marx. The reasonings of Rosa Luxemburg on economic themes had raised many issues, now those of Lenin were considered unarguable. Imperialism was seen as a politico-economic system developed on the basis of monopolies, financial capital, and a labor aristocracy comfortable with capitalism. But according to Lenin, it was also the final stage of capitalism.

Lenin was shot by a frustrated revolutionary, never recovered of his wounds and died in 1924. Leon Trotsky, Nikolai Bukharin, and Yevgeni Preobrazhensky were some of the Soviet theorists that produced significant work on social and economic issues, but soon they were liquidated by Stalin, who apparently found in the Hungarian Eugen Varga a writer on economic issues that he did not need to eliminate. Overall, until the 1950s Lenin's ideas on imperialism based on the need to look for markets were overwhelmingly predominant in the left intelligentsia linked to, at the time, very influential communist parties. In the propaganda of these parties and in the work of authors in the communist sphere of influence the economic theory of Marx had been transformed in just one cell or a few cells in the multicellular organism of "Marxism-Leninism" and it had lost all specificity. Marx's ideas on crises, which undoubtedly were fragmentary and scattered in multiple notebooks when he died, suffered a process of simplification and sorting out. The notion developed that according to Marx there were quite a number of different

[130] Lenin (1963) [1917], *Imperialism, the highest stage of capitalism*, in *Lenin's Selected Works*, 1, 667–766.

types of crises caused by either lack of proportionality between sectors of the economy, overproduction or underconsumption, disturbances in the sphere of finance, or a fall in the rate of profit.[131] This linked to Engels's view that acute crises had been substituted by protracted stagnation, the notion of the dominance of monopolies and financial capital, and reliance on the concept of imperialism as a tool for economic analysis. World War I was seen by many radicals as the confirmation of the criticisms against capitalism and imperialism, but the war passed and capitalism that had failed in Russia did not break in Europe despite that for most Marxists in the 1920s it had reached its limits. The decade saw a roaring expansion of capitalism in America, but serious turbulences in Europe and then the big deluge followed worldwide—the Great Depression in the 1930s, and World War II in the 1940s. But still a revolution to suppress capitalism did not occur. When communists took power, it was mostly because of the influence of the Soviet Red Army during the campaign in which the Wehrmacht was crushed in 1944–1945 in Eastern Europe. Then communist-led revolutions triumphed in 1949 and 1959 where they were not expected, in backward countries where capitalism was rather in its infancy, China and Cuba.

During the 1950s and 1960s colonial empires disappeared, but capitalism continued quite unharmed both in the metropolis and in most of the new independent nations. It was obvious that the views of Luxemburg and Lenin on imperialism were wrong. As Herbert Marcuse said, the concept of imperialism was now useless, and there were certainly no basic US economic interests that would explain the US presence and war in Vietnam.[132]

In 1929 it had been published in Leipzig the book, *Das Akkumulations-und Zusammenbruchsgesetz des kapitalistischen Systems* by Henryk Grossman, which was translated into English only in the 1970s and in a badly abridged version titled *The Law of Accumulation and Breakdown of the Capitalist System*.[133] In this book Henryk Grossman, a

[131] *The capitalist cycle* by Pavel Maksakovsky, originally published in 1928, is an early example of Soviet presentation of ill-digested Marx's ideas. Crises are seen mostly as caused by lack of demand and disproportionality between sectors.

[132] Marcuse (1967), "The obsolescence of Marxism", in Lobkowitz, ed., *Marx and the Western World*, 409–417.

[133] See note 22, on p. 126.

Polish collaborator of the Frankfurt Institute for Social Research, systematized Marx's theory with a detailed exposition of Marx's method and meticulously replied not only to Rosa Luxemburg but also to those who had criticized her, like Otto Bauer, who had denied that the trends elucidated by Marx in the capitalist system were sufficient for its breakdown. Though the book had major strengths and was hailed as a major work by some radical Marxists like Paul Mattick, it did not pay due attention to Lenin's views and Grossmann even criticized Russian writers like Bukharin. Thus, the work was poorly received by most Marxists and ignored by academic economists, despite the fact that arguably it was predicting what started just months later, the Great Depression that affected the capitalist world at large.

During the following decades authors claiming to be followers of the economic theory of Marx mostly developed views that put them quite close to the ideas of Keynes. Indeed, Michael Kalecky was almost explicitly connecting the ideas of Keynes with those of Marx; and others, like Maurice Dobb, Paul A. Baran, Paul M. Sweezy, and Oskar Lange were doing the same thing. A few authors like Paul Mattick, Charles Bettelheim, Victor Perlo, or Geoffrey Piling insisted that the ways Keynes and Marx had understood the capitalist system were very different, and mutually inconsistent, but overall, the ideas of Marx and Keynes were fully mixed up by economists and writers on economic issues who had left-wing political views. The fact that, from the 1960s, Keynes started to be the target of conservative economists like Friedman and Lucas was another reason for the phenomenon of a *contra natura* Keynesian-Marxian economic theory that has been quite prevalent in the field of so-called radical or heterodox economics in the past half century.[134] Hyman Minsky was an important author who illustrates this amalgamation of views. Minsky's book *Stabilizing an unstable economy* takes from Marx the idea that capitalism is unstable and from Keynes the view that despite "problems," capitalism is the economic system to be preserved.[135] Minsky's main thesis in this book and other contributions is that the normal functioning of the market economy in which credit is a key component generates debt that cumulates creating increasingly

[134] To integrate in a consistent theory the views of Marx and Keynes is the explicit purpose of Goldstein & Hillard (2009), in *Heterodox Macroeconomics: Keynes, Marx and globalization*.

[135] Minsky [1986] 2008. *Stabilizing an unstable economy.*

unstable chains of liabilities. Eventually, some minor disturbance destroys the fragile equilibrium in which the economy became a card castle, and everything falls—that is the crisis. At the time of the Great Recession, many left-wing economists found Minsky's views particularly apposite to interpret that crisis.

A particular controversy that has been active since the 1970s among radical economists has been the role of the decline in the profit rate—or the so-called law of the tendency of the profit rate to fall—in the causation of crises. In dozens of papers and books the profit rate was estimated and examined to check whether it had been or not falling during the years leading to crisis. Radical economists who examined the rate of profit in the United States before 2008 and found that it had tendentially increased since the 1980s concluded that the Great Recession could not be caused by that tendency.[136] Andrew Kliman and others replied that by computing properly the rate of profit it was found that, indeed, it had declined.[137] Of course, the controversy never reached any closure. As it happens in the field of neoclassical economics where inconsistent views remain backed by a cloud of heroic assumptions and dark mathematics, in the field of radical or heterodox economics many authors proclaim their views and go ahead whether what they say is found plausible, doubtful, or silly by their colleagues. In natural science knowledge advances by proposing theories and making experiments and predictions which confirm or falsify the theory. In social science to appeal to empirical data is always difficult and many authors theorize—wrongly in my view—that the most important thing is just to elaborate a logically consistent theory.

The Revival of Keynesianism

After a period of decay that probably started in the 1960s and extended to the 1980s, Keynesianism had a kind of slow revival in the late twentieth century and then the Great Recession provided a further stimulus

[136] Many of these views are collected in Friedman, Moseley & Sturr, eds. (2009), *The economic crisis reader*.

[137] Kliman (2012), *The failure of capitalist production: Underlying causes of the Great Recession*; Carchedi & Roberts, eds. (2018), *World in crisis—A global analysis of Marx's law of profitability*.

with even major conversions to the Keynesian faith.[138] However, the revival of Keynesian views in economics had a variety of guises. The labels of New Keynesians, Keynesians, or post-Keynesians were applied to schools that espoused different models to explain economic fluctuations. Most of these models have some link to the ideas of Keynes, but New Keynesians are much closer to the monetarist and the RBC field, while post-Keynesians are more critical of mainstream economics. Jeffrey Sachs, Gregory Mankiw, Larry Summers, Joseph Stiglitz, Olivier Blanchard, and Paul Krugman can perhaps be cited as among the most salient New Keynesians, with each of them representing relatively different approaches to policy.

New Keynesian macroeconomic theories of the business cycle are difficult to grasp by the dispersion and variety of points of view, but they generally have as major components imperfect competition, market imperfections, credit crunches, and other financial disturbances. The practical consequence is that recessions are explained by financial instances and technicalities quite difficult to put into causal terms. Whether business cycles are exogenous or endogenous in the view of new Keynesians would be quite difficult to say.

Such economists like Paul Davidson, James Galbraith, Dean Baker, or Thomas Palley, who should be classified as orthodox Keynesians, or post-Keynesians, are more prone to advice government intervention and fiscal policies of redistribution toward lower incomes. These authors, some of them linked to unions and viewed as left-wing economists, put much more emphasis than the rest of the profession in differential income issues, and often claim in the Keynesian tradition in favor of redistribution policies toward low-income groups to stimulate consumption and economic activity. This view, that at least in part attributes recessions to insufficient demand due to low wages, arrived to modern left-wing economics via modern socialist authors, such as Paul Baran and Paul M. Sweezy, who had taken it from Keynes and Kalecki, and even further back from Lenin, Rosa Luxemburg, and John Hobson. Though these left-wing economists often consider income inequality and low wages as cause of stagnation and recession, most of them see economic crises in general and the 2008 recession in particular as strongly linked to financial turbulence, this in turn due to deregulation of financial activity. These are exogenous factors,

[138] Posner (2009), "How I became a Keynesian: Second thoughts in the middle of a crisis", *New Republic*, Sept. 23.

but many post-Keynesian economists would probably agree with explanations of the business cycle in which endogenous factors also have a role.[139]

Economics on Recessions Since the 1990s

The recessions of the 1970s and the 1980s that, as it was seen in Chapter 2 of this book, were actually national manifestations of worldwide crises, largely dispelled the idea that the business cycle had disappeared, and new ideas were proposed to deal with it. For Lucas and the RBC theorists, the business cycle was real, but it was just a very small nuisance to be expected as an associated fact of the enormous advantages brought by the market economy to make society wealthier. But then a new idea was proposed. Considering that macroeconomic aggregates in Western countries and particularly in the United States presented less volatility in recent decades, it was claimed that recessions had become shorter and expansions larger, and thus the concepts of "the New Economy" and "the Great Moderation" made their appearance. These notions had been somewhat proposed in the 1980s and 1990s, when it had been asserted that in the postwar period macroeconomic aggregates of the US economy presented less volatility, recessions had become shorter, and expansions longer. In a strict sense, though, the concepts of the New Economy and the Great Moderation made their proper appearance after the turn of the century.[140] The general idea embodied in these notions was that recent economic data indicated that sudden and deep fluctuations of the economy were unlikely to be expected because there had been a moderation of business cycles which had basically produced a complete disappearance of crises. That was viewed as an achievement produced by—among other things—intelligent economic policies based on major developments in macroeconomic knowledge. Robert Lucas had indeed proclaimed in his 2003 Presidential Address to the American Economic

[139] See examples in Friedman, Moseley & Sturr, eds. (2009), *The crisis reader.*

[140] Diebold & Rudebusch (1999), *Business cycles—Durations, dynamics, and forecasting*; Blanchard (2006), Macroeconomics; Gordon (2009), *Macroeconomics*; Knoop (2004), *Recessions and depressions*; Bernanke (2004), "Remarks on The Great Moderation by Governor Ben S. Bernanke at the meetings of the Eastern Economic Association, Washington, DC, February 20, 2004".

Association that macroeconomics had at all purposes succeeded "for many decades" in its task of preventing economic depressions.[141]

It is obvious that the circulation and penetration of these notions among mainstream economists was one key reason that the Great Recession was a big surprise for the large majority of the economic profession. As Andrew Haldane, Chief Economist of the Bank of England, explained, out of 27 economic forecasters that produced in 2007 forecasts for the British economy in 2008, few foresaw a slight downturn in 2008 and none foresaw a recession, the recession that was the most severe since the 1930s: "every one of these forecasts was not just wrong but spectacularly so." As Steve Keen has emphasized, by claiming in the early years of the twenty-first century that the economy was in a Great Moderation, the economic establishment could not have been more wrong about the economic future.[142]

The Great Recession that emerged in late 2007 and put large portions of the world economy in shambles for several years pushed the economics profession a long way toward questioning its views on some issues, though not shaking its principles. A good example of this is the work of Nobel laureate microeconomist Michael Spence, who chaired the Commission on Growth and Development sponsored by several governments and the World Bank. Integrating business leaders, politicians, and prominent economists, including Robert Rubin and Robert Solow, the Commission produced several reports before its work formally ended in 2010. In 2011, Spence published *The Next Convergence*, which can be considered a summary of the reflections and conclusions of the Commission.[143] Spence's book illustrates how the world economic and business establishment evolved toward a much more guarded defense of "basic economic principles" such as free markets, business self-regulation, and fiscal soundness; much emphasis is put on the idea that different countries may require different solutions in terms of economic policy. One of the most interesting aspects of *The Next Convergence* is the full acknowledgment of a global economy that for Spence was born with the formation of the General Agreement on Tariffs and Trade (GATT) after World War II.

141 Lucas (2003), "Macroeconomic priorities", *American Economic Review* 93(1), 1–14.

142 Haldane (2016), "The Dappled World"; Keen (2011), *Debunking economics*, xi.

143 Spence (2011), *The next convergence—The future of economic growth in a multispeed world*.

For Spence, as previously noted, this global economy requires not only world-level analyses but also world-level instruments of governance.

While the views of Michael Spence seem to be illustrative of an emerging incorporation of the notion of a world economy into mainstream economics, a very large majority of economists involved in macroeconomic issues continue paying attention to national economies and mostly ignoring the reality of a global economic system. After Paul Krugman raised an uproar by asserting in 2009 that most of what had been done in macroeconomics in the past thirty years was at best irrelevant and at worst harmful, the 2010s were a decade of circumspection in economics and very slow recovery of the world economy. Against the usual view of mainstream economics that in the long run "healthy" economic growth is to be expected, the opinion that long-term stagnation is the most likely perspective for the near future was maintained by outstanding macroeconomists such as Robert Gordon and Paul Krugman.[144] This represents a return to old visions of economic growth eventually transforming itself into stagnation as in the views of Adam Smith, David Riccardo, and John Stuart Mill, all of which believed that languor and quiescence are the likely end of a modern industrial or commercial economy.

The economic controversies triggered by the Great Recession have generally referred to the economic policy to be advised, or have focused on specific macroeconomic themes such as the theory of efficient markets, financial deregulation, or income inequality.[145] Less frequently, the disputes have been on particular factors in the causation of the 2008 financial crisis, but the nature and general causes of business cycles, that is, the answer to the question of why recessions occur, are very hard to find in any controversy on economic issues in the past decade. Indeed, many authors writing on economic issues since the Great Recession, from Robert Lucas to David Harvey, have confessed that they do not believe

[144] Gordon (2012), "Is U.S. economic growth over? Faltering innovation confronts the six headwinds", NBER Working Paper 18315; Krugman (2016), "Review: 'The Rise and Fall of American Growth' by Robert J. Gordon", *The New York Times*, Jan. 31; Griffiths & Luciani, eds. (2012), *North America lost decade?*

[145] For instance Krugman (2009), "How did economists get it so wrong?", *New York Times Magazine*, September 2; Cochrane (2009), "How did Paul Krugman get it so wrong"; Sachs (2009), "The future of capitalism: Rethinking macroeconomics", *Capitalism & Society* 4(3), Article 3.

that recessions have common causes.[146] If that is the case, there is no need to look for explanations of the business cycle, a point of view that was rejected long ago and from very different quarters.[147] However, despite the causal nihilism of many authors, others insist in the role of oil as causal factor in recessions. Problems of distribution of income are often mentioned too, either from positions like those of Ohanian claiming wages are too high or those who from the left claim too low wages as culprits of a chronic weakness of demand.

Ray Fair is one of the few macroeconomists working in recent years with big macroeconometric models in the tradition of the Cowles Commission. In Fair's opinion, DSGE models were generally seen as appropriate for both heuristic and forecasting purposes before the Great Recession, when it was a common opinion among macroeconomists that there had been a convergence of views in the field. But the Great Recession, unpredicted and unforeseen by most macroeconomists, broke that convergence.[148]

The decade of the 2010s was in most countries a protracted period of lukewarm economic growth, a slow recovery from the Great Recession. When the massive turbulences of the Great Recession were far in the rear mirror, it was apparent that the traditional optimism of the economic profession was now damped. Critical voices from the left claimed that the world economy was in a long depression somewhat similar to that of the 1930s.[149] When Donald Trump had been two years in the White House launching commercial wars and boasting to have had the best economy in a very long time, prominent economists started

[146] Robert Lucas declared in 2012 that he had to renounce the view that business cycles are all alike, cited in Kose & Terrones (2015), *Collapse and revival*, 172; authors who favor the view that each recession is a different case: Mankiw (2009), *Principles of macroeconomics*, 5th ed.; Duménil & Lévy (2011), *The crisis of neoliberalism*; Harvey (2010), The crises of capitalism.

[147] Röpke (1936), *Crises and cycles*, ch. IV, §9, contains a strong critique of the notion that "the phenomenon of crises and cycles" is not a general one so that "every crisis and every cycle [is] just an 'historical' event more or less unique in its kind" and therefore "a special theory of crises and cycles" would be pointless, because "nothing useful could be said on crises and cycles in general". Obviously, works like *The business cycle* by Matthews (1959) or *Stabilizing an unstable economy* by Minsky (1986) also looked for general explanations.

[148] Fair (2012), "Has macro progressed?" *Journal of Macroeconomics* 34(1), 2–10.

[149] Roberts (2016), *The Long Depression.*

to see the next recession coming, and quite surprisingly, some of them veered toward considering the merits of protectionist policies.[150] It is now obvious that macroeconomics is a moving ground. Once the COVID-19 pandemic started and the economic crisis triggered by the antipandemic lockdown policies started in the spring of 2020, Paul Krugman was not shy to explain how since 2007 many negative things had been learned about the modern economy. "We've learned that advanced economies are much less stable, much more subject to periodic crises, than almost anyone believed possible."[151]

An Outline of a Causal Model

The experience of more than two centuries of business cycles provides very convincing evidence that the market economy is prone to economic crises, or recessions in modern parlance. These crises are far from being the small nuisances that some mainstream economists have pretended they are. The period of mild recessions in the quarter century after the Second World War was the exception rather than the rule. Economic crises are unequivocally periods in which markets are flooded with unsellable products, which is in clear contradiction with Say's law. That many, probably most in the economic discipline continue asserting that that "law" is a principle of economic science, and that mainstream economics continue mostly ignoring the obvious reality of the instability of our economic system, reveals an antiempirical attitude of the discipline and supports the view that economics is far from being a science.

Statistical data leave no doubt that fluctuations in investment are the main contributor to economic disarray during crises, while analyses going back to Sismondi, Marx, Juglar, Mitchell, and Tinbergen have repeatedly shown the influence of profits as a key determinant of the fluctuations of investment along the business cycle. More than a century ago Mitchell described and provided statistical data on the decline of enterprise earnings, which he described as the encroachment of profits by costs, as a

[150] Hirsh (2019), "Economists on the run—Paul Krugman and other mainstream trade experts are now admitting that they were wrong about globalization", *Foreign Policy*, October 22; Krugman (2019), "What economists (including me) got wrong about globalization", *Bloomberg Opinion*, October 10.

[151] Krugman (2020), "Crashing economy, rising stocks: What's going on? What's bad for America is sometimes good for the market", *New York Times*, April 30.

late-prosperity phenomenon leading to recession. However, Tinbergen was the first who used statistical procedures to show more formally a relation between profits and investment that could be conceptualized as a causal effect. Because it has strong support in empirical data, this view, the macroeconomic centrality of profits, was sustained for some time in mainstream economics by Wesley Mitchell, A. F. Burns, and other authors, but soon disappeared of the discipline.[152] The notion that profits are the key determinant of the condition of prosperity or depression of the economy looks as a seditious idea that was fully dismissed from economics by John Maynard Keynes and Milton Friedman in the 1940s and since that time has been repeatedly ignored. Most post-Keynesian authors who disagree with major tenets of neoclassical economics also reject the view that profits are the key determinant of macroeconomic conditions, and claim that it is not profits but investment the variable that "calls the tune".[153] Thus, they claim it is in investment and financial disturbances where the root of economic troubles needs to be looked for.

The role of profitability as determinant of investment shown by Tinbergen in 1939 has been repeatedly replicated in recent decades by other authors.[154] Several investigators concluded in recent years that the United States is a profit-led economy,[155] which amounts more or less to

[152] Burns (1954), *The frontiers of economic knowledge*; Hultgren (1965), *Cost, prices, and profits—Their cyclical relations*.

[153] Minsky (2008), *Stabilizing an unstable economy*.

[154] Weisskopf (1979), "Marxian crisis theory and the rate of profit in the postwar US economy", *Cambridge Journal of Economics* 3 (4), 341–378; Bhaskar & Glyn (1995), "Expectations and investment: an econometric defense of animal spirits", in Epstein & Gintis, eds., *Macroeconomic policy after the conservative era*, 197–223; Blanchard, Rhee & Summers (1993), "The stock market, profit, and investment", *Quarterly Journal of Economics* 108(1), 115–136. Trofimov (2017), "Profit rates in developed capitalist economies: A time series investigation", *PSL Quarterly Review* 70(280), 85–128; Trofimov (2022), "Determinants of the profit rates in the OECD economies: A panel data analysis of the Kalecki's profit equation", *Structural Change and Economic Dynamics* 61, 380–397.

[155] Barbosa-Filho & Taylor (2006), "Distributive and demand cycles in the US economy: A structuralist Goodwin model", *Metroeconomica* 57(3), 389–411; Rada & Taylor (2006), "Empty sources of growth accounting, and empirical replacements à la Kaldor with some beef", *Structural Change & Economic Dynamics* 17(4), 487–500; Mohun & Veneziani (2008), "Goodwin cycles and the US economy, 1948–2004", in Flaschel & Landesmann, eds., *Mathematical economics and the dynamics of capitalism: Godwin's legacy continued*, 107–130.

the same. This evidence is consistent with the results I have presented elsewhere based on analyses of annual and quarterly data for the period 1947–2015. Data from 275 quarters of the US economy classified into 225 expansion quarters and 50 recession quarters show the following:

(i) during expansion quarters, on average, profits grow faster than wages;
(ii) during recessions quarters, profits drop much faster than wages;
(iii) investment grows in expansion quarters at twice the rate it falls in recession quarters;
(iv) sorting the expansion quarters by its proximity to the end of the expansion shows that several quarters before the end of the expansion, profits stagnate and then fall;
(v) a few quarters after the start of the recession, profits stop declining and start rising;
(vi) investment grows in all expansion quarters, from the trough to the peak, and declines in all recession quarters, from the peak to the trough.

In regression analysis of similar data of 275 quarters of the US economy, with rates of growth of profits and investment and the present value of one variable modeled as a function of the present and lagged values of the other variable, the present and lagged values of the growth of profits before taxes explains close to half of the variation of the growth of investment, with the effect being *positive* and statistically significant in both quarterly and annual data analyses. In the other potential direction of causation, present and past values of investment explain about less than a third of the variation of present profits, with lagged values of investment having a *negative* effect which is statistically significant in the annual but not in the quarterly analysis.

I interpret these results as confirmatory of early views by Mitchell and Tinbergen in the sense that profits are a key element to determine investment and thus macroeconomic conditions of boom or bust. I propose a causal endogenous scheme of the business cycle in which profits and investment are linked in a kind of predator–prey model. Movements in profits are followed some quarters later by movements in investment in the same direction, and movements in investment are followed by movements in profits in the opposite direction.[156] Crises are preceded by drops in profitability. This can be illustrated by the changes of profitability and investment in the US economy before and during the recession of the turn of the century and the Great Recession. As shown in Table 6.1, profitability that had been rising since the mid-1990s dropped in 2000 and again in 2001 and investment followed with a lag of about a year, stagnating in 2001 and significantly declining in 2002 (the NBER dates the US recession as lasting from the first to the fourth quarter of 2001). With profits rising again from 2002 and investment since 2003, the US economy accelerated toward the Great Recession but already in 2004 profitability started declining and this time investment kept growing for three more years until it stagnated in 2007 and dropped from 2.61 trillion in 2007 to 2.05 trillion in 2009 (according to the NBER chronology the Great Recession in the United States lasted from the last quarter of 2007 to the second quarter of 2009).

Explanations of recessions as caused by lack of purchasing power due to a declining share of labor in national income—often proposed by radical economists in recent years—do not match the statistical evidence. Consumption, as well as labor income (wages and salaries), had been increasing before the recessions of 2001 and 2008 and both variables have a stable rate of growth through the business cycle. The steady growth of consumption is nor consistent with a causal role in downturns that appear quite suddenly. Something constant or changing slowly cannot explain a sudden change unless triggering mechanisms are invoked or specifically proposed. The existence of mechanisms of that type goes against the principle of parsimony, or Occam's razor.

Statistical data and models reveal the key role of profits in the business cycle, but equally important is the fact that everything else—except the fantastic microeconomic models of mainstream economics in which profits are zero in equilibrium—indicates the importance of profits as engine and motive of behavior in our monetary economy. As Wesley Mitchell wrote more than a century ago, in our money economy resources are not used, equipment is not employed, and industrial skills are not exercised, "unless conditions are such as to promise a money profit to

[156] The most updated evidence in favor of this model is in my book *Rentabilidad, inversión y crisis* (2017). Most of that evidence is also in my article "Does investment call the tune?", *Research in Political Economy* (2013), 28, 229–259.

Table 6.1 Estimates of profitability and investment in the US economy, 1995–2015. Numbers in **boldface** indicate a decrease with respect to the former year

Year	*Profit rate (%)*	*Investment*
1995	12.2	1.28
1996	12.8	1.40
1997	13.0	1.52
1998	**12.5**	1.66
1999	12.5	1.81
2000	**11.8**	1.96
2001	**11.4**	**1.95**
2002	12.0	**1.89**
2003	12.6	1.99
2004	**12.5**	2.19
2005	**12.4**	2.45
2006	**12.0**	2.61
2007	**11.4**	2.61
2008	**10.5**	**2.49**
2009	10.8	**2.05**
2010	11.6	2.10
2011	**11.4**	2.28
2012	11.7	2.53
2013	11.7	2.70
2014	11.7	2.94
2015	11.9	3.06

Author's computation from the database of the US Bureau of Economic Analysis (BEA). Profit rate estimated following Maito's method (in his chapter in Carchedi and Roberts' *World in Crisis*, 2018) as net operating surplus—estimated as GDP (BEA Table 1.1.5, line 1) minus compensation of employees (Tables 6.2.A and 6.2.B, line 1), net taxes on production (Tables 3.5 and 3.13, line 1), and consumption of fixed capital (Table 1.3, lines 4–10)—divided by fixed reproductive capital (Table 1.1, lines 5–6 and 11–12). Private investment in fixed assets, trillion dollars (From BEA Table 1.5, line 3)

those who direct production".[157] Indeed, to avoid getting lost in a maze of complications when analyzing business cycles "it is necessary to follow constantly the chief clue to business transactions" which is profit. Because every business establishment "is supposed to aim primarily at making money. When the prospects of profits improve, business becomes more

[157] Mitchel (1913), *Business cycles*, 21–22.

active. When these prospects grow darker, business becomes dull."[158] Half a century earlier than Mitchell, Marx had written that profit is "the driving *agency* in capitalist production, and only those things are produced which can be produced at a profit, and they are produced to the extent to which they can be produced at a profit."[159] The pandemic of 2020 has revealed in a surprising way how important is this idea to understand our social reality.

Statistical models also provide evidence—though in my analyses it looked as a weaker one—of another regularity between profits and investment, but this one in the direction from past investment to present profits, with the change in investment showing a *negative* lagged effect on the change in profits—so that a change in investment is generally followed by a change in profits in the opposite direction.[160] This negative association is at odds with the positive link between investment and profits that Keynes, Kalecky, Mathews, Minsky and the Keynesians in general have proposed.[161] The Keynesian view of exogeneity of investment, with "animal spirits" being the prime mover of the economy, does not fit with the evidence that investment follows profits in the same direction but profits follow investment in the opposite direction. Profit squeeze, underconsumption, and animal spirits as determinant of investment are causal explanations commonly proposed for business cycles in general and crises in particular. However, the results of regression models, the leads and lags of profits and investment apparent in the quarterly data of the US economy in past decades, and the fact that profits are more volatile than investment, and investment is more volatile than wages, are inconsistent with such causal explanations.

[158] Mitchel (1923), Chapter 1—Business cycles, in *Business cycles and unemployment*, ed. by the Committee of the President's Conference on Unemployment, and a Special Staff of the NBER, 6.

[159] Economic manuscript of 1861–63, in *MECW* 33, 112.

[160] See an enlightening illustration of this mechanism in the Japanese economy in the chapter by Sato (2018), "Japan "lost" two decades", in Carchedi & Roberts, eds., *World in Crisis*, 157–182.

[161] For more details on the relation between "animal spirits", investment and the so-called marginal efficiency of capital, see the sections on Keynes, Kalecky, and the Keynesians in Tapia (2013), "Does investment call the tune?, *Research in Political Economy* 28, 229–259.

Significant hoards of money pile up during recessions.[162] On the other hand, macroeconomists are aware that "money leads" economic growth. That is, statistical data ordered for instance in an annual series show that the mass of money as defined in specific ways tends to start rising immediately before investment and consumption start growing during the expansion phase of the business cycle. That was the regularity observed in US data that Milton Friedman used as foundation stone for monetarism, as a theory of the business cycle in which money is the key explanatory factor. But as Steve Keen has eloquently explained, monetarism ignores that money is created by banking activity dependent on the demand of the business sector and in that sense is fully endogenous to the economy.[163] As it was observed already in the 1930s by Tinbergen, credit advances to businesses to finance production reach a peak early in each business cycle, but in later phases of the cycle, they are replaced by capital issues. "Neither increase in advances nor issues shows a high correlation with business activity, but their sum does."[164] Thus the conversion of money hoards into investment that expects to yield a revenue as well as the endogenous creation of money by bank credit are key elements of the period of recovery following immediately the slump. The expansion of the money mass early in the recovery also explains the significant and repeatedly observed leads of the money series with respect to business activity that was claimed by Milton Friedman as probably indicative of causal effects.[165]

In the nineteenth century Sismondi, Marx, and Juglar insisted in the role of debt as a key element in the economic processes that recurrently trigger economic crises. During the 1930s Irving Fisher arrived to similar ideas after his disastrous dealing with the Great Depression—but he acknowledged that his views had had precedent in Thorstein Veblen

162 Wilson (2011), "Sales of safes boom as the economy falters: Looking for security in a cube of steel", *New York Times* March 6; Dash & Schwartz (2011), "In cautious times, banks flooded with cash", *New York Times* Oct. 28, A1.

163 Keen (2001), *Debunking economics*, 306–314.

164 Tinbergen (1935), "Suggestions on quantitative business cycle theory", *Econometrica* 3(3), 241–308.

165 According to Milton Friedman data support that "a 1% change in the rate of expansion of the quantity of money tends to produce, on the average, a 2% change in the rate of growth of nominal income"; in Friedman & Heller (1968), *Monetary vs. fiscal policy—A dialogue*, 76.

and Wesley Mitchel.[166] Mainstream economics has paid little attention to these views. Before the Great Depression, modern macroeconomics mostly ignored the effects of private debt, despite evidence that the accumulation of debt by business firms and households has had a major role in each economic crisis. The patterns of growth of credit to households and nonfinancial firms in national economies (Figs. 3.1–3.5, pages 60–64) are strongly suggestive of a key role of debt accumulation in the causation of crisis.[167] Private debt accumulated in many countries in the years before the Great Recession. In Thailand, Malaysia, and Korea a steady buildup of debt reached a peak at the time of the so-called Asian crisis of the late 1990s which in the perspective of this book is a component of the global economic crisis of the turn of the century. In Japan, private debt accumulated steadily since 1974 to 1990, had a two-year plateau and then continued growing until a peak in 1994, from which it declined steadily until 2007. Overall, the Japanese experience suggests that the debt expansion from 1974 to the 1990s was a factor sustaining GDP growth; indeed, when the private nonfinancial debt to GDP ratio declined in 1992 and 1993, GDP growth dropped respectively to 0.8% and −0.5%. At the national level the accumulation of private debt often leads to the crisis and then reverts, as it happened in 1998 in Korea, Malaysia, and Thailand or in Spain, Ireland, or Greece in the Great Recession, or in Brazil in 2015. Other factors must also be at play because, for example, debt peaked in Brazil in 2002 but there was not a recession at the time, and in Chile a recession in 1999 did not interrupt the growth in private debt that continued until 2002. Some preliminary data for debt at the level of the world economy are consistent with the notion that debt growth is an important contributor to economic growth. The average annual rate of credit growth during 1975, 1982, 1991, and 2009—considered years of global recession—has been estimated to be about two-fifths of the annual average observed in non-recession years of the period 1950–2019.[168] Figure 6.1 shows the annual rate of growth of credit to the private sector by banks in the global economy, and the annual

[166] Fisher (1933), "The debt-deflation theory of great depressions", *Econometrica* 1, 337–356.

[167] An isolated voice from the financial industry supporting this claim is Vague (2014), *The next economic disaster*.

[168] Kose, Sugawara & Terrones (2020), "Global recessions", Centre for Applied Macroeconomic Analysis, Australian National University, CAMA Working Paper 10/2020.

growth of WGDP. The two series follow each other quite closely, which clearly suggests the procyclical character of private debt which builds up in expansions and shrinks during crises. Indeed, there are significant drops in the rate of growth of private debt *before* the crises. Figure 6.2 shows how the rate of growth of private debt dropped substantially, even to zero or negative values, before the crises starting in 1975, 1980, 1991, 2001, and 2008. It was growing, though, immediately before 2020, which suggests a different nature of that crisis, clearly connected with the COVID-19 pandemic.

Two important studies of the associations of financial distress, usually connected with credit booms, and recessions in national economies, provide substantial evidence of the links between the crises of the world economy as dated in this book and periods of financial distress. Almost without exception, the 243 half-year episodes of financial distress identified in the OECD countries by Romer and Romer between 1967 and 2012 coincide with the crises of the world economy as dated in this book.[169] Romer and Romer conclude that in advanced economies

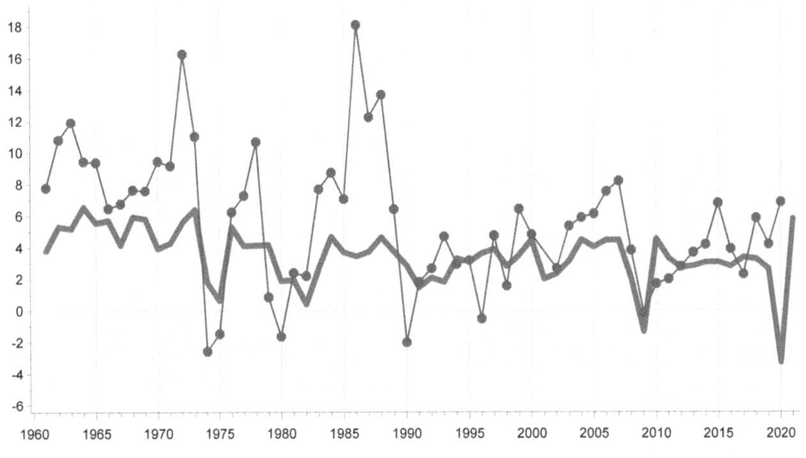

Fig. 6.1 WGDP (thick line) and domestic credit to the private sector by banks in the world economy (dots), both as annual rates of growth. (Author's elaboration from WDI data.)

[169] Romer & Romer (2017), "New evidence on the aftermath of financial crises in advanced countries", *American Economic Review* 107(10): 3072–3118, Table I.

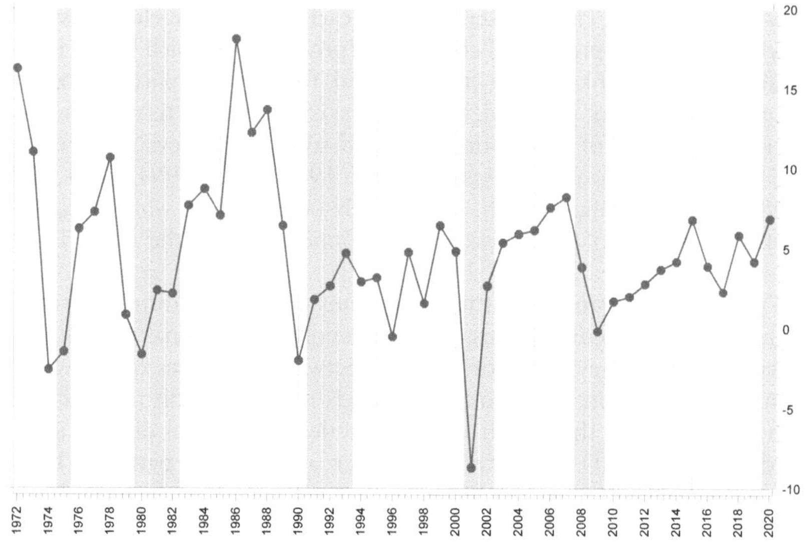

Fig. 6.2 Annual growth of domestic credit to the private sector by banks, and crises as determined by an annual decline in gross capital formation (gray bars). (Author's elaboration from WDI data for the world economy.)

business activity declines significantly after financial distress, with highly persistent effects as measured by real GDP or unemployment. Using a panel of 14 advanced economies in the years 1870–2008 containing 1272 annual observations (about 91 observations per country) Schularick and Taylor found solid evidence on the procyclicality of the financial system and the frequent evolution of credit booms into episodes of financial crisis.[170] They model the risk of financial crises using linear probability and logit models, including as regressors the change in level of credit (total bank loans deflated by the CPI) in each of the former five years. In models including fixed effects for country and year, the year fixed effects are highly statistically significant, which obviously means "that there is a common global time component driving financial crises", which "is not too surprising given the consensus view that financial crises have tended to happen in waves and often afflict multiple countries". These waves are

[170] Schularick & Taylor (2012), "Credit booms gone bust: Monetary policy, leverage cycles, and financial crises, 1870–2008", *American Economic Review* 102(2), 1029–1061.

indeed the crises of the world economy. The models of Schularick and Taylor also show that the increase in the level of credit raises the probability of crises even when fixed effects for country and year are included in the model, which is clearly suggestive of a causal effect of the increase in debt on the emergence of financial crisis. For Schularick and Taylor their historical analysis lend support to the ideas of Minsky and Kindleberger, scholars who argued "that the financial system itself is prone to generate economic instability through endogenous credit booms."

For Steve Keen aggregate demand equals income plus the change in debt, which seems an important contribution to the understanding of macroeconomic issues.[171] The role of debt accumulation in the causation of crisis is granted, but more complex models including hoarding, debt—both private and public—and profit are needed to better understand how these variables interact to trigger the crisis.[172]

Economists and non-economists presently writing on issues related with economic crises and the way to deal with them have multiple views on what causes recessions and expansions. The question of economic crises is the key economic issue, but mainstream economics is built on principles that deny the reality of crises as violent phenomena affecting the economy and markets at large, and allow just for minor fluctuations of particular markets. Many economists are not concerned at all about general macroeconomic issues and have no view on them. The causal outline proposed here is based on the theoretical insights of many authors, put together with a statistical analysis of US data, the consideration of national experiences in recent decades and a parsimonious view of the relations between the major variables involved in the business cycle. It does not include any of the major preconceptions of Say's law or the microfoundations based on methodological individualism that plagues the

[171] Keen (2014), "Secular stagnation and endogenous money", *Real-World Economics Review* 66. See also my comment on Keen, "Money and Say's law—On the macroeconomic models of Kalecki, Keen, and Marx", *Real-World Economics Review* 70, 2015.

[172] See a comprehensive review of opposing views on the role of debt in macroeconomics in the chapter by Michael Roberts (2017) on "Debt matters" in Carchedi & Roberts, eds., *World in crisis*, 197–217. For opposing views on the importance of the federal debt in the editorial pages of *The New York Times*, see Krugman, "Learn to stop worrying and love debt" (December 4, 2020), and "Does America have too much debt?" (Jan 4, 2023), and Appelbaum, "America has a debt problem, and the answer to it starts with Form 1040" (Jan 25, 2023).

business-cycle models of mainstream economics.[173] As causal core of that model, I propose a bidirectional relation between profits and investment, with both effects having different signs. This bidirectional model is consistent with the fact that there are oscillations of both variables. A link between investment and profits with positive effects in both directions as proposed by many Keynesians would imply a circle of positive feedbacks and absolute instability, leading to explosive growth of both variables. The bidirectional causation scheme provides long-run stability to the growth of the economy, though it is just a relative stability at the cost of recurrent periods of economic disarray in which, after a drop in profits, a drop in investment restarts the growth of profits. Thus, crises appear quite as Juglar and Marx saw them, as temporary circumstances restoring, for a while, the normal conditions for the accumulation of capital, which, in turn, will lead to another crisis. Rising debt and mobilization of hoards of money enhance demand and profitability during expansions, the break of chains of debt obligations triggers financial disarray at the end of the boom and the quick increase of unemployment during the crisis reduces wages and favors the deterioration of work conditions, thus facilitating the increase in the rate of exploitation, a higher profitability of business enterprises, and a return to expansion conditions.

Cycles and Tendencies

Richard Goodwin proposed a scheme of the business cycle in which employment and wages are the two variables that follow a predator–prey model. In Goodwin's model a high level of wages and employment leads to low profits, falling investment, falling growth of output, and falling employment; this in turn leads to a drop in the bargaining power of workers, stagnant or falling wages, rising profits and an increase in investment and output which raises the bargaining power of workers leading to high wages and making the cycle to restart.[174] Though the model has

[173] In a methodologically complicated but in many aspects well-argued essay examining *Causality in Macroeconomics*, Kevin D. Hoover (2001) has rejected the idea that microfoundations need to be part of sound macroeconomic models. The attempt by John Hicks (1979) to discuss the general issues of *Causality in Economics* was in my view a very poor one. For more modern and quite sound attempts to deal with causality in science, key authors are Mario Bunge (2011) and Judea Pearl (Pearl & Mackenzie 2019).

[174] Goodwin (1967), "A growth cycle", in Feinstein, ed., *Socialism, capitalism and economic growth*, 54–59.

many things to be commended as it is based on actual mechanisms at work in the business cycle, in essence, it is a profit-squeeze model in which the key element triggering the downturn is the reduction of profits because wages are too high. But statistical data show profits grow much faster than wages in the early expansion and then stagnate and decline before the recession, while wages grow at a roughly constant rate all throughout the cycle. In this aspect, Goodwin's model fits poorly the data.[175]

Goodwin was one of the early critics of Tinbergen's view, based on statistical results, that profits are the key determinant of investment: "if we reverse the direction of causality and say that investment determines profits through the multiplier and income, we rob one of Tinbergen's chief results of much of its significance." For Goodwin this could be done because in business cycles "most things go up and down together, and hence the danger of spurious correlation is very great"[176] Goodwin's critical comments against Tinbergen are based on faulty reasoning, as spurious correlations take place when series trend up together or trend down together, or trend in opposite directions—not when they oscillate following each other or mirroring each other repeatedly. Certainly, as Goodwin said, many things swing up and down "together" in the business cycle but observed lags and statistical analysis can be exploited to provide evidence on whether specific signs of parameter estimates and particular directions of causation have or have not empirical support. Against Goodwin and in support of Tinbergen, the statistical evidence is in favor of a model in which changes in profitability lead and *cause* changes in investment—not the other way around.

Both mainstream economists and radical authors often maintain that different economic crises have different causes, and that it is therefore nonsensical to look for common patterns or common explanations. As previously noted in this book, in pure or applied science it is a well-accepted principle that when studying the causes that determine a phenomenon that occurs repeatedly, rather than looking for the particularities that always exist in a specific case or a particular experiment, the proper strategy is to examine multiple occurrences of the phenomenon

[175] To my knowledge, Goodwin never tried to test his model with actual data.

[176] Goodwin (1964), "Econometrics in business-cycle analysis", in Hansen, *Business cycles and national income*, 433.

and from that multiplicity to try to grasp its essential features and determinants. But in present-day economics, to look for common patterns of economic crises is rather a rarity. Interestingly, the tendency to think that each crisis is different coexists in economics with an ahistorical approach that assumes that business cycles have existed forever, so that any kind of economic disturbance, even one that happened many centuries ago, is to be included when the purpose is to study economic crises.[177]

Empirical data and analyses by a variety of authors show that profits decrease before crises and this decrease is followed by a decrease in investment, which is the key component of the decline in economic activity that constitutes the recession. In all aspects of knowledge, a description poses the question of why things are that way, which often leads to further unanswered questions. That bodies are attracted between them because of the force of gravity is just a description, and if we ask why bodies attract each other—why gravity exists—present-day physics will have no answer for us.

However, in the nineteenth century the most important authors dealing with economic issues, Adam Smith, David Ricardo, John Stuart Mill, and Karl Marx, were all convinced that profitability tends to decline with the pass of time, and they also tried to answer the question of why it would be so. For Smith and Ricardo, the theory of general overproduction "was a heresy" but

> maladjusted production they allowed to be possible, and their theories of crises usually sought to show how maladjustment comes about through the sinking of capital in unremunerative investments. Such lockingup of capital was often held to be one result of 'the tendency of profits to a minimum.' When this tendency has reduced the current rate of profits to an unaccustomed level, the less sagacious capitalists become dissatisfied and embark in ill-considered schemes. There results the production of goods for which no market can be found, business failures, and the loss of confidence—in short, a crisis which extends over all lines of trade.[178]

[177] In *This time is different* Reinhart & Rogoff (2009) analyzed eight centuries "of financial folly" as if credit, markets, capital, and financial crises had been mostly the same since the time of the Crusades. Contrarily, more than a century ago, Mitchell emphasized that business cycles with all the industrial disarray, commercial muddle, and financial crisis they imply are a characteristic of modern industrial economies in which money plays a key role—that is capitalism in today's parlance. See Mitchell (1913), *Business cycles*, 583–586.

[178] Mitchell (1913), *Business cycles*, 4.

Given the scarcity of economic statistics at the time of Smith, Ricardo, Mill, and Marx, we can wonder why these authors were so convinced that profits tend "to a minimum"? Perhaps they had surmised a falling trend from the observations of manufacturers, merchants, and financiers—of which Ricardo was one himself? For Smith it was the competition between different capitals that led to decreasing profits. For Ricardo, the tendency of profits was to decrease because of the increase in wages and rents.[179] With total income composed by profits gained by capitalists, rents paid to landlords and wages earned by workers, decreasing availability of proper land for cultivation and rising population would raise rents and food prices, forcing the rise of wages and the subsequent decline of the profit share in the national income and in the proportion to the total of capital or "stock". Thus, the profit rate would fall. That was Ricardo's view.

Many decades of statistics on price of food have demonstrated that Ricardo's explanation of falling profitability does not make sense, as food has tendentially cheapened. Furthermore, there are many reasons to think the proper partition of national income is no longer a three-part division between profit, rent, and wages, as landlords as a class have not today an independent existence. With national income divided between labor income and capital income, since the mid-twentieth century the share of labor in national income has rather declined wherever data are available.[180] So, why profitability tend to decline? Very wisely Ricardo noticed that with an increasing accumulation of capital a declining rate of profit would be associated for a while with increasing total profit, though *eventually* this would cease, and total profit would fall.[181]

Economic statistics show a decline of both total profits and the rate of profit immediately before crises, coupled with a subsequent drop in investment. Data are much less conclusive "in the long run," as estimates of profit rates show a decline or a rise depending on what is the "long-run" period that is considered (Fig. 6.3). To the present writer, the data available to properly estimate a rate of profit for the global economy are rather poor. Estimates such as the ones by E. E. Maito or Basu et al. (that were cited in Chapter 2) are just preliminary attempts

179 Ricardo (2004) [1817], *On the principles of political economy and taxation*, ch. 6.

180 Piketty (2014), *Capital in the 21st century.*

181 Ricardo, *Principles*, ch. 6.

that, however, suggest a long-run decline for the period with data available. The fact that the rate of economic growth is generally lower in more capitalistically advanced economies and has been secularly declining in the advanced economies themselves can be also interpreted as an indication of a long-term falling tendency in the rate of profit.[182]

In manuscripts that he never tried to publish, Marx referred to "the law of the tendential fall in the general rate of profit with the advance in capitalist production" and judged it as the most important law of political economy. But, is that "law" properly argued by Marx? Is it consistent with the economic reality of the past two centuries? Marxists and radical economists have been arguing about it for decades but a detailed discussion of these controversies is beyond the scope of this chapter.[183]

What national accounts show is that profits increase in the late phases of the recession and then continue rising during expansions, but they decrease at the end of the expansion. This is also the evolution of the profit rate during each cycle. Can these changes and particularly the drop

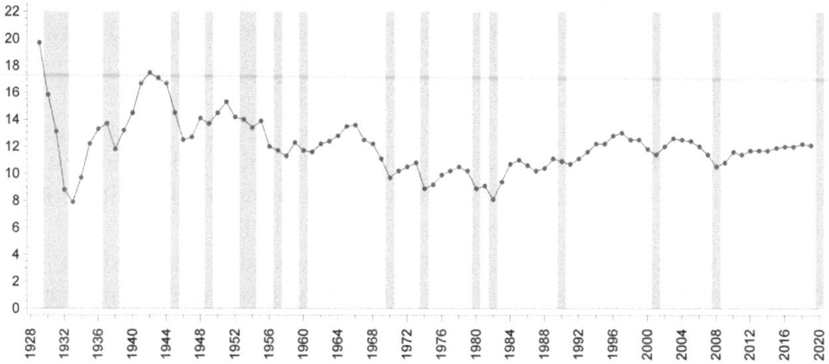

Fig. 6.3 An estimate of the profit rate in the US economy, 1929 to 2020. Gray bars are recession periods according to the NBER chronology. (Author elaboration from the same data sources in Table 6.1)

[182] In *Shaping the World Economy* (1962, ch. 2) Tinbergen shows some data on rates of return on capital in different countries and times that are suggestive of these patterns. In the view of Michio Morishima, in *Marx's Economics* (1973), the rate of growth of GDP—which has tendentially declined wherever data are available—can be interpreted as a proxy for the rate of profit.

[183] See Appendix D.

of profits in the late phase of the expansion be interpreted as manifestations of the tendency of the profit rate to fall? The answer to that question is unclear, as in the way Marx presented his "law" the tendency is a consequence not of the fall in profits but of the rise in the ratio of constant capital to variable capital and this ratio is obviously a variable that changes slowly. The most likely explanation for the decrease in profits observed in the late phases of the expansion is a problem of realization of profits, that is, specific firms that have been selling increasing output during the expansion suddenly notice that they can no longer sell their whole expanded output. That forces to sell at prices that yield a lower profit margin or no margin at all and that manifests itself in national accounts as a decline in profits. Smith, Ricardo, Mills, and Marx agreed on the notion of a tendency of profitability to decline with the advance of capitalist production, but disagreed on the explanation of the phenomenon. Presently, most economists tend to ignore the role of profits both in the macroeconomic fluctuations and in the general long-term trends of the economy, and authors working in the Marxian tradition are largely divided in their views on how to measure the corresponding concepts or even if these concepts can be measured at all. This is obviously a major obstacle for the advancement of knowledge, and evidence indicates that economic theory, whatever its kind, is far from being scientific theory.

Concluding Remarks

Present-day economics reveals an astonishing dispersion of views and agnostic stances on the causes of recession in national economies, thus agnosticism and theoretical chaos will be even worse if the question is about the causes of world economic crises. Those who dare to propose causes of crisis in national economies refer to "oil shocks" because of cartel actions, wars and revolutions, ill-advised actions of governments or central bankers, idiosyncratic events impacting big firms and propagating through networks, or other undefined "shocks" which perhaps generate economic uncertainty.[184]

[184] Hamilton (2009), "Causes and consequences of the oil shock of 2007–08", *Brookings Papers on Economic Activity*, Spring, 215–267; Hamilton (2011), "Historical oil shocks" NBER Working Paper 16790; Schwartz (2010), "Origins of the financial market crisis of 2008", and Butler (2010), "The financial crisis: Blame governments, not bankers", both chapters in Booth, ed., *Verdict on the crash*, 45–50 and 51–59; Gabaix (2011),

The overall result is a situation which from the outside looks as utter conceptual confusion in which, furthermore, a public that asks economists why these things happen and if they can be predicted or prevented, is disappointed by outstanding economists who remain silent or give negative answers. Thus for Edward Leamer, a reputed econometrician, economists' understanding "of causal effects in macroeconomics is virtually nil, and will remain so"[185]; while Eugene Fama and Nicholas Mankiw have the opinions that economists do not know what causes recessions and they cannot be predicted because they do not follow any predictable pattern.[186]

In the view of Ray Fair, macroeconomists have remained mostly looking for internal consistency of their models in their own theoretical paradigm rather than looking for consistency of data and theory.[187] This is also true for many heterodox economists who care little about the empirical data and much more about the consistency of the views of Keynes, Kalecky, Marx, or Minsky. But observing how things work, sorting things and phenomena, and trying to discover patterns of association or evolution are the only ways human beings have to learn by themselves about the real natural or social world. "Theory" is received wisdom produced in the past by others who thought they had learned about patterns in reality, and then invented an explanation of the patterns they thought they had discovered. But these theories are often proved inconsistent with the facts they intend to explain, or can explain only some phenomena but not others that require more general theories. The only attitude that allows for knowledge advancement and rejection of wrong theories is to trust in empirical evidence and to be distrustful about received wisdom. In words of Richard Feynman, a way to define science

"The granular origins of aggregate fluctuations", *Econometrica* 2011 79(3), 733–772; Acemoglu et al. (2012), "The network origins of aggregate fluctuations", *Econometrica* 80(5), 1977–2016; Bloom (2014), "Fluctuations in uncertainty", *Journal of Economic Perspectives* 28(2), 153–176.

[185] Leamer (2010), "Tantalus on the road to asymptopia", *Journal of Economic Perspectives* 24(2), 31–46.

[186] Cassidy (2010), "Interview with Eugene Fama", *New Yorker*, Jan 11; Mankiw (2009), *Principles of macroeconomics*; Mankiw (2010), "Economic view: A call for humility—Trying to tame the unknowable", *New York Times*, March 26, BU6.

[187] Fair (2012), "Has macro progressed?", *Journal of Macroeconomics* 34(1), 2–10.

is to say that it means distrust of experts.[188] Of course, there is a lot of evidence suggesting that in its present stage economic theorizing contains much which is extraneous to science. Economics could be defined, as Steve Keen does, as a pre-science.[189]

To what extent the considerations presented in this chapter about theories on business cycles in national economies can be extended to business cycles of the world economy? The global economy has been rarely an object of investigation or theorizing in economics. But it is probably fair to say that causal theories of the business cycle at the national level can be extended to the world level without much effort. Indeed, I have done it by expanding the view that profitability is the variable leading the boom-and-bust cycle in the world economy, while accumulation of debt and hoarding are also contributing factors with key roles. This is the core of a developing causal outline of a world business cycle based on ideas coming back to Sismondi, Marx, Juglar, Mitchell, Grossman, Schumpeter, Fischer, and Tinbergen. Of course, this has little to do with recent work in mainstream economics that identifies global recessions, in which causality is attributed to oil shocks. This will be discussed more in detail in the next chapter.

[188] Feynman (1998), *The meaning of it all—Thoughts of a citizen scientist*.

[189] Keen (2014), *Debunking economics*, 159.

CHAPTER 7

Nature, Oil, Crises

In a newspaper commentary published when Spain was still dealing with the aftermath of high unemployment and financial troubles of the Great Recession, José Luis Leal, Spain's Minister of Finance during the early 1980s, referred to the economic crises that had occurred during Juan Carlos I reign, which had lasted from 1973 until his abdication in 2014.[1] Leal wrote that Spain had gone through four economic crises, to know, the first and second oil crises of 1973 and 1979, the crisis of 1993, and the worst one, that had started in 2008. This is an example of the chronology often presented for particular countries, which mostly outlines the crises of the world economy posited in this book just ignoring the crisis at the turn of the century. As it is also frequent in the economic literature, the crisis of the mid-1970s and the crisis of the early 1980s are named "oil crises" and implicitly or explicitly attributed to "oil shocks". These "oil shocks" have been often considered in economics as the main explanation for the recessions of recent decades. James Hamilton has been probably

[1] Leal (2014), "Un gran reinado" ["A great reign"], *El País*, June 15, 2014, Negocios, 18.

J. A. Tapia, *Six Crises of the World Economy*,
https://doi.org/10.1007/978-3-031-38735-7_7

the key author in this endeavor.[2] This chapter deals with the validity of these views as well as with other aspects of the relation between nature and economic crises.

Climate Change, the Global Economy, and the *Oikeios* of Jason Moore

Despite many uncertainties, the consensus among geoscientists is that emissions of greenhouse gases are pushing the earth's climate toward severe disturbance because of global warming. What is less known, however, is the evidence showing conclusively that first, economic growth is directly linked to the growth of emissions, and second, that the crises of the world economy proposed here are the only periods in the past half century in which the steady growth in global emissions of CO_2 has slowed down (Fig. 2.8, and Fig. 2.9, pages 26 and 27). Indeed, the same as national economies emit a volume of CO_2 that is highly correlated with economic activity as indexed by GDP, total global emissions of CO_2 are highly correlated with WGDP. Furthermore, at both the national and the world level, the rate of growth of the economy is strongly correlated with the rate of growth of CO_2 emissions.[3] Because CO_2 is produced by almost all economic activities, there is little doubt that these correlations represent causal links.

Authors in the world-system school have provided major insights on these issues. One of them, Jason Moore, has emphasized the need of conceptual language to transcend the misconceptions of the "three supposedly distinctive arenas" conceptualized in science as society, economy, and politics.[4] Following that idea, Jason Moore has proposed

[2] Hamilton (1988), "A neoclassical model of unemployment and the business cycle", *Journal of Political Economy* 96(3), 593–617; Hamilton (2011), "Historical oil shocks", NBER Working Paper 16790. A view from a major oil company in ExxonMobil, "Oil Crises", June 2014.

[3] Both the level of emissions and the rate of growth of atmospheric concentrations of CO_2 are significantly correlated with the rate of growth of the world economy. See Tapia, Ionides & Carpintero (2012), "Climate change and the world economy: Short-run determinants of atmospheric CO_2", *Environmental Science & Policy* 21, 50–62; Tapia & Carpintero (2013), "Dynamics and economic aspects of climate change", in Kang & Banga, eds., *Combating climate change: An agricultural perspective*, 29–58.

[4] Moore (2011), "Ecology, capital, and the nature of our times: Accumulation and crisis in the capitalist world-ecology", *Journal of World-Systems Research* 17(1), 107–146.

to use the term *oikeios,* taken from Theophrastus, to refer to a conceptual unity of nature and society. Indeed, the term *oikeios,* which in Greek is an adjective referring to that which is familiar or homey, brings to consideration the fact that both *economics* and *ecology* have the same Greek root, which is precisely *oikos,* meaning "household" or "home." Both economics and ecology *supposedly* deal with the way things work in "our" home.

Whatever we may think about how heuristically useful can be this *oikeos*, there are some aspects in the consideration of the crises of the world economy that highlight the interest of this concept and the connected frame of thought. Thus, the global slump of the mid-1970s has often been called the Oil Crisis, or the First Oil Crisis, and indeed, as shown in Fig. 7.1, a peak in the world price of oil occurred in 1974. But there were also peaks of oil prices in 1980, 1990, 2000, and 2008, which means that oil prices were rising *in the years immediately before each of the crises of the world economy* posed in this book. Mainstream economics usually blames economic crises on something external to the system, such as governments tinkering with the money supply, regulations, or taxes that strangle business activity or, in the left version, lack of supervision or supervision to prevent speculation and fraud. In the context of real-business-cycle (RBC) theory, unnamed "productivity shocks" are blamed as the determinant of crisis. As it was already mentioned, the econometrician James Hamilton has reported a statistically significant correlation between oil price shocks and recessions in the United States, with nine out of ten recessions in the United States since World War II immediately following a spike in oil prices.[5] Considering that these oil shocks could convincingly be traced to specific exogenous historical events, Hamilton's conclusion was that the evidence "makes it difficult to reject the historical correlation as entirely spurious," meaning that oil price increases might be the shocks that push the economy to recession.[6]

The evidence indicating a correlation between oil price shocks and the five crises of the world economy between the 1970s and the 2010s

[5] Hamilton (2008), "Oil and the macroeconomy", in Durlauf & Blume, eds., *The New Palgrave dictionary of economics*, 2nd ed.; Hamilton (2011), "Historical oil shocks", NBER Working Paper No. 16790.

[6] Hamilton (1988), "A neoclassical model...". See also the interview with Hamilton in Parker, ed. (2007), *The economics of the great depression*, 80–81.

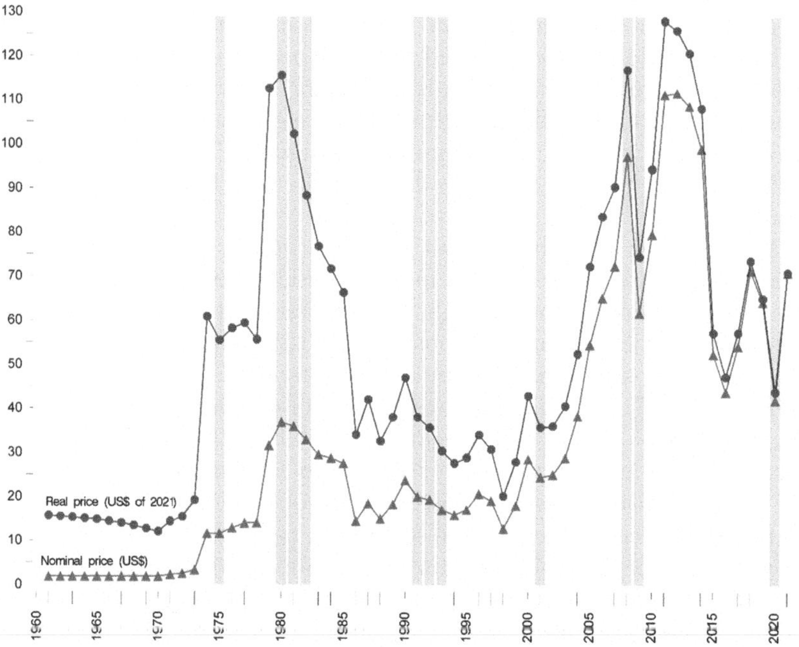

Fig. 7.1 Prices of oil, dollars per barrel in actual dollars (nominal price) and adjusted for inflation (real price, in dollars of 2021), annual means from 1960 to 2021. Gray bars mark the years of world economic crisis as defined by a drop in gross capital formation. (Author's elaboration from data in the WDI database and the BP website, www.bp.com/en/global/corporate/energy-economics/statistical-review-of-world-energy.html, accessed January 2023)

(Fig. 7.1) is solid. Hamilton's basic idea is that non-economic factors—wars, revolutions, or the manipulation of oil markets by cartels for political purposes—constitute shocks that significantly raise oil prices and thus lead to a recession in oil-importing countries. Since most major economies of the world are oil importers, this theory can be easily extended to explain global recessions. Indeed, the view that oil shocks are also responsible for recessions of the global economy was espoused in a publication of the IMF. For its authors, Kose and Terrones, a sharp increase in oil prices drove the global recession of 1975, oil price shocks played significant roles in the global recessions of 1982 and 1991, and in the run up to the global recession of 2009 oil prices "also increased sharply (spiking to

$133 a barrel in July 2008 from $53 in January 2007)."[7] As explained by Kose and Terrones, in considering oil shocks as causes of global downturns they were following ideas that also had been proposed long ago by Olivier Blanchard.[8]

Now, while the correlation between peaks in oil price in international markets and recessions of the global economy is obvious, correlation does not mean causation and there are indeed other explanations that may account for the phenomenon without any implication of causality. Wesley Mitchell explained a century ago that in each period of expansion of capitalism there is a strong increase in the demand for raw materials and energy, raising their prices, which then cease rising and start dropping as soon as the economy stutters, so that demand falls. Among raw materials Mitchell identified minerals—of which oil is one—as the most responsive to economic conditions, so that:

> the crisis of 1907, the depression of 1908, and the revival of 1909, affected the prices of raw materials earlier and more seriously than they affected the prices of manufactured goods. And as between the various classes of raw materials, mineral products record the changes in business conditions more faithfully than any of the other groups.[9]

Half a century before Wesley Mitchell, who was able to back his assertions with statistics, Marx had posed increases of prices of raw materials as an immediate cause of reductions in the general rate of profit. He asserted quite forcefully "the general law that the rate of profit varies inversely with the value of the raw material. This is unconditionally correct, other things being equal, for capital which is newly engaged in a business, and where the investment of capital, the transformation of money into productive capital, takes place for the first time".[10]

Marx saw periods of capital accumulation, business-cycle expansions in the parlance of modern economics, as occasions in which the supply of

[7] Kose & Terrones (2015), *Collapse and revival,* 30, fn. 13, 44–47.

[8] Blanchard (2001), "Close encounters with recessions of the third kind", *Project Syndicate,* March 12.

[9] Mitchell (1913), *Business cycles,* 109.

[10] Marx (2017), *Economic manuscript of 1864–1865* (ed. by F. Moseley), 215. A different translation but with identical meaning in Marx [1894] (1981), *Capital, Volume 3, edited by F. Engels,* 206.

raw materials is often insufficient to meet the rising demand. The more capitalist production is developed, and the more rapid is the process of accumulation in times of prosperity, the greater is the relative overproduction of machinery and other elements of fixed capital, and the more frequent is the relative under-production of raw materials, with the consequent rise of their prices. Marx referred this mostly to raw materials of vegetal or animal origin because they were subject to the influence of climate, long periods of production, or both.[11] However, in the present century the idea is clearly applicable to crude oil, which being the major source of energy becomes increasingly demanded and expensive in each global expansion. Whether or not we are at present in a scenario of peak oil—meaning a situation when the maximum rate of worldwide oil extraction is reached, after which production would begin an irreversible decline—the peaks of oil price preceding the crises of the world economy in the mid-1970s, the early years of the three next decades and 2008 suggest a mechanism in which increasing prices of raw materials, particularly oil, may have contributed to trigger the crises.

A German economist, Martin Stuermer, has analyzed a data set of annual prices and production levels of copper, lead, tin, zinc, and crude oil from 1840 to 2010, finding that price fluctuations of these commodities are primarily driven by demand rather than supply.[12] Stuermer shows that price surges caused by rapid industrialization are a recurrent phenomenon throughout history. Price fluctuations of these mineral commodities were primarily driven by changes in demand rather than by changes in supply. The rise of China as industrial superpower and its effect on prices in recent decades would be a historical phenomenon not very different from industrialization in Britain, the United States, and Japan, which had similar effects on mineral prices in former times. In a similar direction, other authors had found that fluctuations in the price of oil are driven mainly by changes in global demand, rather than being exogenous to the economy, determined by maneuvers of the producer nations, or political events like wars and revolutions. Thus, Robert Barsky and Lutz Kilian have argued

[11] Marx [1894] (1981), *Capital, Volume 3, edited by F. Engels*, Ch. 6, particularly, 214. There is a translation error: it says "overproduction of plant and animal raw materials" when it should say underproduction; see the correct translation in Marx (2017), *Economic manuscript of 1864–1865* (ed. by F. Moseley), 227.

[12] Stuermer (2018), "150 years of boom and bust: What drives mineral commodity prices?", *Macroeconomic Dynamics* 22(3), 702–717.

that variations in oil prices are to a large extent endogenously determined by the demand for oil in international markets; the world economy itself would be only moderately responsive to changes in oil price.[13]

Stuermer data show that peaks in the prices of mineral commodities generally precede downturns of the world economy; these downturns in turn lead to declines of mineral prices. Thus, the recessions of the mid-1970s and the early 1980s caused large declines in demand of tin with subsequent drops in tin prices. Stuermer's graphs show peaks of tin prices in 1974, 1979, 1985, 1989, 2000, 2004, and 2008, that is, a peak coincides or immediately precedes each of the crises of the world economy proposed in this book. But Stuermer says something similar about other minerals. Copper had price peaks in 1974, 1976, 1979, 1989, 2000, and 2006, with the mid-1970s recession causing a strong decline in demand, which led to a serious decline in copper price in 1975. The price of zinc peaked in 1974, 1981, 1984, 1989, 1997, 2000, and 2006. Lead prices peaked in 1974, 1977, 1979, had a plateau in the late 1980s, and peaked again in 2007, immediately before the Great Recession. All this suggests that rising mineral prices due to soaring demand during expansions of the world economy somewhat contributes to trigger the downturn, which in turn, by severely cutting demand, pushes prices down. Overall, price increases of raw materials, particularly minerals and specifically crude oil look much more plausibly endogenous results of the expansion of a world economy in which the supply of natural resources cannot increase at the same rate that demand rises in the booming economy.

Jason Moore has explained how, historically, the transitions from peat and charcoal to coal, and from coal to oil, were major technological revolutions that initiated periods of accelerated accumulation in the history of global capitalism, since cheap energy "powerfully checks the falling rate of profit."[14] Conversely, expensive mineral prices, including oil, reduce profitability and increase the probability of crisis, as clearly illustrated by what happened in the early 1970s, late 1980s, late 1990s, and in the years immediately before the Great Recession.

[13] Barsky and Kilian (2004), "Oil and the macroeconomy since the 1970s", *Journal of Economic Perspectives* 18(4): 115–34; Kilian (2009), "Not all oil price shocks are alike: Disentangling demand and supply shocks in the crude oil market", *American Economic Review* 99(3): 1053–1069.

[14] Moore (2011), "Ecology, capital, and the nature of our times: Accumulation and crisis in the capitalist world-ecology", *Journal of World-Systems Research* 17(1), 107–146.

Peak Oil

The notion of peak oil is maintained by authors who claim that we have reached a point of stagnant or declining supply of oil. Considering the key role of oil and fossil fuels in general as sources of energy in the present economy, the stagnant or even declining supply of oil will create a major constrain for the expansion of the economy, so that economic growth "as we have known it is over and done with".[15] This is not the place to discuss controversies on peak oil which often go into the technicalities of what is or is not oil. Detractors of the peak oil thesis argue that the combustible ethanol for engines that can be produced from harvested vegetable materials is also "oil", which eliminates any rational consideration of foreseeable limits to the supply of energy from fuels. The use of land to produce fuel energy is not new, timber from forests was the basic source of caloric energy for many centuries, but land use to produce biofuel is incompatible with other uses of land. Indeed, it was precisely the destruction of forests in many parts of Europe in the eighteenth and nineteenth centuries that for a while put a break to the growth of industry and commerce and eventually lead to the adoption of coal as main source of energy.[16]

As it was forcefully argued by authors like Marion King Hubbert and Nicholas Georgescu-Roegen, an exponential growth of the economy is not compatible with the limited stock of mineral fields that supply the raw materials for our manufacturing processes.[17] Almost any element in the periodic table will eventually become scarce in the context of ever expanding or just steady use. For instance, copper, a basic element for the manufacturing of many products—a small car has 20 kg of cooper, a hybrid car twice that quantity—has been considered as getting close to a peak of global production. Copper ore grades were in the range of 10–20% until late in the nineteenth century, they dropped to 2–3% in the early twentieth century and in the past two decades have been

[15] Heinberg (2011), *The end of growth*, 1. This book by Richard Heinberg is one of the most elaborated presentations of this view.

[16] Wrigley (2004), *Poverty, progress, and population*, ch. 3 "Two kinds of capitalism, two kinds of growth", 68–86.

[17] Hubbert (1997), "Exponential growth as a transient phenomenon in human history", in Strom, ed., *Societal issues, scientific viewpoints*, 75–84. In *The entropy law and the economic process*, Georgescu-Roegen (1971) kicked off this perspective into mainstream economics, where it was immediately ignored.

just below 1% and slowly declining. Despite prices trending down, with the exception of a notable spike in 2005, attributed to the demand from China, cooper is one of four metals (chromium, manganese, and lead being the others) for which no good substitutes are presently available for their major uses.[18] The idea that scarcity of some particular material will raise prices and thus stimulate the investment in exploration and extraction, eventually bringing prices down, often does not work when specific markets are observed. For instance, the price of gold has been increasing, but world production of gold has basically remained stable since 2001.[19]

At any rate, if the evidence that we have reached peak oil or production peaks in any other mineral raw materials is controversial, what seems to be beyond doubt is that the experience of the past century shows that *price* peaks of raw materials are a basic component of the processes leading to crises of the world economy. These peaks in prices, endogenously generated by the expansion of production during the boom, may contribute to the stagnation and eventual decline in profitability that triggers the crisis. These price peaks were a constant component of economic crises in the past and there is little doubt that they will also be in the future.

Now, economic reasoning suggests that oil prices can influence economic activity in the opposite direction (rising prices will curtail economic growth and falling prices will stimulate expansion) but an effect in the opposite causal direction, from economic activity to oil prices is also very plausible, so that economic expansion will stimulate rising prices and economic contraction will stimulate falling prices. To ascertain the extent to which these potential causal pathways can be operating in the world economy requires a statistical analysis. The evidence suggests that in the past 60 years the annual growth in the price of oil has had an effect on the growth of the WGDP next year and in the opposite direction, so that rising prices inhibited growth and declining prices stimulated it. The effect is barely statistically significant when considering the whole period, it is much stronger considering the period 1961–1990, and is not detectable since 1990 to the present. What is very clearly observable, however, in the period 1991–2021 is a strong correlation between the rate of growth of oil prices and the rate of growth of the world economy.

[18] Kerr (2014), "The coming copper peak", *Science* 343, 722–724.

[19] Kerr (2012), "Is the world tottering on the precipice of peak gold?", *Science* 335, 1038–1039.

This statistically significant correlation must be showing a causal link between the degree of expansion or contraction of the world economy and the increase or decrease of oil prices.[20] This is fully consistent with the notion that oil prices are mostly determined by the status of the world economy or, in economic parlance, they are fully endogenous.

The global economy is largely dependent on the availability of mineral raw materials among which oil is a key one. As shown in this chapter, oscillations of prices of these raw materials are fully consistent with an endogenous dynamics in which demand grows in the periods of expansion of the world economy, driving prices up; conversely, prices of raw materials fall when world demand declines in a recession of the global economy. This is a view supported by the statistical data and it is also a more parsimonious view than the one in which "oil shocks" are seen as exogenous factors to the economy.

[20] For further details on this issue see Appendix C and my unpublished paper on this issue: Tapia (2016), "Oil prices and the world business cycle: A causal investigation".

CHAPTER 8

Long Waves and Social Structures of Accumulation

Nikolai Kondratieff was the Russian economist who in the 1920s proposed that Western capitalist economies had cycles lasting about half a century. Like many other intellectuals in the early years of the USSR, he was jailed during the great purges of the 1930s and executed in 1938. Using data from a variety of economic statistics from Britain, France, and the United States, as well as one German series and two series for the whole world, Kondratieff described synchronized long waves in economic statistics, each one with an upturn and a downturn that divided the wave approximately in half.[1] Later authors denominated these upturns and downturns respectively the A-phase and the B-phase of the long wave. Summarizing the ambiguities in the chronology of the long waves that Kondratieff proposed in his 1926 paper, the first long wave would correspond to 1790–1848, with the peak separating the upswing from the downswing approximately in 1814; the second wave would be 1848–1895, with the peak around 1873; and the third wave would be 1895–1920, with the peak at 1920. Kondratieff argued that he was describing "a succession of long waves", but he was actually describing just two full waves, and half of a third one (Fig. 8.1). "The waves are

[1] Kondratieff (1935), "The long waves in economic life", *Review of Economics & Statistics* 17(6), 105–115.

J. A. Tapia, *Six Crises of the World Economy*,
https://doi.org/10.1007/978-3-031-38735-7_8

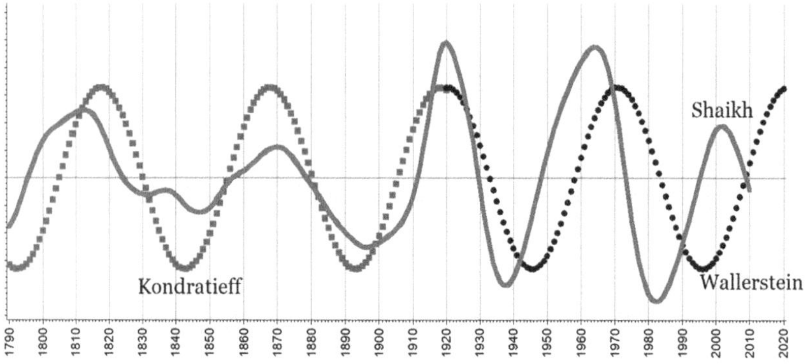

Fig. 8.1 Schematic representation of long waves of the world economy according to Kondratieff (red squares), Wallerstein (black dots), and Shaikh (gray line). More details in the text (Elaboration from data in Kondratief [1935], Wallerstein [1995 and 2011], and the series AvgGoldWaveHP [downloaded 8/2020 from www.anwarshaikhecon.org] which according to Shaikh [2016, 727], is computed by applying the Hodrick-Prescott filter [I checked that the smoothing parameter was $y = 100$] to the residuals of average UK and US wholesale prices in gold detrended with a cubic time trend)

not of exactly the same length, their duration varying between 47 and 60 years."

Mainstream Economists, Marxists, and K-waves

Kondratieff was extremely careful in the presentation of his theory. He acknowledged that the limited amount of data available for his purpose, some 140 years, was "sufficient to decide the question of the existence of long waves," but "not enough to enable us to assert beyond doubt the cyclical character of those waves." However, "the available data are sufficient to declare this cyclical character to be very probable." Kondratieff asserted that the long waves in economic activity coexisted with the business-cycle intermediate waves of 7 to 11 years and the short Kitchin waves of about 3.5 years that had been recently described. Besides providing the raw data for the series conforming to his scheme—that included major economic variables such as imports, exports, coal production and consumption, pig iron production, and wages of miners and textile workers—he mentioned that it was "absolutely impossible [...] to establish long waves in French cotton consumption; in the wool and sugar production of the United States; and in the movement of several other series." At the end of his 1926 paper he argued shrewdly that

> A strict periodicity in social and economic phenomena does not exist at all—neither in the long nor in the intermediate waves. The length of the latter fluctuates at least between 7 and 11 years, i.e., 57 per cent. The length of the long cycles fluctuates between 48 and 60 years, i.e., 25 per cent only.[2]

Kondratieff's claim that the length of business cycles is between 7 and 11 years does not match the classical definition of business cycles according to Burns and Mitchell in which "business cycles vary from more than one year to ten or twelve years".[3] Now, using that definition and Kondratieff computation, the variability of business cycles "of more than one year to ten or twelve years" is $(12 - 2)/1 = 100\%$, so that the cycle Kondratieff was proposing with a variability of $(60 - 48)/48 = 20\%$ was indeed, despite being formed by much longer waves, a much more cyclical and regular fluctuation than the business "cycles" of Mitchell and Burns.

Joseph Schumpeter was the only important author in mainstream economics who supported the idea of long economic cycles or Kondratieff waves, or K-waves as they are often called. Following the presentation of Kondratieff very closely, Schumpeter proposed the coexistence of K-waves of 60 years, together with a shorter decennial Juglar cycle and an even shorter Kitching cycle of 40 months, so that in a beautiful scheme that resembles those of physics representing the harmonics of a sound, three Kitchins add to one Juglar, and six Juglars comprise one Kondratieff.[4]

The long waves that depend as Kondratieff suggested on structural factors proper of capitalism, and the whole Schumpeterian scheme with three coexisting cycles moving harmonically look rather at odds with the Keynesian views emphasizing animal spirits and short-term factors that were predominant in economics after World War II. Interestingly, the long waves proposed by Kondratieff had been rejected in the early 1930s by Leon Trotsky, the theoretician and military leader of the Russian revolution few years before Kondratieff and Trotsky were liquidated by Stalin,

[2] Kondratieff (1935), "The long waves in economic life".

[3] Burns & Mitchell (1946), *Measuring business cycles*, 3.

[4] Schumpeter (1939), *Business cycles*, 210–219.

respectively in 1938 and 1940.[5] In Western mainstream economics, Kondratieff's long waves were taken rather unenthusiastically and never gained more than a consideration as a kind of curiosity, while economists in the Soviet Union and the Eastern bloc paid no consideration to them. However, when Soviet Marxism started to lose its ascendancy on the left intelligentsia of capitalist countries, the K-waves were quite eagerly accepted by two influential Marxist economists, Ernest Mandel and Anwar Shaikh, and by historians, particularly those of the world-economy school.[6] Thus K-waves gained some general acceptance among heterodox economists and social scientists.[7] For authors who accepted the Kondratieffs, as Schumpeter called them, with their phases of expansion and stagnation, each 25–30 years in length, business cycles of a shorter duration would be "the most visible elements" in the development of the capitalist economy, but underlying them the K-waves would provide "a much slower rhythm consisting of alternating long phases of accelerating and decelerating accumulation."[8]

Since Kondratieff himself proposed the upturn of the 3rd long wave extending from the late 1890s to around 1920, and the whole wave should be between 47 and 60 years, most authors following his ideas interpreted World War II in 1939–1945 as part of the declining phase of the 3rd K-wave, so that the period starting in 1945 would be the upturn of the 4th K-wave. But this poses a problem. Kondratieff had put quite explanatory power in his waves, saying that wars "do not come out of a clear sky" and indeed "originate from real, especially economic circumstances," during the "acceleration of the pace and the increased tension of economic life, in the heightened economic struggle for markets and raw materials" of the upturn of long waves. That was indeed very properly fitting for World War I in 1914–1919. But World War II started in 1939 and many social researchers saw it as something that continued the economic malaises of the 1930s. Indeed, authors in the world-system perspective had proposed the 4th Kondratieff starting at the end of the

[5] Arrizabalo (2016), *Capitalismo y economía mundial*, 517–520.

[6] See Mandel's "Long waves", and Shaikh's "Economic crises", both entries in Bottomore et al. eds. (1983), *A dictionary of Marxist thought*, 324–325, and 138–143; Wallerstein (2011), *Modern world-system III*, xvii–xviii.

[7] In *The Great Recession: Profit cycles, economic crises—A Marxist view*, 70; Roberts (2009) provides a "Marxist" version of Schumpeter's scheme of harmonic waves.

[8] Shaikh (1983), "Economic crises".

war, in 1945, with its expanding A-phase lasting until the late 1960s, when the B-phase downturn would have followed[9] (Fig. 8.1). If that is the case, contrarily to Kondratieff views, World War II had occurred in a B-downturn, not in an A-upturn.

Immanuel Wallerstein described the years 1945–1970 as an "extraordinary Kondratieff A-phase expansion," and asserted that the world was at the time he was writing, 1995, "at the tail end of a Kondratieff B-phase that has been going on since 1967–73." That is, the 4th K-wave would have had an A-phase from 1945 to 1970, and a B-phase from 1970 to the mid or late 1990s. Indeed Wallerstein expected that the world economy, "once thoroughly shaken down," would come out of this downturn within five to ten years, and another big A-phase, which would be the start of the 5th K-wave, would start to last circa 2020–2025.[10] Writing in 2009, Wallerstein mentioned again the A-upturn that supposedly had started in 1945 and ended around 1968–1970; however, if he still thought that in 2000 had started an upturn that would last until 2025 he said nothing about it.[11] With the Great Recession starting in 2008, being unarguably the most important economic crisis from the Great Depression of the 1930s, and the early 2010s including major recessions in many economies of Western Europe, and with the whole second decade of the twenty-first century being one of weak economic growth worldwide, the view that the period 2000–2025 is the A-upturn of the 5th Kondratieff—in which supposedly expansion would predominate and recessions would be generally mild—does not look at all plausible.

Also defending the scheme of K-waves, Anwar Shaikh opted however by a different chronology. Guiding himself by the general price level in gold that Kondratieff had used as *one* of the series showing his waves, Shaikh proposed that the 3rd K-wave started not at the end but at the start of World War II, so that the upturn of the 4th K-wave would end in 1968, lasting about three decades. This would be continued with a downturn that would last—departing widely from the Kondratieff scheme, little more than a decade—until 1979. Then the 5th K-wave would start with an upturn until the turn of the century followed by the corresponding

[9] See for instance Shannon (1989), *An introduction to the world-system perspective*, 116; Wallerstein (1995), *After liberalism*, 15.

[10] Wallerstein (1995), *After liberalism*, 19, 40, etc.

[11] Wallerstein (2009), "Crisis of the capitalist system: Where do we go from here?", *MROnline*, November 12.

downturn, which places the Great Recession in the middle of the downturn of the 5th K-wave.[12] Thus for Wallerstein the 4th K-wave downturn started around 1970 and lasted until the end of the century, so that the Great Recession occurred in the upturn of the 5th Kondratieff, while for Shaikh the downturn of the 4th K-wave lasted approximately from the late 1960s to the early 1980s and then the upturn of the 5th K-wave extended until the turn of the century, so that the Great Recession was in the middle of the downturn of the 5th K-wave (Fig. 8.1). Since Shaikh supports his chronology in an index of prices in gold (I checked that for the period 1790–1920 his waves match very well with the waves proposed by Kondratieff) while Wallerstein apparently based his chronology of K-waves on just a general interpretation of economic, political and social events, it could be concluded that Shaikh is giving a more appropriate chronology of the long waves. Now, if that is the case, a number of anomalies appear: first, World War II needs to be interpreted quite counterintuitively as the start of an upturn, which fits Kondratieff's view of wars connected with the expansion phase of the long wave, but not with the common-sense view that World War II was a continuation of the economic troubles of the 1930s; second (see Fig. 8.1), while the first and the second K-waves had had in the chronologies of Kondratieff and Shaikh downturns of about 25 years each (aproximately 1818–1843 and 1868–1893), in the Shaikh chronology the following third and fourth K-wave downturns (in 1920–1937 and 1964–1982) are much shorter; and third, the early years of the twenty-first century before the Great Recession appear as part of a downturn, while judging by available economic indicators the world economy was booming at the time.

Also following the general views of the world-systems school, Minqi Li, Feng Xiao, and Andong Zhu investigated the long-term movements of the rate of accumulation and the rate of profit in the capitalist world economy.[13] Rather inconsistently with the Kondratieff theory that proposes long waves which are coherent between different economic indicators, Minqi Li and his coauthors proposed long waves in profitability which do not overlap with the long waves in accumulation.

[12] Shaikh (2016), *Capitalism—Competition, conflict, crises*, pp. 726–727 and Figure 16.1.

[13] Li, Xiao, & Zhu (2007), "Long waves, institutional changes, and historical trends: A study of the long-term movement of the profit rate in the capitalist world-economy", *Journal of World-Systems Research* 13(1), 33–54.

Thus, for instance they proposed that between 1982 and 2001 there was a "particularly long profit rate 'short cycle', lasting for 19 years [which] encompassed two accumulation short cycles (1983–1991 and 1991–2002)." Based on their findings they also proposed that the aggregate they call World I—an approximation to the world economy formed by weighted averages of the UK, the US, and Japan—would have had a long-wave rate of profit peaking in 1997, while the long-wave rate of accumulation would have had its peak in 2004—both dates are proposed as tentative, though. Most of the statistics of this investigation rely on 10-year moving averages for which Minqi Li and his coauthors do not provide a rationale. With, say, 11-year or 7-year moving averages the inferred chronology could be quite different.

Examining the chronologies of K-waves proposed by other authors reveals even more inconsistencies in dating, measurement, and explanation of the Kondratieff cycles that supposedly would last about half a century. Though the comparison of Shaikh's and Wallerstein's chronologies makes evident major inconsistencies (Fig. 8.1), for both authors the 1970s were part of the downturn of the 4th Kondratieff. Contrarily, Walter W. Rostow interpreted "the extraordinary changes in the world economy during 1972–1976" as the start of the 5th Kondratieff upswing.[14]

Social Structures of Accumulation

In the late 1970s, David Gordon, a radical economist and professor at the New School for Social Research, noted that there was no coherent theory behind the long periods of sustained growth followed by other periods of stagnation, each one spanning several business cycles, that were proposed as components of the so-called Kondratieff cycle. Gordon was convinced that such long waves of growth and stagnation existed and proposed that they "might be explained by the consolidation, flourishing, and decay of successive institutional arrangements which he termed 'social structures of accumulation' (SSAs)."[15] The SSA theory was refined by Gordon

[14] Rostow (1978), *The world economy: History & prospect*, 298; compare with Shannon (1989), *An introduction to the world-system perspective*, 176, and with Wallerstein (1995), *After liberalism*, 15.

[15] Bowles & Weisskopf (1998), "David M. Gordon: Economist and public intellectual (1944–1996)", *Economic Journal* 108, 153–164.

with coauthors Richard Edwards and Michael Reich, though other radical economists including Samuel Bowles, and Thomas Weisskopf have been considered as important contributors to the initial development of the theory.[16] For its proponents, the SSA framework represents "both a theory of stages of capitalism and a theory of economic crisis".[17]

In the view of David Kotz, the SSA theory emerged as a break in the long-wave literature which until the 1970s had followed the ideas of earlier proponents of long waves, for instance, Schumpeter who saw the fluctuations of technological innovation as the ultimate cause of K-waves. The SSA scheme was a new theory to explain long waves. Emerging within the Marxian tradition, says Kotz, in the SSA framework, "long waves are viewed as the outcome of the interaction between the capital accumulation process and the broad set of social institutions which are believed to underpin accumulation".[18] The term "social structure of accumulation" (SSA) is the label for this set of institutions.

For supporters of the SSA notion, a period of strong capital accumulation requires the presence of a set of social institutions "which support or facilitate the accumulation process" and "includes political and ideological structures as well as economic ones". With a viable SSA in place, a long wave expansion starts. However, this expansion contains the causes of its own end, so that eventually both the SSA and accumulation collapse and a long wave contraction starts. During the period of contraction, a new SSA is developed, ultimately put in place, and the process begins again. The basic institutions of capitalism would be "insufficient to yield vigorous growth" because additional institutions conforming the SSA are needed to keep under control the conflicts of capitalism. Without an SSA in place, "productive investments may be avoided, not because the risk is too high relative to the expected return, but because capitalists cannot form any reasonably secure estimate of the expected return".[19]

[16] Lippitt (2010), "Social structure of accumulation theory", in McDonough et al., eds., *Contemporary capitalism and its crises*, Ch. 2, 45–71.

[17] McDonough et al. (2021), "Introduction" to *Handbook on social structure of accumulation theory*, Ch. 1, 9.

[18] Kotz (1987), "Long waves and social structures of accumulation", *Review of Radical Political Economics* 19(4), 16–38.

[19] All the ideas and quotations presented in this paragraph are from Kotz (1987), "Long waves and social structures of accumulation".

In a recent *Handbook on Social Structures of Accumulation Theory* Terrence McDonough explained that, while in the traditional Marxist view the crisis of the 1970s was seen as revealing fundamental tendencies of capitalism (the tendency of the rate of profit to fall due to a rising organic composition of capital, underconsumption, or a profit squeeze due to rapidly rising wages at a low unemployment rate) the new SSA theory did not share the same emphasis on the historical ubiquity of these tendencies:

> A structural crisis [...] would arise due to the breakdown of the institutional framework which conditioned the preceding period of capitalist expansion. One or more of the previously identified classical Marxian crisis tendencies could play a role in the breakdown of a particular SSA, as institutional configurations which held them in check ultimately failed, but an analysis that overlooked the role of the institutional structure in bringing the crisis was inadequate for finding the underlying causes. SSA theory defines recurring structural crisis periods as more serious than downward fluctuations of the ordinary business cycle, but not necessarily as the expression of an ultimate crisis of capitalism.[20]

As shown in this quotation, for SSA theorists, economic crises generally extend for many years, so that they would fill most if not all the B-phase of a K-wave. For instance, many authors who propose the SSA notion would agree that in 2021 the US economy would be still in the extended crisis phase of a global neoliberal SSA that had started in the 1980s and had had in the Great Recession of 2008–2009 its first manifestation.[21] This is the fuzzy concept of economic crisis that is largely at odds with the views of Marx, as it was explained in Chapter 4.

SSA proponents posed three SSAs in the United States since the mid-nineteenth century to the 1970. The first *competitive* SSA would have promoted capital accumulation during the late nineteenth century; the second SSA had been the *monopoly* capitalist SSA of the early twentieth century, until the Great Depression; the third, often labeled, the *postwar* SSA, had been the promoter of growth since the end of World War II until the economic stagnation of the 1970s. After the 1970s, according to

[20] McDonough et al. (2021), "Introduction", in *Handbook on social structure of accumulation theory*, Ch. 1, 10.

[21] McDonough et al. (2021), "Introduction", in *Handbook on social structure of accumulation theory*, Ch. 1, 7.

some sporters of the SSA framework, a *neoliberal* and perhaps global SSA would have emerged, but this notion is controversial among followers of the SSA theory.[22]

The *postwar* SSA that supposedly emerged after World War II in the United States would have involved five institutions: first, a capital-labor accord implying higher wages and benefits; second, *pax Americana*, with significant militarization of the economy in the context of the Cold War and the wars of US supremacy in Korea and Vietnam; third, a capital-citizen accord of which social security assistance and the GI bill would be major components; fourth, muted inter-capitalist competition; and fifth, a favorable financial framework.[23] These institutions, solidly imbricated among them, which makes them to form a structure, would have been both enablers and promoters of solid and sustained GDP growth under Truman, Eisenhower, Kennedy, Johnson, and Nixon. However, for instance in the 1960s, countries so institutionally different with the United States like South Africa, Japan, South Korea, Portugal, Spain and Brazil also had solid and sustained rates of GDP growth, with decadal averages over 6% and annual rates beyond 10% in many particular years. As it is obvious that the US institutions claimed by SSA theorists as facilitators and enablers of strong GDP growth in the United States could not be acting in these and many other countries also having steady growth in these years, authors working in the SSA framework argued the existence of a SSA for each nation. Thus, the frequently heard early criticism of SSA theory—that it was based too exclusively in US history—was answered with applications of the SSA concept to Japan, Greece, Ireland, Canada, South Korea, and other countries.[24]

Major economic troubles emerged in the capitalist world in the mid-1970s and then both at the start and the end of the 1980s recessions occurred in most nations, including the mentioned countries that had had sustained economic growth in the 1960s. As proposed in this book, these were national manifestations of crises of the world economy. Supposedly, for the SSA theorists, each country with its own institutions would have its own SSA so it was remarkable that economic crises occurred quite

[22] Saros (2021), "A comprehensive approach to SSA analysis: An oscillating pattern of crisis in US economic history", in McDonough et al., eds., *Handbook*, Ch. 4.

[23] Lippitt (2006), "Social structure of accumulation theory".

[24] McDonough et al. (2021), "Introduction", in *Handbook*, Ch. 1.

simultaneously in all these countries in which the different institutional arrangements of the national SSA had been supporting growth. It is not a difficult conclusion that the economic interconnections between countries and the existence of a world economy is a much more plausible explanation of these and other instances of events that look very much as manifestations of a global business cycle. Hypothetical K-waves of the world economy connected in a kind of mysterious way with multiple national SSAs are far from being a parsimonious explanation of economic events during the present and the past century.

Early theorists of the notion emphasized that an SSA is a set of "institutions" strongly imbricated among them in "structures".[25] However, the identification of these institutions and structures and the identification of internal links between the institutions supposedly imbricated in a structure are not very accessible to empirical analysis. Even more difficult is to attribute causality to the relation between such entities and other phenomena of economy life. It does not look surprising, therefore, that the SSA framework became soon subject to arguments between its own followers. Thus the sluggish economic growth of the 1980s and 1990s in comparison with the rapid economic growth of the postwar boom left SSA theorists "confused and uncertain as to whether a new SSA had formed".[26] While Minqi Li asserted that a new SSA has formed in the aftermath of the crisis of the postwar SSA in the 1970s, other supporters of the SSA framework like Phil O'Hara, David Kotz, and Martin Wolfson independently denied the formation of a new SSA.[27] In the place of SSAs, theorists of the school started to suggest the existence in the past three decades of other entities appropriately labeled in the jargon of economics with such acronyms like LISs (liberal institutional structures), RISs (regulationist institutional structures) and SSPs (social structures of profitability).[28]

Since the early times of the SSA school when its founder David Gordon was still alive, the theory was presented as a Marxist development,

[25] See for instance Kotz (1987) and the introductory chapters of *Contemporary capitalism and its crises* (2010) and the *Handbook on social structures of accumulation* (2021), both edited by McDonough et al.

[26] Saros (2021), "A comprehensive approach to SSA analysis" in McDonough et al., eds., *Handbook on social structure of accumulation theory*, 69.

[27] McDonough (2010), pp. 36–38.

[28] Saros (2021), "A comprehensive approach to SSA analysis", 70.

though certain aspects of the theory clearly revealed other influences. For instance, the emphasis in presenting the decisions of capitalists to invest as based on expectations clearly connects SSA theory with the animal spirits and the marginal efficiency of capital of Keynes. It seems plausible to describe the SSA theory as a set of Marxist notions "leavened by a certain Keynesianism".[29]

That SSAs have supposedly produced an alternating pattern of "supply-side and demand-side economic crises throughout US history" is presented by Daniel Saros as the "clearest manifestation of an internal mechanism at work within American SSAs". Saros also sees "a tendency for aggregate demand to fall when the balance of power shifts decisively in favor of capitalists, and for profits to be squeezed when non-capitalist groups grow in strength", which in his view "appears to be a recurring theme in American history".[30] In the opinion of the present writer, who sees the economic ideas of Marx and Keynes as deeply contradictory, all these notions strongly suggest that the SSA theory is a *contra natura* amalgamation of Marxian and Keynesian views.

From a theory born from the combination of contradictory views is not surprising to see the emergence of uncountable inconsistencies, discrepancies, and disagreements. SSA theorists have undoubtedly raised many issues which are important and valuable in the analysis of modern capitalism, but putting these issues in the Procrustean bed of SSAs or Kondratiev waves has led to intellectual no-exit aisles. As cogently said by the late Terrence McDonough, "arguing that the Roaring Twenties are central to a period of slow growth seems problematic".[31]

Despite the notion of SSA being quite fuzzy and hard to grasp, the scarce number of instances of this entity to be considered (in the case of the US economy three, perhaps four?) and major disagreements between SSA theorists on the characteristics and even the existence of such "structure" in the most recent decades, the developers of the SSA framework have not been shy in using their notion and elaborating on its supposed characteristics, an exercise that could be compared to a

[29] McDonough (2010), "The state of the art of SSA theory", in McDonough et al., *Contemporary capitalism and its* crises, 39, fn. 14.

[30] Saros (2021), "A comprehensive approach to SSA analysis", 65.

[31] McDonough (2010), "The state of the art of SSA theory", in McDonough et al., *Contemporary capitalism and its crises* 37–38, fn. 13.

consideration of the allotropes of phlogiston or the chemical composition of the interstellar ether when these entities were still considered valid hypotheses in chemistry and physics. Thus, a taxonomy of SSAs has been developed, including "liberal SSAs" and "regulated SSAs", which, furthermore, would tend to alternate;[32] and it has been also theorized that power, which is considered a key element of any SSA, can be or two types, "actual capitalist power" and "underlying capitalist power".[33]

The 1980s saw the opening of China to foreign investment and its quick integration in the world economy that was soon flooded with products manufactured in China often by companies largely owned by investors of the United States, Japan, European countries, or other "capitalist" nations. At the end of the same decade, the 1980s, occurred the breakdown of the Soviet bloc immediately followed by the unexpected disappearance of the Soviet Union and the fast conversion of all these formerly planned economies into market economies. All the former together with further liberalization of the transnational movements of capital and the emergence of low-income countries as major industrial producers made evident that globalization had reached a new stage. Some SSA theorists like David Kotz, Terrence McDonough, and William Robinson argued the formation and strengthening of a *global* neoliberal SSA in the early 1980s. This global SSA would exist at the transnational level, so that the neoliberal SSA would be a transnational entity with nested national structures and a variety of interconnections between the local structure and the neoliberal global structure. While this view obviously implies the necessity of modifying the SSA theory—to admit transnational SSAs—, the notion that institutions differ widely among capitalist countries led to other SSA theorists like Victor Lippit to claim that it is not meaningful to speak of an international or global SSA—as, for instance, the "lifetime" employment system in Japan contrasts markedly with the easy dismissal of employees in the United States. For William Robinson, the national institutional arrangements of capitalism after World War II were largely displaced by the emergence of modern globalization, as movements of capital became quite free from nation-states and capital evolved new power relative to labor and the state, so

[32] McDonough (2021), "Social structure of accumulation theory", in McDonough et al., eds., *Handbook on social structure of accumulation theory*, Ch. 2; 24.

[33] Saros (2021), "A comprehensive approach to SSA analysis", 71.

that nation-states would have shifted from reproducing Keynesian SSAs to fulfill general requirements of the new global accumulation and a new transnational capitalist class.[34] The new global SSA would be superimposed on national structures and governance institutions such as the WTO and the EU would be the most salient among a variety of transnational structures which carry out state-like regulatory functions.[35] This notion of a global neoliberal SSA has led to lengthy discussions and "widespread disagreement that has existed among SSA theorists regarding the nature of the institutional structure that has formed in response to the capitalist crisis of the 1970s and early 1980s."[36] The 2010 volume *Contemporary capitalism and its crises*, significantly subtitled *Social structure of accumulation theory for the twenty-first century*, and the recent *Handbook on Social Structure of Accumulation*, both under the editorial leadership of the late Terrence McDonough, attest the *verbal* richness of these discussions.

If the SSA framework, after many years of development and many hundred pages of theorizing, reveals presently many inconsistencies and appears not to hold water conceptually, the situation is not better from the point of view of statistical evidence. In an econometric chapter of the *Handbook on Social Structure of Accumulations Theory*, Jonathan Goldstein has tried to highlight the relevance of "nonperiodic methods" in an econometric analysis of long swings.[37] In Goldstein view, SSA theory "characterizes long swings associated with accumulation regimes as endogenous, persistent nonperiodic cycles that are mean-reverting around a deterministic trend with structural breaks with the potential for significant deviations from trend". Goldstein claims that complex interactions between adversarial or cooperative social classes, intraclass divisions, the anarchy of production, the government and other institutions, and the business cycle

[34] McDonough (2021), "Social structure of accumulation theory", in McDonough et al., eds., *Handbook*, Ch. 2; Lippitt (2010), "Social structure of accumulation theory", in McDonough et al., eds., *Contemporary capitalism and its crises*, Ch. 2, 45–71.

[35] McDonough (2021), "Social structure of accumulation theory", 23.

[36] Saros (2021), "A comprehensive approach to SSA analysis".

[37] Goldstein (2021), "Econometric analysis of long swings: The relevance of nonperiodic methods", in McDonough et al., eds., *Handbook on social structure of accumulation theory*, Ch. 3, 34–61.

> can result in varied regime dynamics and transitions, and long swings which are highly irregular/heterogeneous, endogenous, regime-specific trend reverting and persistent. Persistence swings which are highly irregular/heterogeneous, endogenous, regime-specific trend reverting and persistent. Persistence in the form of long-lasting autocorrelations (long memory) is associated with slow evolving institutions, policies and social relations. More directly, long swings do not exhibit the regularity in length, amplitude, duration, and symmetry between phases that short-persistence/memory periodic cycles exhibit: long swings are nonperiodic.[38]

If something can be grasped of all the former, it is that Goldstein is trying to argue that the long swings on the basis of the SSA theory are not periodic. Indeed Goldstein clarifies what he means by explaining that in the SSA framework the term "swings" is preferred to "waves" or "cycles", because "swing" connotes a more irregular behavior while "waves" and "cycles" are usually understood as implying periodicity. At any rate, he says, both swings and waves can be regular and irregular and therefore he will use indistinctively these two terms.[39] All this is conceptually confusing. The notion of SSA was born half a century ago as giving a structural basis to the long waves of Kondratiev who, as it was explained in the former section of this chapter, saw the long waves in the development of the capitalist economy as a quite *periodic* oscillation of about half a century duration. Now Goldstein refers to "swings" or "waves" which may or may be not periodic.

Candidly, Goldstein tells his readers that authors using a variety of statistical methods to investigate the issue "for the most part have not found evidence of long swings, with the exception of Goldstein (1999)". Furthermore, it is suggested a reason for this, as "over-differencing, over-smoothed trends, over-adjusted data (outliers), ignoring breaks and imposing a periodic structure in addition to estimation of boundary parameters suggest that recent findings against long swings are biased. In summary, both pre-estimation decisions and the properties of statistical models can severely limit detection of long swings."

Goldstein analyses an annual series of US GDP 1850–2011 and because the SSA literature suggests four long swings, roughly 1848–1890s, 1890s to 1939–1945, 1945–1980, and 1980 to 2010s, he

[38] Goldstein (2021), "Econometric analysis of long swings", 34.

[39] Goldstein (2021) "Econometric analysis of long swings", 34, 54, fn. 2.

computes a model which includes this information using dummy variables, so that break points in 1898, 1946 and 1983 are included in the model. Thus, Goldstein is including in the model the information that supposedly is to be obtained from the analysis of the data. After presenting to the reader a laborious and tortuous analysis of this series 1850–2011, Goldstein concludes that "the existence of a nonperiodic long swing with a period of at least 40 and less than 54 years exists". Grammar clarity does not contribute here to enhance the credibility of the statistical analysis. In the view of the present writer, what Goldstein has accomplished in this chapter is to cover up the lack of statistical substance behind the concept of SSA with a veil of econometric jargon.[40]

Long Waves and the Modern World Economy

As it was shown in Chapter 2 of this book, a variety of statistical series corresponding to the world economy and to multiple national economies show since 1970 to the present the alternate succession of expansions and recessions of a "cycle" which has as one of its features to be of varying length, lasting like the business cycles defined by Burns and Mitchell "from more than one year to ten or twelve years".[41] In this context of macroeconomic fluctuations or "cycles" of quite varying length, K-waves of quite a precise length of about 50 years do not look very believable, and indeed for different authors, these supposed long waves cover different periods. Thomas Kuczyinsky, who half a century ago thoroughly examined the literature in favor of the existence of K-waves, concluded that the evidence supporting the existence of that type of waves, if any, was flimsy.[42] At present, evidence does not look at all

[40] Goldstein's regression estimates of his Eq. 3.6 are presented in Table 3.1 of his chapter. What in the table appears in the column labeled t*D98 seems to be the estimate of β_5 in Eq. 3.6. That estimate is −0.0126 with a standard error of 0.0015 (t or P values are not reported). The estimate is marked with an asterisk (*) which in the footnote of the table is explained as meaning significant at the 0.01 level. It is surprising that an estimate like this, more than 8 times bigger than its standard error, be reported as only significant at the 0.01 level of significance. This is just one of many technical issues I found. Overall, I was unable to reproduce Goldstein's regression estimates of his Eq. 3.6, presented in his Table 3.1.

[41] Burns & Mitchell (1946), *Measuring business cycles*.

[42] Kuczyinsky (1978), "Kondratieff cycles—Appearance or reality?," in Flinn, ed., *Proceedings of the 7th International Economic History Congress, Vol. II*.

supporting the existence of Kondratieff waves in the world economy. Indeed, there are good reasons for that: if waves 50–60 years long existed, statistical evidence conclusively supporting their existence would require a period of observation of at least several centuries. But for most supporters of the world-system view, the world economy is only a few centuries old. If that is the case, K-waves are a kind of Russell's teapot, an entity whose existence cannot be disproved.[43] An additional consideration about the hypothetical K-waves is that their half a century periodicity would give them a sort of magical character. Like a wonder violin that always produces the same pitch wherever the fiddler puts her finger along the vibrating string, the world economy would "vibrate" at the same frequency despite major changes in the vibrating structure—the world economy.

My conclusion on K-waves is that the evidence in favor of its existence is no more convincing than the statistics William Stanley Jevons or Henry L. Moore provided more than a century ago to demonstrate that business cycles are linked to astronomical events.

Perhaps significant of an incipient change in the perspective of the world-system school on K-waves is the recommendation of one of the leading figures of the world-system theory, Giovanni Arrighi, that world-system analysis abandons the idea "of a quantitatively expanding but structurally invariant world capitalist system" which would have Kondratieff cycles as one of the empirical manifestations of such a structural invariance. For Arrighi, "globalization of historical capitalism must instead be represented as involving fundamental structural transformations of the spatial networks in which the system of accumulation has been embedded".[44]

GDP growth has been declining secularly in advanced economies since the early decades following World War II and in recent decades it has declined in so-called emerging economies too. For the available data, the rate of growth of the world GDP shows a statistically significant declining trend.[45] Considering the proportion of investment (gross capital formation) in total global output which oscillated between 26% and 29% in the

[43] See the entry on "Russell's teapot" in Wikipedia.

[44] Arrighi (2003), "Spatial and other 'fixes' of historical capitalism", *Journal of World-Systems Research* 10(2), 527–539.

[45] Regressing the annual rate of growth of WGDP on time (year) using the available data (1961–2021) from the WDI database the slope is negative and highly significant

1970s and reached a minimum of 22.9% in 2002, a long-term decline in the past half century seems also apparent, though a reversal of the trend could be perhaps noticeable in the past decade (Figs. 2.1 and 2.2, pages 14 & 15).[46] On the other hand, as estimated by the World Bank, the volume of money in the global economy (compared with the global output, Fig. 2.6, page 23 has increased steadily from levels between 55% and 60% of WGDP in the late 1960s to 100% at the time of the Great Recession, 125% in 2019 and an amazing 132% in 2020, at the time of the COVID-19 pandemic. The volume of private debt and government debt since the mid-twentieth century to the present has increasing trends in national economies almost without exception. Without much effort and without any need to appeal to K-waves, all this can be interpreted as substantive evidence in favor of a long-term decrease in the rate of accumulation of capital, a long-term increase of the weight of the financial sphere in the global economy during recent decades, and a likely evolution of world capitalism toward more generalized crises.

(parameter estimate ± standard error = −0.041 ± 0.012, t = −3.49, P = 0.0009, R^2 = 0.22).

[46] Regressing gross capital formation as percentage of WGDP on time (year) using the available data (1970–2020), the slope is negative and highly significant (parameter estimate ± standard error = −0.053 ± 0.012, t = −4.40, $P < 0.0001$, R^2 = 0.28).

CHAPTER 9

From the COVID-19 Depression to the War in Ukraine

On June 8, 2020, the Business Cycle Dating Committee of the NBER determined that a peak in economic activity had occurred in the US economy in February 2020. The committee stated that the peak marked the end of the longest expansion in the history of US business cycles since 1854. The committee also determined that a peak in quarterly economic activity had occurred in the last quarter of 2019.[1]

As the lockdown policies implemented in most countries to reduce transmission of the virus that causes COVID-19 started to be put in place in the early months of 2020 the global economy entered a major crisis. In the spring and summer of 2020 national and international economic institutions reported massive losses of output and employment associated with the lockdown. In the United States 26 million people filed unemployment claims in a 5-week period ending April 23, 2020.[2] This was 16% of the 159 million people who were the employed part of the US labor force before the policies to mitigate the coronavirus outbreak severely curtailed the domestic economy. Similar spikes of unemployment

[1] "NBER determination of the February 2020 peak in economic activity", www.nber.org/cycles/june2020.pdf, accessed September 2020.

[2] "The coronavirus crisis—Deluge Continues: 26 million jobs lost in just 5 weeks", *NPR*, April 23, 2020, www.npr.org/sections/coronavirus-live-updates/2020/04/23/841876464/26-million-jobs-lost-in-just-5-weeks.

J. A. Tapia, *Six Crises of the World Economy*,
https://doi.org/10.1007/978-3-031-38735-7_9

occurred everywhere. These were unprecedented figures, much larger in magnitude than those observed during other economic contractions, even those occurring in the 1930s. Troubling news of financial instability that had generated hesitation and some conflict among central bankers when they tried to face a possible meltdown in financial markets were reported by *The Guardian*, but they were scarcely echoed in other media.[3]

Lockdowns of greater or lesser intensity intended to control the pandemic and governments interventions to support incomes were the rule worldwide in the spring of 2020. Apparently, every politician had become Keynesian, nobody dared to argue that the invisible and smart hand of the market would take care of the situation. In the US, after many weeks of lockdowns much less restrictive than the lockdowns of, for instance, many European countries, epidemic data seemed to show improvements ("a flattening of the curve") in the late summer. Authorities at all levels, mostly the Trump administration and the Republican governors, hurried to recommend or implement the removal of COVID-19 control policies. Restrictions on businesses began to be removed early in the summer in the United States and not much later in many other countries except China, and there was some recovery of economic activity, but macroeconomic indicators remained depressed in many countries. The pandemic followed heterogenous paths dependent on country-specific circumstances and dynamics likely linked to the extent and strength of the control measures and policies that were adopted. In Northern Europe, Sweden pursued a minimalist approach, trying to interfere at a minimum with everyday life and business activity, which was severely curtailed in the other Nordics. As reported in February 2023, Denmark had had 1392 COVID-19 deaths per million population, while Norway had had 945, Finland 159, and Sweden 2342 (Table 9.1).

At the time of the final writing of this chapter in March 2023, worldwide reports indicate the COVID-19 pandemic is largely in the rear mirror, though perhaps China could be a special case. In that country extremely drastic policies to restrict the dissemination of the virus and vaccination using local vaccines that being effective at the start of the epidemics apparently were not so effective to avoid the infections by the

[3] Elliott (2020), "ECB's plan to support eurozone banks is underwhelming: Christine Lagarde delivered a disappointing set of measures to mitigate the impact of coronavirus", *The Guardian*, March 12; Tooze (2020), "How coronavirus almost brought down the global financial system", *The Guardian*, April 14.

Table 9.1 COVID-19 deaths per million, since the start of the pandemic to mid-February 2023, selected countries

Peru	6439
USA	3303
Brazil	3242
UK	3235
Spain	2506
Sweden	2234
Switzerland	1625
Finland	1592
Denmark	1392
South Korea	653
Japan	575
Iceland	566
China	61

Source: Oxford University, ourworldindata.org/coronavirus#explore-the-global-situation, accessed 17 February 2023

omicron variant of the COVID-19 virus that appeared later, kept the COVID-19 mortality at a level of 3 deaths per million for many months. Then, after major protests in many Chinese cities against the draconian isolation policies, early in 2023 pandemic lockdowns and controls were mostly removed and COVID-19 deaths quickly rose, increasing the accumulated mortality to 61 per million in just several weeks. These figures were still much lower than the accumulated mortality figures for COVID-19 in February 2023 in many other countries (Table 9.1). Apparently, and judging by the evolution to date, the authoritarian policies of the Chinese government were quite effective to avoid a major impact of the COVID-19 pandemic in the Chinese population.

Reports from many countries in Asia, Africa, and Latin America are too heterogeneous as to allow for a summarized description. Furthermore, statistics from many countries, particularly in Africa, are very unreliable. It would probably be fair to say that the COVID-19 pandemic has basically been left to its own dynamics in many countries of the so-called developing world.

Lockdowns and containment measures caused substantial drops in economic activity in the second quarter of 2020, with unprecedented falls in real GDP in most G20 countries, where overall, GDP dropped by a record 6.9%—as a point of comparison, real GDP had dropped 1.6% in these countries in the first quarter of 2009, the worst time of the Great

Recession.[4] When estimates for the whole year were available, figures were dismal, with WGDP contracting at a rate of 3.3%. Except China, which had a GDP growth of 2.2%, all the major economies of the world contracted: the United States by 3.4%, Japan by 4.5%, Germany by 6.6%, France by 4.6%, India by 6.6%, the UK by 9.3%, Brazil by 3.9%, Russia by 2.7%. In some countries GDP declined in 2020 by almost 10% or even more, that was the case of Argentina and Spain with rates of GDP growth of −9.9% and −10.8%, respectively (Table 3.1, p. 51).

The global economic crisis of 2020 was by its magnitude a world depression. The economic crisis, that became obvious in the early months of 2020, was clearly connected with the isolation policies and restrictions to transport and movements of people that were implemented to curtail the dissemination of the virus. The lockdowns for the COVID-19 pandemic, implemented quite suddenly in most of the world, had a major effect on production and trade and in that sense, the global economic crisis was clearly triggered by a factor extraneous to the economy, an exogenous factor. On the other hand, it is also true that the shock to the economy resulting from the COVID-19 lockdowns fed into economic processes that had been evolving from long before the pandemic struck. For instance, the indebtedness of private households and business enterprises had been growing quickly for several years in many countries and was, in 2019, comparable or higher than before the Great Recession (see Figs. 3.1 to 3.3 in p. 60–62). In 2019 many economic commentators were expecting a recession in 2020. It is of course impossible to know whether such recession would have started in 2020 without the pandemic. What is undeniable is that the monetary flows that in normal conditions are created by business activity suffered a significant stranglement because of the pandemic lockdowns, with the subsequent impact on the financial health of businesses as well as governments. In the fall of 2020 *The New York Times* reported the prospect of a financial abyss for New York City, where the unemployment rate was 16%, personal income tax revenue was expected to drop by $2 billion in 2020, only a third of hotel rooms were occupied, and apartment vacancies in Manhattan had hit a peak.[5]

[4] OECD website, www.oecd.org/economy/g20-gdp-growth-second-quarter-2020-oecd.htm, accessed September 2020.

[5] Rubinstein (2020), "'We're at war': New York City faces a financial abyss", *The New York Times*, September 28.

Pandemic public spending was also pushing the fiscal stance of governments toward positions that would have been unbelievable a few decades ago.[6]

Early in 2021 the estimates of the total mortality caused by the COVID-19 pandemic were 1.5 million, with the death total quickly approaching to 300,000 in the US. By mid-February 2023, estimates of cumulative COVID-19 global mortality had gone up to almost 7 million of which 1.1 million would correspond to the United States.[7] To put these numbers in historical perspective, it can be said that 50–100 million world deaths and half a million deaths in the United States were attributed to the flu pandemic of 1918–1919.[8] At that time the world population was close to 2 billion, that is less than a quarter of its present size, 8 billion. Therefore, compared with the 1918–1919 world flu pandemic, the 2020 COVID-19 pandemic has been a rather mild mortality crisis.

The COVID-19 pandemic with its associated economic crisis was the major event of 2020. But many parts of the world were also hit by other disasters. In Australia, California, Bangladesh, and Central America multiple wildfires and generalized flooding caused major concern and loss of wealth and human lives.[9] Scientists have repeatedly warned that the frequency of "natural" disasters like major hurricanes, floodings, wildfires, and heat waves will increase because of anthropogenic global warming. Indeed, in 2021 natural disasters linked to climate change included exceptional heatwaves across the Western North America and the Mediterranean. In the United States hurricane Ida caused economic losses estimated at US$ 75 billion. Severe flooding caused many deaths in different parts of the world and economic losses estimated to be around US$ 20 billion in both China, in the Henan province, and in Germany.

[6] Tankersley (2020), "Federal borrowing amid pandemic puts US debt on path to exceed World War II—Federal debt, as a share of the economy, hit 98% in the 2020 fiscal year", *New York Times*, September 2.

[7] Oxford University, ourworldindata.org/coronavirus#explore-the-global-situation, accessed February 20, 2023.

[8] Crosby (2003), *America's forgotten pandemic: The influenza of 1918*.

[9] Yeung (2020), "Australia's deadly wildfires are showing no signs of stopping", *CNN*, January 13; Flavelle (2020), "Wildfires hasten another climate crisis: Insurers, facing huge losses, have been pulling back from fire-prone areas across California", *New York Times*, September 2, B1, B4; Earth Observatory NASA, "Intense flooding in Bangladesh".

Table 9.2 Annual growth (%) of final consumption expenditure

Year	*World*		*Euro area*		*United States*	
	Total[a]	*HH and and NPISH*[b]	*Total*	*HH and and NPISH*	*Total*	*HH and and NPISH*
2017	3.0	3.4	1.6	1.8	2.0	2.4
2018	3.2	3.3	1.4	1.5	2.6	2.9
2019	2.6	2.5	1.5	1.4	2.2	2.0
2020	−3.2	−4.8	−5.3	−7.7	−2.1	−3.0
2021	6.2	7.2	3.9	3.8	7.0	8.3

[a]Total final consumption expenditure is the sum of household final consumption expenditure and general government final consumption expenditure
[b]HH and NPISHs final consumption expenditure is the consumption of households and nonprofit institutions serving households
Source WDI database. series codes NE.CON.TOTL.KD.ZG and NE.CON.PRVT.KD.ZG

Canada, the United States, Iran, Afghanistan, Pakistan, Turkey, and Turkmenistan suffered significant drought. In Canada, because of drought, wheat and canola crop production were expected to drop at levels 35% to 40% below 2020 levels. In Greenland it was registered an exceptional melt event and for the first-time ever, rainfall was recorded there.[10]

During 2021, however, with the pandemic more or less under control and lockdowns mostly removed, the world economy quickly recovered. GDP had a major rebound with respect to 2020, with rates of growth as high as 11.7% in China, 5.7% in the United States, 7.0% in France, or 8.9% in India (Table 3.1, p. 51). Once isolation policies were removed, economic activity recovered rapidly. Both because governments *largesse* and because the impossibility of expending money in many common forms of consumption, there were large quantities of cash available for consumption in many countries. Thus, total consumption and private consumption that had contracted strongly in the pandemic year, 2020, quickly rebounded in 2021 (Table 9.2). In the euro area, for instance, household consumption that had increased 1.4% in 2019 and shrank 7.7% in 2020 grew 3.9% in 2021.

In February 2022, when the COVID-19 pandemic started to appear to be mostly gone, a new misery was added to the afflictions of the human race, the war in Ukraine. After years of increasing assertiveness

[10] WMO (2022), *State of the global climate 2021*, 2.

of Russia in the world at large and in the area surrounding its borders in particular, President Putin launched an invasion of Ukraine under excuses related to the status of Russian-speaking populations in Ukraine and the supposed intention of Ukraine to join the EU and NATO, thus completing the encirclement of European Russia by the military alliance led by the United States. It was argued by the Russian government that before the disappearance of the USSR the United States had explicitly given Russia reassurances that NATO would not expand toward the East, which seems to be truth.[11] Actually, in the three decades following the disappearance of the Warsaw Pact and the USSR, NATO significantly expanded toward Russia by incorporation of the states of Eastern Europe. The first incorporation to NATO at the end of the Cold War had been that of East Germany, that joined West Germany in 1990, when the USSR still existed. Poland, Hungary, and the Czech Republic became NATO members in 1999, and in the next five years Bulgaria, Estonia, Latvia, Lithuania, Romania, Slovakia, and Slovenia pursued the same path. Albania, Croatia, and Montenegro followed a few years later. With the war in Ukraine already going on, North Macedonia completed its integration in NATO on March 2020.[12]

The actual expansion of NATO provides some verisimilitude to the Russian claim that NATO is encircling its territory, but the invasion of Ukraine by Russia was a clear aggression which cannot be justified in any way. It generated indeed a quite general rejection in the international community. The United Nations General Assembly adopted on March 2, 2022, a resolution deploring the aggression committed by Russia against Ukraine, with 141 votes in favor, 5 against—Russia, Belarus, Armenia, North Korea, and Syria—and 35 abstentions, including India, China, Cuba, Vietnam, Kazakhstan, Tajikistan, Kyrgyzstan, Iran, Iraq Algeria, South Africa, Namibia, Eritrea, Nicaragua, El Salvador, Bolivia, etc.[13] Two European countries that had traditionally adopted a neutralist approach in the East–West confrontation, Finland and Sweden, requested

[11] National Security Archives, George Washington University, "NATO expansion: What Gorbachev Heard", nsarchive.gwu.edu/briefing-book/russia-programs/2017-12-12/nato-expansion-what-gorbachev-heard-western-leaders-early, accessed March 7, 2023.

[12] NATO, "Enlargement and article 10", www.nato.int/cps/en/natolive/topics_49212.htm, accessed March 7, 2023.

[13] unric.org/en/the-un-and-the-war-in-ukraine-key-information; time.com/6222005/un-vote-russia-ukraine-allies/.

membership in NATO immediately after the Russian attack to Ukraine. After several months of war Ukraine itself applied for NATO membership in September 2022. It has been reported too that Bosnia and Herzegovina, Georgia, and Kosovo have also asserted its willingness to join the Western military alliance.

One year after the war started, there is no clear indication of a possible end. The evolution of the war surprised to many observers who expected a quite defeat of Ukraine in few weeks. When several weeks of war had passed, Ukraine looked to be a much more powerful enemy for Russia than relative size, military strength, and economic power suggested a priori; or perhaps Russia was a much weaker power than it looked before the war started; or perhaps both things.

In the early weeks of the war, NATO countries and many other nations adopted policies to help Ukraine to fight Russia and to put as many obstacles as possible in the Russian efforts to secure financing for its invasion of Ukraine. It does not look however that those efforts have been very successful, as apparently attempts of Western governments to cripple Russian foreign trade have largely failed and the value of Russian exports did not decline, at least in the first half year of war. According to a report published in October 2022 Russian imports had plunged, excepting the imports from some specific countries like China and Turkey that had significantly expanded. Contrarily, Russian exports grew after Russia invaded Ukraine. Compared with the period 2017–2021, monthly exports of Russia to China after the start of the Ukraine invasion expanded 98%, to India 430%, and to Japan 40%. These three countries are not members of NATO but exports of Russia to NATO members also expanded, to Turkey by 213%, to Spain by 112%, to the Netherlands 74%, to Germany 38%, and to Belgium 130%. High prices of oil and natural gas between March and July of 2022 helped Russia to offset revenue lost because of sanctions, indeed Russia received oil payments in those months that largely surpassed payments for the same items in the same months in previous years. Russia has always been and continues to be a leading exporter of nuclear reactors, fertilizer, wheat, and many minerals, like palladium and rhodium required to make catalytic converters for cars, uranium to fuel French nuclear plants, or diamonds for Belgium's diamond industry. As the authors of this report remarked, "as one of the world's most important producers of oil, gas and raw materials, Russia has had longstanding and lucrative trade partnerships. Breaking those ties is not easy."[14]

The former suggests that the world economy is relatively resilient to the major tensions imposed to its existence by the Russian invasion of Ukraine. It is true, however, that since the war started, an obvious reconfiguration of the world system has occurred with a more multipolar power structure being displaced by a quite bipolar configuration. While European countries almost without exception have aligned with the United States and NATO in its support to Ukraine, the two largest countries of the world by population, China and India, have abstained of condemning Russia and indeed to some extent have supported Russia by substantially reinforcing their commercial links with major purchases of fossil fuels—at cheap prices. Chinese imports of Russian oil rose from 0.7 million barrels per day in February to 1 mbpd in November, while Indian imports that were mostly zero in February had increased to 0.9 mbpd in November 2022.[15] The bipolarization of the world system has been also amplified by the anti-Chinese rhetoric in the United States, where the Biden administration has intensified the protectionist policies of Trump—at least versus China.[16] Presently the Biden administration is not shy to manifest its intention to eliminate imports of Chinese semiconductors, solar panels, or many other manufactured products or block the operation of Chinese companies like Huawei or Tiktok, all of which goes against the ideas of free trade and economic openness that the United States preached during decades.

For some observers the COVID-19 pandemic *cum* global economic crisis could perhaps had been the perfect storm making for the end of globalization.[17] Indeed, world exports, that had grown 4.3% in 2018 and 1.2% in 2019 dropped 9.0% in 2020. They however rebounded quickly

[14] Gamio & Swanson (2022), "How Russia pays for war", *New York Times*, October 30.

[15] BBC News, "Ukraine crisis: Who is buying Russian oil and gas?", December 6, 2022, www.bbc.com/news/world-asia-india-60783874, accessed March 7, 2023.

[16] Editorial Board (2023), "Who benefits from confrontation with China", *New York Times*, Sunday Opinion, 9.

[17] Tooze (2020), "The death of globalisation has been announced many times: But this is a perfect storm", *The Guardian*, June 2.

by growing 9.3% in 2021. Exports, that accounted in 2021 for 28.9% of the world economy, had accounted just for 18.9% in 1990.[18]

The fluid situation of recent months does not suggest that globalization is dead or is dying. It could be suddenly dead, however, if a complete breakdown of our worldwide economic system, which is not impossible, occurred. Both private and public debt at stratospheric, unprecedented levels in every nation, do not look like a good omen for the stability of the world economy. In the main component of the world economy, the United States, which in 2021 was 23.9% of the world economy, the national debt grew from less than 6 trillion dollars in 2000 to 31.4 trillion in 2023, that is an expansion more than fivefold; in the same period US GDP about doubled.[19]

And then is the question of war.

In 1873 US President Ulysses S. Grant declared that he thought at some future day,

> the nations of the earth will agree on some sort of congress which will take cognizance of international questions of difficulty and whose decisions will be as binding as the decisions of the Supreme Court are upon us [...]. Transport, education and rapid development of both spiritual and material relationships by means of steam power and the telegraph, all this will make great changes. I am convinced that the Great Framer of the World will so develop it that it becomes one nation, so that armies and navies are no longer necessary.[20]

Humanity faces enormous challenges to be solved if the twenty-first century is not going to be the last of our civilization, and perhaps the last of our species. Whether we follow the path foreseen by President Ulysses Grant and suppress armies and navies or whether we use them to create Armageddon will be the key issue in the remaining years of the present century.

[18] WDI data, accessed March 7, 2023.

[19] Tankersley (2023), "Swelling debt is bipartisan in its origins: Now at 31.4 trillion", *New York Times*, March 7, A1; WDI data, accessed March 7, 2023.

[20] As cited by Schwartzberg (2004) and Streit (1939).

CHAPTER 10

Conclusion

This book has discussed six recent crises of the world economy defined as periods in which the accumulation of capital slows down generating spikes in business failures and mass unemployment. The crises were dated based on observed declines in capital formation, either gross capital formation or gross fixed capital formation (Fig. 10.1). Both procedures identify crisis years in slightly different ways, but yield approximately similar results. Overall, six crises can be identified: the first in the mid-1970s, followed by crises in the early years of each of the next three decades, a fifth crisis at the end of the first decade of the twenty-first century, and the sixth crisis in 2020. While there is some evidence—which has been only briefly mentioned in this book—that crises of the world economy also occurred before World War II, particularly at the end of the nineteenth century and in the early 1930s, the integration of national economies into a global totality developed quickly in the second half of the twentieth century and the evidence for generalized crises of the world economy—in which depressed economic conditions affect most national economies more or less simultaneously—is particularly strong since the 1970s. In fact, over the past 50 years crises of the world economy occurred irregularly but about once per decade.

Since the question of the consequences of an economic organization of our society based on private property of the means of production and business units operating in pursuit of money profits was first posed a few

J. A. Tapia, *Six Crises of the World Economy*,
https://doi.org/10.1007/978-3-031-38735-7_10

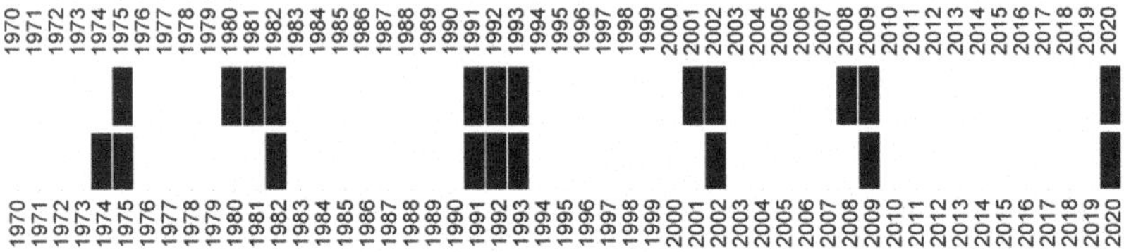

Fig. 10.1 Two chronologies of the six crises of the world economy. In the top panel black bars indicate crisis years as defined by an annual drop in gross capital formation; in the bottom panel, crisis years are defined by an annual drop in gross fixed capital formation. Author's elaboration from WDI data on capital formation in the world economy.

centuries ago, a recurring controversy has opposed those who followed Adam Smith in the view that the market economy is stable and efficient for solving human needs, and those who argue that the market economy is unstable and inefficient. The existence of commercial gluts in which businesses go bankrupt and workers become unemployed and lose income at the same time that markets are flooded with unsold products was highlighted by Simonde de Sismondi as a practical demonstrations that the system is defective. In Marx's analysis the market society, what he called the bourgeois mode of production, appeared as an economic organization based on the permanent accumulation of capital in which an always shrinking minority of capital owners benefited from a steadily expanding majority subjected to alienated work for money—a kind of a wage slavery in which wageworkers were "free to starve" during recurring economic crises.

At the start of the twentieth-century John Hobson, Rosa Luxemburg, and Vladimir Illich Lenin advanced the idea that imperialism and the thrust toward war were the direct result of the expanding forces of modern capitalism. This was followed by two world wars—separated by a Great Depression—and then a Cold War in which Western capitalism led by the United States opposed a large bloc of countries pursuing a different type of economic progress based on anti-capitalist principles. This alternative economic organization and experience lasted seven decades in the Soviet Union and three decades in China and other countries in Eastern Europe and Asia, until the Cold War ended with the demise of the Soviet bloc in Europe. In the 1990s worldwide capitalism expanded its realm to Eastern Europe and to the ruins of the Soviet Union and integrated the

"Asian communism" of China and other countries into global capitalism. China became a key component of the system and commodities produced in China, often by non-Chinese companies, became a very large portion of total global exports.

During the last two decades of the twentieth-century national economies worldwide became much more integrated than any other time in history, and the global economy emerged as a very tangible reality. For some commentators, the system looked stable, more efficient than any other known system, and ready to end history. But then around the turn of the century the crises in Asia and Latin America and ten years later the Great Recession threw cold water on the idyllic image of history supposedly transformed into just a deepening of the American way of life. After the financial and economic turmoil of 2008 and 2009, the 2010s were a decade of low growth worldwide and open stagnation and economic stress for large majorities of the population worldwide. Political systems experienced major changes in many countries and capitalism was increasingly questioned, though mostly by marginal though expanding sectors of the populace. The United States maintained the world hegemony, but it was now very far from being the almost omnipotent political, cultural, and military leader of the free-enterprise system that it had been during the decades following World War II. Since the last years of the twentieth century, the motto that countries that had been formerly peripheral units of the world system were "emerging" in the world economy was increasingly present in the parlance of economists and politicians, in which "emergent" economies displaced the old "developing" or "undeveloped" countries. The so-called BRICS—Brazil, Russia, India, China, and South Africa—were supposedly the five leading emerging economies. Indeed, the BRICS share of the world economy, no matter how it is measured, grew from around a tenth of WGDP to about a quarter of it in the first two decades of the present century (Table 10.1). However, only two of the five BRICS economies, China and India, substantially increased their share of the world output in that period, though India, starting from a tiny level in 2000 was about 3% of the world economy in 2020, while China had tripled its share in the same period to be 17% of the world economy in 2020. Russia, Brazil, and South Africa were each below 2% of the world economy in 2000, and continued below 2% in 2020. Among the BRICS, China is the only obvious emerging power that in 2020 was already a major component of the world economy and is largely integrated economically, though not politically, with the rest of the world.

Table 10.1 Share (%) of the GDP of the five BRICS countries (measured in current dollars or in 2015 US dollars) in WGDP

	BRICS		*China*		*India*		*Russia*		*South Africa*		*Brazil*	
Year	*US$*	*US$2015*	*US$*	*US$2015*	*US$*	*US$2015*	*US$*	*US$2015*	*US$*	*US$2015*	*US$*	*US$2015*
2000	8.1	11.9	3.6	5.7	1.4	1.7	0.8	1.6	0.5	0.5	1.9	2.5
2020	24.2	25.1	17.3	17.8	3.1	3.1	1.7	1.7	0.4	0.4	1.7	2.1

Source: Author's computation from WDI data accessed 25 February 2023

Emergent China, increasingly assertive, gaining economic and military strength every year, became the target of US rhetoric and aggressive trade policies during the presidency of Donald Trump. This stance toward China was mostly continued by the Biden Administration, that in 2021 had to face the undignified withdrawal of United States and other NATO military forces from Afghanistan after 20 years of occupation. The symptoms of decline of the United States as world leader were becoming increasingly obvious when the Russian invasion of Ukraine in February 2022 led to a clear affirmation of the US leadership in guiding NATO countries and other nations to support Ukraine in the war against the Russian aggression. The war has further advanced the antagonism between the United States and China, which has adopted a policy of "neutrality" in the Ukrainian conflict, not condemning the Russian invasion. Whether the growing antagonisms between the US, China, and Russia will evolve or not into a world war is impossible to predict, but is an obvious possibility.

The generalized recessions of national economies clustered in the global economic crises that have been described in this book have disrupted the world economy repeatedly since the 1970s. Despite the assertions of some mainstream economists on the lack of importance of business-cycle fluctuations, each of those crises generated social misery and declining standards of life at least for large minorities. From a purely economic point of view, the idea that the modern free-enterprise system has self-regulatory properties that ensure proper functionality and continuous improvement does not hold water. It has been often argued that capitalism has taken human civilization to new levels that were unthinkable a few centuries ago; that billions have been taken out of poverty in the past several decades; and that the levels of health and technological ability now available to a large fraction of the humans on earth would have not been achieved without the dynamic processes embodied in the capitalist system.[1] Much of that may be true, but it is also undeniably true that capitalism has multiplied social inequality and the technological ability of humans to destroy themselves. Indeed, it has created ingrained dynamics in which the efficient working of the system generates ecological disruption in many aspects and particularly in the warming of the atmosphere and the alteration of the weather patterns which are fundamental for the survival of humans on the planet. Marx viewed with hope the wonderful capacity of capitalism to revolutionize social conditions and develop the *productive* forces. However, today, the existence of many thousands of nuclear weapons that could kill billions and rapidly accelerating climate change that is producing more severe tolls every year make abundantly clear the ability of the system to develop *destructive* forces. Major economic crises occurring at least once per decade, levels of private and public debt at high levels and rising in most countries, the forced interventions of governments and central banks in economic life to avoid chaos, and the mostly failed attempt to create institutions of "global governance" shows quite clearly that the ability of the market economy to regulate itself and produce efficient social outcomes is a myth.

When considered in historical perspective, the idea maintained by left wing critics since the mid nineteenth century that economic crises are the Achille's heel of capitalism, does not look too sound. Certainly, during crises mass joblessness affecting a population that is increasingly composed of men and women who depend on money income from work, generates economic distress and social malaise that shake the ideological foundations of capitalism. However, since the times of Marx, excepting the periods of war the system has proven to be able to skirt these obstacles without too much difficulty. The social services and unemployment insurance systems developed since the early twentieth century in the Nordic countries as the practical reaction of the system to crises were followed in the 1930s by the theoretical justification of this type of government intervention in the economy, Keynesian economics. Then, after World War II the full-blown welfare state developed in Western Europe, North America, and the advanced economies of the Pacific and Asia, and even later in the emerging economies of the rest of the

[1] Field & Taylor (2018), *Is capitalism working? A primer for the twenty-first century.*

world. "The system" also reacted to socioeconomic instability and social distress by generating powerful forces posed to crush any revolt against capitalism. Thus, between the two world wars, in Italy and Germany the anti-capitalist political forces were destroyed by Mussolini's Fascism and Hitler's *Nazionalsocialismus*, both movements that supposedly represented the interest of the nation against their enemies—the "international plutocrats" and their internal allies including the Jews and the Marxists. In more recent experiences, popular revolts, often stoked by economic crises, against regimes in which capitalist exploitation was supported by extremely authoritarian governments—like those of Pinochet's Chile, Botha's South Africa, Franco's Spain, Mubarak's Egypt, Ben Ali's Tunisia, Suharto's Indonesia, or Marcos's Philippines—ended in reformed capitalist regimes with civil liberties and large inequalities, or even led to unreformed dictatorships like that of present day Abdel Fattah el-Sisi in Egypt.

The two world wars led to major changes in the political conformation of the world and to the instauration of regimes that self-defined themselves as socialist in large areas of the world in which capitalism was in early stages of development. Thus World War I saw the demise of three empires and the birth of the first anti-capitalist state, the USSR, while World War II saw the consolidation of state-socialism in the USSR and Eastern Europe and in the next three decades in China, Cuba, Vietnam, and other countries. But capitalism under the political leadership and military supremacy of the United States saved the day by producing material affluence, while state-socialism following the Soviet model resulted in economic stagnation and nightmarish political authoritarianism. The economy of the USSR, strongly committed to a runway arms race that had begun in 1945—when the United States asserted its military supremacy by using nuclear bombs against an already defeated Japan—eventually imploded at the end of the 1980s. Beginning in the mid-1970s, "communist" China eliminated "the iron bowl"—employment safety—and most remains of socialist equalitarianism of Mao's era, intensified the repression of any dissent, opened its doors to international capital, evolved toward levels of inequality greater than those of many "capitalist" countries, and fully integrated into the world market. In the twenty-first century, China became the principal contributor to the destruction of global climate by emissions of greenhouse gasses.

Nationalism rose worldwide and tensions between the United States, China, and Russia, but also between these and other countries created ominous prospects of war, now clearly based on conflicting national interests—which is to say the conflicting interests of the national business and political elites of different countries—rather than any ideological conflict like the one between capitalism and communism that *supposedly* fed the Cold War.

Despite massive privatization of state assets after 1990 in the countries that had been centrally planned economies in eastern and central Europe and in many Western countries where old state-owned companies like railroads, shipyards or coal mines became ruinous and were shrunk and liquidated in the last decades of the 20th century, the long run tendency in the world has been a growing participation of the state in economic life. This occurred through large increases in government indebtedness fed by the participation of the state in the compensation of mass unemployment during recessions, the bailouts required by financial crises, and in some countries, like the US, by massive military spending.

With the passage of time the increasing burden of debt in national budgets and the ascent of conservative forces opposed to social policies have steadily eroded the welfare state. In many countries austerity policies applied in times of high unemployment have crushed almost any possibility of effective fight for better conditions of work or improved social services. These have been also the times of exploding inequality by the enrichment of the world elites. The Great Recession which in many countries extended well into the second decade of the present century was particularly damaging in low-income countries where it triggered social explosions, for instance those of the Arab Spring. But also, in high-income countries like the United States, Greece, Spain, France, or Italy, the Great Recession fed social movements that to some extent questioned the political order and sometimes the sacred principles of the free-enterprise economy. In addition, the Great Recession also stoked pro-capitalist reactions like those embodied in the United States in the Tea Party first and in Trumpism later. The mass mobilizations of 1989 in China opposing the maintenance of the authoritarianism of the Communist Party and denouncing the generalized corruption in the country and the heroic attempt of the people in Hong Kong in 2019 to keep their civil liberties can be also considered part of a general uprising of common people against the ruling of the business and political elites. Regretfully, oppression and direct repression from governments supported by the military or ruling under the disguise of progressivism, populism, or socialism has produced hundreds and even thousands of deaths in recent years in countries as diverse as Egypt, Syria, Myanmar, Nicaragua, Venezuela, and many others.

Economic ideologies of the nineteenth century, even those that were openly antagonistic to each other, agreed that perpetual economic growth was possible and science and technology would bring increasing material affluence to humanity. But in the past century it has become obvious that the steady growth of economic output disrupts the ability of the Earth's ecological systems to regenerate themselves and allow for the sustained maintenance of life. The market system, with its built-in pulsion for growth, has been shown to lead to the exhaustion of natural resources and is arguably the most powerful destroyer of the environmental processes that allow for human and non-human beings to live on Earth. A variety of authors have long noted and demonstrated that continuous and perpetual economic growth is just impossible.[2] In September 2020, the UN Convention on Biological Diversity alerted the world to an ongoing catastrophe of biodiversity collapse that threatens not only to eliminate beloved species and invaluable genetic diversity, but also endangers humanity's food supply, health, and security. It is estimated that one million species of animals and plants are at risk of extinction and the populations of 4,400 monitored mammals, birds, reptiles, amphibians, and fish have declined by 68% since 1970. Stories of catastrophes of the natural world are increasingly frequent in the media.[3]

Climate change, the most peremptory aspect of the progressive destruction of our environment, has become over the past decade the major issue for all concerned about a catastrophic future that is already with us.[4] Politicians and governments have faced climate change through

[2] Boulding (1966), "The economics of the coming spaceship earth," in Jarret, ed., *Environmental quality in a growing economy*, 3–14; Ward & Dubos (1972), *Only one Earth: The care and maintenance of a small planet*; Georgescu-Roegen (1971), *The entropy law and the economic process*; Hubbert (1987), "Exponential growth as a transient phenomenon in human history", in Strom, ed., *Societal issues, scientific viewpoints*, 75–84.

[3] Einhorn (2020), "A 'crossroads' for humanity: Earth's biodiversity is still collapsing", *New York Times*, September 15, A.10; *BBC News* (2020), "Mass deaths of migratory birds reported in New Mexico", September 16; Chappell (2023), "An unusually high number of whales are washing up on US beaches", NPR, February 5.

[4] Speth (2008), *The bridge at the edge of the world*, and Tanuro (2014), *Green capitalism* provide deep insights on the economic aspects of the environmental crisis in general and climate change in particular.

either blatant rejection of scientific facts (à la Trump or Bolsonaro) or through implementation of policies (like the markets for CO_2 emissions enacted in California and the EU) that are ineffective in reducing emissions of greenhouse gases but help cover up the incapacity of governments to do anything practical to slow down climate change. In fact, worldwide and nationally, emissions have been growing *pari pasu* with the economy, following macroeconomic conditions as well as the vagaries of energy policy and deindustrialization in the few countries of North America or Europe in which emissions are declining.[5]

For almost all politicians, social scientists, and media commentators it appears obvious that the higher the level of economic development—measured by income per capita—the easier it will be to deal with environmental problems. But that idea is revealing itself as deeply flawed, as every measure of environmental damage, and particularly the emission of greenhouse gases, is correlated with the level of affluence, so that more economic activity and higher income per person, that is, "economic development", translates into further destruction of nature and faster progress toward climate calamity. The sad reality of our world is that high-income individuals, social groups, and nations who in the short run benefit the most from the global market economy are those contributing the most to push the Earth's climate toward incompatibility with human life. Contributing little to climate change, the poor populations that constitute the majority across the globe are also the most affected by floods, harvest disruptions, and other environmental impacts of climate change fueled by economic growth.

After the turmoil of the Great Recession many social researchers and opinion leaders warned that current economic problems are no longer limited to a national economy, they are global problems that require global solutions and "world governance". A decade later, after four years of protectionist policies by the government of Donald Trump, the subsequent exacerbation of nationalism of all sorts, the commercial, political, and even military conflicts between the great powers and a COVID-19

[5] Spash (2010), "The Brave New World of carbon trading", *New Political Economy* 15(2), 169–95; Tapia & Spash (2019), "Policies to reduce CO_2 emissions: Fallacies and evidence from the United States and California", *Environmental Science & Policy* 94, 262–266; Tapia (2019a), "Fairy tales about climate change", *The Brooklyn Rail*, March; Tapia (2019b), "Why 3508 economists are probably wrong", *The Brooklyn Rail*, May. See also Appendix C in this book.

pandemic that put the world economy on its knees, the world seems as far away as ever from any system of global governance, and running fast in an unclear direction, perhaps toward total disarray. But with or without global governance, the internal dynamics of capitalism will continue generating economic crises and ecological destruction, stoking mass poverty, social unrest, and mass migrations. It seems quite clear that in the absence of a world government, the deepening of these processes significantly increases the risk of a world war. Thus the choice is not between this system and a modification of it that is more stable and efficient, but between this system and another system that must necessarily be very different in order to at least allow a significant portion of the 8 billion human inhabitants of our planet to live in peace with themselves and with nature. For this alternate system to be viable, it must posses certain key features like egalitarianism and democratic functioning, but not the profligate features of Western capitalism, now fully adopted by the governing elites of Eastern "communism." Of course, the cultural and political forces that support the present economic system in its diverse variants, and the influence of nineteenth-century economic ideologies—which despite conflicting views on many things agree on the promise of unlimited material affluence—are so powerful that calls for a different economic system to the one prevailing today in the two major economies of the world, can appear utopian if not delusional. For the present writer, however, the call for a different economic system is based on an objective consideration of facts and evidence that can be analyzed by anyone with the will to do so.

The years 2021 and 2022 were very eventful in terms of economic news. After the dismal economic depression during the pandemic 2020, economists saw with awe the quick recovery of 2021. There were discussions on whether the generous use of government money to support incomes would trigger significant inflation. Then in 2022, a gloomy mood took hold among financial "gurus", economists, and financial institutions which almost unanimously predicted the coming of a new recession soon.[6] There were basically no dissident voices, the only disagreements were around how deep the recession would be. But months passed and the recession did not start, so that forecasts started to be less pessimistic. In the early months of 2023, any talk of a coming recession has been

[6] Rappeport (2022), "World faces high risk of recession, I.M.F. warns", *New York Times*, October 12, B1.

muted, but recent news about layoffs in leading companies—Facebook, Google, 3M, Disney, FedEx—and financial turmoil affecting banks in the United States and Switzerland do not look very positive.[7] At any rate, uncertainty about the future is widespread among economists.[8]

Economic forecasting is particularly difficult, as even the most efficient modeling of past economic data is only a tool which generates probabilistic forecasts that are very far from 100% certain. It is to be agreed that "animal spirits" fulfill a role and generate uncertainty and randomness in economic life, though, as Tinbergen saw half a century ago, they operate under constraints given by the actual evolution of business activity.

A criticism that this book could face is that it does not contribute to the development of practical policies to deal with economic problems. To answer that potential criticism, I would like to refer again to Tinbergen and to other Dutch economist, Tjalling Koopmans, who was, like Tinbergen, a recipient of the Nobel Memorial Prize in Economics.

The notion of the necessity of governmental interventions to amend the inefficiencies of the market system started to be more accepted just after the great political and economic upheavals of the first decades of the twentieth century. Until then, economists had been largely in favor of *laissez faire*, of keeping the hand of authorities out of the economy, letting businessmen and workers to do their jobs. In the years following World War II Jan Tinbergen was a key contributor to the development of macroeconometric models and a general theory of economic policy-making. With an engineering mentality, Tinbergen believed that economists were responsible for making their nations better places; that economies could be managed and developed. A major preoccupation of Tinbergen in his approach to economic policy was to respect the existence of different economic systems and to promote the economic integration of nations in ways that might defeat nationalism and prevent further wars. "Tinbergen's first stated aim of economic policy was the 'maintenance of international peace', coming before those of more conventional economic aims", such as full employment, maximizing per capita income,

[7] Chen et al. (2023), "Are layoffs imminent?", *New York Times*, February 21, B1; Rappeport et al. (2023), "Moving quickly to avert a financial avalanche", *New York Times*, March 14, A1, A12.

[8] Cassidy (2023), "Even the experts don't really know where inflation and jobs are headed", *The New Yorker*, February 28.

etc.[9] It is remarkable how these ideas differ from today's approach to present economic policy which responds to the national interest of each government and thus promotes exclusions and antagonisms that continuously generate conflict and even push our world toward war.

The macroeconometric models that Tinbergen contributed to develop were intended to allow authorities to apply sensible policies to promote the common good, avoiding the damaging instabilities of the economy. The reality is that despite increasing availability of economic statistics and mathematical sophistication of the models, in the five or six decades during which macroeconomic models have been used they have not been found to produce even approximate forecasts of economic outcomes. In any case, already in the 1940s Tjalling Koopmans had a dark and probably more realistic view of the impact of using economic models. For Koopmans, even if macroeconomic models were effective in predicting economic outcomes, considering the way present society is organized "speculation would rush in to anticipate the predicted movements, thus defeating the premises on which the prediction was based and possibly aggravating the fluctuations".[10] Thus, even the well intentioned use of models to develop sound economic policy that can promote stability and the common good fails *ab initio* precisely because of the nature of our present economic system.

A further notion relevant here is what is implied by the existence of a business cycle of the world economy. If, as many things discussed in this book suggest, that cycle is a reality obeying its own laws, national phenomena of whatever kind loose much of its appeal in explaining the cycle and, identically, national economic policies appear as very unclear tools to modify that phenomenon. As Canadian economists investigating the dynamics of the global economy put it in 1997, "if the business cycle is indeed a worldwide phenomenon, then it may not be as responsive to domestic policies or influenced by domestic causes as previously thought".[11]

I started this book with quotations from three women economists. Feminism is a cause viewed with sympathy by all progressive men

[9] Morgan (2019), "Recovering Tinbergen", *De Economist* 167, 283–295.

[10] Koopmans (1941), "The logic of econometric business-cycle research", *Journal of Political Economy* 49(2).

[11] Gregory, Head & Raynauld (1997), "Measuring world business cycles", *International Economic Review* 38(3), 677–701.

and women who believe there should not be discrimination based on gender.[12] But feminism has another dimension that is often overlooked, which is the fact that over the course of history women have often conveyed different values than men. In contrast to the "masculine" force, brutality, violence, intolerance, and rigidity, women have often emphasized the values of understanding, empathy, care, tolerance, and flexibility which are so needed today by humanity. In contrast to the macho style of *by all means necessary,* or *there is nothing more authoritarian than a revolution*, it was women who told us that *it requires less mental effort to condemn than to think,* or that *freedom is always the freedom of the disenter.*

In 2020, when the COVID-19 pandemic was starting to hit peoples and nations worldwide, the Indian writer Arundhati Roy wrote that the virus had eluded immigration controls, biometrics, and digital surveillance, had scorned

> every other kind of data analytics, and struck hardest—thus far—in the richest, most powerful nations of the world, bringing the engine of capitalism to a juddering halt. Temporarily perhaps, but at least long enough for us to examine its parts, make an assessment and decide whether we want to help fix it, or look for a better engine.

Arundhati Roy had also the view that,

> historically, pandemics have forced humans to break with the past and imagine their world anew. This one is no different. It is a portal, a gateway between one world and the next. We can choose to walk through it, dragging the carcasses of our prejudice and hatred, our avarice, our data banks, and dead ideas, our dead rivers and smoky skies behind us. Or we can walk through lightly, with little luggage, ready to imagine another world. And ready to fight for it.[13]

Perhaps this quotation can be a proper way to end this book.

[12] Adichie (2014), *We should all be feminists.*

[13] Roy (2020), "The pandemic is a portal", *The Financial Times*, April 3.

Appendices

APPENDIX A—MONEY LEADS

Data for the years 1970–2020, downloaded in September 2022 from the WDI database of the World Bank show a negligible correlation (−0.14) between the annual rates of growth of WGDP and *m*, broad money measured in inflation-adjusted dollars.[1] Broad money is the monetary aggregate that continues M2, no longer reported by the World Bank (see more about this in Appendix B). However, with the rate of growth of *m* lagged one year its correlation with the rate of growth of WGDP is 0.43, which is statistically significant at a 99% level of confidence ($P < 0.01$). This substantive correlation of the growth of broad money lagged one year with the rate of growth of the world economy shows that "money leads" in the sense that changes in the quantity of money are followed one year later by changes in WGDP in the same direction. Estimating a "monetarist model" in which the annual growth of WGDP (g_t) is a function of the contemporaneous and one-year lagged growth of *m* (that is, $g_{m,t}$ and $g_{m,t-1}$), the estimated equation (standard errors in the bracket

[1] Broad money is defined as "the sum of currency outside banks; demand deposits other than those of the central government; the time savings, and foreign currency deposits of resident sectors other than the central government; banks and traveler's checks; and other securities such as certificates of deposit and commercial paper" (WDI database, metadata, accessed March 2023).

J. A. Tapia, *Six Crises of the World Economy*,
https://doi.org/10.1007/978-3-031-38735-7

below the parameter estimates) is as follows:

$$g_t = 2.22 - 0.03\, g_{m,t} + 0.20\, g_{m,t-1} \quad R^2 = 0.19, \text{Durbin-Watson } d = 1.38$$
$$(0.43)\ (0.06)\quad (0.06).$$

With $n = 49$ observations in the regression, the model predicts about a quarter of the variation of the rate of growth of WGDP and the d relatively close to 2 indicates just a moderate autocorrelation of the residuals. Adding an extra lag or suppressing the lag-zero term does not improve the fit of the model. However, plots of the two rates of growth show clearly that the data for the year 2020 are outliers. Indeed, suppressing the data for that year, the regression results are as follows:

$$g_t = 2.12 - 0.04\, g_{m,t} + 0.18\, g_{m,t-1} \quad R^2 = 0.27, \text{Durbin-Watson } d = 1.62$$
$$(0.34)\ (0.05)\quad (0.05)$$

The model now shows that the growth in broad money predicts 27% of the variation in the growth of WGDP. The suppression of the data for 2020 improves the fit of the model, indicating that 2020 was indeed an atypical year.

Overall, both these regressions and the lagged correlation of the growth of m with the growth of WGDP provide evidence that "money leads" the fluctuations of the world economy. This is a known fact for national economies that was emphasized by Milton Friedman. Friedman and Schwartz found in their historical study of money in the US that:

> on the average of 18 cycles, peaks in the rate of change in the stock of money tend to precede peaks in general business by about 16 months and troughs in the rate of change in the stock of money to precede troughs in general business by about 12 months. The results would be roughly comparable if the comparisons were made with peaks and troughs in a price index rather than in general business. For individual cycles, the recorded lead has varied between 6 and 29 months at peaks and between 4 and 22 months at troughs.[2]

In his 1968 debate with Walter Heller, Friedman was very explicit in explaining his views on the causal role of changes in the stock of money:

[2] Friedman (1983) [1960], *A program for monetary stability*, 87.

> I believe that the rate of change of the money supply by itself [...] has a very important effect on nominal income and prices in the long run. It has a very important effect on fluctuations in nominal and real income in the short run. That's my basic conclusion about changes in the stock of money.[3]

This attribution of a causal effect of the change in the stock of money on the level of economic activity, as indexed by income flows, a basic tenet of monetarism, has been often criticized. One of the most cogent criticisms was that of James Tobin, who emphasized Keynesian dynamics in which autonomous changes in investment are the cause of cyclical fluctuations of output, and the corresponding movements of money precede the movements of output without causing them.[4] Similarly, from a perspective in which investment is not autonomous but depends on profitability, investment spending continues growing during the late phase of an expansion, but the growth of profits slows down, stagnates, and finally reverses, which *ceteris paribus* will tend to reduce the growth of the stock of money. Thus, the slowdown and subsequent reversal in the rate of growth of the stock of money will precede the decline in investment and total output that marks the start of the downturn. Similarly, during the late phases of the recession, the level of profitability starts to increase though investment spending is still stagnant, which will lead to an increase in the rate of growth of broad money, announcing the recovery. In this perspective, as in the Keynesian perspective of Tobin, money leads, but to attribute causality to that relationship is a *post hoc ergo propter hoc* fallacy.

[3] Friedman & Heller (1968), *Monetary vs. fiscal policy—A dialogue*, 50.

[4] Tobin (1970), "Money and income: *Post hoc ergo propter hoc?*", *Quarterly Journal of Economics* 84(2), 301–317.

APPENDIX B—ON MEASURES OF MONETARY AGGREGATES AND DEBT

Figure B1 in this appendix plots M2, one of the aggregates measuring the volume of money in the world economy, as a percentage of WGDP, according to data that were downloaded from the WDI database in November 2012. At that time, the WDI database reported the monetary aggregate M2 for national economies and for the world economy. In a former draft of this book, I commented on the explosive growth of M2 in 2007 and 2008 and said that the series provided a good illustration of Mandelbrot's idea that the representation of economic time series as a trend on which Gaussian deviations are superimposed is frequently invalid.[5]

In the summer of 2013, I noticed the data on money in the world economy in the WDI website had changed. I downloaded the data again and compared them with the data I had before.

Data for the years 2007 and 2008 had been dramatically changed. Table B1 presents the two series of data for M2 as reported in November 2012 and July 2013. They are basically identical except for the years 2007 and 2008, in which they differ, respectively, by several orders of magnitude.

On July 31, 2013, I sent an email to the World Bank to inquire about this startling change in the data reported in the WDI database. On August 6, I received a reply: "Our WDI database is updated quarterly, and data frequently changes (*sic*) as new information comes in and revisions are made. This is a normal occurrence across all indicators. Which countries are you referring to specifically?" The same day, I emailed back explaining that I was referring to the world economy, concretely to the difference of several orders of magnitude between M2 in 2007 and 2008 as reported in November 2012 and July 2013. Specifically, according to the WDI data reported in November 2012, in the year 2008, M2 was estimated as 3.6 billion times bigger than WGDP, while it was only 1.17 times bigger than WGDP as reported in July 2013. I speculated that because the financial crisis estimation of M2 had become particularly difficult, but I stated that I would like to know the opinion of the data managers at the WDI database. Since I did not receive any reply, on September 13 I sent

[5] Mandelbrot & Hudson (2009), *The (mis)behavior of markets: A fractal view of risk, ruin, and reward.*

Fig. B1 Monetary aggregate M2, representing money and "quasi money," as a percentage of WGDP, as reported in the WDI database by the World Bank in 2012. As indicated by the absence of vertical scale and grid, the location of the points for 2007 (1115%) and 2008 (357 billion percent) is arbitrary. (Data from the WDI database, downloaded November 2012.)

a follow-up email asking if they were going to answer my question or if the issue had been archived. I received a short reply telling me one of the data support specialists would reply as soon as possible. However, I did not receive any further information on this issue and I ceased pursuing it.

In May 2019, I checked again the data on monetary aggregates in the world economy reported in the WDI database. M2 was no longer

Table B1 M2 and broad money (BM) in the global economy, as percentages of WGDP

Year	*M2* *Nov 2012*	*M2* *Jul 2013*	*BM* *May 2019*	*Year*	*M2* *Nov 2012*	*M2* *Jul 2013*	*BM* *May 2019*
1960	52.8	53.2		1990	87.9	87.8	87.8
1961	54.4	54.8		1991	89.9	89.8	89.1
1962	55.1	55.4		1992	88.6	88.5	88.2
1963	56.9	57.3		1993	91.6	91.5	92.0
1964	57.2	57.7		1994	91.4	91.4	91.7
1965	57.7	57.7		1995	93.2	93.2	93.3
1966	56.5	56.5		1996	90.6	90.6	90.6
1967	58.9	58.9		1997	90.9	90.9	91.0
1968	59.4	59.4		1998	93.7	93.7	93.4
1969	56.8	56.8	53.5	1999	107.3	107.3	99.6
1970	60.0	60.0	57.2	2000	107.2	107.2	99.8
1971	63.4	63.4	60.6	2001	103.8	104.5	96.0
1972	67.6	67.6	64.7	2002	104.7	105.6	96.7
1973	67.2	67.2	64.6	2003	106.6	107.4	97.5
1974	62.8	62.8	60.7	2004	106.9	107.8	96.4
1975	72.0	72.0	61.9	2005	108.1	109.0	95.7
1976	70.2	70.2	62.3	2006	109.6	110.7	96.5
1977	70.0	70.0	62.6	2007	1115.0	113.2	96.9
1978	73.3	73.3	66.0	2008	357,127,999,020.0	117.7	100.6
1979	66.6	66.6	64.4	2009	127.0	128.8	111.5
1980	65.7	65.7	63.8	2010	124.1	124.9	108.6
1981	67.7	67.6	65.4	2011	125.6	126.0	109.8
1982	70.4	70.3	68.2	2012		130.0	111.9
1983	73.5	73.5	71.6	2013			112.4
1984	74.9	74.9	74.1	2014			114.9
1985	75.9	75.9	75.4	2015			120.0
1986	84.2	84.2	83.6	2016			124.3
1987	88.6	88.6	88.4				
1988	91.9	91.9	92.0				
1989	93.2	93.2	93.3				

Data reported in the WDI database on three different dates

reported, there was now a "Broad Money" measure that was clearly a very similar series (see Table B1 and Figure B2).

The initial huge estimates of M2 in the years around the financial crisis of 2008 may have been a consequence of the changes in the balance sheet of central banks which had enormous increases in assets consisting of devalued securities purchased from financial institutions that

Fig. B2 Monetary aggregates M2 and "broad money" for the world economy as reported in the WDI in database, figures are percentages of the WGDP. M2 as reported in 2012 (hollow squares) and 2013 (triangles) and broad money as reported in 2022. Two values in the M2 series reported in 2012, those corresponding to 2007 and 2008, are suppressed as their inclusion would totally flatten the graph. (The data plotted are those in Table B1)

in exchange got liquid accounts. Furthermore, in 2007 and 2008, because of derivative contracts a number of banks and financial firms received compensation in the form of deposits for payments not received. The combined effect of these and perhaps other processes may have generated a massive expansion of M2. Since many of these financial operations were either never completed or later declared void because of bankruptcies or nationalizations (as in the case of AIG in the US), major adjustments may have been made in the estimates of M2 for these years.

M2 has been for decades one of the accepted measures of the monetary aggregate. The changes in the reported values of that measure and its final substitution by "broad money" are worrying signs that reveal how in many aspects the world economy is hard to assess because of a lack of reliable information. In recent months the WDI database does not provide any data on broad money neither for the EU nor for the Eurozone or for specific European countries such as Germany, Finland, France, or Spain. It provides broad money data, however, for the US, China, Switzerland, Russia, Poland, or Japan.

Bank credit to private individuals or corporation is debt for those who receive the credit. Three measures of domestic credit (DC) available in the WDI are a major source of confusion, as these measures of debt of the private sector are clearly different for some countries while they are identical for others. The three measures, their codes in the WDI database, and the definitions provided in the metadata of the database are the following:

1. DC provided by financial sector (FS.AST.DOMS.GD.ZS) "includes all credit to various sectors on a gross basis, with the exception of credit to the central government, which is net. The financial sector includes monetary authorities and deposit money banks, as well as other financial corporations where data are available (including corporations that do not accept transferable deposits but do incur such liabilities as time and savings deposits). Examples of other financial corporations are finance and leasing companies, money lenders, insurance corporations, pension funds, and foreign exchange companies."
2. DC to private sector by banks (FD.AST.PRVT.GD.ZS) "refers to financial resources provided to the private sector by other depository corporations (deposit taking corporations except central banks), such as through loans, purchases of nonequity securities, and trade credits and other accounts receivable, that establish a claim for repayment. For some countries these claims include credit to public enterprises".
3. DC to private sector (FS.AST.PRVT.GD.ZS) "refers to financial resources provided to the private sector by financial corporations, such as through loans, purchases of nonequity securities, and trade credits and other accounts receivable, that establish a claim for repayment. For some countries these claims include credit to public enterprises. The financial corporations include monetary authorities and deposit money banks, as well as other financial corporations where data are available (including corporations that do not accept transferable deposits but do incur such liabilities as time and savings

deposits). Examples of other financial corporations are finance and leasing companies, money lenders, insurance corporations, pension funds, and foreign exchange companies."

That these definitions are nor operative in practice is shown by Table B2 in which the data for these three measures of credit, as reported in the WDI database in March 2023, are provided for selected countries and for the world economy. Note that for a variety of countries such as Germany, Russia, Switzerland, China, Sweden, or Poland, the aggregates called "DC to the private sector" and the "DC to the private sector by banks" are exactly the same (for example, 128.5% of GDP for Sweden in 2016). For these countries, no data is provided in the WDI database for the series named "DC provided by the financial sector", perhaps because of redundancy. All the former is also true for countries such as India, Pakistan, Peru, or Brazil, not included in Table B2.

The situation is totally different for the United States and Japan, countries for which "DC provided by financial sector" is much greater than "DC to private sector" and this in turn much greater than "DC to private sector by banks." Thus, for instance, as reported in the WDI database, in Japan in 2016 "DC provided by financial sector" was 344.3% of GDP, while "DC to private sector" was 161.8% of GDP, and "DC to private sector by banks" was 102.6% of GDP. For the world at large in 2016, as shown in Table B2, "DC provided by financial sector" was not reported while "DC to private sector" was 125.2% of WGDP and "DC to private sector by banks" was 86.7% of WGDP.

Late in 2022, I emailed the World Bank asking for clarification of these measurements of debt: "I have looked at WDI for figures of credit worldwide and what I found puzzles me, as in the early 1960s [I sent a graph attached] there is a major drop in domestic credit to the private sector. Is that a data error? I do not see any corresponding drop at that time in domestic credit to the private sector by banks. The definitions of these two indicators in the metadata of WDI are almost identical and I am not sure what is the difference between them. Could you please let me know what kind of credit is included in domestic credit to the private sector which is not included in domestic credit to the private sector BY BANKS? I will very much appreciate your answer. Yours sincerely". I never had any answer.

Table B2 Three measures of domestic credit (DC) reported in the WDI, March 2023

Country or area	*Credit measure*	*2014*	*2015*	*2016*
EU	DC provided by financial sector	.	.	.
EU	DC to private sector by banks	92.4	89.7	88.6
EU	DC to private sector	92.4	89.7	88.9
Euro area	DC provided by financial sector	.	.	.
Euro area	DC to private sector by banks	92.6	89.9	88.6
Euro area	DC to private sector	92.6	89.9	88.9
USA	DC provided by financial sector	232.9	227.5	232.6
USA	DC to private sector by banks	49.7	51.1	52.4
USA	DC to private sector	185.4	180.7	183.7
Germany	DC provided by financial sector	.	.	.
Germany	DC to private sector by banks	79.3	78.1	77.3
Germany	DC to private sector	79.3	78.1	77.5
Belgium	DC provided by financial sector	.	.	.
Belgium	DC to private sector by banks	57.9	60.6	62.8
Belgium	DC to private sector	57.9	60.6	63.4
Finland	DC provided by financial sector	.	.	.
Finland	DC to private sector by banks	92.8	94.4	93.9
Finland	DC to private sector	92.9	94.4	94.0
Japan	DC provided by financial sector	342.5	338.7	344.3
Japan	DC to private sector by banks	102.8	101.3	102.6
Japan	DC to private sector	161.7	160.9	161.8
France	DC provided by financial sector	.	.	.
France	DC to private sector by banks	94.1	95.1	96.7
France	DC to private sector	94.1	95.1	97.4
Spain	DC provided by financial sector	.	.	.
Spain	DC to private sector by banks	130.5	119.2	111.4
Spain	DC to private sector	130.6	119.2	111.7
Russia	DC provided by financial sector	.	.	.
Russia	DC to private sector by banks	54.8	55.9	53.1
Russia	DC to private sector	54.8	56.0	53.1
Switzerland	DC provided by financial sector	.	.	.
Switzerland	DC to private sector by banks	165.1	166.8	170.4
Switzerland	DC to private sector	165.1	166.8	170.4
Sweden	DC provided by financial sector	.	.	.
Sweden	DC to private sector by banks	129.4	126.6	128.5
Sweden	DC to private sector	129.4	126.6	128.5
China	DC provided by financial sector	.	.	.
China	DC to private sector by banks	140.2	152.6	156.2
China	DC to private sector	140.2	152.6	156.2

(continued)

Table B2 (continued)

Country or area	*Credit measure*	*2014*	*2015*	*2016*
Poland	DC provided by financial sector	.	.	.
Poland	DC to private sector by banks	52.9	53.6	54.7
Poland	DC to private sector	52.9	53.6	54.7
World	DC provided by financial sector	.	.	.
World	DC to private sector by banks	82.7	85.7	86.7
World	DC to private sector	119.9	123.4	125.2

All figures are percentages of GDP

Oskar Morgenstern stated half a century ago that strictly speaking, economic statistics are not properly scientific observations.[6] They must be used with special care and that is probably applicable especially to such difficult-to-observe quantities as "monetary aggregates" or estimates of debt.

[6] Morgenstern (1959), *International financial transactions and business cycles*, 9; Morgenstern (1950), *On the accuracy of economic observations*, is a more general presentation.

APPENDIX C—ECONOMIC GROWTH AND CLIMATE CHANGE

During the past century, physicists, geoscientists, and climatologists developed the theory of anthropogenic climate change. This theory, today largely accepted worldwide, posits that the average global temperatures and the frequency of extreme weather events will continue increasing toward catastrophic levels if the present evolution is not changed. The key element of the theory is a mechanism that implies physical and chemical mechanisms, i.e., the accumulation in the atmosphere of gases produced by human activities increases the so-called greenhouse effect—the capture of heat radiation reaching Earth from the sun.

Since greenhouse gasses (GHG), mainly carbon dioxide (CO_2) and methane (CH_4), are produced by economic activity of almost any kind, and since economic activity is quantified by indicators of national income such as GDP, it is to be expected that the contribution of an economy to climate change in terms of GHG emissions will be strongly determined by its GDP. Similarly, the change in emissions over time will be strongly correlated with the change in GDP, that is, with economic growth. Figure C1 shows the links between economic activities, GHG emissions, and climate change, suggesting a causal link between the growth of the economy and the processes leading to climate change. That causal link has been largely ignored by economists, social researchers, and opinion leaders. It is not surprising, as since the 1930s, when tools to measure economic growth were developed, there has been general agreement across the political spectrum that economic growth must be the guiding principle of all government policies.

Although there has been significant criticism of this principle,[7] economic growth—often put in the context of millennium goals or so-called "sustainable development"—is still repeatedly presented as the overarching guiding principle.[8] This is not surprising, as in the market economy that prevails worldwide, it is only economic growth that allows for job creation and social contentment in the short run.

[7] Stiglitz, Sen & Fitoussi (2010), *Report by the Commission on the Measurement of Economic Performance and Social Progress*.

[8] Spash (2020), "A tale of three paradigms: Realising the revolutionary potential of ecological economics", *Ecological Economics* 169, 106518.

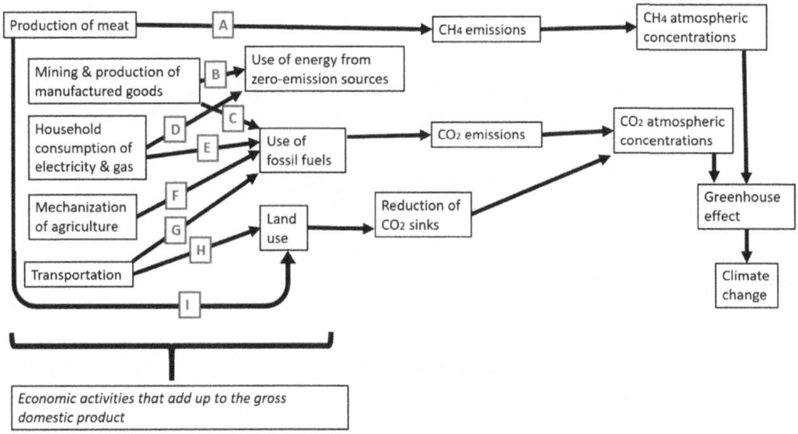

Fig. C1 Causal pathways connecting economic activities to climate change. To simplify the figure, some economic sectors (e.g., finance) and links (e.g., mining & industry → land use) have been omitted

When ecological disruption and climate change were first mentioned as a major threat to humanity, the economic professions were largely reluctant to acknowledge them as a major problem, aligning mostly with politicians and business leaders, who applauded Indian Prime Minister Indira Gandhi who, in Stockholm in 1972, in the first Conference of the United Nations on the Human Environment, claimed that poverty was the greatest source of pollution. In 1992, the *World Development Report* of the World Bank stated that some forms of pollution increase and then decrease with economic growth, in a kind of inverted-U curve. Because this pattern of pollution and income has some resemblance to the pattern of inequality and income that had been suggested in the 1950s by Simon Kuznets, this pollution–income relationship was labeled “environmental Kuznets curve,” or EKC. Since then, tests of this theory for given pollutants have been reported in hundreds of publications that used increasingly complex models to demonstrate or refute the inverted-U pattern, creating what was once described as “a thicket of mathematics and econometrics”.[9] Under the assumption that because the EKC economic growth is ultimately good for the environment, because

[9] Levinson (2000), “The Ups and Downs of the Environmental Kuznets Curve”.

it would eventually cause pollution emissions to abate, economic growth has been encouraged without any regard to its environmental consequences. It was claimed that environmental regulations might actually be damaging the environment, as by reducing economic growth they would be "reducing environmental quality, or at least reducing the rate of improvement".[10] It was probably during the first decade of the present century that the economic profession started to move slowly away from a stance of little or no concern about climate change. The Stern Review on *The Economics of Climate Change* was a 700-page report for the British government in which a team of reputed economists and researchers argued that climate change demanded urgent attention and was worthy of major spending. Controversies on the EKC as applied to different pollutants, including GHG in general and CO_2 in particular, have continued and multiplied since the turn of the century. Many investigations have reached results inconsistent with the EKC hypothesis and consistent with a direct cause–effect link from economic growth to CO_2 emissions.[11] However, apparently this has not weakened the view that economic growth and emissions are either unlinked or linked by an EKC which eventually will make economic growth the cause of *declining* emissions. These views seem to dominate among economists and political leaders, as shown by a number of recent statements. Prominent among them was a paper authored in 2017 by President Obama, in which the years 2008–2015 were described as "the first sustained period of rapid GHG emissions reductions and simultaneous economic growth on record," which for Obama was evidence of the reality of decoupling of GHG emissions and economic growth. Furthermore, as Obama—or whoever wrote the paper for him—said, "although this decoupling is most pronounced in the United States, evidence that economies can grow while emissions do not is emerging around the world'.[12] Perhaps the most important positioning of the economic profession on climate change and its relation with economic growth was the statement published on January 17, 2019, in *The Wall Street Journal*, and signed by 3508 U.S. economists, including

[10] Bartlett (1994), "The high-cost of turning green", *Wall Street Journal*, September 14, A-18.

[11] Saidi & Hammami (2015), "The impact of CO_2 emissions and economic growth on energy consumption in 58 countries", *Energy Reports* 1, 62–70.

[12] Obama (2017), "The irreversible momentum of clean energy", Science 355(6321), 126–129.

four former chairs of the Federal Reserve, 27 Nobel laureate economists, 15 former chairs of the Council of Economic Advisers, and two former secretaries of the U.S. Department of the Treasury. This statement constitutes the clearest illustration of a new stance of the economic profession on climate change policy. On the one hand, it argues in favor of "a robust and gradually rising carbon tax" that will be fully returned to the public and will curb CO_2 emissions; on the other hand, it is said, the policy will stimulate economic growth.[13] Obviously, if economic growth were the cause of rising climate change emissions, to curb emissions and at the same time stimulate economic growth would be quite difficult, not to say impossible. But the aforementioned statements clearly demonstrate that for the economic profession at large, either there is no causal link between growth and climate change or, if there is a causal link, the nature of that link is that implied by the EKC.

The analyses outlined in this appendix reach however opposite views. Evidence in favor of an EKC for emissions per capita is weak, model dependent, and based on models which do not maximize the goodness of fit. Contrarily, the evidence is very solid that emissions of CO_2 are strongly correlated with the size of the economy as measured by GDP; and similarly, economic growth, as measured by the annual increase in real GDP, is strongly correlated with the annual increase of CO_2 emissions. From the usual notions on causality it must be inferred that economic growth causes increasing emissions of CO_2 and, through this mechanism, causes climate change. For the sake of brevity, analyses using GHG rather than CO_2 emissions will not be presented here, but they basically rendered very similar results.

Data analyzed are from the Climate Analysis Indicators Tool (CAIT) of the World Resources Institute, except when a different source is indicated.

Plots of emissions and GDP are apposite to describe the data and illustrate the general ideas on the relation between economic growth and emissions. Figure C2 plots emissions and GDP in the UK and the US. The plot for the UK is fully consistent with the view that emissions can decline while GDP grows, though in most countries, in the long-run emissions and GDP grew together as they did in the United States.

Figure C3 plots CO_2 emissions versus GDP in per capita terms in 28 countries in which they appear to be growing together. Figure C4

[13] Economists' Statement on Carbon Dividends (2019), *Wall Street Journal*, 17 Jan.

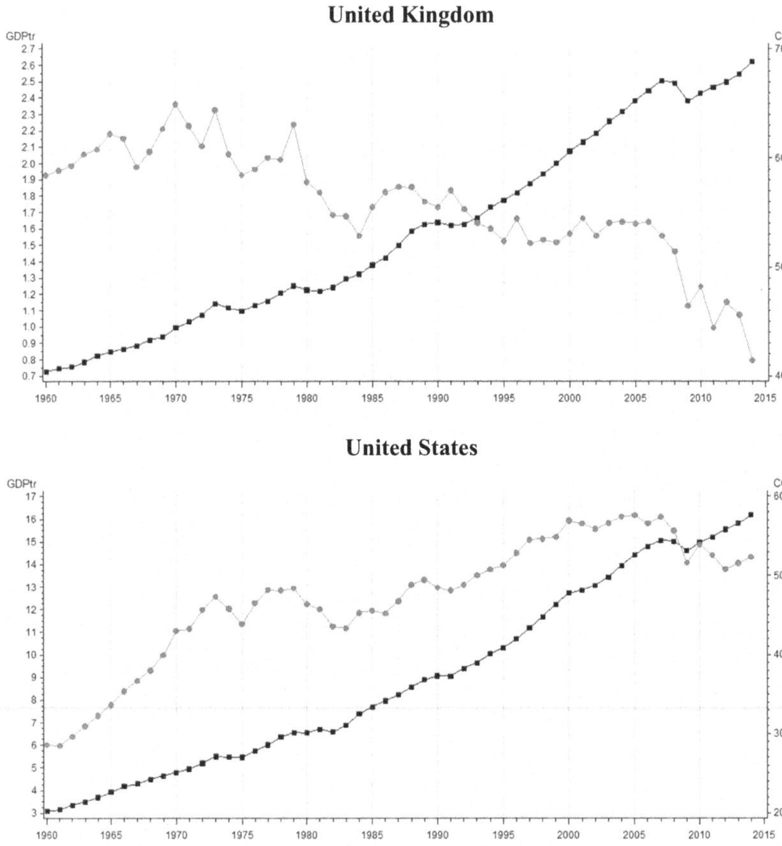

Fig. C2 Real GDP (black squares, trillion US$ of 2010, l.h.s.) and CO_2 emissions (gray dots, megatons, r.h.s.)

however present the same plots for 16 countries in which an inverted-U pattern consistent with the EKC hypothesis looks clear (e.g., Denmark in the first row of Figure 4) or at least suggested (e.g., France). Figures C5 and C6 present emissions and GDP in first differences, for the world economy and for four countries. all the plots are highly suggestive of a strong link between GDP growth and the growth of CO_2 emissions.

Graphs are useful for exploratory analyses, but statistical relations must be quantified with numerical procedures. For the period 1960–2014, the CAIT database includes 7845 pairs of annual emissions of CO_2 and annual GDP; for most countries, there are CO_2 emissions data for 55 years (1960–2014). Assuming a linear link between GDP and emissions, these 7845 observations can be analyzed in several ways, for instance, using all the data in a linear regression

$$E_{ct} = \alpha + \beta Y_{ct} + \varepsilon_{ct} \quad (1)$$

where E_{ct} and Y_{ct} are respectively CO_2 emissions in megatons and GDP in trillion dollars of country c in year t, β is the volume of emissions associated with one trillion dollars of GDP, and ε_{ct} is the error term. This model yields an estimate of 469.7 ± 3.5 megatons (β estimate ± standard error of β), per trillion dollars of GDP ($P < 0.0001$, $R^2 = 0.70$, Durbin-Watson $d = 0.09$).

Regressing annual CO_2 emissions on annual GDP data, that is,

$$E_t = \alpha + \beta Y_t + \varepsilon_t \quad (2)$$

for each of the 186 countries with available data produces a relatively inconsistent picture. For 156 countries, there is a statistically significant positive association of GDP with CO_2 emissions. For example, for the United States the estimate is 164.6 ± 13.6 ($n = 54$, $R^2 = 0.73$, $d = 0.10$), for Uganda 205.3 ± 6.7 ($n = 32$, $R^2 = 0.97$, $d = 0.45$), and for Ukraine 2978.3 ± 513.5 ($n = 26$, $R^2 = 0.57$, $d = 0.05$). Ukraine is the country with the largest CO_2 emissions per dollar of GDP. For 24 countries (Belgium, France, Germany, Luxembourg, Sweden, UK, Zambia, and many ex-Soviet or ex-Yugoslav republics), the regression estimate of the effect of GDP on CO_2 emissions is negative, but the parameter estimate is statistically significant in only 12 of these 24 countries. Thus, for example, for the UK every trillion dollars of GDP is associated with a decrease of 72.9 ± 6.3 megatons of CO_2 emissions ($n = 54$, $R^2 = 0.72$, $d = 0.60$).

Since the series of GDP and emissions are not stationary but strongly trending, the sign of the estimate in these regressions only indicates the direction of the trend in CO_2 emissions in recent decades. Thus, because in the UK in the second half of the twentieth century, CO_2 emissions declined at the same time that GDP increased (Fig. C2), the regression estimate is negative. For a very large majority of the countries, the opposite happened; emissions increased as GDP did (as in the United States, Fig. C2), and for that reason, the estimate is positive.

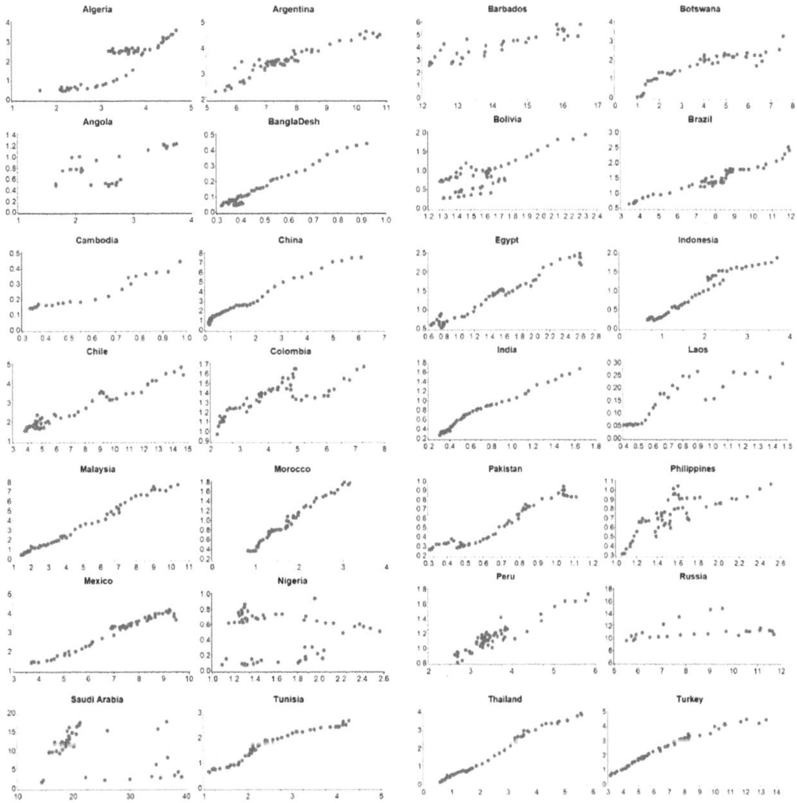

Fig. C3 CO_2 emissions per capita (tonnes, vertical axis) plotted versus GDP per capita (thousand US$2010) in 1960–2014 for 28 countries. Excepting the cases of Russia, Nigeria, and Saudi Arabia, emissions look steadily increasing with economic growth. Note very different scales in the 28 panels. (Author's elaboration from CAIT data.)

As revealed by the values of the Durbin-Watson *d* well below 2.0, all these models with emissions and GDP in levels are strongly influenced by the long-term trends. As both emissions and GDP have strong trends, these series have strong positive autocorrelation which generates spurious relations between variables. In other words, all these are spurious regressions.

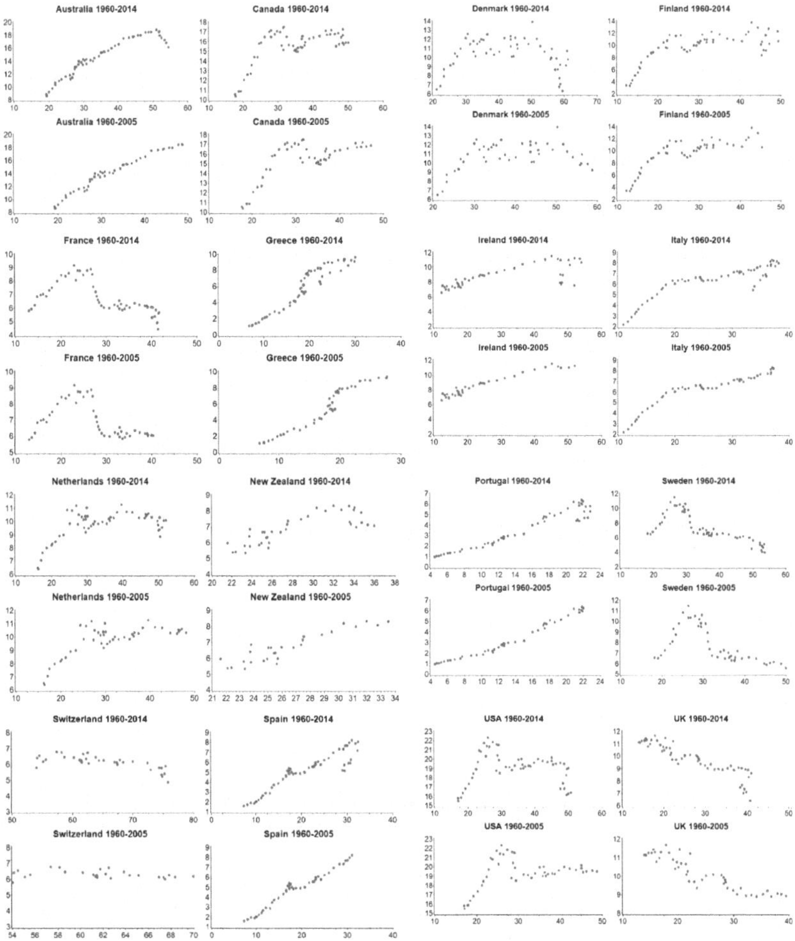

Fig. C4 CO_2 emissions per capita (tonnes) plotted versus GDP per capita (thousand US$2010) in 1960–2014 and 1960–2005 for 16 countries in which the plots are at least suggestive of an inverted-U shape. (Author's elaboration using CAIT data.)

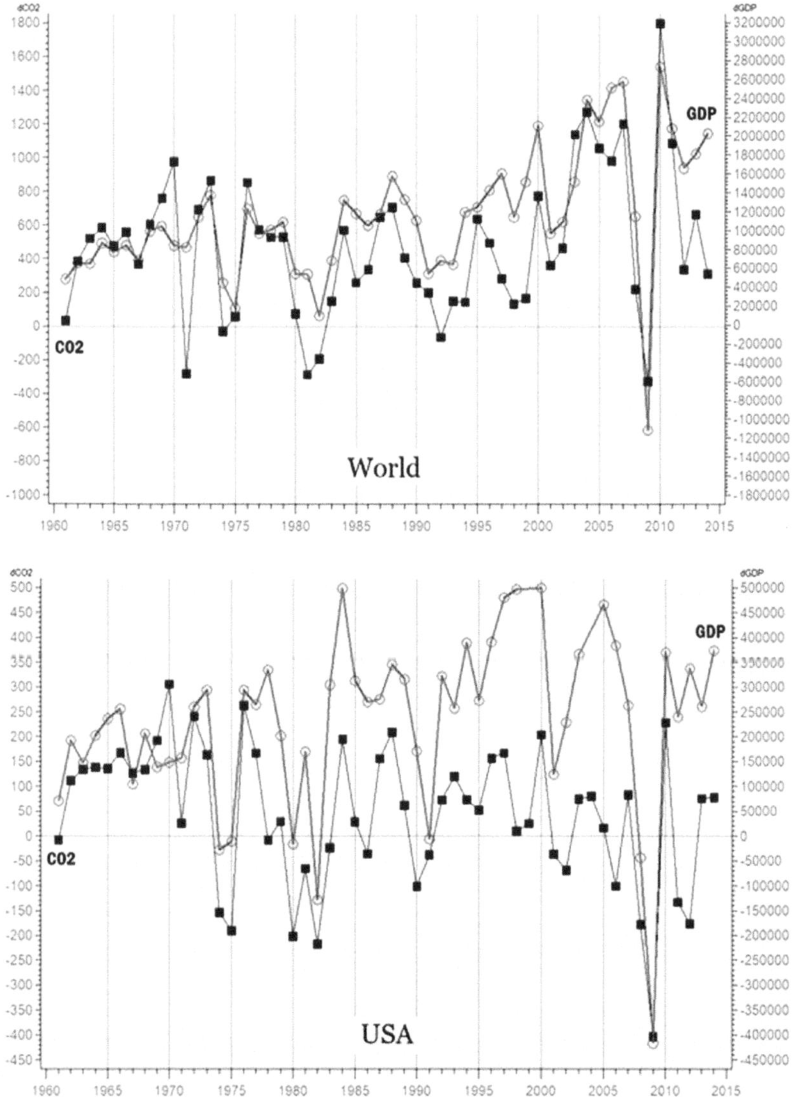

Fig. C5 Annual change in CO_2 emissions (million tonnes, black squares) and GDP (million US 2010 dollars, red circles) for the world and the US economy. (Author's elaboration using CAIT data.)

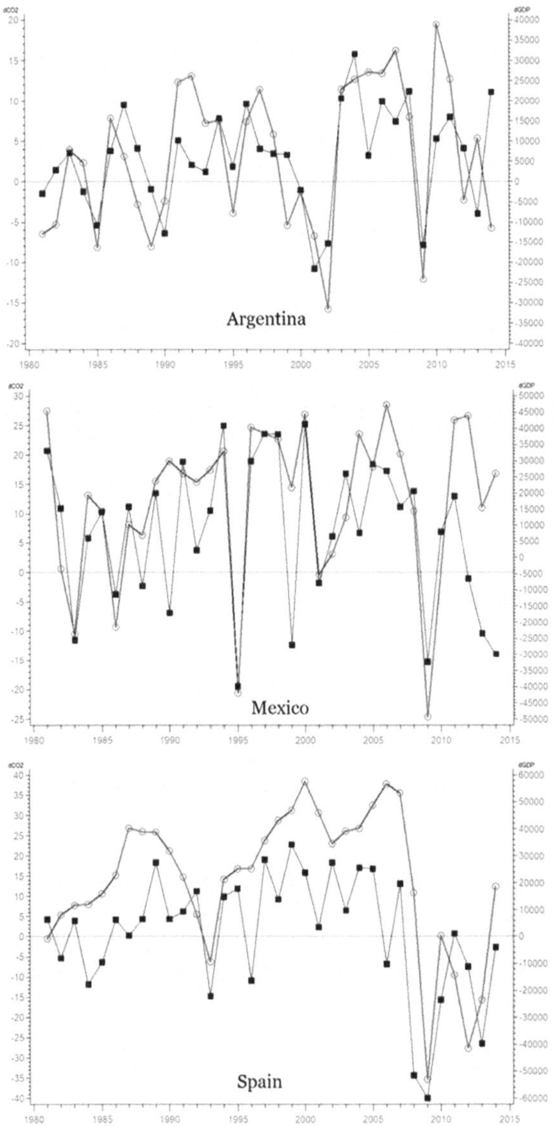

Fig. C6 Annual changes of CO_2 emissions (million tonnes, black squares, left scale) and GDP (million US 2010 dollars, circles, right square) for Argentina, Mexico, and Spain, 1981–2014. (Author's elaboration with CAIT data.)

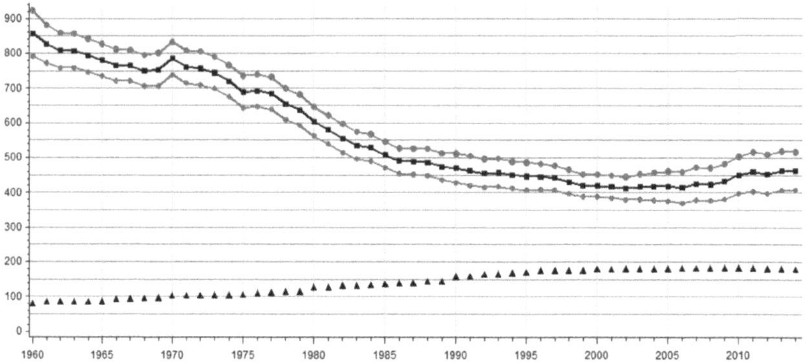

Fig. C7 Estimates of the emissions of CO_2 (in megatons of CO_2 black squares) per trillion dollars of GDP based on regressions of national CO_2 emissions on GDP, for each year in the period 1960–2014. Gray dots are 95% confidence limits for the estimate. Triangles indicate the number of countries included in each regression

One approach to overcome that problem is to regress the annual national emissions for a given year on the national GDP values for that year for all available countries. That is,

$$E_c = \alpha + \beta Y_c + \varepsilon_c \tag{3}$$

where E_c and Y_c are respectively emissions and GDP in a given year for the different countries *c*. That renders 55 regressions. The number of countries for which annual CO_2 emissions exist in the CAIT database has been growing, from 82 in 1960 to 180 in 2014. Figure C.7 shows the regression results, the amount of CO_2 corresponding to one trillion dollars of GDP has declined since the early 1960s, when it was over 800 megatons, to the early years of the 2000s, when it was around 400 megatons. More recently, however, it has increased to around 450 megatons. In these 55 regressions, the Durbin-Watson *d* was in general very close to 2.0, indicating negligible autocorrelation of the residuals. Therefore, the standard errors of these estimates are not underestimated because of autocorrelation. The amount of CO_2 emissions associated with a trillion dollars of GDP, which was declining between 1990 and 2005, has increased since then. The same applies to the analysis of GHG emissions (results not shown).

There are other ways to deal with trends in the variables of a panel. One is the introduction of fixed effects, or linear trends, or both, in the model. Another one is the computation of models with variables in first differences.

In the model

$$E_{ct} = \alpha + \beta Y_{ct} + \gamma_c + \delta_t + \varepsilon_{ct} \quad (4)$$

γ_c and δ_t are respectively fixed effects for each country and each year; E_{ct} is emissions, and Y_{ct} is GDP as in Eq. 1. This analysis with fixed effects for country and year adjusts the results of the regression for the influence of hypothetical time-invariant variables particular to specific nations in the panel, or country-invariant factors linked to the concrete years and time-trends present in the panel.[14]

Time-trends that are common to all the countries in the panel will be also adjusted for by the fixed effect for years. Table C1 shows the results of panel models such as Eq. 4 in which CO_2 emissions are regressed on GDP and country and year fixed effect as explanatory covariates. For the whole sample including 7845 observations, one trillion US$ is associated with 363.8 ± 5.4 megatons of CO_2 emissions ($P < 0.001$ in both cases). Suppressing any of the two fixed effects, or both, the estimates maintain their statistical significance but increase in value between 10 and 25% (results not shown). Adding to the model country-specific linear trends

Table C1 Results of models (parameter estimate β with its standard error) in which CO_2 emissions are regressed on real GDP, fixed effects for country and year, and country-specific linear trends in some specifications

		Estimates			
Sample	*n*	β	*St. error*	R^2	*Country-specific trend*
1960–2014	7845	363.8	5.4	0.87	No
1960–1989	3387	297.8	5.7	0.98	No
1990–2014	4452	594.7	9.0	0.94	No
1960–2014	7845	783.5	7.0	0.98	Yes
1960–1989	3387	43.5	27.3	0.99	Yes
1990–2014	4452	923.0	8.4	> 0.99	Yes

[14] Kennedy (2003), *A guide to econometrics,* 5th ed, 301–306.

for protecting against potential bias due to country-specific trends, that is,

$$E_{ct} = \alpha + \beta\, Y_{ct} + \gamma_c + \delta_t + \mu_c t + \varepsilon_{ct} \tag{5}$$

where μ_c is the country-specific slope and t is year, the β estimate of CO_2 emissions per trillion dollars of GDP more than doubles to 783.5 ± 7.0 (Table C1). Splitting the sample shows that *in the period 1960–1989 the association of emissions with GDP growth is weaker than in the later period 1990–2014.* Indeed, when country-specific linear trends are included in the model computed for the years 1960–1989, the estimate is just 43.5 ± 27.3, with $P = 0.11$, barely within the border or marginal significance. However, the same model computed with data for the years 1990–2014 produces a very significant estimate of 923.0 ± 8.4 megatons of CO_2 per trillion dollars of GDP ($P < 0.0001$).

For short time series like the ones used in this investigation, the first differences, that is, year-to-year changes in the series of annual data, can be considered stationary. A priori, it can be expected that the annual change in CO_2 or GHG emissions will be correlated with the annual change in real GDP, as CO_2 is produced by human activity (Fig. C1), and human activities are largely economic activities that GDP quantifies in terms of monetary value.

Using all the available data ($n = 7761$) to compute the model

$$\Delta E_{ct} = \alpha + \beta\, \Delta Y_{ct} + \varepsilon_{ct} \tag{6}$$

where ΔE_{ct} is the annual change in emissions and ΔY_{ct} is the annual change in GDP in country c, an annual change of one trillion dollars in GDP appears associated with an annual change of 409.2 ± 3.3 megatons of CO_2 emissions ($R^2 = 0.66$). In the case of GHG emissions, fewer data are available ($n = 4323$), but the estimate, 425.5 ± 6.2 CO_2-equivalent megatons of GHG per trillion dollars of GDP ($R^2 = 0.52$), is similar in magnitude.

Decomposing this general relation in partial regressions by country or by year provides interesting insights. Thus, for almost all countries the relation between annual change in CO_2 emissions and annual change in GDP is positive, and for a large majority of countries, it is also statistically significant (results not shown). Not even one country in the sample of 184 countries shows a statistically significant *negative* relation between the annual growth of GDP and the annual change in emissions.

Table C2 shows the cross-correlations between annual changes in CO_2 emissions and real GDP for each year of the period for which data are available. There is a very large positive correlation between both variables, over 0.9 for most years. An interesting finding of this analysis, however, is that much weaker correlations, even sometimes close to zero or negative, coincide with periods of worldwide economic crisis. Thus, for instance, the correlation is quite below 0.8 in 1974, 1975, 1980–1983, 1990–1994, 1997–1999, and 2008.

Estimates of the annual change in CO_2 emissions associated with the annual change in GDP based on data for a unique country or region vary widely. For the world at large, it is 473 ± 57 megatons per trillion dollars of GDP ($P < 0.001$). For the United States, France, the UK, China, and the European Union, the figure is between 600 and 900 megatons of CO_2, while for Uganda it is 243 ± 63 megatons.

All the former results show a statistical association which indeed suggests a causal link, between GDP growth and growth in CO_2 emissions. However, they are not models for testing the EKC hypothesis, which is tested in models whose results are presented in Table C3.

The first six lines of Table C3 present regression estimates for panel models such as

$$e_{ct} = \alpha + \beta\, y_{ct} + \gamma_c + \delta_t + \mu_c t + \varepsilon_{ct} \tag{7}$$

where e_{ct} and y_{ct} are respectively CO_2 emissions per capita and GDP per capita for country c in year t, γ_c, and δ_t are respectively fixed effects for country and year, $\mu_c t$ are country-specific linear trends, and ε_{ct} is the error term. With a sample for 1990–2014 including 4380 observations and a model including country-specific linear trends, regression results reveal a statistically significant effect of GDP per capita on emissions per capita, with one thousand extra US$ of GDP per capita associated with 0.256 ± 0.032 extra tons of CO_2 emissions ($P < 0.001$). For other samples or models without country-specific linear trends, no statistically significant estimate is found for the effect of GDP per capita on emissions per capita.

The EKC hypothesis for CO_2 emissions per capita is based in a regression model such as

$$e_{ct} = \alpha + \beta_1\, y_{ct} + \beta_2 (y_{ct})^2 + \gamma_c + \delta_t + \mu_c t + \varepsilon_{ct} \tag{8}$$

Table C2 Pearson correlations (r) between the annual increase in real GDP (in US$ of 2009) and the annual growth of CO_2 emissions for each year of the period 1961–2014

Year	*r*	*N*	*Year*	*r*	*N*
1961	0.34***	85	1991	0.67***	162
1962	0.95***	87	1992	0.04	163
1963	0.99***	90	1993	0.68***	169
1964	0.99***	88	1994	0.58***	170
1965	0.99***	91	1995	0.89***	172
1966	0.99***	89	1996	0.98***	173
1967	0.94***	98	1997	0.79***	180
1968	0.99***	96	1998	0.67***	180
1969	0.98***	101	1999	0.61***	180
1970	0.54***	99	2000	0.95***	180
1971	−0.94***	108	2001	0.92***	183
1972	0.98***	106	2002	0.85***	183
1973	1.00***	109	2003	0.93***	185
1974	−0.19*	107	2004	0.90***	185
1975	0.35***	110	2005	0.88***	185
1976	0.99***	108	2006	0.87***	185
1977	0.94***	115	2007	0.93***	186
1978	0.90***	116	2008	0.73***	186
1979	0.98***	119	2009	0.83***	187
1980	0.15	119	2010	0.98***	187
1981	−0.83***	132	2011	0.86***	187
1982	0.01	132	2012	0.76***	185
1983	0.67***	137	2013	0.94***	185
1984	0.97***	137	2014	0.72***	183
1985	0.94***	138			
1986	0.90***	141			
1987	0.97***	143			
1988	0.94***	143			
1989	0.93***	148			
1990	0.39***	148			

N is the number of data (countries) that were used to compute the correlation.

in which $(y_{ct})^2$ is squared GDP per capita and everything else as in Eq. 6. With β_1 positive and β_2 negative, when the derivative

$d(e_{ct})/d(y_{ct}) = \beta_1 + 2\beta_2\ y_{ct}$ equals zero, GDP per capita reaches the level $y_{ct} = -\beta_1/2\beta_2$ which is the top of the inverted-U curve hypothesized by the EKC.

Table C3 Results of models with CO_2 emissions per capita (tons) as dependent variable regressed on real GDP per capita (thousand 2010 US$, fixed effects for country and year, and country-specific linear trends (CSLT) when indicated

	Sample	*N*	β_1	β_2	β_3	*CSLT*	$-\beta_1/2\beta_2$	*QIC*
A1	1960–2014	7717	0.044			Yes		7492.6
A2	1960–1989	3337	0.038			Yes		3166.8
A3	1990–2014	4380	0.256***			Yes		4066.4
A4	1960–2014	7717	−0.021			No		7918.7
A5	1960–1989	3337	−0.028			No		3274.0
A6	1990–2014	4380	0.044			No		4369.5
B1	1960–2014	7717	0.253*	−0.002+		Yes	63.3	7601.0
B2	1960–1989	3337	−0.245	0.003		Yes	40.8	3190.9
B3	1990–2014	4380	0.45***	−0.002*		Yes	112.5	4124.0
B4	1960–2014	7717	0.241***	−0.003***		No	40.2	7862.4
B5	1960–1989	3337	0.188*	−0.003***		No	31.3	3266.6
B6	1990–2014	4380	0.253***	−0.002***		No	63.3	4356.2
C1	1960–2014	7717	0.444**	−0.007**	0.00003	Yes		7668.9
C2	1960–1989	3337	−0.291	0.004	−0.00001	Yes		3214.7
C3	1990–2014	4380	0.779***	−0.011***	0.00006***	Yes		4124.0
C4	1960–2014	7717	0.469***	−0.009***	0.00004***	No		7947.7
C5	1960–1989	3337	0.392*	−0.008*	0.00004	No		3288.5
C6	1990–2014	4380	0.427***	−0.006**	0.00003*	No		4356.2

To this basic regression structure of models A1–A6, in models B1–B1, squared GDP per capita is added as covariate, while in models C1–C6 also GDP per capita to the third power is added. β_1, β_2, and β_3 are respectively the effect estimates of GDP per capita to the first, second, and third power. Standard errors adjusted for repeated observations. Since the AIC cannot be computed for this type of models, the QIC is provided as an analogous to AIC to assess the model fit

N = number of observations; *** $P < 0.1$, * $P < 0.05$, ** $P < 0.01$, *** $P < 0.001$. P values computed from standard errors adjusted for repeated country observations. Observations' correspond to 193 countries in the sample period indicated

Models B1 to B6 in Table C3 show results for specifications like Eq. 8. Models B1 and B3–B6 are consistent with the EKC hypothesis, as estimates for β_1 are positive and estimates for β_2 are negative.

An inverted-U distribution of per capita emissions versus per capita GDP is consistent with a quadratic function, but some authors have proposed that rather than in inverted U, the distribution could be *N*-shaped[15] (see, for instance, the graphs for Canada, Finland, or Japan in Fig. C4), which would be consistent with a cubic function. That hypothesis is tested in models C1–C5 of Table C3. As shown there, β_3 in specifications C4–C6 is positive and significant, which is consistent with a distribution in *N*, not with an inverted U.

Another way to test the EKC hypothesis is to compute models such as

$$e_c = \alpha + \beta_1 y_c + \beta_2 (y_c)^2 + \varepsilon_c \tag{9}$$

for specific years using all the available pairs of CO_2 emissions and GDP data, which are just 78 in 1960 but rise up to 186 in 2014. In these models, issues of autocorrelation between successive observations for a given country are solved by the specification of the model which, of course, makes fixed effects unnecessary. In these models, the estimate for β_1 is always positive and significant while β_2 is negative in only a few cases. With a cubic term in the model

$$e_c = \alpha + \beta_1 y_c + \beta_2 (y_c)^2 + \beta_3 (y_{ct})^3 + \varepsilon_c \tag{10}$$

the model computed for specific years between 1960 and 2014 yields a β_2 estimate almost always negative but often not significant, while the estimates for β_1 and β_3 are almost always positive and significant.

An econometric question is whether the models that have been presented are reduced form or structural form equations? In non-econometric terms this question could be posed as: Are these equations simply revealing associations between left-hand-side and right-hand-side variables, or are they revealing causal effects of the right-hand-side variables on the left-hand-side dependent variable? Since economic activities overall generate emissions contributing to climate change (pathways A, C,

[15] Allard et al. (2018), "The N-shaped environmental Kuznets curve: An empirical evaluation using a panel quantile regression approach", *Environmental Science & Pollution Research* 25(6), 5848–5861.

and E to I in Fig. C1) but sometimes economic growth opens up pathways (B and D in Fig. C1) which do not generate emissions and therefore do not contribute to climate change, it appears legitimate to model emissions as a function of GDP, or emissions per capita as a function of GDP per capita either in levels or in first differences. Thus, equations such as those previously presented, when fixed effects are included to adjust results for unknown variables associated with particular years or specific countries, can be seen as structural forms, revealing causal effects.

At any rate, for the sake of argument, it can be thought they are simply reduced-form equations, so that the regression results reveal only statistical associations. These associations are however somewhat inconsistent. Thus we saw that results from models in which emissions or emission growth are a linear function of GDP or GDP growth overall suggest an association of increasing GDP with rising emissions and climate change. But results of models in which emissions per capita are modeled as a function of GDP per capita provide in some cases suggestive evidence that emissions per capita follow a functional form consistent with the EKC, so that GDP growth, eventually, would be either associated or contributing to falling emissions and mitigation of climate change.

This inconsistency is largely solved by comparing the relative strength of the evidence provided by different models. While models based on Eqs. 4, 5, and 6 reveal fairly solid associations of the size of GDP with the volume of emissions and increasing GDP with increasing emissions, models based on specifications like Eq. 8 provide only weak evidence suggesting an EKC for CO_2 emissions. That is so for several reasons.

First, comparing models on the basis of goodness of fit, there is no reason to introduce quadratic or cubic terms in the equation, since, for instance, model A1 compared with models B1 or C1 has a lower QIC value (Table C3), indicating a better fit. The same can be said of model A2 compared with models B2, C2, etc. Thus, the most parsimonious models are those not providing any evidence in favor of the EKC.

Second, in five of the six models including a cubic term (C1 and C3–C6, Table C3) the sign of the parameter estimates (β_1 and β_3 positive, β_2 negative) is not consistent with a curve in inverted U but rather with a curve in N.

Third, the GDP per capita level at which it is supposed that economic growth will begin to be associated with declining emissions depends strongly on sample and model, ranging from US$31,300 (model B5,

Table C3) to US$112,500 (model B3), a value which is almost out of the sample. With variables in logs, the range is even wider.

Fourth, the EKC in inverted U is not robust to sample selection, as changing the sample can make it either appear or disappear. Thus, in model B2 of Table C3, β_1 is negative and β_2 is positive, implying a curve in U, not in inverted U, and since $-\beta_1/2\beta_2 = 40.8$, GDP per capita over US$40,800 would be associated with increasing, not decreasing, emissions. This lack of robustness of the inverted-U functional form to sample selection has been also found when examining the EKC hypothesis for other pollutants.[16] In Fig. C4, in the plot of emissions per capita versus GDP per capita, the pattern suggestive of an inverted-U shape for a number of countries (e.g., Australia, Spain, the Netherlands, etc.) in the sample 1960–2014 mostly disappears when the sample is 1960–2005. This shows that *the inverted-U shape was to a large extent an effect of the economic downturn of the Great Recession*.

Fifth, nonlinear transformations (such as squares and cubes) of non-stationary unit-root series such as GDP per capita imply major uncertainties when they are included in panel regression models, as the statistical theory for such models is fundamentally different from that of models including linear unit-root series.[17]

Sixth, results from models such as Eqs. 7 and 8 do not provide evidence in favor of an inverted-U EKC; rather, they are more consistent with an *N*-shape.

Taken together, these reasons make the evidence in favor of an inverted-U curve very weak, compared with the strong evidence in favor of a direct causal link between GDP and emissions. At the level of GDP per capita and per capita emissions, the evidence in favor of the existence of a specific shape is rather weak, as the goodness of fit of models is best for models without quadratic or cubic terms. Indeed, though also weak as it is only present in one sample (model A3, Table C3), the main support provided by these models is for a linear link, as distributions shaped in

[16] Harbaugh, Levinson & Wilson (2002), "Reexamining the empirical evidence for an environmental Kuznets curve", *Review of Economics & Statistics* 84(3), 541–551.

[17] Wagner (2008), "The carbon Kuznets curve: A cloudy picture emitted by bad econometrics?", *Resource & Energy Economics* 30, 388–408; Schröder& Storm (2020), "Economic growth and carbon emissions: The road to 'Hothouse Earth' is paved with good intentions", *International Journal of Political Economy* 49(2), 153–173.

inverted U or in N come from models which should not be chosen on the basis of goodness of fit.

The most solid evidence of a statistical association between GDP and CO_2 emissions comes from the models based on Eqs. 4, 5, and 6, as presented in the text and in Tables C1 and C2. These results indicate a very strong correlation between GDP and emissions, or between GDP growth and emissions growth. A statistical correlation, however, does not by itself reveal a true cause–effect link. John Stuart Mill and Hans Reichenbach theorized that two things varying together are either causing each other or being caused by a third factor[18]; in more modern terms, a correlation between two variables indicates either a causal link or the presence of a causal fork with a confounder which creates a spurious association.[19] In the present case, is there any reason to believe the correlation of GHG emissions and economic activity is a spurious one due to a confounder variable?

The idea that correlation does not mean causation has sometimes been used as a pretext to ignore causal relations when the existence of a causal link ran counter to powerful preconceptions. For instance, Ignaz Semmelweis observed in the nineteenth century that puerperal fever in childbearing women was much more frequent when childbirth assistance had been given by doctors rather than midwives. He attributed it to the fact that doctors were often present in necropsies just previous to attending childbirth, whereas midwives were not.[20] At the time infectious germs were unknown and the observation by Semmelweis was considered outrageous by doctors who saw it as a spurious correlation, of course not a causal link. Similarly, the causal link between smoking and lung cancer was denied by smoking enthusiasts and the tobacco industry on the claim that the correlation between the two phenomena was simply a spurious association. A gene causing both a proclivity to cancer and a tendency to

[18] Mill (1846), *A system of logic, ratiocinative and inductive: Being a connected view of the principles of evidence and the methods of scientific investigation*; Reichenbach (1956), *The direction of time.*.

[19] Pearl & Mackenzie (2018), *The book of why: The new science of cause and effect.*

[20] Semmelweis (1988) [1855], "The etiology, concept, and prophylaxis of childbed fever", in Buck et al., Carol, E. Llopis, E. Nájera, and M. Terris. *The challenge of epidemiology: Issues and selected readings.*

smoke was posited as a likely explanation.[21] It was also claimed that there is not a causal link between smoking and cancer because "obviously" what causes cancer is not smoking, but the tar of tobacco smoke. Similarly, a reviewer of a previous version of this manuscript claimed that what causes climate change is not economic growth, but the gases that are produced with it.

If highly correlated variations of GDP and CO_2 emissions (Figures C5 and C6) are not evidence of causality, some omitted variable should exist causing the movements of both. But such omitted variable has never been mentioned. Thus, the correlation of these two variables has to be taken as evidence in favor of economic activity causing emissions which, in turn, causes climate change. Despite the enthusiasm of the economic profession and the society at large for economic growth, this troublesome causal link is hard to be denied. Unarguably, the human actions blamed by the IPCC and the scientific community for producing GHG emissions, and thus climate change, are mainly the economic activities quantified by national GDPs and their global aggregate. This is so because economic activities as a rule require energy—today largely produced by burning fossil fuels—and they remove GHG sinks, and in many cases do both. Only a few quantitatively minor pathways lead to energy use that does not contribute to GHG emissions.

In historical experience, economic growth may be associated with some technological changes that reduce emissions per unit of output or emissions per unit of energy use, but other technological changes increase these ratios and the net effect is ambiguous. In the early stages of economic growth, technological change usually implies mechanization, displacement of human labor, and increasing use of both energy and materials. In farming, donkeys, horses, plows, and human manual labor are displaced by agricultural machinery; in mining, construction, or manufacturing, the use of pick and shovel is displaced by machines that do the work of hundreds of workers but require fuel, or electricity—which requires fuel combustion.

Greater quantities of meat, along with comforts such as heating and AC, are increasingly demanded and consumed with rising GDP per capita, again drawing heavily on GHG-producing sources of energy. Reusable beverage containers are displaced by disposable ones, which

[21] Cahuc & Zylberberg (2016), *Le négationnisme économique: et comment s'en débarrasser*; Pearl & Mackenzie (2018), *The book of why*.

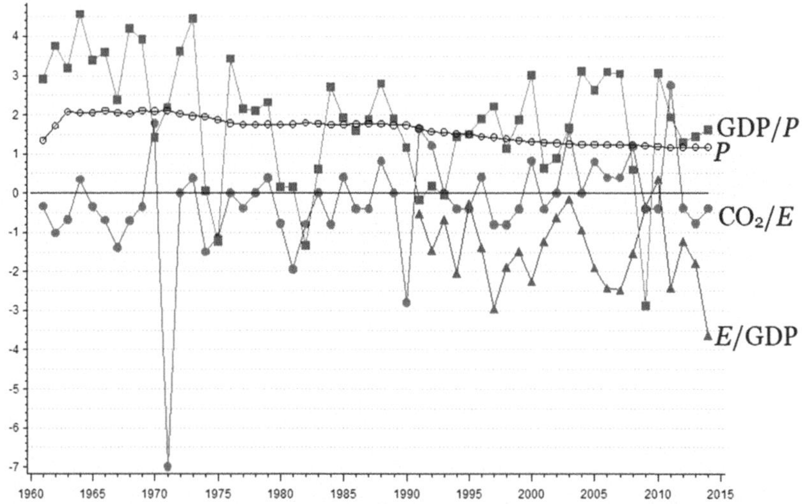

Fig. C8 Rates of annual growth (%) of the four multipliers that yield CO_2 emissions according to the Kaya identity: population (*P*, empty circles), GDP per capita (GDP/*P*, squares), carbon intensity of energy, i.e., emissions of CO_2 per unit or energy used up in the economy (CO_2/E, dots), and energy intensity of the economy, i.e., units of energy per dollar of GDP (*E*/GDP, triangles). (Author's computations from WDI data.)

often imply major inputs of energy (e.g., for the manufacturing or recycling of aluminum cans). Expanding markets and international trade, along with tourism, exponentially expand automobile use and transportation in general, heavily dependent on fossil fuels. All these processes associated with the growth of GDP per capita increase energy consumption, the use of fossil fuels, and the creation of new sources of emissions. Furthermore, a key component of GDP growth is a change in time use, with the displacement of noneconomic activities (sleeping, chatting, playing, etc.) which usually don't produce emissions, by economic activities (producing and marketing commodities) which usually do imply emissions. This is particularly obvious in the upturn of the business cycle, when unemployed workers return to work, or non-employed individuals enter the labor force, and CO_2 emissions, which had dropped during economic downturns, quickly recover.[22]

Total emissions of CO_2 can be deconstructed in several ways. For instance, using the Kaya identity,

$$CO_2 = P \times GDP/P \times CO_2/E \times E/GDP = P \times y \times c \times e,$$

where P is population, E is total energy supplied to the economy, y is GDP per capita, $c = CO_2/E$ is the carbon intensity of the energy supply, and $e = E/GDP$ is the energy intensity of GDP.

If k is the annual rate of growth of CO_2 emissions, by total differentiation of the former equation

$$k = P' + y' + c' + e'$$

where the apostrophe represents the annual rate of growth of the variable. Figure C8 shows P', y', c', and e', that is, the four annual rates of growth which add up to the rate of growth of CO_2 emissions according to the Kaya identity. Figure C8 shows clearly that the two factors contributing to a positive rate of growth of world CO_2 emissions are the growth of GDP per capita and population growth. Population growth has been always positive in the past half-century, although steadily declining since the 1970s, while per capita GDP has increased faster than the population in most of the years and has been positive almost all the time except during a few years of world economic downturn. The energy intensity of the economy (E/GDP) has declined in all years except one since data have been available, in 1990, but the rate of growth of the carbon intensity of energy (CO_2/E) which was mostly negative until 2000, has oscillated around zero thereafter. All this provides no evidence of any decoupling of global emissions of CO_2 from the world economy.

Since population growth decreased steadily from 2.1% in 1969 to 1.2% in 2014, and the rate of growth of world GDP per capita has oscillated in the same period between the deepest contraction of −2.9% and the greatest expansion of 4.6%, the implication is that the rise in global CO_2 emissions between 1960 and 1990s was fundamentally led by growth in GDP per capita. Considering just the most recent period, 2000–2014, per capita GDP grew at a mean annual rate of 1.59%, population at 1.23%,

[22] Peters et al. (2012), "Rapid growth in CO_2 emissions after the 2008–2009 global financial crisis", *Nature Climate Change* 2(1), 2–4.

and the energy content of the economy at 0.32%. The energy content of GDP decreased at a mean annual rate of 1.46%, but this was unable to compensate the other factors, so that CO_2 emissions grew at a mean annual rate of 2.8%, much higher than the annual 1.8% forecasted by Holtz-Eakin and Selden.[23]

Downturns of the global economy or national economies are often considered to be due to political factors exogenous to the economy. If these downturns are viewed as caused by oil shocks or other unknown factors exogenous to the economy, they can be conceptualized as natural experiments that provide strong evidence of a causal link between the economy and GHG emissions, as at both the global and national level, emissions drop in recessions and rise in expansions, procyclically. In the United States, CO_2 emissions dropped in the early 1930s during the Great Depression, again in 1937–1938 during the Roosevelt recession, and again in the recessions of 1975, the early 1980s, and the early 1990s.[24] As illustrated in Figures C2, C5, and C6, major declines in emissions occurred in the world and national economies during the Great Recession and following years of stagnant growth, as well as in the mid-1970s and the early 1980s, all times of global economic turmoil. Figure C6 also illustrates the strong decline of emissions during specific crises of national economies, such as the so-called *tequilazo* in 1995 in Mexico, and the 2001–2002 *corralito* in Argentina.

Consistency of the association and a so-called dose–effect relationship also support the case for a causal effect of economic growth on GHG emissions, and thus, on climate change. The correlations between the size of the economy and the size of GHG emissions, and between the change of GDP and the corresponding change of GHG emissions, are strong and consistently observed across countries and basically in all periods, as well as in the global economy at large. As the world leader in CO_2 emissions, China surpassed the United States in 2006, after a period of about two decades in which China's annual GDP grew several percentage points faster than U.S. GDP. This is further evidence of the causal link between GDP growth and the growth of emissions. It is true that in a handful of countries, emissions and GDP have moved in different directions in

[23] Holtz-Eakin & Selden (1995), "Stocking the fires? CO_2 emissions and economic growth", *Journal of Public Economics* 57(1), 85–101.

[24] Tapia & Carpintero (2013), "Dynamics and economic aspects of climate change", in Kang & Banga, eds., *Combating climate change: An agricultural perspective.*

specific periods, but almost without exception in these countries as in all others, there is still a positive and strong correlation between the annual growth of the economy and the annual change in emissions. Furthermore, in these cases, there are specific reasons—e.g., financialization and deindustrialization in the UK and the US, nuclearization in France—to question the reality of decoupling.

Finally, the fact that atmospheric concentrations of CO_2 grow faster during years in which the global economy expands faster is also evidence in favor of a causal link between economic growth and climate change.[25]

Since the theory of anthropogenic climate change was proposed several decades ago, the causal link between economic growth and climate change has been basically ignored, or indirectly denied by the idea that after reaching some optimal level, economic growth would lead to declining emissions, i.e., the EKC hypothesis. Indeed, to some extent the EKC hypothesis can be seen as one factor contributing to the denialist movement.[26] Climate change could be ignored either because it was not a problem, or because it would be solved by economic growth. However, as has been shown here, the EKC for CO_2 is supported on flimsy evidence from a handful of countries which cannot be generalized to the world economy.

The causal link between economic activity and GHG or CO_2 emissions makes emissions of different countries mostly proportional to the size of their economies. Brazil and Nigeria in 2014 had respective GDPs of 2.4 and 0.5 trillion dollars, while their CO_2 emissions were respectively 0.5 and 0.1 gigatons: the proportionality of both variables is evident. That is despite GDP growth in 2014 being just 0.5% in Brazil and 6.3% in Nigeria. In general, an annual GDP growth of, say, 1% in an economy with a size of 2 trillion dollars, e.g., Italy, will be in terms of climate change 10 times more damaging than a 1% growth of an economy with a size of 0.2 trillion, say Pakistan. Pakistan's population is more than triple that of Italy, but population size has little to do with GHG emissions. If emissions per capita were mostly decoupled from GDP per capita, the growth of national total emissions would occur mostly in countries with a high rate of population growth, but that is not the case. For example, in

[25] Tapia, Ionides & Carpintero (2012), "Climate change and the world economy: Short-run determinants of atmospheric CO_2", *Environmental Science & Policy* 21, 50–62.

[26] Dunlap & McCright (2011), "Organized climate change denial", in Dryzek, Norgard & Schlosberg, eds. *Oxford handbook of climate change and society*.

Table C4 Population, GDP and emissions of CO_2 and greenhouse gases (GHG) in 1990 and 2010 in three countries, in levels and in relative growth

						Relative growth (%)			
Country	*Year*	*Population*	*GDP*	*CO_2*	*GHG*	*Population*	*GDP*	*CO_2*	*GHG*
China	1990	1135.2	0.83	2.18	2.83				
	2010	1337.7	6.1	8.61	9.71	1.18	7.35	3.95	3.43
India	1990	873.3	0.47	0.56	1.14				
	2010	1234.3	1.66	1.71	2.47	1.41	3.53	3.05	2.17
Nigeria	1990	95.2	0.13	0.07	0.39				
	2010	158.5	0.37	0.09	0.46	1.66	2.85	1.29	1.18

Population in millions, GDP in trillion USD dollars of 2010, emissions in gigatons of CO_2 (excluding CO_2 emissions corresponding to land use change or forestry activities, LUCF) or CO_2 equivalents (GHG including LUCF). All data from World Resources Institute except population from the WDI database the period 1990–2010, population growth in China, India, and Nigeria was respectively 18%, 41%, and 66%, while their GDPs multiplied respectively by a factor of 7.3, 3.5, and 2.8, and their CO_2 emissions multiplied respectively by 3.9, 3.1, and 1.3. With the greatest population growth, Nigeria was the one with the smallest growth in emissions; inversely, with the lowest population growth, China had the largest growth in emissions (Table C4). Of course, among these three countries China had by far the largest GDP growth.

The evidence of decoupling between economic growth and climate change emissions is weak, while, contrarily, the evidence of GDP growth causing growing emissions is strong. Despite the assertions in favor of decoupling by prominent people such as President Obama and reputed economists of all tendencies, the evidence is strongly supportive of a causal link between economic growth and climate change. This is a sobering fact that, unfortunately, is strongly supported by the available data. It is also a fact with major policy implications.

APPENDIX D—A NOTE ON THE RATE OF PROFIT

In business practice, the rate of return on capital, rate of return on investment, yield, profitability, or profit rate (the terminology is extensive and often confusing) is usually measured for an annual period: it is the ratio of the flow of profit in a year to the initial investment, that is, to the capital advanced at the start of the period.[27] In Marxian terms, total capital is constant capital c plus variable capital v, and total profit is equal to surplus value s. When considering a complete turnover of a given capital, the profit rate is $r = s / (c + v)$, and dividing the numerator and the denominator of this fraction by v, we arrive at $r = \varepsilon / (q + 1)$, where $\varepsilon = s / v$ is what Marx called rate of surplus value (RSV, also called rate of exploitation), and $q = c / v$ is the organic composition of capital (OCC) or value composition of capital (VCC). In the first volume of *Capital*, Marx defined the OCC as "the value-composition of capital, in so far as it is determined by its technical composition and mirrors the changes of the latter."[28] This definition is problematic, as the technical composition of capital (TCC) is defined in the same place as "the relation between the mass of the means of production employed on the one hand, and the mass of labor necessary for their employment at the other." But the means of production employed is mathematically a vector, a set of quantities of heterogeneous raw materials, tools and machines, and its quantitative change is undefined as soon as old tools, machines or raw materials are no longer used, or new ones are introduced, or the same means of production are used but the quantity of some of them increases while the quantity of others decrease. In all these cases it would be impossible to decide whether the change in the VCC is or is not "mirroring" the change in the TCC, because we cannot say whether the change in the TCC is an increase or a decrease. To avoid the problems derived from this inconsistency, the OCC will be here assumed to be just another name for the VCC, so that VCC = OCC = $q = c / v$.

The profit rate $r = s / (c + v)$ is the annual rate of profit only if s, c and v in the formula refer to a capital with a turnover of one year. If the turnover is greater or smaller, so that n, the number of turnovers of that capital in one year, is greater or smaller than 1, the annual rate of profit

[27] Amer & Amer (1977), *A dictionary of business & economics*; Bannock et al. (1998), *The Penguin dictionary of economics.*

[28] Marx [1867] (1977), ch. 25, 762.

must be computed multiplying the numerator by *n*, so that

$$r = ns/(c + v) = n\varepsilon/(q + 1) \tag{1}$$

where *ns* is the profit produced in one year, $n\varepsilon$ is the annual RSV, and ε is the RSV in one turnover of capital. All this can be clearly inferred from two sources, first, an early letter in which Marx explained to Engels his notions on the profit rate[29]; second, Marx's discussion on the circulation of capital in the manuscripts he wrote between the 1860s and his death in 1883, that Engels edited and published as second volume of *Capital* in 1885. However, in Marx's manuscript of 1864–1865—that Engels edited and published in 1893 as volume 3 of *Capital*—there was a section on the influence of the turnover of capital on the profit rate, in which just the title had been written. It was a major hole in Marx's reasoning in that old manuscript. Engels, who had been a business manager for years, and who had already edited volume 2, could not avoid filling that gap. To make Marx's reasoning more consistent in that context, he wrote a whole chapter, chapter 4, for volume 3 of *Capital.* As Engels explained in his preface to volume 3, "the formula for the profit rate given in chapter 3 needed a certain modification if it was to have general validity".[30] The reasoning behind Eq. 1 here is based in chapter 4 introduced by Engels.

Now, if starting with Eq. 1 we take derivatives with respect to time (t), and use the apostrophe to mean the derivative, so that $r' = \mathrm{d}r\ /\ \mathrm{d}t$, $\varepsilon' = \mathrm{d}\varepsilon\ /\ \mathrm{d}t$, etc., we get the following:

$$r' = \left[\left(n\varepsilon' + n'\varepsilon\right)(q + 1) - n\varepsilon q'\right]/(q + 1)^2 \tag{2}$$

If we now divide Eq. 2 by Eq. 1 and use the asterisk to indicate the rate of change (so that $r^* = r'\ /\ r$ is the rate of change of the rate of profit, $\varepsilon^* = \varepsilon'\ /\ \varepsilon$ is the rate of change of the RSV, etc.), the rate of change of the profit rate is

$$r^* = \varepsilon^* + n^* - \left[q'/(q + 1)\right] \tag{3}$$

Because $q^* = q'\ /\ q$, this can be also written as

$$r^* = \varepsilon^* + n^* - \left[qq^*/(q + 1)\right] \tag{4}$$

[29] Marx to Engels, letter of 30 April 1868 (*MECW* 43, 20–26).

[30] Engels, in Marx [1894] (1981), 94.

Since q is generally much greater than 1, q can be used to approximate $q + 1$ and Eq. 4 becomes

$$r^* = \varepsilon^* + n^* - q^* \tag{5}$$

This expression indicates that the percent change of the profit rate can be approximated by summing the percent change of the RSV (ε^*) and the percent change of the turnover (n^*), and then subtracting the percent change of the OCC (q^*). Thus, for instance, with both the RSV and the turnover being constant (i.e., $\varepsilon^* = n^* = 0$), the decrease in the profit rate equals the percent rise in the OCC. With an RSV rising annually by 3% (i.e., $\varepsilon^* = 0.03 = 3\%$), the turnover increasing annually 4% ($n^* = 4\%$), and the OCC increasing annually by 9% ($q = 9\%$), the profit rate percent change would be $3 + 4 - 9$, that is, $r^* = -2\%$, the profit rate would fall. Now with the same $\varepsilon^* = 3\%$, and $n^* = 4\%$, and a lower $q^* = 6\%$, the percent change of the rate of profit is $3 + 4 - 6 = 1$, the profit rate would increase by 1%. Whether the rate of profit increases or decreases is undefined, though for many plausible values of the variables involved, r will decline.

As Engels himself acknowledged, many of the discussions in volume 3 of *Capital* are sketchy and fragmentary. It could not be any other way because the volume is based on very rough drafts. Marx probably focused most of his thoughts on the evolution of the rate of profit on the expression $r = \varepsilon / (q + 1)$, in which the effect of the turnover is not explicitly considered. From this expression and considering that ε could not grow too much, while q could grow unbounded—and he was very likely right on that—, he concluded that, eventually, r would fall. But he noticed too that other things could also influence r by modifying ε or q, and thus wrote about *factors counteracting* the tendency of r to fall.[31] Reading all he wrote on this *tendency,* that he called a "law", it seems quite clear he was unclear about the problem. He concluded that r tends in the long run to decline *but* it can increase during long periods—a rather vague statement. It was perhaps to counter that vagueness that Engels introduced a sentence, without marking it as such introduction) which left "the possibly misleading impression that Marx definitely concluded

[31] What Marx wrote on these things, with Engels' edition, is in ch. 13 and ch. 14 of *Capital, Volume III*, with further considerations in ch. 15. This corresponds, without Engels's edition, to pages 320–376 in the *Economic manuscript of 1864–1865*, ed. by F. Moseley (Marx 2017).

that the rate of profit would fall in the long run".[32] Furthermore, Marx probably was not paying enough attention to the turnover of capital. If the turnover is considered, then, as Eq. 5 shows, there is not any clear tendency for r, unless we establish other restrictions for the rates of change of ε, n, and q, which are the three factors that have an influence on the rate of change of r.

In his notion that in the long-run the profit rate would fall, Marx was in agreement with major economists like Adam Smith, David Ricardo, and John Stuart Mills, though he gave different reasons for that fall and saw it also in a much less mechanical way, as a complicated tendency. It seems, though, that Marx viewed this tendency as a key reason to expect a breakdown of capitalism. But Rosa Luxemburg commented on this idea that there was still "some time to pass before capitalism collapses because of the falling rate of profit, roughly until the sun burns out."[33] Since that was written more than a century ago, endless controversies on "the law of the tendency of the rate of profit to fall" (whether the "law" was properly argued by Marx, whether it is relevant for expecting an end of capitalism, and whether the empirical evidence is consistent with it) have occurred among Marxists and radical economists.[34] Three recent books on Marxian theory and its application to the modern world have supported the view that the "law" is properly argued by Marx and

[32] Moseley in the introduction to *Marx's economic manuscript of 1864–1865* (Marx 2017, 42).

[33] Luxemburg [1913] (2015), "Anti-critique", in Hudi & Le Blanc, eds., *The complete works of Rosa Luxemburg—Volume II, economic writings 2*, fn. 4.

[34] See the exchanges between Sweezy & Cogoy (1987), *International Journal of Political Economy* 17(2), and between Heinrich, Carchedi and Roberts, Moseley, and Mage in *Monthly Review* (April and December 2013); also Groll & Orzech (1987), "Technical progress and values in Marx's theory of the decline in the rate of profit", *History of Political Economy* 19(4), 591–612; Fichtenbaum (1988), "Did Marx had a theory of the business cycle?, *Nature, Society & Thought* 1(2), 189–200; Reuten (2011), "*Zirkel vicieux* or trend fall? The course of the profit rate in Marx's *Capital III*", *Science & Society* 75(1), 74–90; Reuten & Thomas (2004), "From the 'Fall of the rate of profit' in the *Grundrisse* to the cyclical development of the profit rate in *Capital*", *History of Political Economy* 36(1); Kliman (2012), *The failure of capitalist production*; Astarita (2021), "Teorías marxistas de la crisis, y la crisis de 2007–2009", in Alves & Corsi, eds. *A crise capitalista no século XXI: Um debate marxista*, 145–184. This is just a limited sample of a huge bibliography.

is a key element to understand capitalism.[35] The three books basically ignore the influence of the turnover on the rate of profit.[36] Contrarily, two recent articles by Italian authors have emphasized the importance of the turnover to understand the dynamics of the profit rate.[37] To advance in the understanding and elaboration of these aspects is an important task if Marxian economic theory is to be developed beyond exegetical discussions of Marx's writings.

[35] Mattick Jr (2019), *Theory as critique*; Smith, Butovsky & Watterton (2021), *Twilight capitalism*; Carchedi & Roberts (2022), *Capitalism in the twenty-first century—Through the prism of value.*

[36] Carchedi & Roberts (2022, 94) assert that a shortening of the turnover time increases the surplus value produced per unit of time but does not increase the RSV—which is obvious if the RSV is for one turnover. It seems they are implying, though, that an increase in the turnover does not raise the rate of profit. Paul Mattick Jr (2017, 230) claims that Cogoy demonstrated mathematically that the profit rate has to fall in the long-run because the rise in the RSV cannot ultimately compensate for the rise in the OCC. In my view, however, Cogoy's demonstration fails as soon as the starting assumption of a constant number of workers (a very restrictive assumption) is removed.

[37] Veronese Passarella & Baron (2015), "Capital's humpback bridge", *Cambridge Journal of Economics* 39(5), 1415–1441; De Marco (2023), "Marx's general rate of profit: How turnover time, accumulation and rate of surplus value affect the formation of prices of production", *Capital & Class*, 47(4), 1–32.

APPENDIX E—DATA

See Table E1.

Table E1 World economy aggregates as estimated by the World Bank

Year	*DCPS bB*	*DCPS*	*GFCF t2015$*	*GFCF t2015$*	*GCF t2010$*	*GCF t2015$*	*gY*	*gY_*	*HNPISHs FCE*	*Y t2010$*	*Y t2015$*	*BrM*	*Ypc 2015$*
1960	32.6	204.0									10.9	50.0	3588
1961	33.9	199.6						3.8			11.3	51.6	3677
1962	35.6	56.0						5.3			11.9	52.4	3806
1963	37.9	58.8						5.2			12.5	53.9	3922
1964	38.9	60.4						6.6			13.3	54.1	4095
1965	40.4	62.2						5.5			14.1	54.4	4235
1966	40.6	61.5						5.7			14.9	53.4	4385
1967	41.7	64.2						4.2			15.5	55.5	4475
1968	42.3	65.5						5.9			16.4	55.8	4646
1969	43.0	65.0						5.8			17.4	53.2	4815
1970	45.3	69.4					3.5	3.9	58.6		18.0	57.3	4902
1971	47.4	73.0					4.3	4.3	58.8		18.8	60.6	5005
1972	52.2	78.3	6.1		6.4		5.7	5.6	58.6	24.5	19.9	64.7	5181
1973	54.5		6.5		7.0		6.5	6.4	57.7	25.9	21.2	64.5	5406
1974	52.2		6.4		7.1		2.0	1.8	57.3	25.5	21.5	60.7	5398
1975	51.1		6.3		6.5		0.6	0.6	58.4	25.1	21.7	61.8	5334
1976	51.5		6.6		7.0		5.3	5.3	58.1	26.5	22.8	62.3	5518
1977	53.1	73.0	6.9		7.3		3.9	4.1	58.2	27.4	23.8	62.6	5645
1978	56.4		7.3		7.7		3.9	4.1	58.0	28.3	24.7	66.1	5778

(continued)

Table E1 (continued)

Year	*DCPS bB*	*DCPS*	*GFCF t2015$*	*GFCF t2015$*	*GCF t2010$*	*GCF t2015$*	*gY*	*gY_*	*HNPISHs FCE*	*Y t2010$*	*Y t2015$*	*BrM*	*Ypc 2015$*
1979	54.6		7.6		8.1		4.1	4.2	57.9	29.4	25.8	64.5	5914
1980	52.7		7.7		8.1		1.9	1.9	58.1	29.9	26.3	63.8	5922
1981	53.0	73.9	7.7		8.0		1.9	1.9	57.7	30.2	26.8	65.3	5932
1982	53.9	76.7	7.5		7.5		0.4	0.4	58.9	30.1	26.9	68.1	5850
1983	56.6	81.4	7.5		7.5		2.4	2.6	59.7	31.0	27.6	71.5	5900
1984	58.7	84.1	7.8		8.3		4.5	4.7	59.4	32.5	28.9	74.0	6069
1985	60.7	89.0	8.2		8.5		3.7	3.7	59.6	34.0	29.9	75.6	6186
1986	69.2	100.1	8.5		8.9		3.4	3.4	59.5	35.2	31.0	83.9	6288
1987	74.9	106.7	9.0	9.3	9.3		3.7	3.7	59.3	36.6	32.1	88.8	6408
1988	81.4	111.4	9.6	9.8	10.1		4.6	4.6	59.0	38.4	33.6	92.2	6589
1989	83.5	116.8	10.1	10.4	10.3		3.7	3.8	58.6	40.6	34.9	93.3	6719
1990	79.5		10.5	10.7	11.2		2.9	2.9	58.7	43.0	35.9	87.9	6794
1991	79.8		10.4	10.6	11.1		1.4	1.5	58.9	43.6	36.4	89.7	6780
1992	80.3		10.2	10.4	10.8		1.8	2.1	59.1	42.6	37.2	88.3	6813
1993	82.5	123.2	10.0	10.3	10.4		1.5	1.8	59.5	41.6	37.8	91.9	6830
1994	82.2	121.2	10.2	10.7	10.8		3.0	3.3	59.4	43.0	39.1	91.3	6950
1995	82.3	121.6	10.6	11.0	11.2	9.9	3.1	3.1	58.9	45.2	40.3	92.6	7058
1996	79.0	121.4	11.2	11.8	11.7	9.8	3.4	3.6	59.2	47.3	41.7	89.9	7209
1997	79.7	124.4	11.6	12.4	12.2	10.4	3.7	3.9	59.4	49.2	43.4	90.4	7385
1998	78.7	130.1	11.9	12.7	12.2	10.1	2.6	2.8	59.8	49.9	44.6	92.8	7487
1999	80.9	139.4	12.3	13.2	12.6	10.3	3.2	3.5	60.0	52.1	46.2	99.0	7648

Year	*DCPS bB*	*DCPS*	*GFCF t2015$*	*GFCF t2015$*	*GCF t2010$*	*GCF t2015$*	*gY*	*gY_*	*HNPISHs FCE*	*Y t2010$*	*Y t2015$*	*BrM*	*Ypc 2015$*
2001	72.7	124.0	12.9	14.0	13.2	10.7	1.9	2.0	60.4	55.0	49.2	95.5	7941
2002	72.9	121.1	12.9	13.9	13.1	11.4	2.2	2.3	60.4	55.9	50.3	96.2	8024
2003	74.5	124.8	13.2	14.4	13.6	11.4	3.0	3.2	60.0	56.9	51.9	97.0	8173
2004	75.5	124.6	13.9	15.2	14.6	12.8	4.4	4.5	59.2	58.8	54.2	95.8	8435
2005	77.0	125.3	14.8	16.1	15.3	13.3	3.9	4.0	58.9	61.0	56.4	95.1	8668
2006	79.2	127.9	15.6	17.1	16.2	14.5	4.4	4.5	58.2	63.6	59.0	95.9	8945
2007	82.1	128.1	16.3	17.9	17.2	16.1	4.3	4.5	57.6	66.3	61.6	96.2	9231
2008	83.5	120.1	16.4	18.0	17.1	16.3	1.9	2.1	57.3	66.7	62.9	99.7	9306
2009	84.5	124.8	14.9	16.2	14.8	15.0	−1.7	−1.3	58.2	63.2	62.0	110.5	9072
2010	82.2	119.7	15.5	16.6	16.2	16.4	4.3	4.5	57.1	66.5	64.9	107.6	9370
2011	81.1	115.3	16.2	17.4	17.0	17.3	3.1	3.3	56.5	69.1	67.0	108.9	9568
2012	81.2	116.1	16.7	17.5	17.3	17.5	2.5	2.7	56.5	70.6	68.8	111.1	9709
2013	81.8	118.2	17.1	17.8	17.6	18.1	2.7	2.8	56.5	72.3	70.8	111.6	9863
2014	82.7	119.8	17.6	18.3	18.2	18.9	2.8	3.1	56.5	74.0	72.9	114.1	10,043
2015	85.7	123.2	17.9	18.8	18.6	19.4	2.9	3.1	56.7	75.9	75.2	119.0	10,232
2016	86.7	124.9	18.2	19.1	18.8	19.9	2.6	2.8	57.0	78.0	77.3	123.0	10,396
2017	85.7	126.1	18.9	19.8	19.6	20.9	3.2	3.4	56.6	80.8	79.9	121.3	10,625
2018	87.9	125.6	19.6	20.5	20.2	21.8	3.1	3.3	56.1	83.1	82.5	122.4	10,853
2019	89.2	131.1		21.0		22.5		2.6	56.3		84.7	125.1	11,019
2020	98.6	147.4		20.0		21.6		−3.3	55.3		81.9	143.5	10,549
2021								5.8			86.7		11,057

Total domestic credit to the private sector (DCPS) and DCPS by banks (DCPSbN); gross fixed capital formation (GFCF), gross capital formation (GCF), annual percent growth or WGDP (gY, gY_), households and nonprofit institutions serving households, final consumption expenditure (HNPISHs FCE); WGDP (Y), broad money (BrM), WGDP per capita (Ypc). Figures are percentages of WGDP except when indicated to be monetary aggregates in trillion US$ of 2010 (t2010$) or trillion US$ of 2015 (t2015$). The series ending in 2021 or 2020 were downloaded from the WDI database in 2022, the series ending in former years were downloaded in 2020.

References

Acemoglu, Daron, V. M. Carvalho, A. Ozdaglar, and A. Tahbaz-Salehi. 2012. The network origins of aggregate fluctuations. *Econometrica* 80(5), 1977–2016.

Adelman, Ira. 1960. Business cycles—Endogenous or stochastic? *Economic Journal* 70, 783–796.

Adichie, Chimamanda Ngozi. 2014. *We should all be feminists.* New York, Vintage.

Aglietta, Michel. 1982. La crisis: ¿Un desafío para los economistas? *Mientras Tanto* 13, 93–120.

Allard, Alexandra, Johanna Takman, Gazi Salah Uddin, and Ali Ahmed. 2018. The N-shaped environmental Kuznets curve: An empirical evaluation using a panel quantile regression approach. *Environmental Science and Pollution Research* 25(6), 5848–5861.

Ammer, C., and D. S. Ammer. 1977. *Dictionary of business and economics*. New York, Free Press.

Anonymous. 1991. Review of the month—Where are we going? *Monthly Review* 42(10), 1–15.

Anonymous. 2021. Japan recession lasted for 19 months through May 2020, government panel says. *The Japan Times*, December 1, www.japantimes.co.jp/news/2021/12/01/business/economy-business/japan-recession, accessed September 2022.

Appelbaum, B. 2013. In surprise, Fed decides to maintain pace of stimulus. *New York Times*, September 18, A1, B5.

Arrighi, Giovanni. 1994. *The long twentieth century: Money, power, and the origins of our times*. London, Verso.

J. A. Tapia, *Six Crises of the World Economy*,
https://doi.org/10.1007/978-3-031-38735-7

Arrighi, Giovanni. 2004. Spatial and other "fixes" of historical capitalism. *Journal of World-Systems Research* 10(2), 527–539.

Arrizabalo Montoro, Xabier. 2016. *Capitalismo y economía mundial—Bases teóricas y análisis empírico para la comprensión de los problemas económicos del siglo XXI*. Madrid, Instituto Marxista de Economía.

Arrow, Kenneth, Bert Bolin, Robert Costanza et al. 1995. Economic growth, carrying capacity, and the environment. *Science* 268(5210), 520–521.

Astarita, Rolando. 2009. *El capitalismo roto*. Madrid, La Linterna Sorda.

Baby, Jean. 1976. *Los orígenes de la controversia chino-soviética*. Madrid, Emiliano Escolar.

Bagus, Philipp. 2011. Morgenstern's forgotten contribution: A stab to the heart of modern economics. *American Journal of Economics & Sociology* 70(2), 540–562.

Bannock, G., R. E. Baxter, and E. Davis. 1998. *The penguin dictionary of economics*. London, Penguin.

Barbosa-Filho, Nelson H., and Lance Taylor. 2006. Distributive and demand cycles in the US economy: A structuralist Goodwin model. *Metroeconomica* 57(3), 389–411.

Barsky, Robert B., and Lutz Kilian. 2004. Oil and the macroeconomy since the 1970s. *Journal of Economic Perspectives* 18(4), 115–134.

Bartlett, Bruce. 1994. The high-cost of turning green. *Wall Street Journal*, September 14, A 18.

Bernstein, Jeremy. 1973, "The secrets of the old one", I & II. *The New Yorker*, March 10, 44–101, March 17, 44–91.

Blanchard, Olivier. 2001. Close encounters with recessions of the third kind. *Project Syndicate*, March 12, www.project-syndicate.org/commentary/close-encounters-with-recessions-of-the-third-kind-2001-03.

Basu, Deepankar, J. Huato, J. Lara Jauregui, and E. Wasner (2022). World profit rates, 1960–2019. University of Massachusetts Amherst, Economics Department Working Paper Series 318, https://doi.org/10.7275/43yv-c721.

BBC. 2020. Mass deaths of migratory birds reported in New Mexico. *BBC News*, September 16, 2020, at www.bbc.com/news/world-us-canada-54183430, accessed September 2020.

Bernanke, Ben S. 1983. Nonmonetary effects of the financial crisis in the propagation of the Great Depression. *American Economic Review* 73(3), 257–276.

Bernanke, Ben S. 2004. Remarks on the great moderation by Governor Ben S. Bernanke at the meetings of the Eastern Economic Association, Washington, DC, February 20, 2004, available July 2020 at www.federalreserve.gov/boarddocs/speeches/2004/20040220/.

Besomi, Daniel. 2005. Clément Juglar and the transition from crises theory to business cycle theories. Paper prepared for a conference on the occasion of the centenary of the death of Clément Juglar, Paris, December 2, www.unil.ch/files/live/sites/cwp/files/users/neyguesi/public/D._Besomi_, accessed October 2020.

Besomi, Daniel. 2012. Clément Juglar and his contemporaries on the causes of commercial crises. *Revue européenne des sciences sociales* 47(143), 17–47.

Bhaduri, Amit, and S. Marglin. 1990. Unemployment and the real wages: The economic basis for contesting political ideologies. *Cambridge Journal of Economics* 14, 375–393.

Bhaskar, V., and A. Glyn. 1995. Expectations and investment: An econometric defense of animal spirits. In: G. A. Epstein and H. Gintis, eds., *Macroeconomic policy after the conservative era: Studies in investment, saving and finance.* Cambridge, Cambridge University Press, 197–223.

Blake, William J. 1939. *An American looks at Karl Marx: Elements of Marxian economic theory and its criticism.* New York, Cordon.

Blanchard, Olivier. 2006. *Macroeconomics.* Upper Saddle Rivel, NJ, Pearson/Prentice Hall.

Blanchard, Olivier, C. Rhee, and L. Summers. 1993. The stock market, profit, and investment. *Quarterly Journal of Economics* 108(1), 115–136.

Bloom, N. 2014. Fluctuations in uncertainty. *Journal of Economic Perspectives* 28(2), 153–176.

Boddy, Rafford, and J. Crotty. 1975. Class conflict and macro policy: The political business cycle. *Review of Radical Political Economics* 7(1), 1–19.

Boldrin, Michael, and M. Horvath. 1995. Labor contracts and business cycles. *Journal of Political Economy* 103(5), 972–1004.

Boulding, Kenneth E. 1966. The economics of the coming spaceship earth. In: H. Jarret, ed., *Environmental quality in a growing economy.* Baltimore, MD, Johns Hopkins University Press.

Bowles, Samuel, and R. Edwards. 1985. *Understanding capitalism: Competition, command, and change in the US economy.* New York, Harper & Row.

Bowles, Samuel, and Thomas E. Weisskopf. 1998. David M. Gordon: Economist and public intellectual (1944–1996). *Economic Journal* 108, 153–164.

Brenner, Robert, 2020. *The boom and the bubble: The US in the world economy.* London, Verso.

Bronfenbrenner, M. 1969. *Is the business cycle obsolete? Based on a conference of the Social Science Research Council Committee on Economic Stability.* New York, Wiley-Interscience.

Burns, Arthur F. 1954. *The frontiers of economic knowledge.* New York, Princeton University Press.

Burns, Arthur F., and W. C. Mitchell. 1946. *Measuring business cycles.* New York, NBER.

Burns, Arthur F., ed. 1952. *Wesley Clair Mitchell: The economic scientist.* New York, NBER.

Butkiewicz, James L., and Scott Ohlmacher. 2021. Ending bretton woods. *The Economic Historian*, November 28, at economic-historian.com, accessed November 2022

Butler, E. 2010. The financial crisis: Blame governments, not bankers. In: P. Booth, ed., *Verdict on the crash: Causes and policy implications*. London, Institute of Economic Affairs, 51–59.

Cabrera de León A et al. 2018. Austerity policies and mortality in Spain after the financial crisis of 2008. *American Journal of Public Health* 108(8), 1091–1098, retraction in 109(7), e17.

Cahuc, Pierre, and André Zylberberg. 2016. *Le négationnisme économique: et comment s'en débarrasser*. Paris, Flammarion.

Carchedi, Guglielmo, and Michael Roberts, eds. 2017. *World in crisis*. Chicago, Haymarket.

Carchedi, Guglielmo, and Michael Roberts. 2013. A critique of Heinrich's, 'Crisis theory, the law of the tendency of the profit rate to fall, and Marx's studies in the 1870s'. *Monthly Review*, December, monthlyreview.org/commentary/critique-heinrichs-crisis-theory-law-tendency-profit-rate-fall-marxs-studies-1870s/, accessed October 2020.

Carchedi, Guglielmo & Michael Roberts. 2022. *Capitalism in the 21st century: Through the prism of value*. London, Pluto Press.

Cassidy, John. 2010. After the blowup—Interview with Eugene Fama. *The New Yorker*, January 11, www.newyorker.com/news/john-cassidy/interview-with-eugene-fama.

Cassidy, John. 2023. Even the experts don't really know where inflation and jobs are headed. *The New Yorker*, February 28, www.newyorker.com/news/our-columnists/its-ok-to-be-confused-about-this-economy, accessed 28 February 2023.

Castro, Vitor. 2015. The Portuguese business cycle: Chronology and duration dependence. *Empirical Economics* 49(1), 325–342.

CEIC Website. 2022. Data on Russian exports of crude oil. www.ceicdata.com/en/indicator/russia/crude-oil-exports, accessed November 1.

Chappell, Bill. 2023. An unusually high number of whales are washing up on U.S. beaches. *NPR*, February 5, news.wgcu.org/2023-02-05/an-unusually-high-number-of-whales-are-washing-up-on-u-s-beaches, accessed March 2023.

Chen, Brian X., Emma Goldberg, and Ron Lieber. 2023. Are layoffs imminent? Here's how to prepare. *New York Times*, February 21, B1.

Clarke, Simon. 1994. *Marx's theory of crisis*. New York, St. Martin's Press.

Clegg, John, and A. Benanav. 2011. The economic crises in fact and fiction: Paul Mattick. *Brooklyn Rail*, June, brooklynrail.org/2011/06/express/the-economic-crisis-in-fact-and-fictionpaul-mattick-with-john-clegg-and-aaron-benanav.

Cochrane, John. [2009] 2011. How did Paul Krugman get it so wrong. *Economic Affairs* 31(2), ricardo.ecn.wfu.edu/~cottrell/ecn272/cochrane.pdf, accessed October 2020.

Cogoy, Mario. 1987a. Marx and the accumulation of capital. *International Journal of Political Economy* 17(2), 11–17.

Cogoy, Mario. 1987b. The falling rate of profit and the theory of accumulation: A reply to Paul Sweezy. *International Journal of Political Economy* 17(2), 54–74.

Cornia, Giovanni Andrea. 2016. The mortality crisis in transition economies. Bonn, Institute for the Study of Labor (IZA).

Cornia, Giovanni A., and R. Paniccià, eds. 2000. *The mortality crisis in transitional Economies*. New York, Oxford University Press.

Crosby, Alfred W. 2003. *America's forgotten pandemic: The influenza of 1918*, 2nd ed. New York, Cambridge University Press.

Dash, E., and N. D. Schwartz. 2011. In cautious times, banks flooded with cash. *New York Times*, October 28, A1.

De Marco, Guido. 2023. Marx's general rate of profit: How turnover time, accumulation and rate of surplus value affect the formation of prices of production, *Capital & Class*, 47(4), 1–32.

Diebold, Francis X., and G. D. Rudebusch. 1999. *Business cycles: Durations, dynamics, and forecasting*. Princeton, Princeton University Press.

Dore, Mohammed H. I. 1993. *The macrodynamics of business cycles: A comparative evaluation*. Cambridge, Blackwell.

Dore, Mohammed H. I. 1997. Stylized facts. In: D. Glasner, and T. F. Cooley, eds., *Business cycles and depressions—An encyclopedia*. New York, Garland, 662–664.

Duménil, Gerard, and D. Lévy. 2011. *The crisis of neoliberalism*. Cambridge, MA, Harvard University Press.

Duque Garcia, Carlos Alberto. 2022. Economic growth and the rate of profit in Colombia 1967–2019: A VAR time-series analysis. *Review of Radical Political Economics* 54(3), 1–19.

Easterlin, Richard A. 2003. *Happiness in economics*. London, Edward Elgar.

Easterlin, Richard A. 2004. *The reluctant economist—Perspectives on economics, economic history, and demography*. New York, Cambridge University Press.

Eckes, Jr, Alfred E., and Thomas W. Zeiler. 2003. *Globalization and the American century*. Cambridge, Cambridge University Press.

Economists' statement on carbon dividends: The largest public statement of economists in history. 2019. *Wall Street Journal*, January 17.

Editorial Board. 2023. Who benefits from confrontation with China. *New York Times*, Sunday Opinion, 9.

Einhorn, C. 2020. A 'crossroads' for humanity: Earth's biodiversity is still collapsing. *New York Times*, September 15, A.10.

Elliott, Larry. 2020. Christine Lagarde delivered a disappointing set of measures to mitigate the impact of coronavirus. *The Guardian*, March 12, www.theguardian.com/world/2020/mar/12/ecbs-plan-to-support-eurozone-banks-is-underwhelming, accessed July 2020.

Encyclopedia.com. Oil crises, www.encyclopedia.com/history/dictionaries-thesauruses-pictures-and-press-releases/oil-crises, accessed October 2020.

Engels, Friedrich. [1847] 1969. The principles of communism. In: *Marx & Engels—Selected works*, 1. Moscow, Progress Publishers, 81–97.

Engels, Friedrich. [1848] 2010. Letter to Karl Marx, 4 March 1848. *Marx & Engels collected works*, 40. London, Lawrence & Wishart Electric Book, 279–282.

Engels, Friedrich [1894] 2010. *Anti-Dűhring: Herr Eugen Dühring's revolution in science* (trans. E. Burns). In: *Marx & Engels Collected Works*, 25. London, Lawrence & Wishart, 5–312.

England, Minnie Throop. 1912. Fisher's theory of crises: A criticism. *Quarterly Journal of Economics* 27(1), 95–106.

England, Minnie Throop. 1913a. Economic crises. *Journal of Political Economy* 21(4), 345–354.

England, Minnie Throop. 1913b. An analysis of the crisis cycle. *Journal of Political Economy* 21(8), 712–734.

England, Minnie Throop. 1915. Promotion as the cause of crises. *Quarterly Journal of Economics* 29(5), 748–767

Esteva, Gustavo. 1992. Development. In: W. Sachs, ed., *The development dictionary: A guide to knowledge as power*. London, Zed Books.

ExxonMobil. 2014. "Oil CRISES," June 2014, available July 2020 at exxonmobil.com/Benelux-English/about_who_history_esso_oilcrisis.aspx.

Fair, Ray C. 2004. *Estimating how the macroeconomy works*. Cambridge, MA, Harvard University Press.

Fair, Ray C. 2012. Has macro progressed? *Journal of Macroeconomics* 34(1), 2–10.

Feldstein, Martin, and Summers, Larry. 1977. Is the rate of profit falling? *Brookings Papers on Economic Activity* 1, 211–228.

Feldstein, Martin, ed. 1991. *The risk of economic crises*. Chicago, University of Chicago Press.

Feynman, Richard P. 1998. *The meaning of it all: Thoughts of a citizen scientist*. Reading, MA, Addison-Wesley.

Fichtenbaum, Rudy. 1988. Did Marx had a theory of the business cycle? *Nature, Society & Thought* 1(2), 189–200.

Field, Jacob, and Matthew Taylor. 2018. *Is capitalism working? A primer for the 21st century*. London, Thames & Hudson.

Fisher, Irving. 1933. The debt-deflation theory of great depressions. *Econometrica* 1, 337–356.

Flavelle, C. 2020. Wildfires hasten another climate crisis—Insurers, facing huge losses, have been pulling back from fire-prone areas across California. The marketplace has largely collapsed. *New York Times*, September 2, B1, B4.

Foley, Duncan. 2010. The political economy of post-crisis global capitalism. Paper prepared for the economy and society conference at the University of Chicago, December 3–5, 2010.

Fonseca, Gonçalo L. 1998. The general glut controversy, www.hetwebsite.net/het/essays/classic/glut, accessed February 2023.

Frank, Andre Gunder, and K. Barry. 1992. The five thousand year world system: An interdisciplinary introduction. *Humboldt Journal of Social Relations* 18(1), 1–79.

Freeman, J. 2019. Has the recession been cancelled? The strength of the U.S. economy continues to confound the liberal establishment. *The Wall Street Journal*, April 26.

Friedman, G., F. Moseley, and C. Sturr, eds. 2009. *The economic crisis reader: Readings in economics, politics, and social policy*. Boston, Dollars & Sense.

Friedman, Milton. 1940. Review of Tinbergen's *Business cycles in the United States. American Economic Review* 30(4), 657–660.

Friedman, Milton. 1969. Money and business cycles. In: *The optimum quantity of money, and other essays*. Chicago, Aldine.

Friedman, Milton. 1983. *A program for monetary stability*. New York, Fordham University Press.

Friedman, Milton, and Anna J. Schwartz. 1963. *A monetary history of the United States 1867–1960*. New York, NBER/Princeton University Press.

Friedman, Milton, and Walter W. Heller. 1968. *Monetary vs. fiscal policy—A dialogue*. New York, W. W. Norton.

Frisch, Ragnar. 1933. *Propagation problems and impulse problems in dynamic economics*. Oslo, Universitetets Økonomische Institutt.

Gabaix, Xabier. 2011. The granular origins of aggregate fluctuations. *Econometrica* 79(3), 733–772.

Galbraith, John K. 1961. *The great crash 1929*. New York, Time.

Gamio, Lazaro, and Ana Swanson. 2022. How Russia pays for war. *The New York Times*, October 30, www.nytimes.com/interactive/2022/10/30/business/economy/russia-trade-ukraine-war.html, accessed 15 February 2023.

Georgescu-Roegen, Nicholas. 1971. *The entropy law and the economic process*. Cambridge, MA, Harvard University Press.

Ghenne, Christopher, Beth Herron, David Stewart, and Robert Morison. 2021. *Fighting money laundering with intelligent automation*. International Institute for Analytics/SAS Institute.

Glasner, David. 1997a. Adam Smith. In: D. Glasner, and T. F. Cooley, eds., *Business cycles and depressions: An encyclopedia*. New York: Garland, 627–629.

Glasner, David. 1997b. David Ricardo. In: D. Glasner, and T. F. Cooley, eds., *Business cycles and depressions: An encyclopedia*. New York, Garland, 580–582.

Goldfarb, Z. 2014. Why Robert Gordon thinks economic growth is over. *The Washington Post*, March 2.

Goldstein, Jonathan P., and Michael G. Hillard, eds. 2009. *Heterodox macroeconomics: Keynes, Marx and globalization*. New York, Routlede.

Goldstein, Jonathan P. 2021. Econometric analysis of long swings: The relevance of nonperiodic methods. In: Terrence McDonough, Cian McMahon, and David M. Kotz, eds., *Handbook on social structure of accumulation theory*. Cheltenham, Edward Elgar, Ch. 3, 34–61.

Goodwin, Richard M. Econometrics in business-cycle analysis. In: A. H. Hansen, *Business cycles and national income*, 2nd ed. London, George Allen & Unwin, 417–468.

Goodwin, Richard M. 1967. A growth cycle. In: C. H. Feinstein, ed., *Socialism, capitalism and economic growth*. Cambridge, Cambridge University Press, 54–59.

Gordon, Robert J. 2009. *Macroeconomics*. Boston, Addison-Wesley.

Gordon, Robert. 2012. Is US economic growth over? Faltering innovation confronts the six headwinds. NBER Working Paper 18315.

Gorton, Gary. 2012. *Misunderstanding financial crises: Why we don't see them coming*. New York, Oxford University Press.

Government of Japan, Cabinet Office. 2013. The provisional determination of business-cycle peak and trough, August 21, 2013, www.esri.cao.go.jp/en/stat/di/130821rdates.html, accessed September 2022.

Gregory, A. W., A. C. Head, and J. Raynauld. 1997. Measuring world business cycles. *International Economic Review* 38(3), 677–701.

Greider, William. 1987. *Secrets of the temple: How the Federal Reserve runs the country*. New York, Simon & Schuster.

Griffiths, Rudyard, and Luciani, Patrick, eds. 2012, *North America lost decade? Paul Krugman and David Rosenberg vs. Lawrence Summers and Ian Bremmer—The Munk Debate on the North American economy*. Toronto, Anansi.

Groll, Shalom, and Z. B. Orzech 1987. Technical progress and values in Marx's theory of the decline in the rate of profit: an exegetical approach. *History of Political Economy* 19(4), 591–612.

Groseclose, Erwin. 1961. *Money and man: A survey of monetary experience*. New York, Frederick Ungar.

Grossman, Henryk. 1924. *Simonde de Sismondi and his economic theories* (trans. by J. Vertegaal of the original published in Warsaw in 1924), www.vcn.bc.ca/~vertegaa/grossman.pdf, accessed July 2020.

Grossman, Henryk. 1941. Schumpeter's *Business cycles*. *Studies in Philosophie and Social Science* 9(1), 181–189.

Grossmann, Henryk. [1929] 1979. *La ley de la acumulación y del derrumbe del sistema capitalista: Una teoría de la crisis* (ed. by Jorge Tula on a transl. by J. Berend, I. del Carril, and J. Aricó). Mexico, Siglo XXI.

Haberler, Gustav. 1937. *Prosperity and depression: A theoretical analysis of cyclical movements*. Geneva, League of Nations.

Hagiwara, Shinjiro. 2013. The demise of the Keynesian regime, financial crisis, and Marx's theory. In: Yagi et al., eds., *Crises of global economies and the future of capitalism*. New York, Routledge, 91–108.

Haldane, Andrew. 2016. The Dappled Word. Shackle Biennial Memorial Lecture, www.bankofengland.co.uk/speech/2016/the-dappled-world, accessed May 2023.

Hamilton, James D. 1988. A neoclassical model of unemployment and the business cycle. *Journal of Political Economy* 96(3), 593–617.

Hamilton, James D. 2007. Interview. In: R. E. Parker, ed., *The economics of the Great Depression: A 21st century look back at the economics of the interwar era*. Cheltenham, Edward Elgar, 81 *et seq*.

Hamilton, James D. 2008. Oil and the macroeconomy. In: S. N. Durlauf, and L. E. Blume, eds., *The New Palgrave dictionary of economics*, 2nd ed. London, Palgrave Macmillan.

Hamilton, James D. 2009. Causes and consequences of the oil shock of 2007–2008. *Brookings Papers on Economic Activity*, Spring, 215–267.

Hamilton, James D. 2011. Historical oil shocks. NBER Working Paper 16790.

Harrison, Joseph. 1978. *An economic history of modern Spain*. Manchester, Manchester University Press.

Hart, Jeffrey A., and Joan Edelman Spero. 2010. *The politics of international economic relations*, 7th ed. Boston, Wadsworth.

Harbaugh, William T., Arik Levinson, and David Molloy Wilson. 2002. Reexamining the empirical evidence for an environmental Kuznets curve. *Review of Economics & Statistics* 84(3), 541–551.

Harvey, David (2010). The crises of capitalism, www.youtube.com/watch?v=qOP2V_np2c0.

Heinberg, Richard. 2011. *The end of growth: Adapting to our new economic reality*. Gabriola Island, BC, New Society Publishers.

Heinrich, Michael. 2012. *An introduction to the three volumes of Karl Marx's Capital*. New York, Monthly Review Press.

Heinrich, Michael. 2013. Crisis theory, the law of the tendency of the profit rate to fall, and Marx's studies in the 1870s. *Monthly Review*, April, monthlyreview.org/2013/04/01/crisis-theory-the-law-of-the-tendency-of-the-profit-rate-to-fall-and-marxs-studies-in-the-1870s/, accessed October 2020.

Heisenberg, Werner. 1971. *Physics and beyond: Encounters and conversations* (transl. by A. Pomerans). New York, Harper & Row.

Hexter, Maurice Beck. 1925. *Social consequences of business cycles*. Boston, Houghton Mifflin.

Hicks, John. 1979. *Causality in macroeconomics*. Canberra, Canberra Australian National University Press.

Hilferding, Rudolf. [1910] 1981. *Finance capital: A study of the latest phase of capitalist development* (ed. by T. Bottomore on a transl. by M. Watnick and S. Gordon). London, Routledge & Kegan Paul, available July 2020 at www.marxists.org/archive/hilferding/1910/finkap/.

Hirsh, M. 2019. Economists on the run—Paul Krugman and other mainstream trade experts are now admitting that they were wrong about globalization. *Foreign Policy*, October 22, available July 2020 at getpocket.com/explore/item/economists-on-the-run?utm_source=pocket-newtab.

Hobsbawm, Eric. 1994. *Age of extremes—The short 20th century*. London, Michael Joseph.

Holtz-Eakin, D., and T. Selden. 1995. Stocking the fires? CO_2 emissions and economic growth. *Journal of Public Economics* 57(1), 85–101.

Hoover, Kevin D. 2001. *Causality in macroeconomics*. New York, Cambridge University Press.

Hubbert, Marion K. 1987. Exponential growth as a transient phenomenon in human history. In: M. A. Strom, ed., *Societal issues, scientific viewpoints*. New York, American Institute of Physics, 75–84.

Hull, G. H. 1926. *Industrial depressions: Their causes analysed and classified with a practical remedy for such as result from industrial derangements*. New York, Codex.

Hultgren, Thor. 1965. *Cost, prices, and profits: Their cyclical relations*. New York, NBER.

Huntington, Ellsworth. 1920. *World-power and evolution*. New Haven, Yale University Press.

Kalecki, Michał. 1954. *Theory of economic dynamics—An essay on cyclical and long-run changes in capitalist economy*. London, George Allen & Unwin.

Kalecki, Michał. 1984. The mechanism of the business upswing. In: J. B. Foster, and H. Szlajter, eds., *The faltering economy—The problem of accumulation under monopoly capitalism*. New York, MR Press, 127–133.

Keen, Steve. 2001. *Debunking economics*, 2nd ed. New York, Zed Books.

Keen, Steve. 2014. Secular stagnation and endogenous money. *Real-World Economics Review* 66.

Kennedy, Peter. 2003. *A guide to econometrics*, 5th ed. Cambridge, MIT Press.

Kenway, P. 1998. Crises. In: J. Eatwell, M. Milgate, and P. Newman, eds., *The New Palgrave: A dictionary of economics*. London, Macmillan, 724–726.

Kerr, R. A. 2012. Is the world tottering on the precipice of peak gold? *Science* 335, 1038–1039.

Kerr, R. A. 2014. The coming copper peak. *Science* 343, 722–724.

Keynes, John M. 1936. *The general theory of employment, interest, and money*. London, Macmillan.
Keynes, John M. 1939. Professor Tinbergen's method. *Economic Journal* 49(195), 558–568.
Keynes, John M. 1987. *The general theory and after: Part I, preparation: Collected writings of John Maynard Keynes, 13, pt. 1* (ed. by D. Moggridge). Cambridge, Cambridge University Press.
Kilian, Lutz. 2009. Not all oil price shocks are alike: Disentangling demand and supply shocks in the crude oil market. *American Economic Review* 99(3), 1053–1069.
Kim, Kyun. 1988. *Equilibrium business cycle theory in historical perspective*. Cambridge, Cambridge University Press.
Klein, Phillip A. 1997. Growth cycles. In: D. Glasner, and T. F. Cooley, eds., *Business cycles and depressions—An encyclopedia*. New York, Garland, 289.
Kliman, Andrew. 2012. *The failure of capitalist production—Underlying causes of the Great Recession*. London, Pluto Press.
Knoop, T. A. 2004. *Recessions and depressions: Understanding business cycles*. Westport, CT, Praeger.
Kondratieff, Nikolai D. 1935. The long waves in economic life. *Review of Economics & Statistics* 17(6), 105–115.
Koopmans, Tjalling. 1941. The logic of econometric business-cycle research. *Journal of Political Economy* 49(2):157–181.
Koopmans, Tjalling C. 1947. Measurement without theory. *Review of Economic Statistics* 29(3), 161–172.
Kose, M. Ayham, N. Sugawara, and M. E. Terrones. 2020. Global recessions. Centre for Applied Macroeconomic Analysis, Australian National University, CAMA Working Paper 10/2020.
Kose, M. Ayhan, and Marco E. Terrones. 2015. *Collapse and revival: Understanding global recessions and recoveries*. Washington, DC, IMF.
Kotz, David M. 1987. Long waves and social structures of accumulation: A critique and reinterpretation. *Review of Radical Political Economics* 19(4), 16–38.
Krugman, Paul, and R. Wells. 2006. *Economics*. New York, Worth Publishers.
Krugman, Paul. 2008. Synchronized sinking. *New York Times*, August 23, krugman.blogs.nytimes.com/2008/08/23/synchronized-sinking/.
Krugman, Paul. 2009. A Dark Age of macroeconomics (wonkish). *New York Times*, January 27, archive.nytimes.com/krugman.blogs.nytimes.com/2009/01/27/a-dark-age-of-macroeconomics-wonkish/.
Krugman, Paul. 2009. How did economists get it so wrong? *New York Times Magazine*, September 2.
Krugman, Paul. 2016. Review: 'The Rise and Fall of American Growth' by Robert J. Gordon. *New York Times*, January 31.

Krugman, Paul. 2019. What economists (including me) got wrong about globalization. *Bloomberg Opinion*, October 10, available July 2020 at www.bloomberg.com/opinion/articles/2019-10-10/inequality-globalization-and-the-missteps-of-1990s-economics.

Krugman, Paul. 2020. Crashing economy, rising stocks: What's going on? What's bad for America is sometimes good for the market. *New York Times*, April 30.

Krugman, Paul. 2020. Learn to stop worrying and love debt. *New York Times*, December 4, 2020, A27.

Krugman, Paul. 2023. "Does America have too much debt? *New York Times*, January 4, 2023, www.nytimes.com/2023/01/24/opinion/us-debt-deficit-economy.html, accessed March 2, 2023.

Kuczyinsky, Thomas. 1978. Kondratieff cycles—Appearance or reality? In M. Flinn, ed., *Proceedings of the 7th international economic history congress, II.* Edinburgh, Edinburgh University Press.

Kuczyinsky, Thomas. 1987. Marx and Engels on long waves. In: T. Vasko, ed., *The long-wave debate.* Berlin, Springer-Verlag, 35–47.

Kurth, J. 2011. A tale of four crises: The politics of great depressions and recessions. *Orbis* 55(3), 500–523.

Kuznets, Simon. 1966. *Modern economic growth: Rate, structure, and spread.* New Haven, Yale University Press.

Laeven, Luc, and Fabian Valencia. 2008. Systemic banking crises: A new database. IMF Working Paper 08/224.

Laeven, Luc, and Fabián Valencia. 2012. Systemic banking crises database: An update. IMF Working Paper 12/163.

Latouche, S. 1992. Standard of living. In: W. Sachs, ed., *The development dictionary: A guide to knowledge as power.* London, Zed Books.

Leal, José Luis. 2014. Un gran reinado. *El País* (Madrid), June 15, Negocios 18.

Leamer, Edward E. 2010. Tantalus on the road to asymptopia. *Journal of Economic Perspectives* 24(2), 31–46.

Leijonhufvud, Axel. 1967. Keynes and the Keynesians: A suggested interpretation. *American Economic Review* 57(2), 401–410.

Lenin, Vladimir I. [1917] 1963. *Imperialism, the highest stage of capitalism.* In *Lenin's selected works*, Progress Publishers, 1963, Moscow, Volume 1, 667–766, available August 2020 at www.marxists.org/archive/lenin/works/1916/imp-hsc/.

Levinson, Arik. 2000. The ups and downs of the environmental Kuznets curve. Paper for the UCF/Center Conference on Environment, November 30–December 2, Orlando, FL.

Li, Minqi, Feng Xiao, and Andong Zhu. 2007. Long waves, institutional changes, and historical trends: A study of the long-term movement of the profit rate in the capitalist world-economy. *Journal of World-Systems Research* 13(1), 33–54.

Li, Minqi. 2011. The rise of the working class and the future of the Chinese revolution. *Monthly Review* 63(2), 38.

Lippitt, Victor D. 2010. Social structure of accumulation theory. In: Terrence McDonough, Michael Reich, and David M. Kotz, eds. *Contemporary capitalism and its crises—Social structure of accumulation theory for the 21st century*. Cambridge, Cambridge University Press, 2010, Ch. 2, 45–71.

Lucas, Robert E. 1977. Understanding business cycles. *Carnegie-Rochester Conference Series on Public Policy* 57, 29.

Lucas, Robert E. Macroeconomic priorities. *American Economic Review* 93(1), 1–14.

Luxemburg, Rosa. [1897] 2013. The industrial development of Poland. In: Peter Hudis, ed., *The complete works of Rosa Luxemburg: Volume I—Economic writings I* (transl. D. Fernbach, J. Fracchia, G. Shriver). London, Verso.

Luxemburg, Rosa [1913] 2015. *The accumulation of capital, or what the epigones have made out of Marx's theory—An anti-critique*. In: P. Hudis, and P. Le Blanc, eds., *The complete works of Rosa Luxemburg—Volume II, economic writings 2* (transl. N. Gray and G. Shriver). London, Verso.

Luxemburg, Rosa. 2013. *Introduction to political economy*. In: *The complete works of Rosa Luxemburg—Volume I: Economic writings 1* (ed. by P. Hudis, transl. George Shriver). London, Verso.

Maclachlan, F. C. 1999. The Ricardo-Malthus debate on underconsumption: A case study in economic conversation. *History of Political Economy* 31(3), 563–574.

Mage, Shane. 2013. Response to Heinrich—In defense of Marx's law. *Monthly Review*, December, monthlyreview.org/commentary/response-heinrich-defense-marxs-law/, accessed October 2020.

Maier, Mark, and T. Easton. 1999. *The data game: Controversies in social science statistics*. Armonk, NY, M.E. Sharpe.

Maito, Esteban E. 2013. The historical transience of capital: The downward trend in the rate of profit since the XIX century, gesd.free.fr/maito14.pdf, accessed August 2020.

Maito, Esteban E. 2018. The tendency of the rate of profit to fall since the nineteenth century and a world rate of profit. In: G. Carchedi, and M. Roberts, eds., *World in crisis*. Chicago, Haymarket, 129–156.

Maksakovsky, Pavel. [1928] 2009. *The capitalist cycle: An essay on the Marxist theory of the cycle* (transl. by R. Day). Chicago, Haymarket.

Malthus, Thomas Robert. 1836. *Principles of political economy*. London, online ed., available June 2020 at oll.libertyfund.org/titles/2188.

Mandel, Ernest. 1983. Long waves. In: T. Bottomore, L. Harris, V. G. Kiernan, and R. Miliband, eds., *A dictionary of Marxist thought*. Cambridge, MA, Harvard University Press, 324–325.

Mandel, Ernest. Introduction. In: Marx, Karl [1894] 1981. *Capital—A critique of political economy. Volume 3, edited by Friedrich Engels* (transl. by D. Fernbach). London, Penguin, 9–90.

Mandelbrot, Benoit B., and R. L. Hudson. 2009. *The (mis)behavior of markets: A fractal view of risk, ruin, and reward.* New York, Basic Books.

Mankiw, N. G. 2009. *Principles of macroeconomics*, 5th ed. Mason, OH, South Western.

Mankiw, N. G. 2010. A call for humility—Trying to tame the unknowable. *New York Times*, March 26, B6.

Marcuse, Herbert. 1967. The obsolescence of Marxism. In: N. Lobkowitz, ed., *Marx and the western world.* Notre Dame, University of Notre Dame Press, 409–417.

Mardani, Abbas, Dalia Streimikiene, Fausto Cavallaro, et al. 2019. CO_2 emissions and economic growth: A systematic review of two decades of research from 1995 to 2017. *Science of the Total Environment* 649, 31–49.

Marx, Karl, and Frederick Engels. [1848] 1969. *Manifesto of the communist party* (transl. S. Moore, F. Engels). Marx and Engels *Selected Works*, Volume One, Moscow, Progress Publishers, 98–137, available at www.marxists.org/archive/marx/works/1848/communist-manifesto/.

Marx, Karl. [1848] 2010. Letters to F. Engels. March 2 & 5, 1848. *Marx & Engels Collected Works* 40, London, Lawrence & Wishart, 277–279, 282–284.

Marx, Karl. [1852]. Pauperism and free trade—The approaching commercial crisis [1852], *Marx & Engels collected works*, 11. London, Lawrence & Wishart, 357–363.

Marx, Karl. [1855] 2020. The crisis in trade and industry [1855]. *Marx & Engels Collected Works*, 13. London, Lawrence & Wishart 571–578.

Marx, Karl [1855]. The commercial crisis in Britain" [1855]. *Marx & Engels collected works*, 13. London, Lawrence & Wishart, 585–589.

Marx, Karl. [1859] 2010. Population, crime, and pauperism. *New-York Daily Tribune*, September 16, 1859. *Marx & Engels Collected Works*, 16. London, Lawrence & Wishart, 487–491.

Marx, Karl [1867] 1977. *Capital—A critique of political economy, Volume 1* (transl. by B. Fowkes). New York, Vintage Books.

Marx, Karl [1885] 1991. *Capital—A critique of political economy, Volume 2, edited by Friedrich Engels* (transl. by D. Fernbach). London, Penguin.

Marx, Karl [1894] 1981. *Capital—A critique of political economy. Volume 3, edited by Friedrich Engels* (transl. by D. Fernbach). London, Penguin.

Marx, Karl. 1968. *Theories of surplus value.* Moscow, Progress.

Marx, Karl. 2017. *Economic manuscript of 1864*–1865 (ed. by F. Moseley, transl. by B. Fowkes). Chicago, Haymarket.

Marx, Karl. 2010 [1848]. On the question of free trade. *Marx & Engels Collected Works*, 6. London, Lawrence & Wishart, 450–465.

Marx, K and F. Engels. 2010 [1848] Manifesto of the communist party. *Marx & Engels Collected Works*, 6. London, Lawrence & Wishart, 477–520.

Marx, Karl. [1861–1863] 2010. Economic manuscript of 1861–1863. *Marx & Engels Collected Works*, 32. London, Lawrence & Wishart.

Matthews, R. C. O. 1959. *The business cycle*. Chicago, University of Chicago Press.

Mattick Jr, Paul. 2011. *Business as usual: The economic crisis and the failure of capitalism*. London, Reaktion.

Mattick Jr, Paul. 2019. *Theory as critique: Essays on* Capital. Chicago, Haymarket.

Mattick, Paul. 1934. The permanent crisis: Henryk Grossman's interpretation of Marx's theory of capitalist accumulation. *International Council Correspondence* 1(2), 1–20.

Mattick, Paul. 1969. *Marx and Keynes: The limits of the mixed economy*. Boston, P. Sargent.

Mattick, Paul. 1978. *Economics, politics, and the age of inflation*. White Plains, M. E. Sharpe.

Mattick, Paul. 1981. *Economic crisis and crisis theory* (transl. from the German by P. Mattick Jr). White Plains, NY, M. E. Sharpe.

McDonough, Terrence. 2010. The state of the art of SSA theory. In: Terrence McDonough, Michael Reich, and David M. Kotz, eds., *Contemporary capitalism and its crises—Social structure of accumulation theory for the 21st century*. Cambridge, Cambridge University Press, 2010, Ch. 1.

McDonough, Terrence. (2021), Social structure of accumulation theory. In: Terrence McDonough, Cian McMahon, and David M. Kotz, eds., *Handbook on Social Structure of Accumulation Theory,* Cheltenham, Edward Elgar, Ch. 2, 15–33.

McDonough, Terrence, Cian McMahon & David M. Kotz, eds. 2021. Introduction. In: Terrence McDonough, Cian McMahon, and David M. Kotz, eds., *Handbook on social structure of accumulation theory*. Cheltenham, Edward Elgar, Ch. 1, 1–14.

McNally, David. 2010. *Global slump: The economics and politics of crisis and resistance*. Oakland, CA, PM Press.

Medio, Alfredo. 1987. Trade cycle. In: J. Eatwel, M. Milgate, and P. Newman, eds., *The New Palgrave—A dictionary of economics*. New York, Macmillan, 666–671.

Mill, John Stuart. 1846. *A system of logic, ratiocinative and inductive: Being a connected view of the principles of evidence and the methods of scientific investigation*. New York, Harper.

Mills, John. 1868. On credit cycles and the origin of commercial panics. *Transactions of the Manchester Statistical Society*, 5–40, archive.org/details/oncreditcyclesor00manc/page/n21/mode/2up, accessed September 2020.

Minsky, Himan P. [1986] 2008. *Stabilizing an unstable economy.* New York, McGraw-Hill.

Mitchell, Wesley C. 1913. *Business cycles.* Berkeley, University of California Press.

Mitchell, Wesley C. 1923. Chapter 1, Business cycles. In: Committee of the President's Conference on Unemployment, and a Special Staff of the NBER, ed. *Business cycles and unemployment.* New York, McGraw-Hill/NBER, 7–20.

Mitchell, Wesley C. 1927. *Business cycles: The problem and its setting.* New York: NBER.

Mitchell, Wesley C. 1937. *The backward art of spending money, and other essays.* New York, McGraw-Hill.

Mitchell, Wesley C. 1941. *Business cycles and their causes.* Berkeley, University of California Press.

Mitchell, Wesley C. 1944. Test of free enterprise: Depression-proof economy is sought. *The New York Times*, September 18.

Mitchell, Wesley C. 1944. The role of money in economic history. *Journal of Economic History* 4(sup), 61–67.

Mitchell, Wesley C. 1949. *Lecture notes on types of economic theory as delivered by professor Wesley C. Mitchell.* New York, August M. Kelley.

Mitchell, Wesley C. 1951. *What happens during business cycles: A progress report.* New York, NBER.

Mohun, Simon, and Roberto Veneziani. 2008. Goodwin cycles and the US economy, 1948–2004. In: P. Flaschel, and M. Landesmann, eds., *Mathematical economics and the dynamics of capitalism: Godwin's legacy continued.* New York, Routledge, 107–130.

Moore, J. W. 2011. Ecology, capital, and the nature of our times: Accumulation and crisis in the capitalist world-ecology. *Journal of World-Systems Research* 17(1), 107–146.

Morgan, Mary S. 1990. *The history of econometric ideas.* Cambridge, Cambridge University Press.

Morgan, Mary S. 2019. Recovering Tinbergen. *De Economist* 167, 283–295.

Morgenstern, Oskar. 1950. *On the accuracy of economic observations.* Princeton, Princeton University Press.

Morgenstern, Oskar. 1959. *International financial transactions and business cycles.* Princeton, Princeton University Press.

Morishima, Michio. 1973. *Marx's economics.* Cambridge, Cambridge University Press.

Moseley, Fred. 2000. The rate of profit and stagnation in the US economy. In: R. Baiman, H. Boushey, and D. Saunders, eds., *Political economy and contemporary capitalism.* Armonk, NY: M.E. Sharpe, 59–67.

Moseley, Fred. 2013. Critique of Heinrich: Marx did *not* abandon the logical structure. *Monthly Review*, December, monthlyreview.org/commentary/critique-heinrich-marx-abandon-logical-structure/, accessed October 2020.

Münchau, Wolfgand. 2010. *The meltdown years: The unfolding of the global economic crisis.* New York, McGraw-Hill.

NASA Earth Observatory. 2020. Intense flooding in Bangladesh, at earthobservatory.nasa.gov/images/147057/intense-flooding-in-bangladesh, accessed September 2020.

National Public Radio. 2020. The coronavirus crisis—Deluge continues: 26 million jobs lost in just 5 weeks. *NPR*, April 23, www.npr.org/sections/coronavirus-live-updates/2020/04/23/841876464/26-million-jobs-lost-in-just-5-weeks.

NBER 2020. Determination of the February 2020 peak in economic activity, at www.nber.org/cycles/june2020.pdf, accessed September 2020.

Nordhaus, William D. 1974. The falling share of profits. *Brookings Papers on Economic Activity* 1, 169–217.

Obama, Barak (2017). The irreversible momentum of clean energy. *Science* 355(6321), 126–129, https://doi.org/10.1126/science.aam6284.

Ohanian, Lee E. 2008. Back to the future with Keynes. *Federal Reserve Bank of Minneapolis Quarterly Review* 32(1), 10–16.

Oppenlaender, K. H. 1997. Characteristics and classification of business cycle indicators. In: K. H. Oppenlaender, ed., *Business cycle indicators.* Avebury, Aldershot, 25–32.

Panitch, Leo. 2013. Crisis of what? *Journal of World-Systems Research* 19 (2), 129–135.

Parker, R. E. ed., *The economics of the Great Depression: A 21st century look back at the economics of the interwar era.* Cheltenham, UK, Edward Elgar.

Pass, C., B. Lowes, L. Davis, and S. J. Kronish. 1991. *The Harper-Collins dictionary of economics.* New York, Harper.

Pearl, Judea, & Dana Mackenzie. 2019. *The Book of Why: The New Science of Cause and Effect.* New York, Basic Books.

Perlo, Victor. 1973. *The unstable economy: Booms and recessions in the U.S. since 1945.* London, Lawrence & Wishart.

Peters, G. P. et al. 2012. Rapid growth in CO_2 emissions after the 2008–2009 global financial crisis. *Nature Climate Change* 2(1), 2–4.

Pigou, Arthur C. 1927. Wage policy and unemployment. *Economic Journal* 37(147), 355.

Piketty, Thomas. 2014. *Capital in the 21st century.* Cambridge, MA, Harvard University/Belknap Press.

Pilling, Geoffrey. 1987. *The crisis of Keynesian economics A Marxist view.* London, Croom Helm.

Plosser, Charles I. 1989. Understanding real business cycles. *Journal of Economic Perspectives* 3(3), 51.

Posner, Richard A. 2009. How I became a Keynesian: Second thoughts in the middle of a crisis. *New Republic*, September 23, available July 2020 at newrepublic.com/article/69601/how-i-became-keynesian.

Prescott, Edward C. 1986. Theory ahead of business cycle measurement. *Federal Reserve Bank of Minneapolis Quarterly Review* 10, 9–22.

Rada, Codrina, and Lance Taylor. 2006. Empty sources of growth accounting, and empirical replacements à la Kaldor with some beef. *Structural Change & Economic Dynamics* 17(4), 487–500.

Rappeport, Alan. 2022. World faces high risk of recession, I.M.F. warns. *New York Times*, October 12, B1.

Rappeport, Allen, Lauren Hirsch, Jeanna Smialek, and Jim Tankersley. 2023. Moving quickly to avert a financial avalanche. *New York Times*, March 14, A1, A12.

Reichenbach, Hans. 1956. The direction of time (ed. by Maria Reichenbach). Berkeley, University of California Press.

Reinert, K. A., and R. S. Rajan. 2009. *The Princeton encyclopedia of the world economy.* Princeton, NJ, Princeton University Press.

Reinhart, Carmen M., and K. Rogoff. 2009. *This time is different: Eight centuries of financial folly.* Princeton: Princeton University Press.

Reuten, Geert, and P. Thomas. 2011. From the 'fall of the rate of profit' in the *Grundrisse* to the cyclical development of the profit rate in *Capital. Science & Society* 75(1), 74–90.

Reuten, Geert. 2011. *Zirkel vicieux* or trend fall? The course of the profit rate in Marx's *Capital III. History of Political Economy* 36(1), 163–186.

Ricardo, David. [1817] 2004. *The principles of political economy and taxation.* Mineola, NY, Dover.

Rickards, James. 2012. *Currency wars: The making of the next global crisis.* New York, Penguin.

Robbins, Lionel R. 1945. *An essay on the nature and significance of economic science.* London, Macmillan.

Robert, J. 1992. Production. In: W. Sachs, ed., *The development dictionary: A guide to knowledge as power.* London, Zed Books.

Roberts, Michael. 2009. *The great recession: Profit cycles, economic crises—A Marxist view.* London, Author's Edition.

Roberts, Michael. 2012. A world rate of profit, gesd.free.fr/mrwrate.pdf.

Roberts, Michael. 2016. *The long depression.* Chicago, Haymarket.

Roberts, Michael. 2017. Chapter 13—Debt matters. In: G. Carchedi, and M. Roberts, eds., *World in crisis: A global analysis of Marx's law of profitability.* Chicago, Haymarket, 197–217.

Robinson, Joan. 1979. *The generalisation of the general theory, and other essays.* London, Macmillan.

Robinson, Joan. 1971. *Freedom & necessity: An introduction to the study of society.* New York, Routledge.
Röpke, Wilhelm. 1936. *Crises and cycles.* London, William Hodge.
Romer, Christina D., and Romer, David H. 2017. New evidence on the aftermath of financial crises in advanced countries. *American Economic Review* 107(10), 3072–3118.
Rostow, Walter W. 1978. *The world economy: History and prospect.* Austin, University of Texas Press.
Rothbard, Murray N. 1959. Why the business cycle happens, available July 2020 at mises.org/library/how-business-cycle-happens.
Rothkopf, D. J. 2008. *Superclass: The global power elite and the world they are making.* New York, Farrar, Straus and Giroux.
Routh, Guy. 1975. *The origin of economic ideas.* White Plains, M. E. Sharpe.
Rowe, D. E. and R. J. Schulmann. 2007. *Einstein on politics—His private thoughts and public stands on nationalism, Zionism, war, peace, and the bomb.* Princeton, Princeton University Press.
Roy, Arundhati. 2020. The pandemic is a portal. *The Financial Times*, April 3, www.ft.com/content/10d8f5e8-74eb-11ea-95fe-fcd274e920ca, accessed March 15, 2023.
Rubinstein, D. 2020. 'We're at war': New York City faces a financial abyss. *The New York Times*, September 28, www.nytimes.com/2020/09/28/nyregion/nyc-budget-coronavirus.html.
Ruhm, Christopher J. 2000. Are recessions good for your health?" *Quarterly Journal of Economics* 115(2), 617–650.
Rumyantsev, A. 1963. *Crisis and the capitalist cycle—A symposium.* New Delhi, People's Publishing House.
Sachs, Jeffrey D. 2009. The future of capitalism: Rethinking macroeconomics. *Capitalism and Society* 4(3), Article 3.
Saidi,Kais, and Sami Hammami. 2015. The impact of CO_2 emissions and economic growth on energy consumption in 58 countries. *Energy Reports* 1, 62–70.
Salinari, Giambattista, and Federico Benassi. 2022. The long-term effect of the Great Recession on European mortality. *Journal of Population Research* 39(3), 417–439.
Samuelson, Paul A. [1947] 1966. *Foundations of economic analysis.* Cambridge, MA, Harvard University Press.
Saros, Daniel E. 2021. A comprehensive approach to SSA analysis: An oscillating pattern of crisis in US economic history. In: Terrence McDonough, Cian McMahon, and David M. Kotz, eds., *Handbook on social structure of accumulation theory.* Cheltenham, Edward Elgar, Ch. 4.
Samuelson, Paul A. 1957. *Economics,* 7th ed. New York, McGraw-Hill.

Sato, Takuya. 2018. Japan "lost" two decades: A Marxist analysis of prolonged capitalist stagnation. In: G. Carchedi, and M. Roberts, eds., *World in crisis*. Chicago, Haymarket, 157–182.
Say, Jean Baptiste. 1880 [1826]. *A treatise on political economy, or the production, distribution, and consumption of wealth* (transl. from the 4th French ed. by C. R. Prinsep). Philadelphia, Claxton, Kemsen & Haffelfingee.
Schirwitz, Beate. 2009. A comprehensive German business cycle chronology. *Empirical Economics* 37(2), 287–301.
Schröder, Enno, and Servaas Storm. 2018. Why "green growth" is an illusion. Institute for New Economic Thinking web. www.ineteconomics.org/perspectives/blog/why-green-growth-is-an-illusion, accessed September 2020.
Schröder, Enno, and Servaas Storm. 2020. Economic growth and carbon emissions: The road to 'Hothouse Earth' is paved with good intentions. *International Journal of Political Economy* 49(2), 153–173.
Schularik, Moritz, and Alan M. Taylor. 2012. Credit booms gone bust: Monetary policy, leverage cycles, and financial crises, 1870–2008. *American Economic Review* 102(2), 1029–1061.
Schumpeter, Joseph A. 1934. *The theory of economic development: An inquiry into profits, capital, credit, interest, and the business cycle* (transl. from the German by R. Opie). Cambridge, MA, Harvard University Press.
Schumpeter, Joseph A. 1939. *Business cycles: A theoretical, historical and statistical analysis of the capitalist process*. New York, McGraw-Hill.
Schumpeter, Joseph A. 1954. *History of economic analysis*. New York, Oxford University Press.
Schwartz, Anna J. 2010. Origins of the financial market crisis of 2008. In: P. Booth, ed., *Verdict on the crash: Causes and policy implications*. London, Institute of Economic Affairs.
Schwartzberg, J. E. 2004. *Revitalizing the United Nations: Reform Through Weighted Voting*. New York and The Hague, Institute for Global Policy.
Semmelweis, Ignaz. 1988. The etiology, concept, and prophylaxis of childbed fever. In: Carol Buck, E. Llopis, E. Nájera, and M. Terris. *The challenge of epidemiology: Issues and selected readings*, Washington, D.C., Pan American Health Organization (PAHO/WHO), 49–59.
Sen, Amartya. 1994. The political economy of hunger. In: I. Serageldin, and P. Landell-Mills, eds., *Overcoming global hunger*. Washington, DC, World Bank, 85–90.
Shaikh, Anwar. 1983. Economic crises. In: T. Bottomore, L. Harris, V. G. Kiernan, and R. Miliband, eds., *A dictionary of Marxist thought*. Cambridge, MA, Harvard University Press, 138–143.
Shaikh, Anwar. 2011. The first great depression of the 21st century. *Socialist Register* 47.

Shaikh, Anwar. 2016. *Capitalism—Competition, conflict, crises.* New York, Oxford University Press.

Shannon, T. R. 1989. *An introduction to the world-system perspective.* Boulder, CO, Westview Press.

Sherman, Herman 2001. The business cycle theory of Wesley Mitchell. *Journal of Economic Issues* 35(1), 85–98.

Sims, Christopher A. 2012. Statistical modelling of monetary policy and its effects: Nobel Prize lecture. *American Economic Review* 102(4), 1187–1205.

Sismondi, M. S. d. 1847. *Political economy and the philosophy of government: A series of essays from the works of M. de Sismondi with an historical notice of his life and writings, by M. Mignet.* London: John Chapman.

Smith, Adam. [1776] 1937. *An inquiry into the nature and causes of the wealth of nations* (ed. by E. Cannan). New York, Modern Library.

Smith, Murray E. G., Jonah Butovsky & Josh Watterton. 2021, *Twilight Capitalism: Karl Marx and the Decay of the Profit System.* Black Point, Nova Scotia, Fernwood Publishing.

Sokal, Alan. 2010. *Beyond the hoax: Science, philosophy and culture.* New York, Oxford University Press.

Solow, Robert M. 2014. Thomas Piketty is right: Everything you need to know about "Capital in the Twenty-First Century". *The New Republic*, April 22, www.newrepublic.com/article/117429/capital-twenty-first-century-thomas-piketty-reviewed, accessed July 2020.

Solow, Robert. 2010. Prepared statement, House Committee on Science and Technology Subcommittee on Investigations and Oversight, Building a Science of Economics for the Real World, July 20, available July 2020 at www.govinfo.gov/content/pkg/CHRG-111hhrg57604/pdf/CHRG-111hhrg57604.pdf.

Soon, Lau Teik. 1980. The Soviet-Vietnamese treaty: A giant step forward. *Southeast Asian Affairs*, 1980, 54–65.

Sowell, Thomas. 1963. The general glut controversy reconsidered. *Oxford Economic Papers* 15(3), 193–203.

Sowell, Thomas. 1972. *Say's Law: An historical analysis.* Princeton, Princeton University Press.

Spash, Clive L. 2010. The Brave New World of carbon trading. *New Political Economy* 15(2), 169–195.

Spash, Clive L. 2020. A tale of three paradigms: Realising the revolutionary potential of ecological economics. *Ecological Economics* 169, 106518.

Spence, Michael. 2011. *The next convergence: The future of economic growth in a multispeed world.* New York, Farrar, Straus & Giroux.

Speth, James Gustave. 2008. *The bridge at the edge of the world: Capitalism, the environment, and crossing from crisis to sustainability.* New Haven, CN, Yale University Press.

Stiglitz, Joseph, Amartya Sen, and Jean Paul Fitoussi. 2010. Report by the commission on the measurement of economic performance and social progress, ec.europa.eu/eurostat/documents/8131721/8131772/Stiglitz-Sen-Fitoussi-Commission-report.pdf.

Stillman, S. 2006. Health and nutrition in Eastern Europe and the former Soviet Union during the decade of transition: A review of the literature. *Economics & Human Biology* 4(1), 104–146.

Streit, C. 1940. *Union now: The proposal for inter-democracy federal union*. London: Harper & Brothers.

Stuermer, Martin. 2014. 150 years of boom and bust: what drives mineral commodity prices. Paper presented at the Philadelphia 2014 Meeting of the American Economic Association, 2014.

Summers, Lawrence H. 1986. Some skeptical observations on real business cycle theory. *Federal Reserve Bank of Minneapolis Quarterly Review* 10, 23–27.

Summers, Lawrence. 2019. The right policy as recession looms. *The Washington Post*, January 7.

Sweezy, Paul M. 1987. Some problems in the theory of capital accumulation. *International Journal of Political Economy* 17(2), 38–53.

Tankersley, Jim. 2020. Federal borrowing amid pandemic puts US debt on path to exceed World War II—Federal debt, as a share of the economy, hit 98% in 2020. *New York Times*, September 2, www.nytimes.com/2020/09/02/business/us-federal-debt.html?auth=login-email&login=email.

Tankersley, Jim. 2023. Swelling debt is bipartisan in its origins: Now at 31.4 trillion. *New York Times*, March 7, A1.

Tanuro, Daniel. 2014. *Green capitalism: Why it can't work*. Halifax, Fernwood.

Tapia, José A. 2015. Money and Say's law: On the macroeconomic models of Kalecki, Keen, and Marx. *Real-World Economics Review* 70.

Tapia, José A. 2016, "Oil prices and the world business cycle: A causal investigation", available at mpra.ub.uni-muenchen.de/68978/1/MPRA_paper_68978.pdf.535937.

Tapia, José A. 2017. *Rentabilidad, inversión y crisis: teorías económicas y datos empíricos*. Madrid, Maia.

Tapia, José A. 2017–2018. Climate change—What is to be done? Parts 1, 2, and 3. *The Brooklyn Rail*, November, December, and February, brooklynrail.org/2017/11/field-notes/Climate-Change-What-is-to-be-Done, brooklynrail.org/2017/12/field-notes/Climate-Change-What-is-to-be-Done-Part-2-Climate-and-the-Economy, brooklynrail.org/2018/02/field-notes/Climate-Change.

Tapia, José A. 2018. Investment, profit and crises—Theories and evidence. In: G. Carchedi, Guglielmo, and M. Roberts, eds., *World in crisis—A global analysis of Marx's law of profitability*. Chicago, Haymarket, 78–128.

Tapia, José A. 2019a. Fairy tales about climate change. *The Brooklyn Rail*, March, brooklynrail.org/2019/03/field-notes/Fairy-Tales-About-Climate-Change.

Tapia, José A. 2019b. Why 3508 economists are probably wrong. *The Brooklyn Rail*, May, brooklynrail.org/2019/05/field-notes/Why-3508-Economists-Are-Probably-Wrong.

Tapia, José A. Oil prices and the world business cycle: A causal investigation. Working Paper, Drexel University, mpra.ub.uni-muenchen.de/68978/1/MPRA_paper_68978.pdf.

Tapia Granados, José A. 2005. Increasing mortality during the expansions of the US economy, 1900–1996. *International Journal of Epidemiology* 34(6), 1194–1202.

Tapia Granados, José A. 2012. Statistical evidence of falling profits as cause of recession: A short note. *Review of Radical Political Economics* 44(4), 484–493.

Tapia Granados, José A. 2013. Does investment call the tune? Empirical evidence and endogenous theories of the business cycle. *Research in Political Economy* 28, 229–259.

Tapia Granados, José A., and A. V. Diez Roux. 2009. Life and death during the great depression. *Proceedings of the National Academy of Sciences of the USA* 106, 17290–17295.

Tapia Granados, José A., and C. L. Spash. 2019. Policies to reduce CO_2 emissions: Fallacies and evidence from the United States and California. *Environmental Science & Policy* 94, 262–266.

Tapia Granados, José A., and E. L. Ionides. 2017. Population health and the economy: Mortality and the Great Recession in Europe. *Health Economics* 26(12), e219–e235.

Tapia Granados, José A., E. L. Ionides, and Ó. Carpintero. 2012. Climate change and the world economy: Short-run determinants of atmospheric CO_2. *Environmental Science & Policy* 21, 50–62.

Tapia Granados, José A., and Ó. Carpintero. 2013. Dynamics and economic aspects of climate change. In: M. S. Kang, and S. S. Banga, eds., *Combating climate change: An agricultural perspective*. New York, CRC Press.

Tatom, J. A. 1997. Recessions (supply-side) in the 1970s. In: D. Glasner, and T. F. Cooley, eds., *Business cycles and depressions: An encyclopedia*. New York, Garland, 569–572.

Thomas, Dorothy S. 1927. *Social aspects of the business cycle*. New York, Knopf.

Ticktin, Hillel. 2017. The permanent crisis, decline and transition of capitalism. *Critique* 43(3), 359–386.

Tinbergen, Jan. 1935. Suggestions on quantitative business cycle theory. *Econometrica* 3(3), 241–308.

Tinbergen, Jan. 1939. *Statistical testing of business-cycle theories. Volume I "A method and its application to investment activity"*. Geneva, League of Nations.

Tinbergen, Jan. 1939. *Statistical testing of business-cycle theories. Volume II "Business cycles in the United States of America 1919–1932"*. Geneva, League of Nations.

Tinbergen, Jan. 1950. *The dynamics of business cycles: A study in economic fluctuations* (transl. and adapted by J. J. Polak). Chicago, University of Chicago Press.

Tinbergen, Jan. 1952. Comments [on Orcutt's 'Toward partial redirection of econometrics']. *Review of Economics and Statistics* 34(3), 205–206.

Tinbergen, Jan. 1962. *Shaping the world economy: suggestions for an international economic policy.* New York, Twentieth Century Fund.

Tobin, James. 1970. Money and income: post hoc ergo propter hoc? *Quarterly Journal of Economics* 84(2), 301–317.

Tooze, Adam. 2020. How coronavirus almost brought down the global financial system. *The Guardian*, April 14, at www.theguardian.com/business/2020/apr/14/how-coronavirus-almost-brought-down-the-global-financial-system, accessed September 2020.

Tooze, Adam. 2020. The death of globalisation has been announced many times: But this is a perfect storm. *The Guardian*, June 2, at www.theguardian.com/commentisfree/2020/jun/02/end-globalisation-covid-19-made-it-real, accessed August 2020.

Tortella Casares, Gabriel. 1998. *El desarrollo de la España contemporánea: Historia económica de los siglos XIX y XX.* Madrid, Alianza.

Trofimov, Ivan D. 2017. Profit rates in developed capitalist economies: A time series investigation. *PSL Quarterly Review* 70(280), 85–128.

Trofimov, Ivan D. 2022. Determinants of the profit rates in the OECD economies: A panel data analysis of the Kalecki's profit equation. *Structural Change and Economic Dynamics* 61, 380–397.

Turgeon, Lynn. 1996. *Bastard Keynesianism: The evolution of economic thinking and policymaking since World War II.* Westport, CT, Greenwood Press.

Tylecote, A. 1993. *The long wave in the world economy: The present crisis in historical perspective.* London, Routledge.

Vague, Richard. 2014. *The next economic disaster: Why it's coming and how to avoid it.* Philadelphia, University of Pennsylvania Press.

Veronese Passarella, Marco, and Hervé Baron. 2015. Capital's humpback bridge: 'financialisation' and the rate of turnover in Marx's economic theory. *Cambridge Journal of Economics* 39(5), 1415–1441.

Wagner, M. 2008. The carbon Kuznets curve: A cloudy picture emitted by bad econometrics? *Resource and Energy Economics* 30, 388–408.

Wallerstein, Immanuel. 1984. *The politics of the world-economy: The states, the movements and the civilizations.* Cambridge, Cambridge University Press.

Wallerstein, Immanuel. 1995. *After liberalism.* New York, The New Press.

Wallerstein, Immanuel. 2009. Crisis of the capitalist system: Where do we go from here? *MROnline*, November 12, available August 2020 at mronline.org/2009/11/12/crisis-of-the-capitalist-system-where-do-we-go-from-here/s.

Wallerstein, Immanuel. 2011. *Modern world-system III: The second era of great expansion of the capitalist world-economy, 1730s–1840s.* Berkeley, CA, University of California Press.

Wallerstein, Immanuel. 2013. Interview with G. Williams on the origins of world-systems analysis. *Journal of World-Systems Research* 19(2), 202–210.

Ward, Barbara, and Rene J. Dubos. 1972. *Only one Earth: The care and maintenance of a small planet—An unofficial report commissioned by the Secretary-General of the UN Conference on the Human Environment.* Harmondsworth, Penguin.

Weisskopf, Thomas E. 1978. Marxist perspectives on cyclical crises. In Union for Radical Political Economics (ed.), *U.S. capitalism in crisis,* New York, URPE, 241–260.

Weisskopf, Thomas E. 1979. Marxian crisis theory and the rate of profit in the postwar US economy. *Cambridge Journal of Economics* 3(4), 341–378.

Wemheuer, Felix. 2011. Sites of horror: Mao's great famine; Dikötter, Frank. Response. *The China Journal* 66, 155–164.

Wikipedia. Oil crisis, en.wikipedia.org/wiki/Oil_crisis, accessed October 2020.

Wikipedia. Russell's teapot, en.wikipedia.org/wiki/Russell%27s_teapot, accessed October 2020.

Wilson, M. 2009. Sales of safes boom as the economy falters: Looking for security in a cube of steel. *New York Times*, March 6.

WMO, World Meteorological Organization. (2022). *State of the global climate 2021.* Geneva, WMO.

Wrigley, E. A. 2004. *Poverty, progress, and population.* New York, Cambridge University Press.

Yagi, Kiichiro, Nobuharu Yokokawa, Hagiwara Shinjiro, and Gary Dymski, eds. 2013. *Crises of global economies and the future of capitalism—Reviving Marxian crisis theory.* New York, Routledge.

Yarbrough, B. V, and R. M. Yarbrough. 2006. *The world economy: International trade.* Mason, OH, Thompson South-Western.

Yeung, J. 2020. Australia's deadly wildfires are showing no signs of stopping. *CNN*. January 13, at www.cnn.com/2020/01/01/australia/australia-fires-explainer-intl-hnk-scli/index.html, accessed September 2020.

Yueh, L. 2014. G20 summit: Much promised, less delivered. *BBC News*, November 16, www.bbc.com/news/business-30073281, accessed September 2020.

Zarnowitz, Victor. 1985. Recent work on business cycles in historical perspective: A review of theories and evidence. *Journal of Economic Literature* 23(2), 523–580.

Index

J. A. Tapia, *Six Crises of the World Economy*,
https://doi.org/10.1007/978-3-031-38735-7

Acknowledgments

This book has had a long gestation and has benefited from my discussions, conversations, and exchanges with many people. To start with, I must mention Rolando Astarita, who has taught economics at the Universidad de Buenos Aires and at the Universidad de Quilmes for many years. He was my coauthor in the 2011 book *La Gran Recesión y el capitalismo del siglo XXI*. We have kept a quite fluid communication since that time, and he gave me many valuable comments on several chapters of this book.

I got a Ph.D. in economics twenty years ago, at the New School for Social Research, where I was particularly fortunate to have as my dissertation advisor Duncan Foley, who since then has been a colleague and friend with whom I have had many exchanges, some of which left its mark on this book. It was also in New York City that I met Guido de Marco, who was at the time a student of economics at the New School, and Paul Mattick then the editor of the *International Journal of Political Economy*. Both gave me valuable comments on previous drafts of this book. Guido helped me a lot with the math of Appendix D. Michael Roberts (a pen name) has been an important influence on me through his writings, when we got involved in email exchanges or in very stimulating conversations the few times when we were able to meet in London, New York, or Bilbao. Ed Ionides, my coauthor in several papers, was also

J. A. Tapia, *Six Crises of the World Economy*,
https://doi.org/10.1007/978-3-031-38735-7

helpful with some statistical issues that are part of this book. My acknowledgment to all of them. Of course, all the errors, omissions, and blunders in this book are my only responsibility.

I want to finish mentioning Encarna Hidalgo, Benigno Asensio, and Ana Diez Roux, three persons who have nothing to do with this book, but who have been always very important to me, even more in these troubling times of existential threats of various origins.

About the Author

José A. Tapia Granados is a professor of politics at Drexel University, Philadelphia, where he teaches courses on international political economy, political economy of climate change, social development, and political parties. With degrees in economics, medicine, and public health, he worked formerly for the Spanish Social Security system, the publishing industry, the World Health Organization, and the University of Michigan. His books in Spanish and English cover economic topics (*Rentabilidad, inversión y crisis,* Madrid, Maia, 2017), environmental matters (*Chernobyl and the mortality crisis in Eastern Europe and the former USSR*, Berlin, De Gruyter, 2022), and climate change (*Cambio climático: ¿Qué hacer?*, Madrid, Maia, 2021). He coauthored with Rolando Astarita a book on the Great Recession (*La Gran Recesión y el capitalismo del siglo XXI*, Madrid, Catarata, 2011). His publications include papers in *PNAS*, *Demography*, *Research in Political Economy*, *Health Policy*, *International Journal of Political Economy*, *Journal of Health Economics*, *Ensayos de Economía*, *Environmental Science & Policy*, *Review of Radical Political Economics*, *Revista de Economía Crítica*, *Lancet*, *International Journal of Epidemiology,* and other journals. He has written on music, politics, and social issues in *Mientras Tanto*, *MundoClasico*, *Rebelión*, *Capitalism-Nature-Socialism*, and *The Brooklyn Rail.*

J. A. Tapia, *Six Crises of the World Economy*,
https://doi.org/10.1007/978-3-031-38735-7

The manufacturer's authorised representative in the EU is Springer Nature Customer Service Centre GmbH, Europaplatz 3, 69115 Heidelberg, Germany. If you have any concerns regarding our products, please contact ProductSafety@springernature.com

Printed and bound by CPI Group (UK) Ltd, Croydon, CR0 4YY

01/10/2026

02225894-0015